McGRAW-HILL MATHEMATICS

Math in my World

DOUGLAS H. CLEMENTS

KENNETH W. JONES

LOIS GORDON MOSELEY

LINDA SCHULMAN

 McGraw-Hill
School Division

New York   Farmington

PROGRAM AUTHORS

Dr. Douglas H. Clements

Kenneth W. Jones

Lois Gordon Moseley

Dr. Linda Schulman

CONTRIBUTING AUTHORS

Christine A. Fernsler

Dr. Liana Forest

Dr. Kathleen Kelly-Benjamin

Maria R. Marolda

Dr. Richard H. Moyer

Dr. Walter G. Secada

MULTICULTURAL AND EDUCATIONAL CONSULTANTS

Rim An

Sue Cantrell

Mordessa Corbin

Dr. Carlos Diaz

Carl Downing

Linda Ferreira

Judythe M. Hazel

Roger Larson

Josie Robles

Veronica Rogers

Telkia Rutherford

Sharon Searcy

Elizabeth Sinor

Michael Wallpe

Claudia Zaslavsky

COVER PHOTOGRAPHY Jade Albert for MMSD.

PHOTOGRAPHY CREDITS All photographs are by the McGraw-Hill School Division (MMSD), and Scott Harvey for MMSD except as noted below.
Table of Contents iii: t. Runk/Schoenberger/Grant Heilman Photography, Inc.; m. Sandy Fox for MMSD; • iv: Jeff Dunn/Stock Boston, Inc.; • t.r. Alain Pitcairn/Grant Heilman Photography, Inc.; m. Liba Taylor/Panos Pictures; b. Lori Adamski Peak/Tony Stone Images; • vi: t. © Photo Disc, Inc.; m. David Lissi/The Picture Cube; • vii: m. Jeff Greenberg/Photo Researchers, Inc.; b. Doug Armand/Tony Stone Images; • viii: t. Kent & Donna Dannen; m. Ron Pacchiana; b. William R. Sallaz/Duomo; • vix: t. David Young-Wolff/Photo Edit; b. Nicolas Russel/The Image Bank; • x: t. Jerry Jacka Photography; m. Jeffry W. Myers/Stock Boston, Inc.; • xi: t. Superstock, Inc.; m. Camerique/The Picture Cube; **Chapter 1** 1: Kindra Clineff/The Picture Cube, Inc.; • 1: Paul Degreve/FPG International; • 2: t.l. Christopher Arend/Alaska Stock; • 3: Anne Nielsen for MMSD; • 14: Sandy Fox for MMSD; • 15: Jacob Taposchaner/FPG International; • 17: Wolfgang Bayer/Bruce Coleman, Inc.; • 20: Jim Brandenburg/Minden Pictures; • 21: Tom Brakefield/Bruce Coleman, Inc.; • 22: Merlin B. Tuttle; • 26: b. Nigel J. Dennis/Photo Researchers, Inc.; t. Russ Kinne/Comstock; m. Franz Lanting/Minden Pictures; • 28: t.l. Robert Winslow/Viesti Associates, Inc.; m.l. Wardene Weiss/Bruce Coleman, Inc.; b.l. Nancy Adams/Tom Stack & Associates; t.r. Alan D. Carey/Photo Researchers, Inc.; m.r. J.S. Flannery/Bruce Coleman, Inc.; b.r. Runk/Schoenberger/Grant Heilman Photography, Inc.; • 29: b.r. D. Young-Wolff/PhotoEdit; • 34: t.l. David Jennings/The Image Works; t.m. Kevin Vandivier/Viesti Associates, Inc.; b.m. Hoyer/Snowdon/Focus/Woodfin Camp & Associates; r. The British Museum; • 34-35: b.r. Runk/Schoenberger/Grant Heilman Photography, Inc.; **Chapter 2** 36: t.l. Bullaty Lomeo/Photo Researchers, Inc.; t.m Ed Malles/Gamma Liaison; t.r. Lee Snider/The Image Works; b.l. Richard Pasley/Stock Boston, Inc.; b.m. Carl Rosenstein/Viesti Associates, Inc.; b.r. Leslie Cashen/Uniphoto Picture Agency; i. Jeff Dunn/Stock Boston, Inc.; • 37: t.l. Bill Wisser/Gamma Liaison; t.m. Craig Aurness/Woodfin Camp & Associates; b.l. N. Neveux/Westlight; t.r. Joe Cornish/Tony Stone Worldwide; b.m. C.C. Lockwood/D. Donne Bryant Stock Photo; b.r. Lee Snider/The Image Works; • 38: r. Institut Royal des Sciences Naturelles; • 48: Eric Jordan/ADP Photo Lab; • 56: John Welzenbach/The Stock Market; • 57: m. Bruce Berman for MMSD; 60: t.r. Superstock, Inc.; • 61: b. Superstock, Inc.; • 63: Jeff Greenberg/PhotoEdit; • 66: Richard Hutchings/PhotoEdit; • 68: Kindra Clineff/ The Picture Cube; • 70: m.l. Sobel/Klonsky/The Image Bank; b.r. E.R. Degginger/Bruce Coleman, Inc.; • 75: l. Courtesy of The Metropolitan Club; m.l. Kunio Owaki/The Stock Market; m.r. Coutesy of Dr. Michael P. Doss; r. Tom Carroll/FPG International; • 76: b. Tom Tracy/The Stock Market; t. Cary Wolinsky/Stock Boston, Inc.; i. Greig Cranna/Stock Boston, Inc.; • 77: b. Cliff Hollis/Gamma Liaison; **Chapter 3** 78-79: Eric Horan/Gamma Liaison; • 83: t.r. Susan Van Etten/PhotoEdit; • 84: Ronald Glassman; • 91: Peter Cade/Tony Stone Images; • 94: t.r. Kids Only Market; • 96: Lawrence Migdale; • 107: m.l. Ronald Sheridan/Ancient Art & Architecture Collection; m. D. Donne Bryant; b.m.r. Boltin Picture Library; b.r. Boltin Picture Library; i. Fun-Tronics, Inc.; t.m.r. World Stat International, Inc. 1994; • 114: m.r. Stephen Ogilvy for MMSD; t.r. Stephen Ogilvy for MMSD; b.l. Runk Schoenberger/Grant Heilman Photography, Inc.; t.l.i. Alan Pitcairn/Grant Heilman Photography, Inc.; • 120: Brown Brothers; **Chapter 4** 124 :i. Ken Kaminsky/Uniphoto Picture Agency; • 124: t.l. Comstock; t.m. Nubar Alexanian/Stock Boston; b.r. Jim Zuckerman/Westlight; b.l. Churchill & Klehr; • 124-125: Herbert W. Booth III/Gamma Liaison; • 125: t.l. Tony Freeman/PhotoEdit; t.m.l. Alan Schein/The Stock Market; t.m.r. Churchill & Klehr; t.r. Kevin Horan/Stock Boston; b.r. Eric Roth/The Picture Cube; • 126: Mary Jo Kidder; • 127: t.l. Mark E. Gibson; • 129: Susan Noonan/Motor Week; • 130: David Barnes/The Stock Market; • 140: r. Rainer Grosskopf/Tony Stone Images; t. Art Brewer/Tony Stone Images; l. Comstock; • 146: Tom Bean/The Stock Market; • 147: Pascal Quittemelle/Stock Boston, Inc.; • 149: World Stat International, Inc. 1994; • 152: Joe Stancampiano/National Geographic Society; • 154: Jamaican Tourist Board; • 156-157: b. Superstock, Inc.; • 156: t.r. Michael Heron for MMSD; • 160: Liba Taylor/Panos Pictures; • 161: Kathleen Campbell/Gamma Liaison; • 164: t.r. Xavier Rossi; t.l. Lori Adamski Peak/Tony Stone Images; **Chapter 5** 166-167: Zane Williams/Tony Stone Images; • 166: i. David Lissy/The Picture Cube; • 167: b.r. Scott Harvey for MMSD; • 168: Ronald Sheridan/Ancient Art & Architecture Collection; • 169: Churchill & Klehr; • 174: Sonya Jacobs/The Stock Market; • 179: Australian Tourist Council; • 182: b.l. Sandra Fox for MMSD; 182: t.l. Frank Siteman/PhotoEdit; m. Bob Randall for MMSD; t.r. Chip Henderson For MMSD; b.r. David Madison/Tony Stone Images; • 184: t.l. Jim Powell for MMSD. t.r. Michael Nelson/FPG International; • 185: Jim Powell for MMSD; • 188: Courtesy of Dave Chin. • 189: b. Stephen Wilkes/The Image Bank; • 192: © Photo Disc, Inc.; • 194: b.l. Ron Pacchiana; m.l. Sonlight Images for MMSD; t.r. Stephen Ogilvy for MMSD; m.r. David Young-Wolff/PhotoEdit; • 195: Bill Waltzer for MMSD; • 200 :t. Brown Brothers; **Chapter 6** 202-203: Zefa-Craddock/The Stock Market; • 202: Frank Siteman/The Picture Cube, Inc.; • 207: Kean/Archive Photos; • 212: t.l. National Postal Museum/Smithsonian Institution; • 213: b.r. National Postal Museum/Smithsonian Institution; • 217: Churchill & Klehr; • 218: Courtesy of Baxter Lane Co.; • 220: Superstock, Inc.; • 222: "Barbie (R) Doll" (c)1998 Mattel Inc. All Rights Reserved; • 223: Rob Crandall/Stock Boston, Inc.; • 226: t.l. Churchill & Klehr; b.r. Runk/Schoenberger/Grant Heilman, Inc.; • 228: t. David Young-Wolff/PhotoEdit; • 230: t.m.r. Lee E. Battaglia/Photo Researchers, Inc.; b.l. Joe Viesti/Viesti Associates; b.m.r. David Ulmer/Stock Boston, Inc.; • 233: Myrleen Ferguson/PhotoEdit; • 236: l. Laurie Evans/Tony Stone Images; • 236: b.m. Laurie Evans/Tony Stone Images; • 236: t.m.r. Laurie Evans/Tony Stone Images; m.m.r. G.I. Bernard/Earth Scenes; m. R.J. Mathews/Unicorn Stock Photos; t.l. G.I. Bernard/Earth Scenes; b.r. G.I. Bernard/Earth Scenes; b.m.r. Bohdan Hrynewych/Stock Boston, Inc.; t.r. Ravi Shekhar/Dinodia Picture Agency; **Chapter 7** 195: t. Elisa Leonelli/Tony Stone Worldwide; • 240-241: Superstock, Inc.; • 240: i. Richard Nowitz/Tony Stone Worldwide; • 243: t.r. Michael Newman/PhotoEdit; • 246: t. Clair Hain; • 247: t. Bob Torrez/Tony Stone Images; • 249: t. Stock Montage, Inc.; • 262: m.l. Jeff Greenberg/Photo Researchers, Inc.; b.r. Jeffry W. Myers/Uniphoto; • 262-263: Young-Wolff/PhotoEdit; • 264: t.l. George Kufrin/FPG International; b.r. Tom Brakefield/The Stock Market; b.m.r. Bill Ross/Westlight; t.m.r. Ron Watts/Westlight; • 270-271: b.l. Robert Landau/Westlight; • 271: b. Doug Armand/Tony Stone Worldwide; • 272-273: R.W. Jones/Westlight; **Chapter 8** 280: Kent & Donna Dannen; • 282: t.r. Catherine Ursillo/Photo Researchers, Inc.; • 285: Wernher Krutein/Gamma Liaison; • 286: t. Lawrence Migdale/Stock Boston, Inc.; • 290: m.m. Zefa/The Stock Market; t. Andrew J. Martinez/Photo Researchers, Inc.; m.r. Superstock, Inc.; b.r. R.W. Jones/Westlight; b.l. Pecolatto/Photo Researchers, Inc.; m.l. Gilbert S. Grant/Photo Researchers, Inc.; • 291: Ron Pacchiana;

(continued on page 560)

ILLUSTRATION CREDITS Winky Adam: 40, 41, 81, 119 • Bernard Adnet: 265, 297, 309 • Laurie Anzalone: 14, 15, 33 • George Baquero: 58, 289, 338, 361, 367, 395 • Ken Bowser: 363, 364, 371, 374, 380, 383, 384, 390, 392, 393, 394, 477 • Tom Cardamone: 11, 63, 107, 153, 173, 207, 213, 245, 277, 329, 343, 385, 429, 453 • Jean Cassels: 406, 414, 415, 420 • Anthony Cericola: 209, 210, 214, 270, 404, 405, 424 • Brian Dugan: 241, 251, 252, 254, 270, 386, 387, 393, 394 • Jonathan Evans: 273, 292 • Deborah Haley: 470 • John Hart: 182, 183 • Linda Helton: 170 • Robin Hotchkiss: 97, 115, 150, 151, 163, 264, 486 • Pat Isaza: 54 • WB Johnston: 203, 253, 368, 372, 373, 374 • Brian Jensen: 1, 42, 64, 65, 108, 109, 284, 286, 298, 300, 410, 436, 472 • Laszlo Kubinyi: 22 • Andy Levine: 171, 172, 180, 196, 198, 498 • Claude Martinot: 429 • Paul Mirocha: 2,3,287, 296 • Sam Nougorodoff: 400 • Miles Parnell: 13, 29, 34, 139, 158, 159, 161, 275, 276, 282, 283, 310. 311, 312 • Michael Racz: 402, 403, 417 • Victoria Raymond: 126, 127, 137 • Douglas Schneider: 340-347, 350, 352-354, 356 • Remy Simard: 230, 446, 447 • Kenneth Spengler: 39, 50, 51, 71, 281, 308, 309 • Gary Torrisi: 319. 320, 323, 324, 336, 355, 356 • Joe VanDerBos: 470 • Dale Verzaal: 290 • Nina Wallace: 206, 207, 212, 220, 222-225, 232, 379, 378, 499, 513, 514, 517-520, 522, 529 • Jonathan Weisbach: 224 • Susan Williams: 83. 100. 181, 199, 242-244, 246, 248, 252, 266, 269, 335, 453, 458, 472, 475 • Yemi: 329, 445, 460 • Rose Zgodzinski: 70, 125, 136, 137, 174, 176, 177, 179, 180, 195, 197, 198 • Jerry Zimmerman: 457

McGraw-Hill School Division

A Division of The McGraw-Hill Companies

Copyright © 1998 McGraw-Hill School Division,
a Division of the Educational and Professional Publishing Group of The McGraw-Hill Companies, Inc.

McGraw-Hill School Division,
1221 Avenue of the Americas
New York, New York 10020

Printed in the United States of America
ISBN 0-02-109470-5 / 3
2 3 4 5 6 7 8 9 043/071 02 01 00 99 98 97

Contents

3 Addition and Money

4 Subtraction

5   Time, Data, and Graphs

6   Understanding Multiplication

7 Multiplication Facts

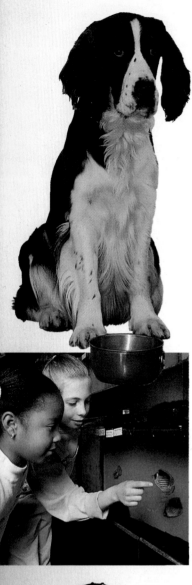

10 Geometry

11   Fractions, Decimals, and Probability

12 Multiply and Divide by 1-Digit Numbers

ADDITION AND SUBTRACTION FACTS

Wild Animals

In this chapter, you will learn about many kinds of wild animals, such as whales, bees, and birds. You will see how mathematics can be used to describe these animals.

What Do You Know ?

1 Are there more elephants than zebras? How do you know?

2 There are 5 lions hiding behind the rocks. How many lions are there in all? How did you find the answer?

3 Portfolio When do you count to solve a problem? When do you add? Give examples.

Addition Facts

Imagine watching whales swim right by you. On a whale-watching trip, they will. If 7 whales come up on one side of the boat and 2 come up on the other side, how many whales come up in all?

$7 + 2 = \blacksquare$

Count on to add mentally.

Think: Start at 7. Count on 8, 9.

0 1 2 3 4 5 6 7 8 9 10

Cultural Note

In Canada, Inuit artists carve figures out of soapstone.

Read: Seven plus two is equal to nine.

$7 + 2 = 9 \leftarrow$ **sum**
↑ ∟ **addend**
addend

Nine whales come up in all.

Talk It Over

▶ Count on to find 2 + 7. Is it easier to count on from 7 or from 2? Why?

▶ Would you count on to find 9 + 8? Why or why not?

What if 8 more whales come up around the boat. How many whales are there now?

$9 + 8 = \blacksquare$

Use a double to help you recall the sum.

There are 17 whales now.

> $8 + 8 = 16$
> and 1 more is 17.

More Examples

A $9 + 3 = 12$

Think: Start at 9.
Count on 10, 11, 12.

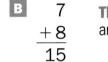

8 9 10 11 12 13 14

B
$$\begin{array}{r} 7 \\ +\ 8 \\ \hline 15 \end{array}$$

Think: $7 + 7 = 14$
and 1 more is 15.

Check for Understanding
Find the sum. Tell how you did it.

1 $9 + 1$ **2** $2 + 8$ **3** $8 + 3$ **4** $3 + 6$ **5** $1 + 8$

6 $9 + 9$ **7** $7 + 6$ **8** $5 + 6$ **9** $6 + 6$ **10** $5 + 4$

11
$$\begin{array}{r} 8 \\ +6 \\ \hline \end{array}$$
12
$$\begin{array}{r} 9 \\ +8 \\ \hline \end{array}$$
13
$$\begin{array}{r} 7 \\ +5 \\ \hline \end{array}$$
14
$$\begin{array}{r} 8 \\ +8 \\ \hline \end{array}$$
15
$$\begin{array}{r} 6 \\ +2 \\ \hline \end{array}$$
16
$$\begin{array}{r} 5 \\ +5 \\ \hline \end{array}$$
17
$$\begin{array}{r} 7 \\ +7 \\ \hline \end{array}$$

THINK CRITICALLY: Analyze   Explain your reasoning.

18 When do you use counting on to find a sum? Why?

19 How can you use the sum of $8 + 8$ to help you find the sum of $7 + 8$?

Turn the page for Practice.

Practice

Find the sum.

1 5 + 1　　**2** 4 + 4　　**3** 3 + 7　　**4** 6 + 8　　**5** 1 + 2

6 9 + 4　　**7** 7 + 7　　**8** 5 + 8　　**9** 4 + 8　　**10** 5 + 3

11
$$\begin{array}{r} 2 \\ +6 \\ \hline \end{array}$$
12
$$\begin{array}{r} 9 \\ +2 \\ \hline \end{array}$$
13
$$\begin{array}{r} 5 \\ +7 \\ \hline \end{array}$$
14
$$\begin{array}{r} 8 \\ +8 \\ \hline \end{array}$$
15
$$\begin{array}{r} 6 \\ +2 \\ \hline \end{array}$$
16
$$\begin{array}{r} 5 \\ +5 \\ \hline \end{array}$$
17
$$\begin{array}{r} 6 \\ +4 \\ \hline \end{array}$$

18
$$\begin{array}{r} 4 \\ +9 \\ \hline \end{array}$$
19
$$\begin{array}{r} 9 \\ +6 \\ \hline \end{array}$$
20
$$\begin{array}{r} 6 \\ +7 \\ \hline \end{array}$$
21
$$\begin{array}{r} 1 \\ +8 \\ \hline \end{array}$$
22
$$\begin{array}{r} 9 \\ +3 \\ \hline \end{array}$$
23
$$\begin{array}{r} 9 \\ +7 \\ \hline \end{array}$$
24
$$\begin{array}{r} 4 \\ +7 \\ \hline \end{array}$$

25 What is the sum of 5 and 8?　　**26** How much is 9 plus 8?

27 What is the sum of 7 and 1?　　**28** How much is 6 plus 6?

Find the rule. Then complete the pattern.

29 8, 9, 10, ■　　　　　　**30** 4, 6, ■, 10, ■

31 3, 6, 9, ■　　　　　　**32** 17, 19, ■, 23, ■

Algebra Complete the table.

33

Rule: Add 3.	
Input	Output
5	8
6	■
7	■
8	■
9	■

34

Rule: Double + 1.	
Input	Output
2	5
4	■
5	■
7	■
9	■

35

Rule: ■	
Input	Output
1	2
3	6
4	8
6	12
8	16

········· **Make It Right** ·····················

36 Eli counted on to find the sum of 8 and 3. Tell what the error is and correct it.

8 + 3 = ■

Think: Count on 8, 9, 10.
8 + 3 = 10

Fighting Facts Game!

Play with a partner.

Play the Game

▶ Write two addends on each index card.

▶ Make two equal piles of cards. Place them facedown.

▶ Each of you takes one pile.

▶ Take a card from the top of your own pile and place it faceup.

▶ The player with the greater sum wins the round and keeps both cards.

▶ Play until you have gone through the cards once.

You will need
• *index cards*

more to explore

Using Letters for Numbers

Algebra Ruby has 8 whale posters. She buys a few more. Now she has 13 posters. How many posters did she buy?

You can use a letter to stand for an unknown number.

$$8 + P = 13 \leftarrow \textbf{number of posters in all}$$

number of posters she had — **number of posters she bought**

Think: $8 + 5 = 13$
$P = 5$

Ruby bought 5 posters.

Write a number sentence to solve.
Karl spent $9 on a Whale Watcher shirt. He also bought a button. He spent $14 in all. How much did the button cost?

More Addition Facts

You can make a ten to help you find sums mentally.

Work Together

Work with a partner. Make a
ten-frame from an egg carton.

Spin the spinner two times to get
two addends.

Put red counters for the first
addend in the carton. Use yellow
counters to show the second
addend.

Find the total. Write a number
sentence.

Take turns. Repeat the activity
several times.

▶ How did you combine the counters? How
did this method help you to find the sum?

You will need
- *0–9 spinner*
- *egg carton*
- *scissors*
- *18 two-color counters*

KEEP IN MIND
Check that
your partner
understands
your methods.

Make Connections

Joan and Le Roi used a ten-frame to find these sums.

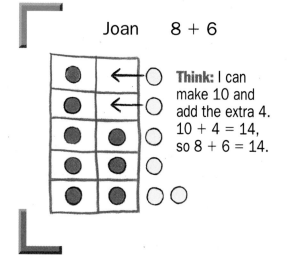

Joan   8 + 6

Think: I can
make 10 and
add the extra 4.
10 + 4 = 14,
so 8 + 6 = 14.

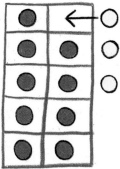

Le Roi   9 + 3

Think: Adding 9 is the
same as adding 10 and
subtracting 1.
10 + 3 = 13,
13 − 1 = 12,
so 9 + 3 = 12.

▶ Why do you think Le Roi decided to add 10 and subtract 1 rather than add 9?

▶ Why is it helpful to put the greater addend in the ten-frame first?

Check for Understanding

Find the sum. Tell how you did it.

1 6 + 5   **2** 8 + 5   **3** 3 + 7   **4** 9 + 4   **5** 6 + 7

THINK CRITICALLY: Analyze   **Explain your reasoning.**

6 How can you add 9 + 8 mentally?

Practice

Write an addition sentence.

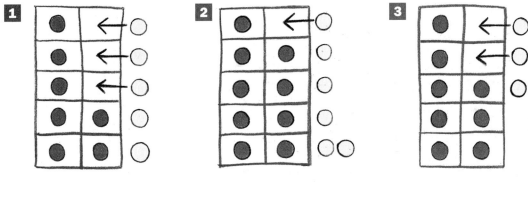

Add.

4 6 + 8   **5** 8 + 2   **6** 6 + 6   **7** 5 + 8   **8** 2 + 7

9 4 + 5   **10** 7 + 6   **11** 3 + 8   **12** 8 + 8   **13** 9 + 4

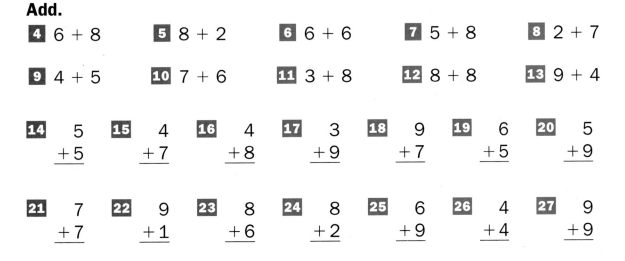

14 5 +5	**15** 4 +7	**16** 4 +8	**17** 3 +9	**18** 9 +7	**19** 6 +5	**20** 5 +9

21 7 +7	**22** 9 +1	**23** 8 +6	**24** 8 +2	**25** 6 +9	**26** 4 +4	**27** 9 +9

Properties of Addition

You can use cubes to explore addition properties.

Work Together

Work with a partner.

Show 4 red cubes, 3 blue cubes, and 5 yellow cubes.

Write a number sentence for the cubes. Find the sum.

Change the order of the cubes. Write another addition sentence.

Repeat the activity with a different number of each color.

KEEP IN MIND
▶ Compare your work to others'.
▶ Be prepared to talk about what you discover.

Talk It Over

▶ What methods did you use to add three numbers?

▶ Did the way you ordered the cubes change the sum? How do you know?

Make Connections
These addition properties can help you add mentally.

Order Property of Addition

$5 + 1 = 6$

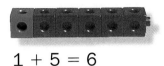

$1 + 5 = 6$

Think: The order of the addends is changed, but the sum is the same.

Grouping Property of Addition

Note: Always do what is in the parentheses ( ) first.

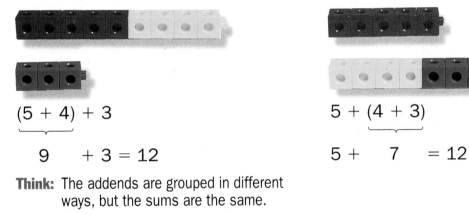

$(5 + 4) + 3$

$9 \quad + 3 = 12$

$5 + (4 + 3)$

$5 + \quad 7 \quad = 12$

Think: The addends are grouped in different ways, but the sums are the same.

Check for Understanding
Find the sum. Then use the Order Property to write a different number sentence.

1 $2 + 3$ **2** $6 + 2$ **3** $7 + 8$ **4** $9 + 3$

Use the Grouping Property to find the sum two different ways.

5 $6 + 3 + 4$ **6** $5 + 4 + 9$ **7** $4 + 4 + 7$ **8** $1 + 2 + 3 + 5$

THINK CRITICALLY: Analyze

9 *journal* How can the properties you learned help you find $7 + 8 + 3$ mentally?

10 **What if** one addend is zero. How does the sum compare with the addends? Give examples.

Turn the page for Practice. ➡

Practice

Write two number sentences. Tell which property the model shows.

1

2

3

Write *true* or *false*. If false, write the correct statement.

4   The Order Property of addition can help you find $3 + 8$ when you know that $8 + 3 = 11$.

5   When you add zero and any other number, the sum is zero.

6   Parentheses tell which numbers you add first.

7   Changing the way you group the addends changes the sum.

Add.

8   $5 + 4$ 　　9 $9 + 1$ 　　10 $0 + 7$ 　　11 $8 + 9$

12   $5 + 4 + 3$ 　　13 $7 + 0 + 6$ 　　14 $2 + 8 + 4$ 　　15 $1 + 9 + 8$

16   $2 + 4 + 0 + 6$ 　　17 $1 + 2 + 8 + 7$ 　　18 $6 + 1 + 2 + 6$

19	20	21	22	23	24	25
5	2	7	1	3	1	2
6	0	5	8	8	7	6
+5	+9	2	2	6	5	5
		+0	+7	+1	+3	+4

Algebra **Find the missing number.**

26   $3 + 6 = 6 + \blacksquare$ 　　27 $9 + \blacksquare = 9$ 　　28 $4 + \blacksquare = 8 + 4$

29   $5 + \blacksquare + 5 = 10$ 　　30 $6 + 8 + 4 = 10 + \blacksquare$ 　　31 $3 + 8 + 7 = \blacksquare + 8$

Problem Solving

32 The Milford town library ordered 5 books on the lives of animals and 3 books on animal care. How many books on animals did the library order altogether?

33 The Wildlife Center Nursery has 6 newborn rabbits and 8 goslings. It also has 2 orphaned black bear cubs. How many baby animals are in the nursery?

34 **Write a problem** that can be solved by addition. Solve the problem. Ask others to solve it.

35 Write an addition sentence with three addends and a sum of 12. Each addend must be 6 or less.

36 The red nature trail is 2 miles long. The green nature trail is 4 miles long. How long are both trails together?

37 **Data Point** Make a class line plot showing favorite zoo animals. Which animal is the most popular?

Cultural Connection The Magic Square

In Chinese legends, Emperor Yu saw this **magic square** on the back of a turtle about 4,000 years ago. The numbers are shown as knots. The sum of the numbers in each row, column, or diagonal is the same.

What are the numbers in the magic square? What is the magic sum?

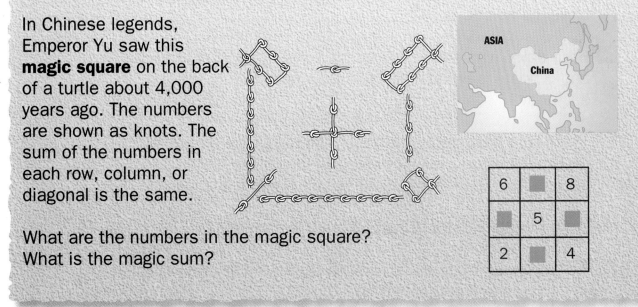

Addition and Subtraction Facts **11**

Find the sum mentally.

1 5 + 6   **2** 0 + 8   **3** 7 + 7   **4** 8 + 9   **5** 8 + 5

6 9 + 3   **7** 4 + 5   **8** 3 + 8   **9** 5 + 6   **10** 3 + 3

| **11** $\begin{aligned}9\\ +5\\ \hline\end{aligned}$ | **12** $\begin{aligned}4\\ +7\\ \hline\end{aligned}$ | **13** $\begin{aligned}6\\ +6\\ \hline\end{aligned}$ | **14** $\begin{aligned}9\\ +7\\ \hline\end{aligned}$ | **15** $\begin{aligned}8\\ 6\\ +2\\ \hline\end{aligned}$ | **16** $\begin{aligned}7\\ 2\\ +8\\ \hline\end{aligned}$ | **17** $\begin{aligned}9\\ 0\\ +1\\ \hline\end{aligned}$ |

Find the sum. Then use the Order Property to write a different number sentence.

18 8 + 7   **19** 2 + 6   **20** 9 + 4   **21** 7 + 6   **22** 2 + 9

Find the missing number.

23 7 + ■ = 7   **24** 5 + 6 = ■ + 5   **25** (3 + 4) + 7 = ■ + 7

26 5 + 4 + 5 = 10 + ■   **27** 4 + ■ + 8 = 12   **28** 5 + 6 + 3 = ■ + 6

Solve.

29 Lou watches birds at his feeder. On Tuesday he saw 4 cowbirds, 3 cardinals, and 6 sparrows. How many birds did he see in all?

30 Each day 6 whale-watching boats leave the harbor at noon and 2 boats leave at 3 o'clock. How many boats leave each day?

31 Janet built a birdhouse for purple martins. There is room for 6 families on the first floor, and 6 families on the second floor. How many families can live in the house?

32 Write all the addition facts that have a sum of 10.

33 Choose three numbers less than 10. Describe how you can find the sum.

Number Puzzles

You can use what you have learned about addition to solve puzzles.

If [rabbit] + [rabbit] = 10 and [cat] + [cat] = 8, then what is [rabbit] + [cat]?

Think: $5 + 5 = 10$ So [rabbit] = 5. $4 + 4 = 8$ So [cat] = 4.

$5 + 4 = 9$

So [rabbit] + [cat] = 9.

Solve. Explain your thinking.

1 If [cat] + [cat] = [cat], then what is [cat]?

2 If [fish] + 7 = 10, then what is [fish] + [fish]?

3 If [butterfly] + [fish] = 4 and [butterfly] + [butterfly] + [butterfly] = [fish], then what is [butterfly]?

4 If [turtle] + [owl] + [squirrel] = 9 and [owl] + [squirrel] = 5, then what is [turtle]?

5 If [pig] + 5 = [bird] and $3 + 4 =$ [bird], then what is [pig]?

6 If [elephant] + [elephant] + [elephant] = 6 and [bird] + [elephant] = 9, then what is [bird]?

7 If [penguin] + [caterpillar] = 6 and [caterpillar] + [caterpillar] = [penguin], then what is [caterpillar]?

8 **Write your own** number puzzle. Solve it. Then give it to others to solve.

real-life investigation
APPLYING ADDITION

Animal Inventory

What types of animals live in your neighborhood? Work in a group to take a survey of the types of mammals, birds, or reptiles you see in your neighborhood. What do you think is the most common type of animal?

▶ Decide where and when you will look.

▶ Set a time limit.

▶ Decide how you will record your data.

▶ Do a count of all the animals that you see.

DECISION MAKING

Counting Animals

1 How many different types of animals did you count?

2 How many animals did you count in all?

3 What types of animals were most common?

4 **What if** you were going to do this investigation again. Decide where and when you would do it. Tell why.

Report Your Findings

5 [Portfolio] Prepare a report on the data you gathered. Include the following:

▶ Tell how you chose where to look. How did your group share the work of counting and keeping track of time?

▶ Display your data using charts, graphs, or pictures. Give totals.

6 Share your findings and compare them to the findings of other groups.

Revise your work.
▶ Is the data accurate and is it displayed correctly?
▶ Is your report organized and clear?
▶ Did you proofread your work?

MORE TO INVESTIGATE

PREDICT how your data would change if it were summer.

EXPLORE why animals live in the areas where you saw them.

FIND what the rarest animal ever found in your neighborhood is.

Subtraction Facts

Frank Mazotti, wildlife biologist, University of Florida Institute

Frank says that crocodiles are shy, but they can be dangerous when protecting their nests. There are 12 nests in a park. Frank has only looked at 9 nests. How many nests does he need to look at?

$12 - 9 = $ ■

Count up to subtract mentally.

Think: Start at 9.
Count up—10, 11, 12.

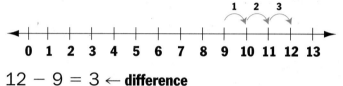

$12 - 9 = 3 \leftarrow$ **difference**

Read: Twelve minus nine is equal to three.

You can also count back to find the difference.

Think: Start at 12.
Count back to 9—11, 10, 9.

Frank needs to look at 3 nests.

More Examples

A
$$\begin{array}{r} 8 \\ -6 \\ \hline 2 \end{array}$$

Think: Start at 6.
Count up—7, 8.

B $11 - 4 = 7$

Think: Start at 11. Count back 4—10, 9, 8, 7.

Check for Understanding

Find the difference.

1 $12 - 8$ **2** $11 - 9$ **3** $10 - 3$ **4** $10 - 8$ **5** $9 - 6$

THINK CRITICALLY: Analyze   Explain your reasoning.

6 If you change the order of the numbers in a subtraction sentence, do you always get the same difference? Give an example.

Practice

Find the difference.

1 $6 - 5$ **2** $6 - 2$ **3** $5 - 2$ **4** $11 - 8$ **5** $13 - 4$

6 $10 - 6$ **7** $7 - 5$ **8** $12 - 3$ **9** $8 - 5$ **10** $9 - 0$

11 $\begin{array}{r} 4 \\ -0 \\ \hline \end{array}$ **12** $\begin{array}{r} 9 \\ -3 \\ \hline \end{array}$ **13** $\begin{array}{r} 8 \\ -6 \\ \hline \end{array}$ **14** $\begin{array}{r} 8 \\ -3 \\ \hline \end{array}$ **15** $\begin{array}{r} 7 \\ -6 \\ \hline \end{array}$ **16** $\begin{array}{r} 9 \\ -4 \\ \hline \end{array}$ **17** $\begin{array}{r} 12 \\ -\ 6 \\ \hline \end{array}$

Algebra **Write + or − to make a true number sentence.**

18 $6 \bullet 2 = 8$ **19** $8 \bullet 8 = 0$ **20** $7 \bullet 5 = 12$ **21** $4 \bullet 5 = 9$

22 $12 \bullet 4 = 8$ **23** $6 \bullet 3 = 9$ **24** $14 \bullet 8 = 6$ **25** $8 \bullet 7 = 15$

MIXED APPLICATIONS
Problem Solving
Pencil & Paper   Calculator   Mental Math

26 Cuban crocodiles grow to be about 12 feet long. Chinese alligators are rarely longer than 5 feet. About how much longer do Cuban crocodiles grow?

27 By the time an American crocodile is one year old, it can be 18 inches long. How many inches does it grow in its first year? See INFOBIT.

28 A one-year-old American crocodile weighs about 4 pounds. A two-year-old crocodile can weigh between 9 and 12 pounds. What is the most it can gain in 1 year?

> **INFOBIT**
> American crocodiles are only about 9 inches long when they hatch.

mixed review

1 $6 + 7$ **2** $0 + 5$ **3** $9 + 6$ **4** $8 + 3$

5 $6 + 4 + 7$ **6** $5 + 4 + 1$ **7** $8 + 0 + 9$ **8** $2 + 5 + 8$

More Subtraction Facts

You can use ten to help you find differences mentally.

Work Together

Work with a partner. Make a ten-frame from an egg carton.

Model 12 − 5.

Show 12. Then take away 5.

How many are left?

Write a number sentence.

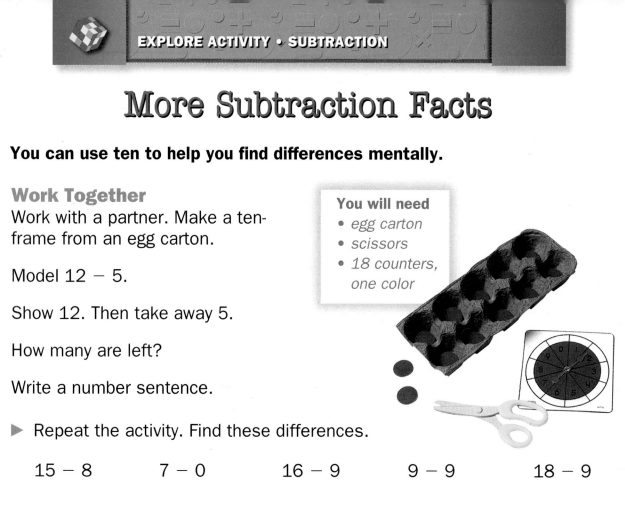

You will need
- *egg carton*
- *scissors*
- *18 counters, one color*

▶ Repeat the activity. Find these differences.

15 − 8	7 − 0	16 − 9	9 − 9	18 − 9

▶ Explain your methods. Did you always use the ten-frame? Why or why not?

▶ How did you use the ten-frame to find the difference?

Make Connections

Harvey and Kiki used ten-frames to find these differences.

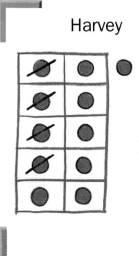

Harvey   11 − 4

Think: 11 = 10 + 1
So you can subtract
from 10 and add 1.
10 − 4 = 6,
6 + 1 = 7,
so 11 − 4 = 7.

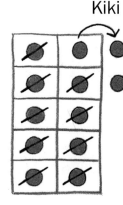

Kiki   12 − 9

Think: Subtracting 9 is
the same as subtracting
10 and adding 1.
12 − 10 = 2,
2 + 1 = 3,
so 12 − 9 = 3.

► What is the difference when you subtract a number from itself? Write a subtraction sentence as an example.

► What is the difference when you subtract zero from a number? Write a subtraction sentence as an example.

Check for Understanding

Find the difference. Tell how you did it.

1 17 − 9   **2** 16 − 8   **3** 7 − 7   **4** 6 − 0   **5** 12 − 6

THINK CRITICALLY: Summarize

6 Journal What if a friend asked, "How do you subtract?" Write an explanation.

Practice

Write a subtraction sentence.

1   **2**   **3**

Subtract.

4 15 − 9   **5** 12 − 7   **6** 8 − 8   **7** 13 − 6   **8** 7 − 3

9 10 − 5   **10** 11 − 2   **11** 9 − 0   **12** 15 − 8   **13** 5 − 0

14	**15**	**16**	**17**	**18**	**19**	**20**
6	13	11	16	12	14	3
− 5	− 4	− 9	− 9	− 5	− 9	− 3

21	**22**	**23**	**24**	**25**	**26**	**27**
10	9	15	16	11	10	15
− 7	− 2	− 7	− 8	− 8	− 4	− 9

Extra Practice, page 484

Choose the Operation

One wolf pack has 9 wolves in it.
Another pack has 15 wolves.
How many more wolves are in the larger pack?

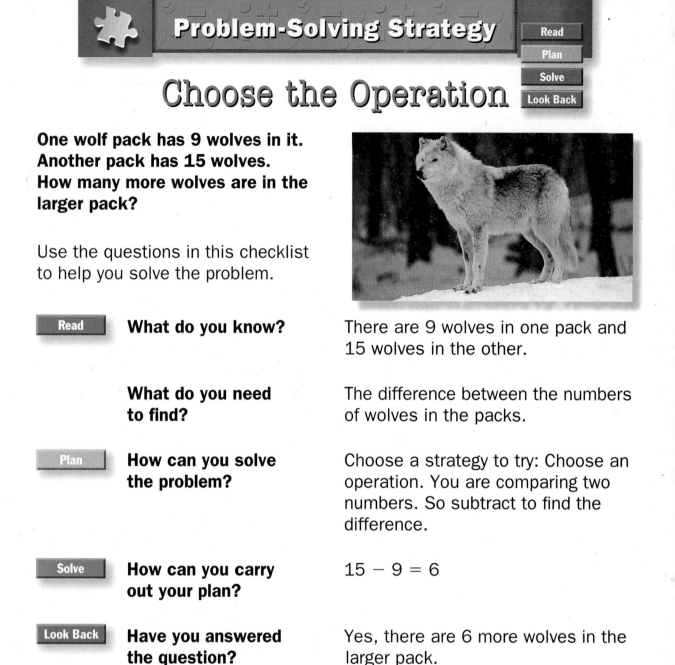

Use the questions in this checklist to help you solve the problem.

Read **What do you know?**
There are 9 wolves in one pack and 15 wolves in the other.

What do you need to find?
The difference between the numbers of wolves in the packs.

Plan **How can you solve the problem?**
Choose a strategy to try: Choose an operation. You are comparing two numbers. So subtract to find the difference.

Solve **How can you carry out your plan?**
$15 - 9 = 6$

Look Back **Have you answered the question?**
Yes, there are 6 more wolves in the larger pack.

Check for Understanding

1 What if 7 new pups were born in the smaller pack. How many wolves are in that pack now? Tell how you would solve the problem.

THINK CRITICALLY: Generalize **Explain your reasoning.**

2 Tell when you would add to solve a problem. Tell when you would subtract.

Problem Solving

Pencil & Paper *Calculator* *Mental Math*

1 Ahmik followed the wolf pack for 6 miles on Monday and for 8 miles on Tuesday. On which day did he follow them farther?

2 There were 8 wolves in another pack. Nine pups were born this season. How many wolves are in the pack now?

3 A wolf pup weighs about 16 ounces at birth. A coyote pup weighs about 9 ounces. About how much more does a wolf pup weigh than a coyote pup?

4 Kamil carries 3 pounds of food, 4 pounds of clothes, and 6 pounds of equipment in his pack. How many pounds does he carry?

5 **Logical reasoning** Fang, Fido, Buck, and Lobo are walking in a line. Fang is between Buck and Lobo. Lobo is not in the lead. Fido is next to Lobo. Buck is in front of Fang. Fido is last. In what order are they walking?

6 Sara is keeping track of a wolf pack that lives in the north woods. She needs to tag 12 wolves for her study. She has already tagged 7 wolves. How many more wolves does she need to tag?

Use the table for problems 7–11.

7 Write *true* or *false.* A rabbit usually lives longer than a beaver.

8 How much longer does an elk live than a deer?

9 **Data Point** Use the table on page 530 in the Databank to find an animal with a life span about 9 years shorter than a wolf's.

10 How much shorter is the life span of a rabbit than that of a wolf?

11 **Write a problem** using some of the information in the table. Solve it and have others solve it.

Average Life Span (in years)	
Wolf	12
Rabbit	5
Elk	15
Deer	8
Beaver	5

Extra Practice, page 484

Fact Families

Joseph counted 6 red bats on the bottom branch and 7 red bats on the top branch. Yama counted 7 bats on the top and 6 bats on the bottom.

Cultural Note

The ancient Maya honored bats by naming a city Tzinacent Lan, or Bat City.

▶ Find the total number of bats.

$6 + 7 = 13$ or $7 + 6 = 13$

There are 13 bats in all.

▶ **What if** 6 of the 13 bats are male. How many bats are female?

$13 - 6 = 7$ Seven of the bats are female.

▶ **What if** 7 bats flew away. How many bats would be left?

$13 - 7 = 6$ There would be 6 bats left.

These 4 related facts are called a **fact family:**

$6 + 7 = 13$ $13 - 7 = 6$

$7 + 6 = 13$ $13 - 6 = 7$

Fact families can help you remember addition and subtraction facts and solve related problems.

Talk It Over

▶ Why do we say that number sentences in a fact family are related?

▶ Do all fact families have the same number of addition and subtraction sentences in them? Give examples to prove your answer.

In the evening some of the 13 bats fly away to feed on insects. Joseph and Yama see that only 4 are left. How many bats flew away?

Joseph and Yama use related facts in different ways to find the missing number.

■ + 4 = 13   **Think:** If 4 + 9 = 13,
              then 9 + 4 = 13.
              ■ = 9

13 − ■ = 4   **Think:** If 13 − 4 = 9,
              then 13 − 9 = 4.
              ■ = 9

Both Joseph and Yama find that 9 bats flew away.

More Examples

A 6 + ■ = 14

Think: If 14 − 6 = 8,
          then 6 + 8 = 14.
          ■ = 8

B 12 − ■ = 9

Think: If 9 + 3 = 12,
          then 12 − 3 = 9.
          ■ = 3

Check for Understanding

Write a fact family for the group of numbers.

1 5, 8, 13   **2** 2, 0, 0   **3** 2, 7, 9   **4** 6, 6, 12

5 7, 7, 14   **6** 3, 9, 12   **7** 1, 5, 6   **8** 7, 9, 16

Find the missing number.

9 9 + ■ = 10   **10** 11 − ■ = 8   **11** ■ + 4 = 9   **12** ■ − 8 = 8

13 7 + ■ = 13   **14** 10 − ■ = 5   **15** ■ + 3 = 10   **16** ■ − 3 = 3

THINK CRITICALLY: Analyze   **Explain your reasoning.**

17 Tell how you can use an addition fact to check the answer to 9 − 7 = ■.

Practice

Write a fact family for the group of numbers.

1 7, 1, 8   **2** 6, 2, 8   **3** 9, 9, 18   **4** 7, 0, 0   **5** 7, 8, 15

Find the sum. Then write a related subtraction fact.

6 $9 + 3$ **7** $5 + 6$ **8** $2 + 7$ **9** $4 + 4$ **10** $3 + 8$

11 $0 + 4$ **12** $7 + 8$ **13** $6 + 7$ **14** $7 + 7$ **15** $8 + 4$

Find the difference. Then write a related addition fact.

16 $5 - 4$ **17** $10 - 5$ **18** $7 - 4$ **19** $12 - 3$ **20** $9 - 9$

21 $14 - 8$ **22** $18 - 9$ **23** $6 - 0$ **24** $16 - 8$ **25** $15 - 6$

Algebra Find the missing number.

26
$$\begin{array}{r} 4 \\ +7 \\ \hline \blacksquare \end{array}$$
27
$$\begin{array}{r} \blacksquare \\ -6 \\ \hline 8 \end{array}$$
28
$$\begin{array}{r} 3 \\ +\blacksquare \\ \hline 3 \end{array}$$
29
$$\begin{array}{r} \blacksquare \\ +7 \\ \hline 14 \end{array}$$
30
$$\begin{array}{r} 8 \\ -\blacksquare \\ \hline 1 \end{array}$$
31
$$\begin{array}{r} 5 \\ +\blacksquare \\ \hline 7 \end{array}$$
32
$$\begin{array}{r} \blacksquare \\ -9 \\ \hline 8 \end{array}$$

33 $8 + 5 = \blacksquare$ **34** $9 - \blacksquare = 4$ **35** $\blacksquare + 8 = 12$ **36** $8 + \blacksquare = 13$

· · · · · · · · · · · · · · · **Make It Right** · · · · · · · · · · · · · · ·

37 Maria wrote this fact family. Tell what the error is and correct it.

$9 + 5 = 14$ $5 + 9 = 14$ $9 - 5 = 4$ $9 - 4 = 5$

MIXED APPLICATIONS

Problem Solving

38 Nancy counts 4 adult bats and 6 babies. How many bats does Nancy count in all?

39 Otto spots 7 bats. Doris spots 4 more bats than Otto does. How many bats does Doris spot?

40 Twelve people are supposed to meet to go bat spotting. Only 8 people show up. How many people do not come?

41 **Write a problem** that can be solved by addition. Then change the problem so it can be solved using a related fact.

Going in Circles Puzzle!

Copy the puzzle.

Each number in the two inside circles is an addend. Each sum is shown in the outside circle.

Use addition or subtraction facts to find the missing numbers.

Draw a new puzzle using different numbers. Trade with a friend. Complete each other's puzzles.

more to explore

Missing Numbers

Algebra

You can use what you know about addition and subtraction to find missing numbers.

$$35 + 16 = \blacksquare + 35$$

Think: Use the Order Property of addition.

$$\blacksquare = 16$$

Find the missing numbers.

1 $42 + 23 = 23 + \blacksquare$

2 $65 + \blacksquare = 65$

3 $56 - \blacksquare = 56$

4 $45 - 45 = \blacksquare$

5 $(34 + 27) + 78 = 34 + (\blacksquare + 27)$

Part 1   Act It Out

Salim and Mary see 9 zebras and 5 elephants drinking at a water hole in Kenya. When 8 lions come, the zebras leave. How many animals are at the water hole after the zebras leave?

Work Together

Solve. Be prepared to explain your methods.

1 How could you act out this problem to solve it?

2 How many animals were at the water hole before the lions came?

3 How many animals are at the water hole after the zebras leave?

4 **What if** 4 of the lions leave and 6 hyenas come. How many animals are at the water hole now?

5 **Make a decision** What other strategies could you have used to solve these problems? Explain.

Part 2   Write and Share Problems

Amy used the data in the table to write a problem.

Animals at the Water Hole	
Animal	**Number**
Zebra	9
Elephant	5
Lion	8
Hyena	6
Gnu	18
Wild dog	12
Impala	15

There are 12 wild dogs. If 6 hyenas scare off 6 wild dogs, how many dogs are left?

6 Solve Amy's problem.

7 Change Amy's problem so it is either easier or harder to solve. Do not change any of the data in the table.

8 Solve the new problem and explain why it is easier or harder to solve than Amy's.

9 Use information from the table to write an addition and a subtraction problem.

10 Trade problems. Solve at least three problems written by your classmates.

11 What was the most interesting problem that you solved? Why?

Amy Blankenship
Hawthorne Elementary School
Indianapolis, IN

Turn the page for Practice Strategies. ➡

Menu

**Choose four problems and solve them.
Explain your methods.**

1 Four of the young males in a herd of elephants left to live by themselves. There had been 13 elephants in the herd. How many are there now?

2 Tía's class has raised enough money to adopt 7 wild horses. The local herd has 15 horses. How many horses are left to be adopted?

3 Cowbirds lay their eggs in the nests of other birds. Ian checks the nests of 7 sparrows and 9 thrushes for cowbird eggs. How many nests does he check?

4 Rangers free 6 ferrets on the prairie. They had already freed 8 other ferrets in the same area. How many ferrets have they freed in all?

5 Dianne follows a band of chimps for 3 miles to a termite mound. From there the chimps travel 2 miles to the river. They travel another 4 miles to some fruit trees. For how many miles does Dianne follow them?

6 Harry tags 5 rainbow trout as part of a study. Gail tags 4 trout. They free most of them. They keep 1 trout to study back at the lab. How many trout do they let go?

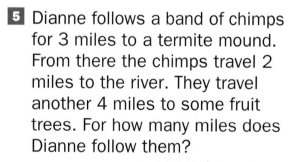

Choose two problems and solve them. Explain your methods.

7 Keisha wants to spend between $10 and $15 on animal patches. She wants to buy at least two different types of patches. Which patches can she buy?

Sale! Animal Patches	
No more than two of each type of patch to a customer	
Eagle	$3
Panda	$4
Elephant	$7

8 **Spatial reasoning** Sort the shapes. Tell how you did it. How else can you sort them?

9 Write two statements describing the data in the line plot.

Which Animal Do You Like?

	X			
X	X			
X	X		X	
X	X	X	X	
X	X	X	X	
X	X	X	X	
X	X	X	X	X
X	X	X	X	X
Tiger	Bear	Gorilla	Bison	Leopard

10 **At the Computer** Use the stamps in a drawing program to create a picture involving addition or subtraction. Trade pictures with others. Write an addition or subtraction sentence that describes the picture.

Language and Mathematics

Complete the sentence. Use a word in the chart.

1 The ■ of 7 and 8 is 15.

2 The numbers 4 and 5 in the number sentence 4 + 5 = 9 are called ■.

3 The ■ between 14 and 8 is 6.

4 Changing the ■ of the addends does not change the sum.

5 Related facts using the same three numbers are called a ■.

Vocabulary
difference
addends
sum
fact family
order

Concepts and Skills

Add.

6 6 + 4   **7** 8 + 5   **8** 0 + 8   **9** 9 + 9   **10** 7 + 6

11 4 + 4 + 3   **12** 3 + 6 + 2 + 6   **13** 5 + 4 + 7   **14** 3 + 5 + 7 + 1

Subtract.

15 16 − 8   **16** 16 − 7   **17** 17 − 9   **18** 13 − 6   **19** 9 − 9

Add or subtract.

20 18
  − 9

21   9
  +4

22   6
   5
  +4

23   8
  −0

24   2
   0
  +9

25 17
  − 8

26   4
   6
  +6

Find the missing number.

27 7 + 4 = ■ + 7   **28** 14 − ■ = 7   **29** ■ + 3 = 3

Write a fact family for the group of numbers.

30 4, 6, 10   **31** 5, 8, 13   **32** 7, 9, 16

Think critically.

33 Analyze. Tell what the error is. Then correct it.
(5 + 2) + 3 = 7

34 Summarize. Write *true* or *false*. Give examples to show why.

a. A fact family may have only two related facts.

b. Whenever you add a number and zero, the answer is always zero.

c. You can add to check a subtraction problem.

d. When you subtract a number from itself, the answer is always the number.

MIXED APPLICATIONS
Problem Solving

Pencil & Paper   Calculator   Mental Math

35 Frank spots 6 cardinals while bird-watching in the morning. He spots some sparrows in the afternoon. He spotted 14 birds in all. How many sparrows did he spot?

36 A beaked whale grows to about 15 feet in length. Mr. Blake is about 6 feet tall. How would you find how much longer the whale is than Mr. Blake?

37 Mabel finds that the garden snake she has been studying grew 2 inches. The last time she measured, it was 5 inches long. What operation can you use to find how long Mabel's snake is now?

38 Jenny works three days a week at the Weis Ecology Center. She works 5 hours on Monday, 7 hours on Tuesday, and 6 hours on Friday. How many hours does Jenny work for the center a week?

39 Samuel entered a Walk-for-Wildlife fund-raising event in town. He walked 4 miles across town to the park and 4 miles back. How many miles did he walk in all?

40 Mrs. Sutter is repairing a fence at the local animal shelter. She has a wooden board 15 feet long. She needs a 7-foot board. How many feet should she cut off to make her repair?

Add or subtract.

1 6 + 6   **2** 8 + 1   **3** 4 + 7   **4** 9 + 7

5 12 − 7   **6** 15 − 6   **7** 10 − 5   **8** 16 − 9

9
$$\begin{array}{r} 16 \\ -\ 8 \\ \hline \end{array}$$

10
$$\begin{array}{r} 5 \\ +9 \\ \hline \end{array}$$

11
$$\begin{array}{r} 3 \\ 4 \\ +6 \\ \hline \end{array}$$

12
$$\begin{array}{r} 8 \\ -0 \\ \hline \end{array}$$

13
$$\begin{array}{r} 14 \\ -\ 7 \\ \hline \end{array}$$

Write a fact family for the group of numbers.

14 4, 6, 10   **15** 5, 6, 11   **16** 6, 8, 14   **17** 8, 9, 17

Find the missing number.

18 ■ + 6 = 6

19 ■ − 7 = 0

20 2 + 5 = ■ + 2

21 3 + (6 + 2) = (3 + ■) + 2

Solve.

22 An adult fox weighs about 14 pounds. A ringtail monkey weighs about 6 pounds. How would you find out how much more the fox weighs than the monkey?

23 During the first hour Kanda observed the water hole, 6 elephants came. During the second hour, 9 came. What operation would you use to find how many came in all?

24 There were 18 adult elephants and 9 baby elephants in the herd. How many more adults than babies were there?

25 At the Wild Animal Park, Sean saw 4 lions, 5 leopards, 2 tigers, and 3 cheetahs. How many cats did he see in all?

What Did You Learn?

Use the information below. Write a word problem for addition and one for subtraction. Solve. Show all your work.

Hanna wants to be a naturalist. She counts the animals she sees at a local pond.

Animal	Number
Chipmunk	12
Squirrel	18
Rabbit	9
Blue jay	5
Hawk	2
Turtle	4

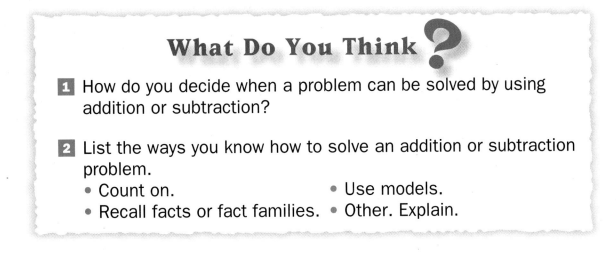

················· **A Good Answer** ·················

• tells one addition story and one subtraction story

• clearly shows how you used addition and subtraction to solve the problems

You may want to place your work in your portfolio.

What Do You Think?

1 How do you decide when a problem can be solved by using addition or subtraction?

2 List the ways you know how to solve an addition or subtraction problem.
- Count on.
- Recall facts or fact families.
- Use models.
- Other. Explain.

The Story of Honey

1 Honeybees are one of only two insects that people use as farm animals. The other is the silkworm.

2 Bees use wax to make honeycombs. They build six-sided cells in which they store honey.

3 The Egyptians used beeswax for candles and for cosmetics. We still use it for these and many other uses.

4 Honey is a sweet liquid made by bees from the nectar of flowers. It takes the nectar from more than a million flowers to make 1 pound of honey.

5 People keep bees for the honey and beeswax they make and to use them to help plants reproduce.

6 One bee stops at about 600 flowers each trip. As bees collect the nectar, they pollinate the plants.

▶ What are some things we do with honey?

▶ Why do farmers keep bees near their crops?

How Much Honey?

A beekeeper has five hives. Each month, the hives produce the number of pounds of honey shown in the chart.

Hive 1	Hive 2	Hive 3	Hive 4	Hive 5
3	4	1	2	3

1 How much honey do the hives produce each month in all?

2 Which hive do you think has the most honeybees? Why?

3 From which three hives would you collect honey to have exactly 7 pounds of honey? Is there more than one answer? Explain.

4 Another beekeeper has three hives. The three hives produce a total of 10 pounds of honey each month.

Hive 1	Hive 2	Hive 3
3	4	▮

How much honey does Hive 3 produce each month?

At the Computer

Honey We Use

	X			
X	X			
X	X		X	
X	X	X	X	
X	X	X	X	
X	X	X	X	
X	X	X	X	X
X	X	X	X	X
X	X	X	X	X
Bottled Honey	**Cereal**	**Cookies**	**Bread**	**None**

5 Make a list of how you use honey. Combine your list with others to create a class list.

6 Use graphing software to draw a class line plot showing the different ways you use honey.

7 Write two statements about the class based on the line plot.

PLACE VALUE AND NUMBER SENSE

Where Do You Live?

Where do you call home? From desert to seaside, from city to farm, people live and work together. In this chapter, you will see how math helps people organize their communities.

What Do You Know **?**

1 How many new members did Volunteer Your Time sign up? How did you use the table to find out?

2 Which program got the greatest number of new members? How many new members are there?

3 Portfolio The program with the most new members wins a blue ribbon. Second place wins a red ribbon. Third place wins a yellow ribbon. The rest win green ribbons. Explain how you would decide which ribbon to give to each program.

Ridgemont Community Center	
Program	**New Members**
Elder Care	27
Tutor Your Classmates	63
Volunteer Your Time	37
Sports Roundup	46
Read for Fun	127

Numbers in the World

Before people invented numbers, they used objects to help keep track of things. Some people carved notches on bones. Others made piles of stones.

Today we use numbers in many ways.

Work Together
Work in a group.

▶ Make a list of ways numbers are used every day. For example, your address may use numbers.

▶ Sort the items on your list into these groups: Money, Measures, Names, or Counts.

▶ Display your groups in a list, on a graph, or on a line plot.

Make Connections
Marta's group recorded their ideas about numbers and how they are used on a line plot.

Cultural Note
Over 22,000 years ago, people in Zaire marked the Ishango (ee-SHAN-goh) bone. It may have been a lunar calendar.

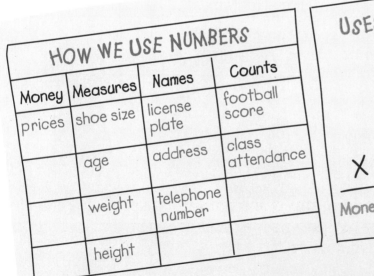

HOW WE USE NUMBERS

Money	Measures	Names	Counts
prices	shoe size	license plate	football score
	age	address	class attendance
	weight	telephone number	
	height		

USES FOR NUMBERS

Money Measures Names Counts

▶ What does their line plot tell you?

▶ Did you list any of the same uses for numbers as Marta's group did? any different uses?

· ·

Check for Understanding
Tell how the number is used.

1 Alphonso is 49 inches tall.

2 My phone number is 555-4567.

3 I see a flock of 32 geese.

THINK CRITICALLY: Analyze Explain your reasoning.

4 Journal Make a list of the numbers that are special to you. Group them and tell why you grouped them that way.

Practice
Tell how the number is used.

1 **2**
PROD 5.99
MEAT 6.27
GROC 11.99
GROC 1.95
TOTAL 26.20

3 **4**
WELCOME TO
FAIRFIELD
POP. 32,657

For ex. 5–9, write the letter of the reasonable number.

5 number of students in a class   **a.** 22,300

6 a person's age   **b.** 07456

7 population of a town   **c.** 5

8 zip code   **d.** 82

9 players on a basketball team   **e.** 25

10 **Data Point** Use the data from the group lists to make a line plot for the whole class. What was the most common use for numbers chosen by your class?

Ordinals

Have you ever marched in a local parade? The Orange Festival takes place each year in Winter Haven, Florida. Who is first in line? In which position is Pablo?

You can use **ordinal numbers** to tell the positions of people or things that are in order.

Betty is first in line. Pablo is eighth.

More Examples

A *M* is the 13th letter of the alphabet.

B Yellowstone National Park was the first national park in the world.

Check for Understanding

Use the word NEIGHBORHOOD for ex. 1–3.

1 In which position is the letter *G*?

2 Which letter is sixth?

3 Which letter is 12th?

4 Write a word with *t* in the second position.

THINK CRITICALLY: Analyze

5 If you are the tenth person in line, how many people are before you? Can you tell how many are after you? Why or why not?

6 How are ordinal numbers and counting numbers different? How are they the same?

Practice

Tía placed the cap she got at the Orange Festival on her shelf first.

Name the position of the item.

1 pennant   **2** cup   **3** T-shirt   **4** belt bag

5 Which item is sixth on the shelf?   **6** Which item is fourth on the shelf?

7 In which position is the last item?   **8** Which item is fifth on the shelf?

9 **What if** Tía decides to wear the cap. In which positions
are the belt bag and mug now?

MIXED APPLICATIONS
Problem Solving

10 **What if** Maria goes to the end of the line on page 40 to talk to Erin. In which position will Lara be then?

11 Suppose a plane is 21st in a line to take off at a busy airport. How many planes are in front of it?

12 The parade began with 12 bands. Three bands have played already. How many bands have yet to play?

13 **Write a problem** that uses ordinal numbers about your class. Solve it. Then give it to others to solve.

mixed review

1 5 + 5   **2** 6 + 2   **3** 9 − 5   **4** 6 + 7   **5** 9 + 3

6 14 − 7   **7** 8 − 3   **8** 6 + 5   **9** 15 − 8   **10** 18 − 9

Counting

Neighborhood gardens not only feed people but help them get to know one another. Look at this plan. How many corn plants will there be?

C	C	C	C	C	C	C	C	C	C	
C	C	C	C	C	C	C	C	C	C	
P	P	P	P	P	B	B	B	B	B	C corn
P	P	P	P	P	B	B	B	B	B	P peas
P	P	P	P	P	B	B	B	B	B	T tomato
P	P	P	P	P	B	B	B	B	B	B bean
P	P	P	P	P	B	B	B	B	B	
T	T	T	T	T	T	T	T	T	T	

You can skip-count by twos to find the answer.

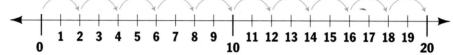

There are 20 corn plants.

Even numbers end in 0, 2, 4, 6, 8.
There is an even number of corn plants.

How many bean plants does the garden have? You can skip-count by fives to find the answer.

There are 25 bean plants.

Odd numbers end in 1, 3, 5, 7, 9.
There is an odd number of bean plants.

Check for Understanding
Find the missing numbers. Tell how you counted.

1 6, 8, 10, ■, 14, ■, ■

2 10, 15, 20, ■, ■, 35, ■

THINK CRITICALLY: Analyze

3 What pattern do you see for odd and even numbers when you skip-count by fives? by tens? by hundreds?

Practice

Find the missing numbers. Tell how you counted.

1 20, 22, ■, ■, ■, 30, ■

2 60, ■, ■, 90, ■, ■, 120

3 15, ■, ■, 30, ■, 40

4 ■, ■, 40, 45, ■, ■, 60

5 5, 7, 9, ■, ■, ■, 17

6 ■, ■, 400, ■, 600, ■, 800

7 42, ■, ■, 72, ■, ■, 102

8 425, ■, ■, 725, ■, 925

Complete the pattern. Are the numbers *even* or *odd*?

9 32, 34, 36, ■, ■, ■, ■

10 5, 10, 15, ■, ■, ■, ■

11 15, 17, 19, ■, ■, ■, ■

12 350, 360, 370, ■, ■, ■, ■

MIXED APPLICATIONS
Problem Solving
Pencil & Paper | Calculator | Mental Math

Use the plan on page 42 for problems 13–14.

13 Josie planted peas in the garden. How would you skip-count to find the number of pea plants? How many plants are there?

14 **What if** 3 of the tomato plants in the garden died. How many would be left? Explain how you found out.

15 **Spatial reasoning** Suppose you folded the figure to form a box. Would it look like this box?

16 Fold a paper square in half. Unfold it and count the parts. Refold it, fold it in half again, and count the parts. Continue folding and counting until you cannot fold it anymore. What pattern do you discover?

mixed review

Write a fact family for the group of numbers.

1 4, 5, 9   **2** 6, 0, 6   **3** 7, 8, 15   **4** 1, 8, 9   **5** 9, 9, 18

6 5, 9, 14   **7** 6, 4, 10   **8** 3, 3, 6   **9** 3, 8, 11   **10** 7, 9, 16

Extra Practice, page 486

Place Value and Number Sense   **43**

Building to Hundreds

You can use place-value models to show numbers in different ways.

You will need
- *ones, tens, and hundreds place-value models*

Work Together

Work with a partner. Model the numbers using ones, tens, and hundreds. Record your results on a place-value chart.

Hundreds   Tens   Ones

Show 27 using:
▶ only ones models.

▶ tens and ones models.

Show 153 using:
▶ only tens and ones models.

▶ hundreds, tens, and ones models.

Choose your own 2-digit and 3-digit numbers. Repeat the activity with the new numbers.

Compare your numbers and models with those of others.

KEEP IN MIND
Think about the relationship between the models.

Make Connections

Place-value charts can help you understand numbers greater than 100.

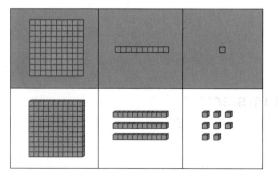

hundreds	tens	ones
1	3	8

You can think of 138 as: 1 hundred 3 tens 8 ones
or 13 tens 8 ones
or 138 ones

▶ How are ones, tens, and hundreds models related to one another?

▶ **What if** you change the order of the digits in the number above. What other numbers can you make?

▶ Choose one of these new numbers and tell how you would model it.

Check for Understanding
Write the number.

1 **2** **3**

4 9 tens 6 ones   **5** 17 tens 6 ones

THINK CRITICALLY: Analyze

6 How may the symbol $///$ be different from the number 111?

Practice
Write the number.

1 **2**  **3**

4 5 hundreds 3 tens 6 ones   **5** 13 tens 4 ones

6 **Logical reasoning** There is a 3-digit mystery number. The sum of its digits is 8. The last digit is 4. The first two digits have a difference of 0. What number is it? Make up your own number riddle. Have others solve it.

Ones, Tens, and Hundreds

Is your town famous for one thing? Battle Creek, Michigan, makes the most cereal—about 235 truckloads a day!

You can show and name this number in different ways.

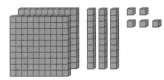

hundreds	tens	ones
2	3	5

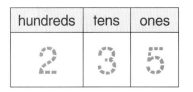

Expanded Form: 200 + 30 + 5

Standard Form: 235

Word Name: two hundred thirty-five

More Examples

A

3 hundreds 7 ones
300 + 7
307
three hundred seven

B

3 hundreds 7 tens
300 + 70
370
three hundred seventy

Check for Understanding
Write the number.

1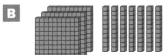

2

3

4 forty-seven

5 600 + 80 + 2

6 9 hundreds 3 tens

THINK CRITICALLY: Generalize **Explain your reasoning.**

7 How does place value help you to name numbers?

Practice

Write the number.

1.

2.

3.

4. sixty-eight

5. 1 hundred 3 tens

6. 200 + 70 + 6

7. nine hundred eighty

8. 3 hundreds 9 ones

9. 700 + 80

10. two hundred six

11. 4 hundreds 6 tens

12. 700 + 70 + 7

Write the word name.

13. 272

14. 404

15. 635

16. 394

17. 860

Write the number in expanded form.

18. 38

19. 79

20. 194

21. 350

22. 203

MIXED APPLICATIONS
Problem Solving

23. Give an example of a number in the hundreds that you use every day.

24. Breakfast cereal is shipped in cartons of 100 boxes. If there are 742 cereal boxes, how many full cartons are there?

25. **What if** the 742 boxes were put in cases of 10 boxes each. How many cases would be filled?

26. Choose three digits from 0 through 9. Use the digits to write as many different numbers as you can.

mixed review

1.
$$\begin{array}{r} 6 \\ 6 \\ +4 \\ \hline \end{array}$$

2.
$$\begin{array}{r} 9 \\ 7 \\ +2 \\ \hline \end{array}$$

3.
$$\begin{array}{r} 6 \\ 0 \\ +8 \\ \hline \end{array}$$

4.
$$\begin{array}{r} 5 \\ 5 \\ +5 \\ \hline \end{array}$$

5.
$$\begin{array}{r} 3 \\ 8 \\ +9 \\ \hline \end{array}$$

6.
$$\begin{array}{r} 8 \\ +7 \\ \hline \end{array}$$

7.
$$\begin{array}{r} 6 \\ +5 \\ \hline \end{array}$$

8.
$$\begin{array}{r} 9 \\ +4 \\ \hline \end{array}$$

9.
$$\begin{array}{r} 6 \\ +6 \\ \hline \end{array}$$

10.
$$\begin{array}{r} 9 \\ +8 \\ \hline \end{array}$$

Compare and Order Numbers

Beverly places police officers into the city's zones based on how many calls come in from each zone. Which of these zones has the most officers? Which zone has the least?

Officers Assigned	
Zone	Number of Officers
2	109
4	117
6	110

Atlanta Chief of Police Beverly Harvard responds to numbers and to community input.

A number line can help you order numbers.

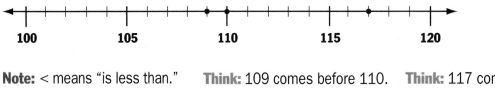

| 100 | 105 | 110 | 115 | 120 |

Note: < means "is less than."
> means "is greater than."

Think: 109 comes before 110.
109 is less than 110.
109 < 110

Think: 117 comes after 110.
117 is greater than 110.
117 > 110

Zone 4 has the most officers. Zone 2 has the least.

Another way to order numbers is to compare digits.

Line up the ones.
Start from the left.

Compare the first digits.

117
109
110

Compare the second digits.

117
109
110

Compare the third digits.

117
110

Think: They are the same.

Think: 0 < 1
So 109 is least.

Think: 7 > 0
So 117 > 110.

You can write the number of officers in order from greatest to least.

117, 110, 109

Write in order from greatest to least.

1 542, 548, 545, 540

2 $167, $76, $193, $162

THINK CRITICALLY: Generalize

3 Is the whole number with the greatest number of digits always the greatest whole number? Why or why not?

Practice

Compare. Write >, <, or =.

1 98 ● 89

2 142 ● 77

3 237 ● 237

4 674 ● 675

5 87 ● 85

6 122 ● 94

7 $52 ● $52

8 456 ● 654

Write in order from least to greatest.

9 $122, $42, $56

10 564, 453, 465

11 812, 810, 818, 900

12 356, 365, 65

13 792, 790, 907

14 215, 176, 301, 251

MIXED APPLICATIONS
Problem Solving

15 A police force is not just officers. Citizens do many things, like fixing computers. A police force has 417 officers and 276 citizens. Which group is larger?

16 **Data Point** Use the table on page 531 in the Databank. Write the home run totals in order from greatest to least.

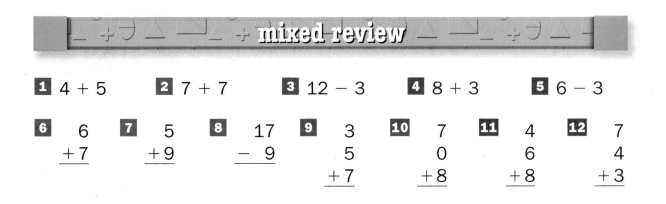

mixed review

1 4 + 5

2 7 + 7

3 12 − 3

4 8 + 3

5 6 − 3

6
$$\begin{array}{r} 6 \\ +7 \end{array}$$

7
$$\begin{array}{r} 5 \\ +9 \end{array}$$

8
$$\begin{array}{r} 17 \\ -\ 9 \end{array}$$

9
$$\begin{array}{r} 3 \\ 5 \\ +7 \end{array}$$

10
$$\begin{array}{r} 7 \\ 0 \\ +8 \end{array}$$

11
$$\begin{array}{r} 4 \\ 6 \\ +8 \end{array}$$

12
$$\begin{array}{r} 7 \\ 4 \\ +3 \end{array}$$

Make a Table

Read | **Raising money to help others makes you feel great! Three classes want to sell snacks to raise money for a food bank. From the survey results, which snack should they sell?**

They need to find out:
▶ Which snack is most popular?

Plan | Collect and organize data on snack choices in a table.

Solve | Ask several people what snack they would buy. Then organize the data in a table.

They should decide to sell fruit.

Look Back | Does the answer make sense?

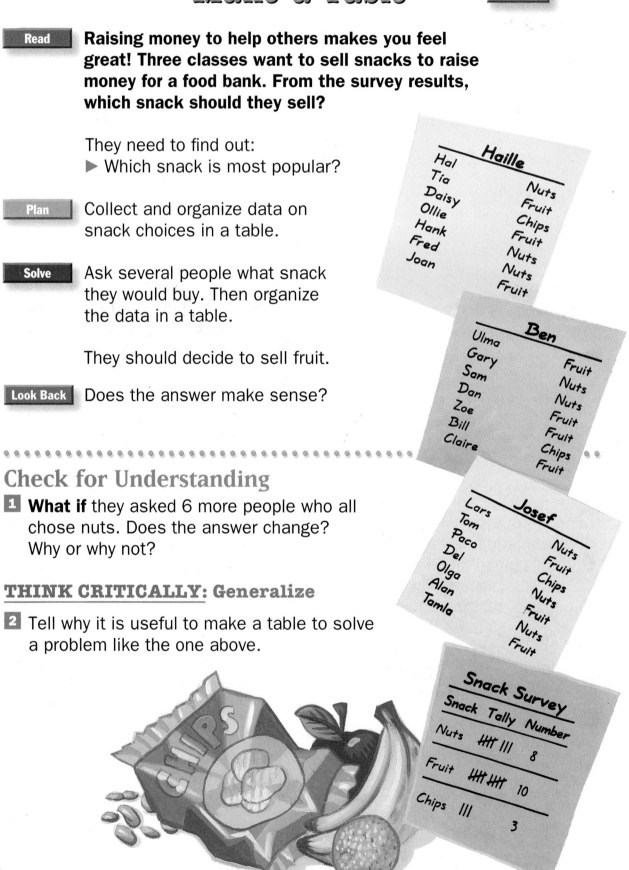

Haille

Hal	
Tia	Nuts
Daisy	Fruit
Ollie	Chips
Hank	Fruit
Fred	Nuts
Joan	Nuts
	Fruit

Ben

Ulma	
Gary	Fruit
Sam	Nuts
Dan	Nuts
Zoe	Fruit
Bill	Fruit
Claire	Chips
	Fruit

Josef

Lars	
Tom	
Paco	Nuts
Del	Fruit
Olga	Chips
Alan	Nuts
Tamla	Fruit
	Nuts
	Fruit

Check for Understanding

1 **What if** they asked 6 more people who all chose nuts. Does the answer change? Why or why not?

THINK CRITICALLY: Generalize

2 Tell why it is useful to make a table to solve a problem like the one above.

Snack Survey

Snack	Tally	Number
Nuts	⊬⊬ III	8
Fruit	⊬⊬ ⊬⊬	10
Chips	III	3

Problem Solving

Use the data on page 50 for problems 1–2.

1 Which type of snack is most popular with boys?

2 How many more girls chose fruit over nuts or chips?

3 **Logical reasoning** How can you sort these objects? Use your imagination.

pencil	wheel	clock
tree	sun	telephone
book	ball	bat

4 Several friends finished a race in this order: Dee came in tenth, Evie was sixteenth, Martin was fifth, Frank was twelfth, and Irene was third. Write the names in the order they finished the race.

5 Chips are shipped in packages of ten bags each. If 23 packages are delivered to the school, how many bags are there?

6 **Data Point** Survey your class to find out the most popular type of snack. Make a table to show your results.

7 Joshua earned $17 raking leaves. He paid $8 for a new seat for his bicycle. How much money did he have left?

8 **Write a problem** that you can solve with a table. Trade your problems with a classmate and solve.

9 Andrea wants to buy a 10-pack of colorful pens. About how much money will she need in order to buy the pens?

　a. $2　**b.** $20　**c.** $200

10 Felix wants to read 18 books as part of a readathon at his library. He has already read 9 books. How many more books does he have to read to meet his goal?

11 Jared and Hannah decided they would buy something different for a snack. Jared ordered 1 bloop, 1 blam, and 1 bing. Hannah bought 2 blangs and 1 blapper. How much did each friend spend?

What-Is-Its for Sale	
Item	**Price**
bloop	10¢
blam	8¢
blang	5¢
blapper	3¢
bing	1¢

Match the use to a reasonable number.

1 soccer score
2 length of a room in feet
3 price of a car

a. 19,799
b. 35
c. 3

Use the word ALPHABET for ex. 4–5.

4 In which positions is the letter *A*?

5 Which letter is third?

Complete the pattern. Are the numbers *even* or *odd*?

6 Count by twos.
8, ■, 12, ■, 16, ■, ■

7 Count by tens.
15, ■, 35, ■, ■, 65, ■

Write the number.

8 six hundred five

9 9 hundreds 6 tens

10 700 + 30 + 5

Compare. Write >, <, or =.

11 86 ● 68

12 245 ● 267

13 683 ● 687

Write in order from least to greatest.

14 245, 324, 76

15 653, 649, 656, 650

Copy and complete the table for problems 16–19.

16 How many students chose mangoes as their favorite?

17 Which fruit was chosen by the most people?

18 How many more people chose grapes than plums?

Favorite Fruit		
Apples	‖‖‖ ‖‖‖ ‖‖‖	15
Grapes	‖‖‖ ‖‖‖ I	11
Plums	‖‖‖ III	8
Mangoes	‖‖‖ ‖‖‖	10
Oranges	‖‖‖ ‖‖‖ ‖‖‖ III	18

19 Tell how you can rearrange the table to make it easier to compare numbers.

20 Journal Write a letter to another student telling him or her how you order the numbers 56, 560, and 506 from greatest to least.

Use Place-Value Models

You can use a computer to show models for numbers. You can regroup your models when necessary.

Use the computer to stamp out a model of a number with hundreds, tens, and ones. The number box keeps count as you stamp.

⬛ = 1,000	▦ = 100	▮ = 10	▫ =1	🔲 ⬆1⬇

Show Hide 🖥 (2) Hundreds (1) Ten (5) Ones

▶ How would the model shown above change if you were to regroup the ones as tens? the tens as hundreds?

▶ How would it change if you were to regroup the hundred as tens?

Show the models. Regroup to show the fewest models. Name the number.

1 4 tens 12 ones   **2** 3 hundreds 25 tens 23 ones   **3** 234 ones

THINK CRITICALLY: Analyze

4 Tell how you would use these tools to help you compare numbers.

WHAT'S OUR NUMBER?

What would it be like counting with another number system?

Take a census of your school. A census is a count of every person in a community. Use tokens instead of numbers to record all of the people at your school.

Work Together

▶ Work in five small groups. Decide which group will count each number.
  a. students in lower grades
  b. students in upper grades
  c. teachers
  d. other staff
  e. volunteers and student teachers

▶ Decide what tokens your group will use for 1, 10, and 100.

▶ Decide on a plan for collecting your data. Will you visit classrooms and offices? get copies of lists? make phone calls?

▶ Take your part of the census. Then combine it with the data collected by the other groups.

Cultural Note
Ancient Sumerians used tokens to count sheep. The tokens were like place-value models. Their size and shape determined their value.

| 1 | 10 | 100 |

You will need
• *clay for ones, tens, and hundreds tokens*

Taking the Census

1 How can you use shape, size, or other attributes to make your tokens stand for place values?

2 How can your group divide up tasks to make the census taking easier?

3 How did you make sure you did not count anyone twice or leave anyone out?

4 After each group does part of the census, what do you need to do to find the total number of people in the school?

Report Your Findings

5 Portfolio Prepare a report that explains how you used tokens to take the census. Include the following:

▶ Describe how the token number system and our number system are alike. How are they different?

▶ Explain any problems you had using the tokens. How did you solve them?

6 Share your report and compare your conclusions with those of other groups.

Revise your work.

▶ Is your report well organized and clear?
▶ Is the data accurate?
▶ Did you proofread your work?

MORE TO INVESTIGATE

PREDICT what will be needed when tokens are used to count numbers greater than 999.

EXPLORE the different kinds of number symbols invented by early civilizations.

FIND an example of another number system that is still used today.

Round Numbers

Fred takes the school bus each day. It may take Fred 26 minutes to get home one day, and 33 minutes another day. However, he tells his friends that his ride takes about 30 minutes.

Sometimes you do not need an exact number. You can round the numbers to tell about how many.

Work Together

Work in a group. Use the number lines. Take turns.

> **You will need**
> • *0–9 spinner*

Spin the spinner twice to make a 2-digit number.

Note: To **round** to the nearest ten means to find the ten closest to that number.

Between which two tens is the number? Which ten is it closer to?

```
   10      30      50      70      90
0      20      40      60      80      100
```

Record your answers in a chart. Repeat three times.

Number	Between	Closer to

Spin the spinner three times to make a 3-digit number.

Between which hundreds is the number? Which hundred is it closer to?

```
    100     300     500     700     900
0       200     400     600     800     1,000
```

Record your answers in a chart. Repeat three times.

Talk It Over

▶ How did you decide which number to round to?

▶ Why did Fred round 26 and 33 to 30?

Making Connections

Here is how three students rounded numbers to the nearest ten or to the nearest hundred.

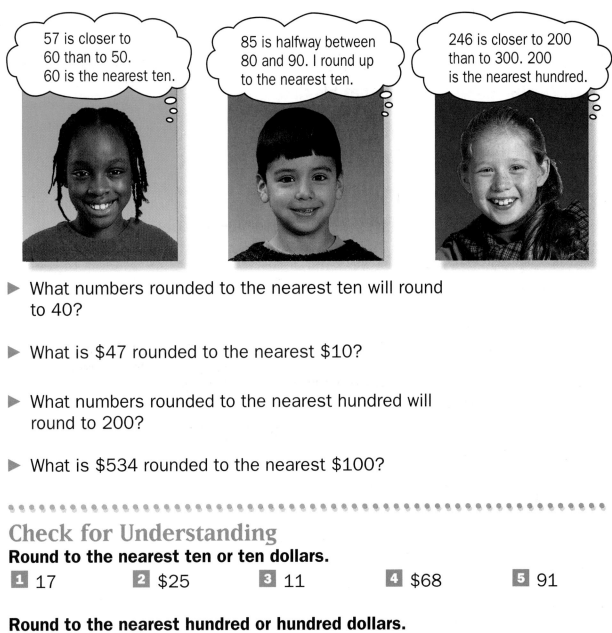

57 is closer to 60 than to 50. 60 is the nearest ten.

85 is halfway between 80 and 90. I round up to the nearest ten.

246 is closer to 200 than to 300. 200 is the nearest hundred.

▶ What numbers rounded to the nearest ten will round to 40?

▶ What is $47 rounded to the nearest $10?

▶ What numbers rounded to the nearest hundred will round to 200?

▶ What is $534 rounded to the nearest $100?

Check for Understanding

Round to the nearest ten or ten dollars.

1 17 **2** $25 **3** 11 **4** $68 **5** 91

Round to the nearest hundred or hundred dollars.

6 123 **7** 301 **8** $350 **9** 749 **10** $190

THINK CRITICALLY: Analyze Explain your reasoning.

11 What are some situations when a rounded number can be used?

12 Write a rule about when to round numbers up and when to round them down.

Turn the page for Practice.

Practice

Round to the nearest ten or ten dollars.

1 5   **2** 21   **3** $16   **4** 49   **5** 65

6 87   **7** 78   **8** 35   **9** $97   **10** 4

Round to the nearest hundred or hundred dollars.

11 104   **12** $255   **13** 415   **14** 281   **15** 647

16 290   **17** 503   **18** $56   **19** 25   **20** $850

21 What numbers round to 50 when rounded to the nearest ten?

22 What numbers round to 700 when rounded to the nearest hundred?

23 What numbers round to 0 when rounded to the nearest ten? to the nearest hundred?

24 What numbers round to 100 when rounded to the nearest ten? to the nearest hundred?

25 Which number does not round to 50?
a. 48   **b.** 45   **c.** 44   **d.** 54

26 Which number does not round to 80?
a. 74   **b.** 84   **c.** 76   **d.** 82

27 Which number does not round to 300?
a. 275   **b.** 356   **c.** 326   **d.** 314

28 Which number does not round to 100?
a. 125   **b.** 143   **c.** 97   **d.** 165

29 How can 94 round to both 90 and 100?

···············**Make It Right**···············
30 Jodie tried to round 549 to the nearest hundred. Tell what the error is and correct it.

549 rounds to 550.
550 rounds to 600.

Round and Sort Game!

Play with a partner.

First, partners use different colors to copy a set of these numbers on index cards:

516	255	597	125	259	176	492	104	342
95	484	235	565	385	602	352	150	426

Next, label the envelopes with these numbers:

100	200	300	400	500	600

Play the Game

▶ Mix up your set of cards. Place them facedown. Pick a card.

▶ Round to the nearest hundred to decide into which envelope the card should go.

▶ Pick another card from your set. Repeat the activity.

▶ The first partner to place three cards in any one envelope wins.

You will need
- *index cards*
- *5 envelopes*
- *blue crayon and red crayon*

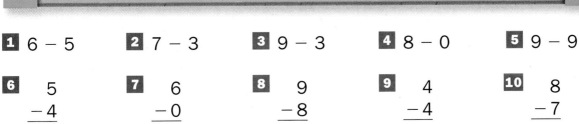

mixed review

1 6 − 5   **2** 7 − 3   **3** 9 − 3   **4** 8 − 0   **5** 9 − 9

6   5   **7**   6   **8**   9   **9**   4   **10**   8
     −4   −0   −8   −4   −7

Thousands

How many is one thousand? Can you imagine one thousand people, one thousand days, or one thousand pennies?

Work Together
Work in a group to explore *one thousand.*

Each member counts a row of ten squares on the graph paper. Cut the row out.

Tape rows together to make a hundreds model.

How can you use your hundreds models to show *one thousand*?

Build your model of *one thousand* using hundreds models. Compare your model with those of others.

You will need
- *scissors*
- *tape*
- *centimeter graph paper*

Note: 10 tens = 1 hundred
10 hundreds = 1 thousand

Talk It Over
▶ What was the same about making a ten row, a 100 square, or a 1,000 model?

▶ How is your thousands model like that of others? How is it different?

▶ How could you show 1,246 using your models?

Make Connections

You can use a place-value chart to organize your models.

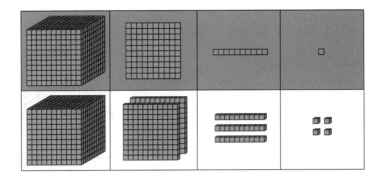

You can think of the number in different ways:

1 thousand 2 hundreds 3 tens 4 ones

1,000 + 200 + 30 + 4

1,234   **Think:** Use a comma after the thousands place.

▶ How else could you model this number?

Check for Understanding
Write the number.

3 3,000 + 60

4 3,000 + 100 + 40

5 4 thousands 3 hundreds
5 tens 1 one

6 4 thousands 7 hundreds
9 ones

THINK CRITICALLY: Analyze

7 **What if** you needed to count one thousand pennies.
How many piles of ten pennies would you have? How
many piles of one hundred?

Turn the page for Practice. ➡

Practice

Write the number.

1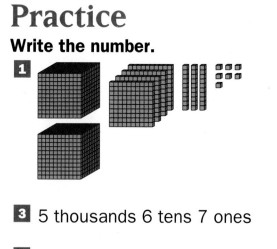

2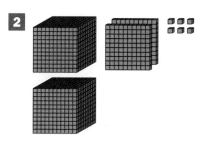

3 5 thousands 6 tens 7 ones

4 6 thousands 2 hundred 7 tens

5 9 thousands 1 ten 5 ones

6 1 thousand 6 hundreds 5 ones

7 3,000 + 600 + 50 + 5

8 9,000 + 70 + 3

Algebra Use the rule to complete the table.

9

Rule: Find the number 10 more.	
Input	Output
75	■
153	■
990	■
1,192	■

10

Rule: Find the number 1,000 less.	
Input	Output
2,341	■
1,039	■
5,097	■
3,153	■

Write the expanded form.

11 6,784   **12** 2,985   **13** 8,900   **14** 5,078

15 7,777   **16** 9,802   **17** 4,009   **18** 3,050

Write the value of the underlined digit.

19 4,<u>7</u>56   **20** 9,8<u>0</u>6   **21** <u>8</u>,967   **22** 6,02<u>3</u>   **23** <u>4</u>,325

Write the number that comes before or after.

24 2,657; ■   **25** ■; 5,678   **26** 3,339; ■   **27** ■; 4,098

28 ■; 3,980   **29** 1,099; ■   **30** ■; 2,911   **31** 999; ■

Problem Solving

Use the boxed numbers for problems 32–34.

27 7,851 8,745
567 879

32 Which number would be a reasonable number of students in an elementary class?

33 Name two things the numbers have in common.

34 What is the value of the 7 in the greatest number?

35 **Make a decision** Which of these two prizes is greater: two thousand, five hundred fifty dollars or $2,500?

36 Which reservation is home to the greater number of Navajo? See INFOBIT.

INFOBIT
The Fort Apache, Arizona reservation is home to about 9,900 Navajo—about 7,000 live on the reservation in San Carlos, Arizona.

Cultural Connection Roman Numerals

Ancient Romans used letters to name numbers.

I	V	X	L	C
1	**5**	**10**	**50**	**100**

When a letter is repeated, add.

II   **XX**   **CC**
$1 + 1 = 2$ $10 + 10 = 20$ $100 + 100 = 200$

When a letter of less value is to the right of a letter of greater value, add.

XI   **LX**
$10 + 1 = 11$ $50 + 10 = 60$

When a letter of less value is to the left of a letter of greater value, subtract.

IX   **XL**
$10 - 1 = 9$ $50 - 10 = 40$

Write the number.

1 VIII   **2** CCX   **3** LXVI   **4** XXII   **5** LXIII   **6** CCLI

Numbers to Hundred Thousands

A post office in Lawton, Oklahoma, handles about 256,000 pieces of mail a day.

You can use a place-value chart to help you read and write greater numbers.

Each group of 3 digits is called a **period.**

Thousands Period			Ones Period		
Hundred Thousands	Ten Thousands	Thousands	Hundreds	Tens	Ones
2	5	6	0	0	0

Expanded Form: 200,000 + 50,000 + 6,000

Standard Form: 256,000

Word Names: two hundred fifty-six thousand or 256 thousand

More Examples

A 12,305

10,000 + 2,000 + 300 + 5
twelve thousand, three hundred five

B 405,090

400,000 + 5,000 + 90
four hundred five thousand, ninety

Check for Understanding
Write the number.

1 two hundred thirty-four thousand, three hundred forty-four

2 6 ten thousands 3 thousands 7 hundreds 4 ones

3 400,000 + 30,000 + 8,000 + 60 + 3

THINK CRITICALLY: Analyze

4 Name some things counted in hundred thousands.

Practice

Write the word name.

1 36,902   **2** 90,670   **3** 290,502

For ex. 4–8, write the letter of the matching number.

4 six hundred forty thousand, sixty   **a.** 17,505

5 101 thousands 3 tens   **b.** 700,654

6 eight thousand, two   **c.** 101,030

7 17 thousands 5 hundreds 5 ones   **d.** 640,060

8 700,000 + 600 + 50 + 4   **e.** 8,002

9 Find 10 more than 64,821.   **10** Find 10 less than 137,915.

11 Find 100 more than 23,563.   **12** Find 100 less than 4,882.

13 Find 1,000 more than 54,524.   **14** Find 1,000 less than 423,067.

more to explore

Millions

You can use this chart to name numbers to millions.

Millions			Thousands			Ones		
Hundreds	Tens	Ones	Hundreds	Tens	Ones	Hundreds	Tens	Ones
		2	9	8	0	4	0	1

Think: 2,980,401
two million, nine hundred eighty thousand, four hundred one

Write the number. Use a place-value chart for help.

1 five million, eighty thousand, nine

2 eight million, two thousand, thirty

3 nine million, one thousand, seven

4 Name some things that are counted in millions.

Compare and Order Greater Numbers

Does your playground need new equipment? Many do. Suppose a town got these bids to build new equipment. Which is the lowest estimate?

Company	Estimated Cost
Fun Construction	$142,000
Monkey Bars, Inc.	$135,500
Slides-R-Us	$137,500

You can compare the numbers.

Line up the ones. Start from the left. Compare to find the first place the digits are different.
$142,000
$135,500
$137,500

Compare the other numbers.
$135,500
$137,500

Order the numbers from greatest to least.
$142,000; $137,500;
$135,500

Think: 4 > 3
So $142,000 is the greatest.

Think: 5 < 7
So $135,000 < $137,500.

Monkey Bars, Inc., made the lowest bid.

Check for Understanding
Compare. Write >, <, or =.

1 7,465 ● 9,786   **2** 23,087 ● 25,420   **3** 53,809 ● 52,897

4 152,060 ● 152,110 **5** 338,124 ● 338,124 **6** 108,675 ● 108,657

Write in order from greatest to least.

7 805,403; 99,089; 879,607   **8** 592,423; 599,007; 599,123

THINK CRITICALLY: Generalize

9 Explain how you can use comparing numbers to round a number to the nearest thousand. Give an example.

Practice

Compare. Write >, <, or =.

1 12,768 ● 9,210   **2** 25,600 ● 24,598   **3** 35,089 ● 35,199

4 55,672 ● 55,670   **5** 67,980 ● 101,211   **6** 143,000 ● 143,000

Write in order from least to greatest.

7 38,900; 37,100; 42,897   **8** 72,340; 72,459; 72,390

9 561,777; 560,987; 559,781   **10** 987,002; 987,500; 987,005

Algebra Which numbers at right can be used to complete the number sentence?

321,651	100,987	34,276
152,804	123,456	400,500
121,902	12,345	254,965

11 ■ > 123,456   **12** ■ < 123,456

MIXED APPLICATIONS

Problem Solving

Pencil & Paper   Calculator   Mental Math

13 The Tops Roofing Company charges $12,999 to put a roof on the band shell. The Johnson Roofing Company charges $13,500. Which company charges less?

14 Mr. Ling manages the amusement park. He needs to replace 520 light bulbs. Light bulbs come in boxes of 100 bulbs. Does he need to buy 5 boxes or 6 boxes?

15 **Make a decision** Which number is a reasonable population for a large city?
a. 745,000   **b.** 7,450
c. 750   **d.** 75

16 **Write a problem** that can be solved by comparing numbers. Solve it. Give it to someone else to solve.

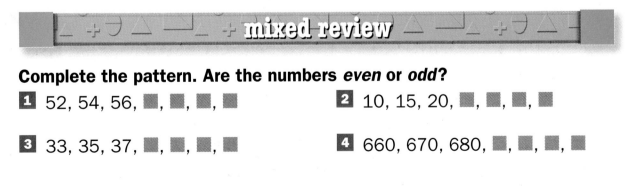

mixed review

Complete the pattern. Are the numbers *even* or *odd*?

1 52, 54, 56, ■, ■, ■, ■   **2** 10, 15, 20, ■, ■, ■, ■

3 33, 35, 37, ■, ■, ■, ■   **4** 660, 670, 680, ■, ■, ■, ■

Problem Solvers at Work

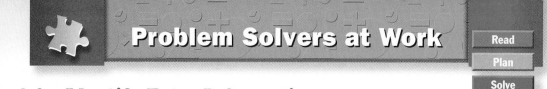

Read
Plan
Solve
Look Back

Part 1   Identify Extra Information

The concert in Millerton City Park lasted four nights.
The tickets cost $3 each.

Millerton City Park Concert	
Day	**Number of People**
Thursday	578
Friday	620
Saturday	932
Sunday	830

Work Together
Solve. Be prepared to explain your methods.

1 On which day did the greatest number of people go to the concert?

2 What information is not needed to solve the problem?

3 **What if** the concert had been rained out on Saturday. On which day would the greatest number of people have been at the concert?

4 **Make a decision** Next year, the conductor wants to hold the concert on two nights only. On which two nights should she hold the concert? Why?

Part 2 Write and Share Problems

Patrick wrote a problem that uses the data in the chart.

SUPER BAND CONCERT

School Auditorium

Saturday and Sunday at 8:00 P.M.

Tickets $5⁰⁰

There were 898 people at the concert on Saturday and 989 people on Sunday. It was very hot! It was at 8 p.m. Tickets were $5 each. Which night did more people come?

Patrick McLaughlin
Shaughnessy School
Lowell, MA

5 What information in Patrick's problem is not needed to solve the problem?

6 Rewrite the problem leaving out the extra information.

7 Solve the new problem. Explain how you solved it.

8 **Write a problem** of your own. Include some extra information.

9 Trade problems. Solve at least three problems written by your classmates.

10 What was the most interesting problem you solved? Why?

Menu

Choose four problems and solve them. Explain your methods.

1 Michael and Kendra bought tickets for the school dance. Whose ticket has the greater number?

Kendra
Centerville
chool Dance
156702

Michael
Centerville
School Dance
156710

2 Ann's address is 383 Main Street. Does she live on the odd or even side of the street? Between which two house numbers could her house be?

3 There is 1 boy more than there are girls in the marching band. There are 8 girls. How many people are there in the band?

4 Mr. Bottino has a choice of two prizes. Which prize do you think he should take? Why?

Pick the Prize of Your Choice!
$250
or
$250 rounded to the nearest hundred

5 Mr. Lisa, the baseball coach, wants to buy T-shirts for the team. If they cost $5 each, how much will 10 T-shirts cost? What method did you use?

6 Mrs. Fallon raises gerbils. She has 15 for sale. Lakeland School buys 8. How many does she have left? What operation did you use?

Choose two problems and solve them. Explain your methods.

7 Jodi's team took a vote to choose the color for a team uniform. Use the information in this line plot to write a short article for the team newsletter. Be sure to tell what the results were.

Vote for Team Color			
		X	
	X	X	
	X	X	
	X	X	X
	X	X	X
X	X	X	X
X	X	X	X
Yellow	**Green**	**Blue**	**Red**

8 **Logical reasoning** How many cuts will the lumberjack make to get 4 pieces? 5 pieces? 6 pieces? What pattern did you find? Use the pattern to predict the number of cuts to get 27 pieces.

9 Use an almanac and a map to find three small towns near you. Compare the population numbers for the years 1980 and 1990. Did the population increase or decrease between those dates?

10 **At the Computer** Use a drawing program to arrange circles on the screen to make the triangle shown. It points to the right. Then move only three of the circles to make a triangle that points to the left.

Language and Mathematics

Complete the sentence. Use a word in the chart.

1 Use an ■ number to tell the position of a person on a line.

2 675 is an ■ number.

3 In the number 475, the ■ of the 7 is 70.

4 In the number 245, the 2 is in the hundreds ■.

Vocabulary
ordinal
place
value
round
odd
even

Concepts and Skills

Use the word CALCULATOR for ex. 5–6.

5 In which position is the letter *U*?

6 Which letter is in the ninth position?

Find the missing numbers. Tell how you counted.

7 25, 30, ■, ■, 45, ■, ■, ■, 65

8 125, 225, ■, ■, 525, ■, 725, ■

Write the number.

9 2 hundreds 3 tens 5 ones

10 one thousand, twenty-eight

11 76 thousands

12 700,000 + 7,000 + 800 + 6

13 64 rounded to the nearest 10

14 254 rounded to the nearest hundred

15 $189 rounded to the nearest hundred dollars

Compare. Write >, <, or =.

16 567 ● 675

17 734 ● 713

18 940 ● 904

Write in order from least to greatest.

19 1,243; 1,387; 990; 1,900

20 4,216; 642; 680; 96

Think critically.

21 Analyze. Kate wrote the number this way. Tell what the error is and correct it.

$$300 + 6 = 36$$

22 Analyze. Write *true* or *false*. The number you round to must always have the same number of digits as the number rounded. Give an example.

MIXED APPLICATIONS

Problem Solving

Pencil & Paper | Calculator | Mental Math

23 Irene buys postage stamps in rolls of 100 stamps. How many stamps will she get in 9 rolls?

24 Mr. Wong says he is in his eighties. What is the youngest he could be? What is the oldest?

25 Mr. Balma got four prices for a car. Which was the least?
a. $15,000 **b.** $14,900
c. $14,580 **d.** $14,200

26 Mrs. Casey pays her bills in order from greatest to least. Which bill will she pay first? $45, $8, $65, $369, $95

27 Nine of the 40 stores in the mall are shoe stores. Four shoe stores close. How many shoe stores are left? What information did you *not* need to solve this problem?

28 Craig stood in a line to buy tickets for the Rocks and Stones concert. He was 65th in line. How many people were in front of him?

Copy and complete the table for problems 29–33.

29 How many people chose tennis?

30 How many more people chose basketball than chose tennis?

31 Six more people chose basketball than chose baseball. Show this on the table.

32 Which sport was chosen the least?

33 Write a statement that describes the information in this table.

Favorite Sport		
Sport	**Tally**	**Number**
Soccer	ЖЖ ЖЖ ‖	12
Hockey	ЖЖ ‖	6
Football	ЖЖ ЖЖ	10
Baseball	■	■
Tennis	ЖЖ ‖	7
Basketball	ЖЖ ЖЖ ЖЖ	15

Use the word *thousand* for ex. 1–2.

1 In which position is the letter *u*?

2 Which letter is in the eighth position?

Find the missing numbers.
Tell how you counted.

3 45, 55, ■, ■, 85, ■, ■, 115

4 102, 104, ■, ■, 110, ■, 114, ■

Write the number.

5 5 thousands 3 hundreds 6 ones

6 400,000 + 60,000 + 200 + 4

7 fifty-one thousand, one hundred

8 25 thousands

9 55 rounded to the nearest 10

10 $328 rounded to the nearest hundred dollars

Compare. Write >, <, or =.

11 208 ● 802　　**12** 625 ● 618

13 603 ● 630　　**14** 745 ● 745

Write in order from least to greatest.

15 28; 208; 82; 67

16 5,371; 99; 1,694; 5,186

Solve.

17 Sara read 28 books. Tomás read 13 books, and Sun-Li read 8 books. How many more books did Tomás read than Sun-Li? What information do you *not* need to solve this problem?

18 Ms. Timmer bought 5 packages of pencils for her class. Each package contained 100 pencils. How many pencils did she buy?

Copy and complete the table for problems 19–20.

19 How many more times did Erin go to the mall than José?

20 Who went to the mall the greatest number of times?

Visits to the Mall		
	Tally	Number
Erin	ЖЖ ЖЖ II	
Rob	III	3
José	ЖЖ III	8
Tamia	ЖЖ ЖЖ ЖЖ	

What Did You Learn?

Some of the Tallest Places to Live SOURCE: *THE GUINNESS BOOK OF RECORDS*

Gingerbread House
Des Moines, Iowa
52 feet high

John Hancock Center
Apartment Building
Chicago, Illinois
1,127 feet high

Tepee
Montana
43 feet high

Hotel Westin at
Renaissance Center
Detroit, Michigan
748 feet high

▶ Write the heights of the places in order. Explain your method.

▶ Write four sentences that compare the heights.

················ A Good Answer ·······················
- correctly describes how to write the heights in order
- tells how the heights compare with one another using
  the words *taller than* and *shorter than*

You may want to place your work in your portfolio.

What Do You Think?

1 Can you read, write, and compare 3-digit and 4-digit
numbers? If not, what do you find difficult to do?

2 List the ways you might compare or order numbers.
- Use a place-value chart.
- Use a number line.
- Use place-value models.
- Other. Explain.

3 How do you know which place to round a number to?

Aqueducts

One of the first great modern aqueducts was the Croton Aqueduct. It was built for New York City in 1842.

All living things need water. Towns and cities have often used nearby rivers, lakes, or wells for their water. Other places, however, have had to go to great lengths to be sure they had a good supply of water.

An *aqueduct* is a channel or pipe built to carry water. Often pumps are used to move the water along.

▶ Why did places like Carthage, New York, and Los Angeles need to build aqueducts?

▶ How does your community get its water?

The longest modern aqueduct is the California State Water Project. It supplies water for Los Angeles, California, and several other cities.

Who Went Farthest?

Length of Aqueducts (in miles)			
Ancient		**Modern**	
Nineveh	50	Old Croton	38
Carthage	87	New Croton	120
Aqua Marcia (Rome)	58	California State Water Project	826

1 Which is longer—the longest ancient aqueduct or the longest modern aqueduct?

2 Which is longer—the Old Croton Aqueduct or the New Croton Aqueduct?

3 List the aqueducts in order from shortest to longest.

At the Computer

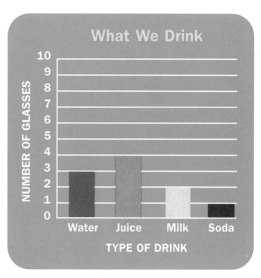

Survey your class to find out what they drink. Ask them to estimate how many glasses of each type of drink they have each day.

4 Use a spreadsheet program to make a table of your survey data. You can also use a graphing program to make a bar graph to compare the data.

5 Use the information from the table and the graph to write a paragraph about which drinks you would buy for a class party.

CHAPTER 3

ADDITION AND MONEY

THEME

Let's Go Shopping

Whether you wander in a toy store or dash to the corner for milk, you are a shopper. You will see that people may not need a store to shop, but they do need to add.

What Do You Know?

1 Kyle has 27 comic books in his collection. If he buys 12 more books, how many will he have in the collection?

2 Sanna buys one book and one grab bag. Is $2.00 enough to pay for them? Tell why.

3 Portfolio Choose two items. What is the total cost? Make a drawing of the coins or bills you could use to pay for your items.

Books 75¢ each

Grab bags 60¢ each

Bags of marbles $1.00 each

Comic books 50¢ each

Baseball cards 15¢ each

Add Whole Numbers

Big parties need big shopping lists! Here is one of the dessert lists for the Fall Festival. How many juice bars are needed?

Shopping List

Orange juice bars	500
Grape juice bars	300
Ice cream cups (mixed flavors)	600

Add: 500 + 300

You can use patterns to find sums mentally.

5 + 3 = 8
50 + 30 = 80
500 + 300 = 800

Think: 5 ones + 3 ones = 8 ones
5 tens + 3 tens = 8 tens
5 hundreds + 3 hundreds = 8 hundreds

800 juice bars are needed.

What if you buy 600 orange juice bars and 400 grape juice bars. How many juice bars do you buy?

6 + 4 = 10
60 + 40 = 100
600 + 400 = 1,000

Think: 6 ones + 4 ones = 10 ones = 1 ten
6 tens + 4 tens = 10 tens = 1 hundred
6 hundreds + 4 hundreds = 10 hundreds = 1 thousand

You buy 1,000 juice bars.

Talk It Over

▶ How did you use the addition facts to find the sums mentally?

▶ What pattern did you use to find the sums mentally?

After the festival all that is left are 46 orange juice bars and 52 grape juice bars. How many juice bars are left in all?

Add: 46 + 52

Sometimes you can add mentally by starting with tens.

$$
\begin{array}{r}
46 \\
+52 \\
\hline
98
\end{array}
$$

Think: Start with tens.
40 + 50 = 90
6 + 2 = 8

98 juice bars are left.

More Examples

A
$$
\begin{array}{r}
77 \\
+51 \\
\hline
128
\end{array}
$$

Think: Start with tens.
70 + 50 = 120
7 + 1 = 8

B
$$
\begin{array}{r}
605 \\
+180 \\
\hline
785
\end{array}
$$

Think: Start with hundreds.
600 + 100 = 700
80 + 0 = 80
5 + 0 = 5

Check for Understanding
Copy and complete the pattern.

1 3 + 4 = ■
30 + 40 = ■
300 + 400 = ■

2 7 + ■ = 12
70 + ■ = 120
700 + ■ = 1,200

3 1 + 8 = ■
■ + 80 = 90
100 + ■ = ■

Add mentally. Explain your method.

4
$$
\begin{array}{r}
20 \\
+50
\end{array}
$$

5
$$
\begin{array}{r}
600 \\
+300
\end{array}
$$

6
$$
\begin{array}{r}
60 \\
+74
\end{array}
$$

7
$$
\begin{array}{r}
200 \\
+526
\end{array}
$$

8
$$
\begin{array}{r}
302 \\
+172
\end{array}
$$

THINK CRITICALLY: Analyze Explain your reasoning.

9 How would you add 320 + 72 mentally?

Turn the page for Practice. ➡

Practice

Copy and complete the pattern.

1
$4 + 5 = \blacksquare$
$40 + 50 = \blacksquare$
$400 + 500 = \blacksquare$

2
$6 + 2 = \blacksquare$
$60 + 20 = \blacksquare$
$600 + 200 = \blacksquare$

3
$2 + \blacksquare = 10$
$20 + \blacksquare = 100$
$200 + \blacksquare = 1,000$

4
$3 + 4 = \blacksquare$
$\blacksquare + 40 = 70$
$\blacksquare + \blacksquare = 700$

5
$8 + \blacksquare = 16$
$\blacksquare + 80 = \blacksquare$
$\blacksquare + \blacksquare = 1,600$

6
$9 + \blacksquare = 15$
$90 + 60 = \blacksquare$
$\blacksquare + \blacksquare = \blacksquare$

Add mentally.

7
30
$+\,20$

8
100
$+\,600$

9
70
$+\,14$

10
87
$+\,20$

11
24
$+\,71$

12
400
$+\,700$

13
500
$+\;\,28$

14
407
$+\,301$

15
640
$+\,150$

16
326
$+\,451$

17
306
$+\,602$

18
640
$+\;\,34$

19
400
200
$+\,300$

20
500
200
$+\,500$

21
602
113
$+\,200$

22 $40 + 50$

23 $70 + 60$

24 $50 + 32$

25 $83 + 70$

26 $600 + 200$

27 $400 + 800$

28 $603 + 124$

29 $245 + 302$

30 $500 + 40$

31 $350 + 30$

32 $306 + 203$

33 $563 + 403$

34 $200 + 600 + 200$

35 $500 + 60 + 20$

36 $400 + 320 + 4$

Find the missing digit.

37 $6\blacksquare + 23 = 83$

38 $20 + \blacksquare 1 = 61$

39 $\blacksquare 3 + 70 = 103$

40 $101 + \blacksquare 00 = 701$

41 $600 + \blacksquare 5 = 675$

42 $7\blacksquare 5 + 60 = 765$

················· **Make It Right** ·····················
43 Ben added mentally. Tell what
the error is and correct it.

$810 + 104 = 950$

Problem Solving

44 At the Fall Festival people bought 302 cheeseburgers and 320 plain hamburgers. Which type of burger was more popular?

45 Mr. Reed buys more than a gross of pencils. What is the least number of pencils that he could have bought? See INFOBIT.

INFOBIT
A **gross** is 144 items. Many items are shipped by the gross.

46 Cara sold 105 festival T-shirts and 50 caps. How many items did she sell in all?

47 Mrs. Ramsey bought 320 large pretzels and 400 small pretzels for her booth. How many pretzels did she buy in all?

48 About 400 people came to the festival on Saturday. About 600 other people came to the festival on Sunday. About how many people came to the festival over those two days?

49 **Logical reasoning** Ashley, Lisa, and James buy ice cream. No two of them buy the same flavor. Neither girl buys a fruit flavor. Lisa always buys chocolate. What flavor does Ashley buy?

Ice Cream Flavors

Vanilla
Chocolate
Strawberry

---

more to explore

Zigzag Addition
Here is another method for adding 63 + 31 mentally.

Think: $63 + 30 = 93$
$93 + 1 = 94$

Add mentally. Explain your method.
1 42 + 20   **2** 33 + 10   **3** 24 + 61   **4** 53 + 43

5 72 + 13   **6** 22 + 36   **7** 163 + 20   **8** 245 + 300

Estimate Sums

Yesterday one of Dino's restaurants used 188 heads of lettuce. His other restaurant used 172 heads. About how many heads of lettuce should Dino buy at the market today?

Estimate: 188 + 172

Round each number so you can find the sum mentally.

Think: 188 + 172
↓   ↓
200 + 200 = 400 ← Round to the hundred.

So 188 + 172 is about 400.

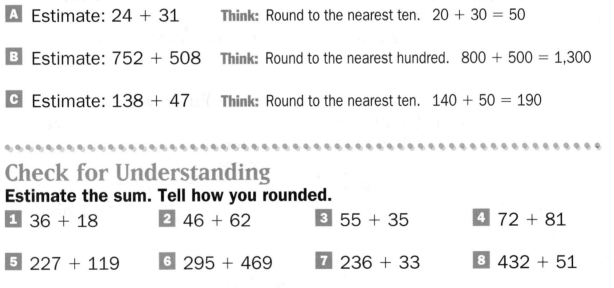

Cultural Note
Fruits and vegetables from all over the world pass through the Hunts Point Market on their way into New York City.

Dino should buy about 400 heads of lettuce.

More Examples

A Estimate: 24 + 31   **Think:** Round to the nearest ten. 20 + 30 = 50

B Estimate: 752 + 508   **Think:** Round to the nearest hundred. 800 + 500 = 1,300

C Estimate: 138 + 47   **Think:** Round to the nearest ten. 140 + 50 = 190

Check for Understanding
Estimate the sum. Tell how you rounded.

1 36 + 18   **2** 46 + 62   **3** 55 + 35   **4** 72 + 81

5 227 + 119   **6** 295 + 469   **7** 236 + 33   **8** 432 + 51

THINK CRITICALLY: Analyze **Explain your reasoning.**

9 Journal Tell how you could round the numbers in ex. 8 another way to estimate the sum. What would the estimate be?

Practice

Estimate the sum. Round to the nearest ten.

1 36 + 26   **2** 64 + 81   **3** 58 + 75   **4** 63 + 59

5 78 + 42   **6** 45 + 12   **7** 633 + 38   **8** 836 + 41

Estimate the sum. Round to the nearest hundred.

9 273 + 318   **10** 166 + 952   **11** 387 + 438   **12** 744 + 123

13 253 + 128   **14** 680 + 861   **15** 340 + 76   **16** 582 + 27

**Algebra Estimate. Write > or < to make a true sentence.
Explain your reasoning.**

17 46 + 19 ● 70   **18** 31 + 54 ● 90   **19** 197 + 149 ● 300

20 13 + 52 ● 60   **21** 387 + 462 ● 800   **22** 615 + 835 ● 1,500

MIXED APPLICATIONS
Problem Solving

23 Last year one restaurant used 409 cases of pizza sauce. The other restaurant used 310 cases. How many cases did the two restaurants use in all?

24 **Make a decision** One party needs 330 rolls. The other party needs 222 rolls. The buyer orders 500 rolls. Did she order enough?

25 On one day Dino sold 59 lunch specials in one restaurant. He sold 66 lunch specials in the other restaurant. About how many lunch specials did he sell in all?

26 **Data Point** Maria bought two cases of oranges. She received fewer than 140 oranges but more than 120 oranges. What size orange was in each case? See the Databank on page 533.

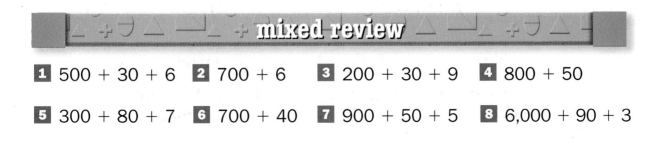

mixed review

1 500 + 30 + 6   **2** 700 + 6   **3** 200 + 30 + 9   **4** 800 + 50

5 300 + 80 + 7   **6** 700 + 40   **7** 900 + 50 + 5   **8** 6,000 + 90 + 3

Add 2- and 3-Digit Numbers

You can use what you know about place value and estimation to play a game finding sums.

Work Together
Work with a partner as a team to play Target 100.

Take turns. Spin the spinner four times. Use the digits to write two 2-digit numbers.

Model each number. Then combine them to find the sum. Record your results.

The team with the sum closer to 100 scores 1 point. Continue to play until a player has 5 points.

Next play Target 1,000. Spin the spinner 6 times to create 3-digit numbers. The team with the sum closer to 1,000 scores 1 point.

Make Connections
Sabrina and Medgar spun 524 and 318. They used models to find the sum.

> **You will need**
> - *place-value models*
> - *0–9 spinner*

Note: Remember to regroup when you can.

Here is how Sabrina and Medgar found the sum.

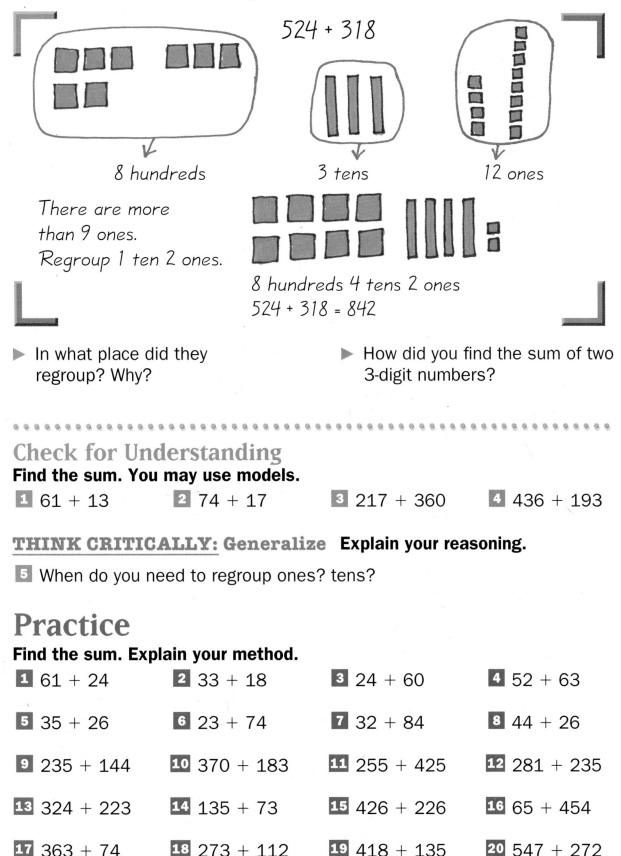

524 + 318

8 hundreds

3 tens

12 ones

There are more than 9 ones.
Regroup 1 ten 2 ones.

8 hundreds 4 tens 2 ones
524 + 318 = 842

▶ In what place did they regroup? Why?

▶ How did you find the sum of two 3-digit numbers?

Check for Understanding
Find the sum. You may use models.

1 61 + 13   **2** 74 + 17   **3** 217 + 360   **4** 436 + 193

THINK CRITICALLY: Generalize   Explain your reasoning.

5 When do you need to regroup ones? tens?

Practice
Find the sum. Explain your method.

1 61 + 24   **2** 33 + 18   **3** 24 + 60   **4** 52 + 63

5 35 + 26   **6** 23 + 74   **7** 32 + 84   **8** 44 + 26

9 235 + 144   **10** 370 + 183   **11** 255 + 425   **12** 281 + 235

13 324 + 223   **14** 135 + 73   **15** 426 + 226   **16** 65 + 454

17 363 + 74   **18** 273 + 112   **19** 418 + 135   **20** 547 + 272

Add 2-Digit Numbers

Colleen's Gardens is a shop with a page on the Internet. If Colleen gets 55 E-mail orders for sweet grass braids and 67 orders for potpourri, how many items does she need to ship?

Add: 55 + 67

Estimate the sum. **Think:** 60 + 70 = 130

In the last lesson you used models to find the exact sum. Here is another method.

Colleen Heminger-Cordell, a Sisseton-Wahpeton Sioux business owner, Marvin, SD

Step 1
Add the ones.
Regroup if necessary.

$$\begin{array}{r} \overset{1}{5}5 \\ +67 \\ \hline 2 \end{array}$$

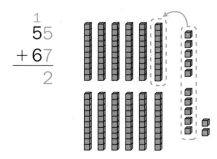

Think: 3 ones + 7 ones = 10 ones
10 ones = 1 ten 0 ones

Step 2
Add all the tens.
Regroup if necessary.

$$\begin{array}{r} \overset{1}{5}5 \\ +67 \\ \hline 122 \end{array}$$

Think: 5 tens + 6 tens + 1 ten = 12 tens
12 tens = 1 hundred 2 tens

Colleen needs to ship 122 items.

Check for Understanding

Add. Estimate to check the reasonableness of your answer.

1 65 + 8   **2** 98 + 5   **3** 81 + 76   **4** 47 + 54

THINK CRITICALLY: Generalize **Explain your reasoning.**

5 How can you use an estimate to check if your answer is reasonable?

Practice

Add. Remember to estimate.

1 24
+ 3

2 17
+ 4

3 56
+ 2

4 63
+ 7

5 32
+ 9

6 44
+29

7 29
+78

8 41
+25

9 39
+80

10 43
+77

11 50 + 70

12 97 + 3

13 48 + 76

14 75 + 8

15 60 + 96

16 91 + 17

17 13 + 36

18 82 + 59

19 53 + 47

20 5 + 90

21 37 + 6

22 8 + 65

23 13 + 3

24 17 + 29

25 68 + 36

26 69 + 74

MIXED APPLICATIONS
Problem Solving

Pencil & Paper   Calculator   Mental Math

27 Colleen's shop got 92 E-mail orders on Saturday and 95 on Sunday. On which day did she get more orders?

28 **Write a problem** using items you could buy or sell at a gift shop. Solve it. Ask others to solve it.

29 Henry sells about 150 belts each day. So far he has made 92 black belts and 71 brown belts. Has he made enough belts? How do you know?

30 Tara is paying her bills. She wants to pay them in order from greatest to least. Which bill should she pay first?
$55, $9, $75, $239, $65

mixed review

1 4
+1

2 6
−6

3 2
+7

4 13
− 9

5 9
+8

6 14
− 7

7 9 + 3

8 10 − 4

9 8 + 7

10 7 − 2

11 18 − 9

Add 3-Digit Numbers

In Monopoly you can spend huge piles of play money. Suppose you are down to $286. The other players pay you $118 in rent. Now how much do you have?

Add: 286 + 118

Estimate the sum.   **Think:** 300 + 100 = 400

Find the exact sum.

Step 1	**Step 2**	**Step 3**
Add the ones. **Regroup if necessary.**	**Add all the tens.** **Regroup if necessary.**	**Add all the hundreds.** **Regroup if necessary.**

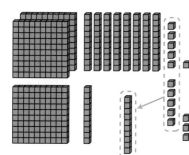 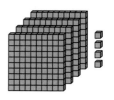

$$\begin{array}{r} \overset{1}{}286 \\ +118 \\ \hline 4 \end{array}$$

Think: 14 ones = 1 ten 4 ones

$$\begin{array}{r} \overset{11}{286} \\ +118 \\ \hline 04 \end{array}$$

Think: 10 tens = 1 hundred 0 tens

$$\begin{array}{r} \overset{11}{286} \\ +118 \\ \hline 404 \end{array}$$

404 is close to the estimate of 400. So the answer is reasonable.

You have $404 now.

Talk It Over

▶ When did you need to regroup? Why?

▶ How did you record the regrouping?

Suppose you have $692 and the other players owe you $514 in rent. How much money will you have after they pay you?

Add: 692 + 514

Estimate.   **Think:** 700 + 500 = 1,200

Then find the exact sum.

Step 1
Add the ones.
Regroup if necessary.

```
  692
+ 514
    6
```

Step 2
Add all the tens.
Regroup if necessary.

```
   1
  692
+ 514
   06
```

Think: 10 tens =
1 hundred 0 tens

Step 3
Add all the hundreds.
Regroup if necessary.

```
   1
  692
+ 514
1,206
```

Think: 12 hundreds =
1 thousand 2 hundreds

You will have $1,206 after they pay you.

More Examples

A
```
   1
  670
+ 585
1,255
```

B
```
    1
  365
+  29
  394
```

C
```
    1
  174
+ 716
  890
```

D
```
   11
  578
+ 927
1,505
```

Check for Understanding
Add. Estimate to check the reasonableness of your answer.

1
```
  187
+ 108
```

2
```
  175
+ 120
```

3
```
  297
+  48
```

4
```
  715
+ 560
```

5
```
  749
+ 857
```

THINK CRITICALLY: Generalize Explain your reasoning.

6 What is the greatest number of places the sum can have when you add two 3-digit numbers? Give an example.

Turn the page for Practice. ➡

Practice

Add. Remember to estimate.

1 236 + 19

2 320 + 675

3 569 + 350

4 809 + 71

5 381 + 410

6 779 + 101

7 960 + 57

8 147 + 88

9 214 + 286

10 764 + 577

11 608 + 94

12 465 + 70

13 897 + 7

14 365 + 758

15 621 + 345

16 185 + 91

17 191 + 508

18 89 + 635

19 915 + 207

20 Find the sum of 37 and 545.

21 Find the sum of 653 and 409.

22 What is 502 plus 439?

23 What is 756 plus 879?

24 What is 705 more than 210?

Algebra Complete the table.

25

Rule: Add 200.				
Input	135	346	573	924
Output	▪	▪	▪	▪

26

Rule: ▪				
Input	253	327	446	563
Output	293	367	486	603

Find the sums that are greater than 500.
Write _under_ for the others.

27 206 + 242

28 127 + 143

29 792 + 483

30 484 + 159

31 397 + 319

32 208 + 69

33 573 + 122

34 309 + 135

35 399 + 258

········· **Make It Right** ·········

36 Zachary added 639 and 519.
Tell what the error is and correct it.

639
+ 519
1,148

Least Sum Game!

First, make one card for each of the numbers 1 through 9.

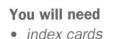

You will need
- *index cards*

Next, make a game sheet and a scorecard for each player.

Play the Game

▶ Mix up the cards. Place them facedown. Pick a card. Each player writes the number in one of the boxes.

▶ Continue until all six boxes are filled.

▶ Find the sum. Compare it with the other player's. The player with the least sum scores 1 point.

▶ If the sums are the same, each player gets a point.

▶ Mix up the cards and continue playing until one player gets 5 points.

How did you decide where to place the numbers?

Game Sheet
Round 1:

Round	1	2	3	4	5
Player 1					
Player 2					

Sample

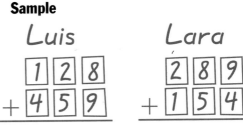

Luis   Lara

443 < 587
So Lara scores 1 point.

more to explore

Using Front Digits to Estimate

Here is another way to estimate a sum. Add the front digits. Write zeros for the other digits.

Estimate: 345 + 862   **Think:** 300 + 800 = 1,100

Use front digits to estimate the sum.

1 38 + 90   **2** 46 + 29   **3** 324 + 463   **4** 823 + 412

Column Addition

Suppose you can pick out a toy at the Kids Only Market. If there are 498 games, 265 dolls, and 562 other toys, how many items can you choose from?

Add: 498 + 265 + 562

Estimate.   **Think:** 500 + 300 + 600 = 1,400

Find the exact sum. You can use pencil and paper.

Cultural Note
The Granville Island Kids Only Market is in Vancouver, British Columbia, Canada.

Step 1
Add the ones.
Regroup if necessary.
```
  1
 498
 265
+562
   5
```

Step 2
Add all the tens.
Regroup if necessary.
```
 21
 498
 265
+562
  25
```

Step 3
Add all the hundreds.
Regroup if necessary.
```
 21
 498
 265
+562
1,325
```

Check by adding up.
```
 498
 265
+562
1,325
```

Think: 8 + 2 = 10
       10 + 5 = 15

Think: 6 + 6 = 12
       1 + 9 = 10
       10 + 12 = 22

Think: 2 + 2 = 4
       4 + 4 = 8
       8 + 5 = 13

 You can also use a calculator.   498 + 265 + 562 = **1325.**

You can choose from 1,325 items.

Check for Understanding
Add. Explain your method.

1 571 + 452 + 169   **2** 918 + 706 + 74   **3** 347 + 227 + 86 + 534

THINK CRITICALLY: Analyze **Explain your reasoning.**

4 Why can you check an answer by adding up?

Practice

Add. Remember to estimate.

1	28	**2**	383	**3**	310	**4**	123	**5**	672
	30		83		350		270		411
	+ 30		+ 204		+ 509		+ 402		+ 298

6 638 + 567 + 832 **7** 513 + 124 + 43 **8** 605 + 140 + 30 + 100

9 189 + 271 + 68 **10** 20 + 30 + 40 **11** 20 + 21 + 13 + 40

12 414 + 287 + 523 **13** 812 + 607 + 735 + 992

Choose two or three numbers from the box that give the sum.

14 148   **15** 1,265   **16** 629

84	123
839	9	565
417	64

MIXED APPLICATIONS
Problem Solving

17 There were 945 people at the market on Friday, 832 on Saturday, and 915 on Sunday. Josh says over 2,000 people visited the market. Is he correct? How do you know?

18 **Spatial reasoning** Which item would not fit in the trunk of a small car?
  a. home video game player
  b. handheld video game
  c. full-size arcade game

19 Hillary traveled 202 miles to Vale. She returned home, then traveled 121 miles to Vista. How far did she travel?

20 **Write a problem** using three or more addends. Solve it. Ask other students to solve it.

mixed review

1 6 + (9 + 1)   **2** (7 + 2) + 6   **3** 9 + (3 + 2)

4 9 + (4 + 5)   **5** (4 + 4) + 4   **6** 4 + (5 + 3)

Draw a Picture

Read   **Carl and his father plan a trip to an outlet mall and a craft fair.**

The mall is 33 miles from Carl's house. The craft fair is 7 miles beyond the mall. How many miles will they travel round trip?

Plan   You can use the information in the problem to draw a picture.

Solve   Use the picture to find the distance from Carl's house to the craft fair.

Then find the distance for the round trip.

They will travel 80 miles.

Look Back   How could you solve this problem another way?

$$33 + 7 = 40 \qquad 40 + 40 = 80$$

Check for Understanding
Draw a picture to solve.

1 The shoe store is to the right of the entrance to the mall. The bakery is to the right of the shoe store and to the left of the music store. Which store is farthest from the entrance?

THINK CRITICALLY: Analyze

2 Tell how the picture helped you solve problem 1.

1 Kuni needs to go to the drugstore and the bookstore. How many blocks will he need to walk to go to both places and back home?

2 **Make a decision** Kuni and Sean want to go to the music store and the market together. Where should they meet? Explain your thinking.

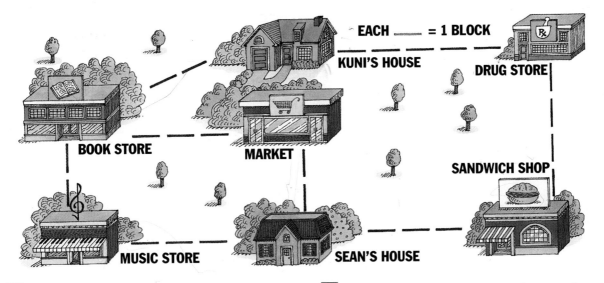

EACH ___ = 1 BLOCK

KUNI'S HOUSE

DRUG STORE

BOOK STORE

MARKET

SANDWICH SHOP

MUSIC STORE

SEAN'S HOUSE

3 At the drugstore Kuni buys 2 boxes of crayons. One box has 64 crayons. The other box has 48 crayons. About how many crayons does he buy in all?

4 The music store has 375 rock CDs, 355 classical CDs, and 372 rap CDs. For which type of music does the store have the most CDs?

5 Mary Anne, Gail, Denise, and Li are in a race. Mary Anne is 6 meters ahead of Gail. Denise is 4 meters behind Mary Anne. Gail is 9 meters behind Li. In what order are the runners from first to last?

6 Lois walks out her front door. She turns right and walks 5 blocks. She turns left and walks 6 blocks. She turns left again and goes 5 blocks. She then turns left and goes 6 blocks. Where is she?

7 Harry rides 8 miles to the market. Then he goes 9 miles farther to the feedstore. He takes a shortcut that makes his trip back only 12 miles. How many miles does he save?

8 **Write a problem** that involves shopping and could be solved by drawing a picture. Solve your problem. Ask others to solve it.

Add Greater Numbers

Suppose you go to a trading card sale.
You want to buy only nonsports cards.
How many are there to choose from?

Add: 9,265 + 3,569

Estimate the sum.

Think: 9,000 + 4,000 = 13,000

Type of Card	Number of Cards for Sale
TV stars	9,265
Football	2,750
Cartoons	3,569
Baseball	6,967
Other sports	9,225

You can use pencil and paper to find the exact sum.

Step 1
Add the ones.
Regroup if necessary.

$$\begin{array}{r} 1 \\ 9,265 \\ +3,569 \\ \hline 4 \end{array}$$

Step 2
Add all the tens.
Regroup if necessary.

$$\begin{array}{r} 11 \\ 9,265 \\ +3,569 \\ \hline 34 \end{array}$$

Step 3
Add all the hundreds.
Regroup if necessary.

$$\begin{array}{r} 11 \\ 9,265 \\ +3,569 \\ \hline 834 \end{array}$$

Step 4
Add all the thousands.
Regroup if necessary.

$$\begin{array}{r} 11 \\ 9,265 \\ +3,569 \\ \hline 12,834 \end{array}$$

Think: 12 thousands =
1 ten thousand 2 thousands

 You can also use a calculator.   9,265 + 3,569 = *12834.*

There are 12,834 nonsports cards to choose from.

Check for Understanding
Add. Explain your method.

1 6,057 + 4,792   **2** 3,905 + 812   **3** 7,495 + 6,546 + 3,892

THINK CRITICALLY: Analyze

4 How can you decide whether to use pencil and paper or a calculator? Give examples.

Practice

Add. Remember to estimate.

1   1,858
    + 2,402

2   5,027
    + 1,650

3   2,010
    + 1,050

4   1,911
    +   786

5   6,001
    + 3,105

6 147 + 1,121

7 1,328 + 1,252

8 6,804 + 8,075

9 2,764 + 3,427

10 3,565 + 698

11 6,974 + 97 + 895

Add mentally. Explain your method.

12 200 + 48 + 700

13 301 + 90 + 2,002

14 220 + 30 + 40 + 700

15 2,000 + 400 + 74 + 3,100

MIXED APPLICATIONS
Problem Solving

Instead of buying cards, some collectors swap cards. Here is what one collector had before and after a convention.

Type of Card	Number Before	Number After
Movie cards	4,075	2,862
TV series cards	1,201	2,701
Superhero cards	1,842	1,876
President cards	1,209	1,927

16 About how many cards did the collector have before the convention? after it?

17 Which type of card did the collector have fewest of before the convention? after it?

18 Brian has 305 superhero cards and 254 cartoon cards. He gets 100 Batman cards for his birthday. How many cards does he have now?

19 One booth sells over 5,000 cards. Two other booths sell at least 2,000 cards each. What is the least number of cards that all of the booths could have sold?

mixed review

Round to the nearest hundred.

1 878

2 384

3 521

4 456

5 98

6 217

Add mentally.

1 67 + 20   **2** 29 + 30   **3** 102 + 13   **4** 60 + 103

5 103 + 23   **6** 120 + 230   **7** 400 + 121   **8** 220 + 510

Estimate how many.

9 sweaters and vests

10 shirts and jeans

11 vests and shirts

12 sweaters and jeans

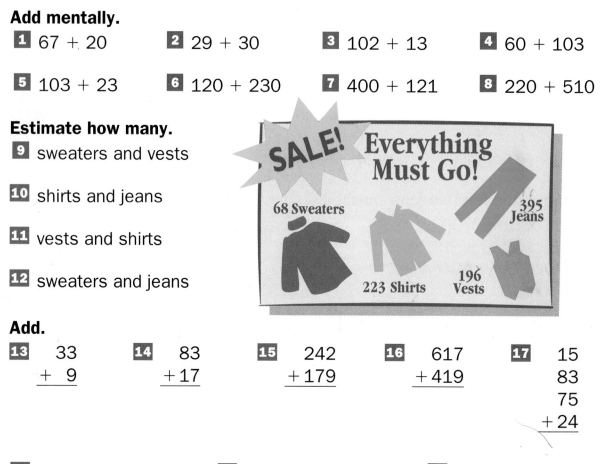

SALE! Everything Must Go!

68 Sweaters
395 Jeans
223 Shirts
196 Vests

Add.

13
```
  33
+  9
```

14
```
  83
+ 17
```

15
```
  242
+ 179
```

16
```
  617
+ 419
```

17
```
  15
  83
  75
+ 24
```

18 527 + 72   **19** 706 + 112   **20** 1,411 + 32 + 875

Solve.

21 For the Harvest Dance the PTA buys 500 large paper cups and 800 medium paper cups. How many paper cups does the PTA buy in all?

22 A bookstore receives 2 boxes of books. Each box has 24 books. The owner needs 40 books for a special order. Does he have enough? Why or why not?

23 **Make a decision** Mrs. Toro needs about 75 pounds of clay. Clay comes in 50-, 30-, or 10-pound sacks. Which sacks should Mrs. Toro buy?

24 Amy drives 16 miles from home to the market. Later she drives 5 miles farther to the mall. Then she drives home. How many miles does she drive in all?

25 Journal Explain how to find 398 + 702 in as many different ways as you can.

"Make a Ten" to Add Mentally

If you want to grow tulips in the spring, you have to plant them in the fall. If you order 43 plain tulips and 29 parrot tulips from a catalog, how many bulbs do you order?

Add mentally: 43 + 29

Add a number to one addend to make a ten. Subtract the same number from the other addend.

$$\begin{array}{c} 43 + 29 \\ {\scriptstyle -1\downarrow \quad \downarrow +1} \\ 42 + 30 = 72 \end{array}$$

You order 72 bulbs in all.

Add mentally.

1 19 + 71   **2** 33 + 9   **3** 29 + 15   **4** 19 + 67

5 66 + 29   **6** 25 + 39   **7** 55 + 49   **8** 39 + 74

9 86 + 8   **10** 45 + 18   **11** 69 + 27   **12** 28 + 74

Use the shopping list for problems 13–15.

13 How many herbs are there?

14 How many flowers?

15 How many berry plants?

16 Ana adds 41 and 26 mentally. She thinks 41 is close to 40. What does she need to add to 26 to find the sum?

Berries: 39 Strawberry plants
           21 Blueberry plants
           12 Raspberry plants
Herbs: 9 Parsley plants
           24 Basil plants
Flowers: 29 Marigolds
           36 Pansies

What to Buy?

Stores use inventories to find out how many of each item they have. In this activity you will work in teams to do an inventory of the school supplies in your classroom.

▶ Think about what you use at school. Decide which items you will count.

▶ Decide how you will record your data.

▶ Create an inventory.

Memo Book

Doing an Inventory

1 With your team make a list of the school supplies you will count.

2 Develop a plan for how you will count the supplies, then record and display the data.

3 Of which type of supply does your class have the most? the least?

Report Your Findings

4 **Portfolio** Prepare a report on what you learned. Include the following:

▶ Describe how you chose items to count. How did you share the work of counting and recording?

▶ Make a display or poster of your inventory.

5 Share your findings and compare them with those of other groups.

Revise your work.
▶ Is your display neat and easy to understand?
▶ Is the data accurate and is it displayed correctly?
▶ Did you proofread your work?

MORE TO INVESTIGATE

PREDICT the cost of the supplies used each month by your class.

EXPLORE how your school purchases school supplies.

FIND which item on your list is used the most.

Count Money and Make Change

Suppose your team sells snacks during an after-school soccer game to earn money for uniforms.

You will need
- *play money— bills and coins*

Work Together

Work with a partner. Choose an item from the snack bar.

Then use play money to give one coin or bill that you could use to buy the snack.

Your partner then counts on to find the change you should receive and gives you your change.

Count your change to be sure it is correct.

Take turns choosing items and making change.

KEEP IN MIND
Be prepared to share your methods for making change with the class.

Talk It Over

▶ Describe how you decided what coin or bill to use to pay for this item.

▶ Describe how you found the amount of change.

Snacks

Peanut butter crackers	55¢
Cheese crackers	65¢
Peanuts (small package)	50¢
Peanuts (large package)	75¢
Raisins (small box)	45¢
Raisins (large box)	90¢
Granola bar	$1.10

Make Connections

Jesse uses a five-dollar bill to pay for a granola bar that costs $1.10. His partner counts up to find the change.

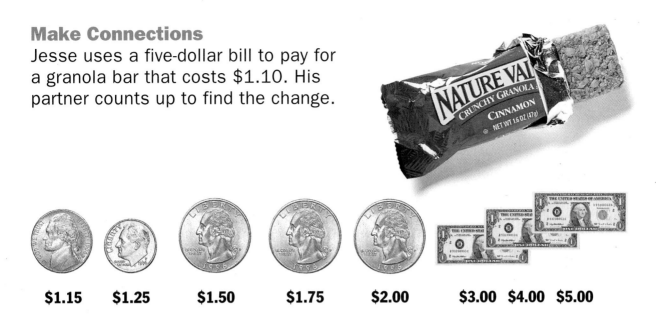

| $1.15 | $1.25 | $1.50 | $1.75 | $2.00 | $3.00 $4.00 $5.00 |

Jesse then counts the amount of change he receives.

$1.00 → $2.00 → $3.00 → $3.25 → $3.50 → $3.75 → $3.85 → $3.90

Jesse receives $3.90 in change.

Check for Understanding

Write the money amount.

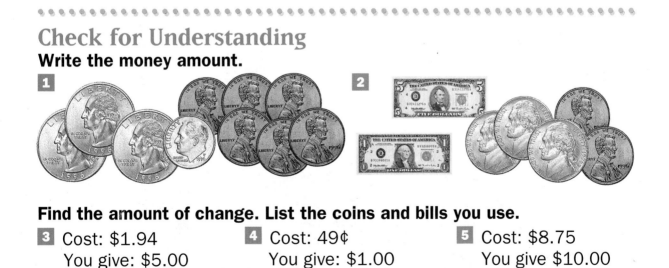

1   **2**

Find the amount of change. List the coins and bills you use.

3 Cost: $1.94
You give: $5.00

4 Cost: 49¢
You give: $1.00

5 Cost: $8.75
You give $10.00

THINK CRITICALLY: Generalize   **Explain your reasoning.**

6 How do you know that you have used the least number of coins and bills to buy an item?

Turn the page for Practice. ➡️

Practice

Write the money amount.

1

2

3 1 five-dollar bill, 3 one-dollar bills, 3 dimes

4 3 one-dollar bills, 7 quarters, 3 pennies

Write the coins and bills needed to make the amount.

5 35¢ **6** 97¢ **7** $1.12 **8** $5.80 **9** $7.30 **10** $9.78

Find the amount of change. List the coins and bills you use.

11 Cost: 17¢
You give: $1.00

12 Cost: $7.61
You give: $10.01

13 Cost: $3.28
You give: $5.03

What if a vending machine runs out of quarters. What coins could it give in change?

14 Cost: 65¢
You give: $1.00

15 Cost: $1.25
You give: $2.00

16 Cost: 50¢
You give: $1.00

What if a vending machine runs out of dimes. What coins could it give in change?

17 Cost: 65¢
You give: 75¢

18 Cost: $1.40
You give: $2.00

19 Cost: 35¢
You give: $1.00

·················· **Make It Right** ··················

20 Marco gave Camille $1.00 to buy an apple for 40¢. Camille counted on to find the change for Marco.

40¢   50¢   75¢ $1.00

Tell what the error is and correct it.

Use the price list for problems 21–23.

21 Beth pays for sunflower seeds with 3 quarters. She gets 4 dimes as change. What can you say about her change?

22 Nathan has 1 dollar and 1 quarter. He wants to buy juice and some nuts or seeds. What can he buy?

23 Vince spent exactly 1 nickel, 3 quarters, and 2 dimes. What did Vince buy?

24 In what year had vending machines been used in the United States for 100 years? See INFOBIT.

Fruit and Nut Snacks	
1 apple	40¢
1 pear	50¢
1 pkg sunflower seeds	55¢
1 pkg mixed nuts	75¢
juice, small	60¢
juice, large	90¢

INFOBIT
The first vending machines were used in the United States in 1888.

Cultural Connection Money Around the World

Many different objects have been used for money in the past:

- Cacao beans in Mexico
- Cowrie shells in Thailand and India
- Metal objects in Liberia and Sierra Leone
- Bars of salt in eastern Africa
- Copper bracelets in Nigeria

1 Why do you think different kinds of money were used by the different cultures?

2 Suppose you were going to pick a classroom object to use as money. What would you choose? Why?

Compare, Order, and Round Money

You can have lots of fun designing and decorating with stamps. Some of them can be expensive. Which stamp costs the most? the least?

Compare the prices.

Step 1
Compare the three amounts.

$8.55   **Think:** 8 > 5, so
$5.99 $8.55 > $5.99 and
$5.25 $8.55 > $5.25.

Step 2
Compare the other two amounts.

$5.99   **Think:** 9 > 2, so
$5.25 $5.99 > $5.25.

Step 3
Write the amounts in order from greatest to least.

$8.55, $5.99, $5.25

The balloon stamp costs the most. The cake stamp costs the least.

What if you want to buy a stamp that costs about $5.00. Which price rounds to $5.00?

Round each amount to the nearest dollar.

$8.55 → $9.00 $5.99 → $6.00 $5.25 → $5.00

The price of the cake stamp rounds to $5.00.

Check for Understanding
Write in order from greatest to least.

1 $0.47, $0.53, $0.48   2 $2.57, $2.50, $3.05   3 $8.95, $9.75, $9.52

Round to the nearest dollar.

4 $4.25   5 $1.76   6 $8.51   7 $9.83   8 $8.42

THINK CRITICALLY: Analyze   Explain your reasoning.

9 Todd says that you can round both a $12.35 stamp and a $10.25 stamp to $10. How did he round the prices?

Practice

Compare. Write >, <, or =.

1 $2.90 ● $3.12

2 $2.81 ● $2.96

3 $5.42 ● $4.09

4 $1.87 ● $1.93

5 $4.25 ● $4.25

6 $3.54 ● $0.58

Write in order from least to greatest.

7 $3.41, $8.92, $5.39

8 $1.95, $1.59, $1.75

9 $0.36, $3.06, $0.63

10 $5.76, $5.66, $7.66, $6.53

11 $6.70, $3.67, $3.72, $6.07

Round to the nearest dollar.

12 $3.35

13 $7.54

14 $4.06

15 $2.56

16 $9.75

Round to the nearest ten dollars.

17 $14.34

18 $48.20

19 $90.17

20 $39.61

21 $88.02

MIXED APPLICATIONS
Problem Solving

Use the price list for problems 22–26.

22 Which rubber stamp set costs about $5.00?

Rubber Stamp Sets	Price
All About Bears	$7.50
Alphabet	$4.79
Have a Party!	$8.39
Stars	$9.95

23 Which rubber stamp set costs the most?

24 Which rubber stamp sets cost more than $5.00?

25 Could you buy all of the stamp sets for under $35? How do you know?

26 **Write a problem** using the information in the list. Solve it. Ask others to solve it.

mixed review

Write in order from least to greatest.

1 302; 321; 231; 608

2 1,926; 2,962; 1,957

3 171; 127; 172; 167

Add Money

Making the team is fun, but it can cost money. If you decide to order the cap and T-shirt when you sign up, how much will it cost?

Add: $9.95 + $6.55 + $7.75

Estimate. Round each amount to the nearest dollar.

Think: $10 + $7 + $8 = $25

You can use pencil and paper to add.

SOCCER
REGISTRATION FORM WITH FEES

SIGN UP FEE	$9.95
T-SHIRT	$6.55
TEAM CAP	$7.75

Step 1
Line up the decimal points.

$$\begin{array}{r} \$9.95 \\ 6.55 \\ + \ 7.75 \end{array}$$

Step 2
Add each place.
Regroup if necessary.

$$\begin{array}{r} {\scriptstyle 2\ 1} \\ \$9.95 \\ 6.55 \\ + \ 7.75 \\ \hline \$24.25 \end{array}$$

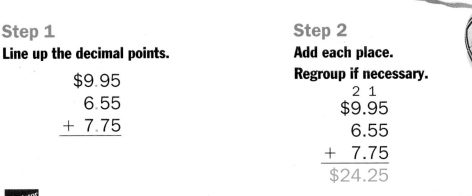

You can also use a calculator.   9.95 + 6.5 + 7.75 = **24.25**

The total cost is $24.25.   **Note:** Remember to enter the decimal point.

- -

Check for Understanding

Add. Estimate to check if your answer is reasonable.

1	**2**	**3**	**4**	**5**
$0.20	$0.79	$6.57	$7.94	$6.00
+ 0.55	+ 0.98	+ 1.41	3.38	3.59
			+ 2.72	+ 0.10

THINK CRITICALLY: Generalize   Explain your reasoning.

6 How is adding money like adding whole numbers?

7 Why do you line up the decimal points before adding?

Practice

Add. Remember to estimate.

1　$0.73
　　+　0.52

2　$0.53
　　+　0.69

3　　$4.88
　　+　3.98

4　　$9.37
　　　9.72
　　+　9.18

5　　$93.05
　　　74.73
　　+　　3.67

6 $0.23 + $0.90　　　**7** $9.02 + $5.83　　　**8** $2.20 + $8.98

Add mentally. Explain your method.

9 $0.20 + $0.50　　　**10** $0.53 + $0.60　　　**11** $1.24 + $1.54

MIXED APPLICATIONS
Problem Solving

Use the price list for problems 12–13.

12 About how much do a team bag, a headband, and a belt cost, including delivery?

13 Make a decision You have a $10 gift certificate. Which items would you choose? What is the cost of your order? Remember to include delivery charges.

14 Data Point What is the favorite type of clothes in your class? Make a class graph. Place your name in the correct column.

Item Description	Price
Wristbands (pair)	$2.25
Baseball cap	$5.15
Belt	$7.50
Headband	$1.99
Workout socks (pair)	$6.25
Team bag	$8.79
Delivery charges per item	$0.75

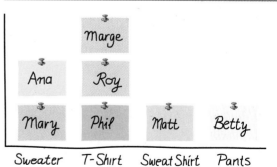

---

mixed review

Complete the pattern.

1 25, 35, 45, ■, ■

2 60, ■, 80, 90, ■

3 12, 15, ■, 21, ■

4 12, 14, 16, ■, ■

5 30, ■, 36, 39, ■

6 7, 9, ■, 13, ■

Problem Solvers at Work

Read
Plan
Solve
Look Back

Part 1 Finding Estimates or Exact Answers

Rebecca and Mrs. Fleming have a budget of $100 for costumes and props for the play. They plan to purchase them at the local thrift store.

Costume	Price	Props	Price
Snow White	$10.95	Plastic apple	$0.50
Queen	$12.95	Mirror	$5.00
Old Woman	$6.25	Set of dishes	$6.50
Prince	$8.00	Broom	$1.50
Huntsman	$4.00	Tablecloth	$2.50
7 Dwarfs	$35.00		
(7 costumes at $5.00 each)			

Work Together

Solve. Be prepared to explain your methods.

1. Which character costs the most to costume?

2. Which costs more, props or costumes?

3. What is the total cost of the costumes?

4. Is the cost of the costumes and the props within the budget? Why or why not?

5. **What if** the budget is only $80. What changes will they have to make?

6. Which problems did you answer with an estimate? Which needed an exact answer? Tell why.

7. **Make a decision** They could rent costumes from another school for about $75. Which would you choose? Expain you reasoning.

Part 2 Write and Share Problems

Rahul used the information in the table on page 112 to write this problem.

8 Solve Rahul's problem.

9 Did you use an estimate or an exact answer to solve the problem? Why?

10 **Write a problem** about the show that can be solved either by an estimate or by an exact answer.

11 Trade problems. Solve at least one problem written by your classmates that uses an estimate and one that needs an exact answer.

12 What was the most interesting problem that you solved? Why?

If you have $15.00, is that enough to buy all the props?

Rahul Bhambhani
Pauline O'Rourke School
Mobile, AL

Turn the page for Practice Strategies.

Part 3 Practice Strategies

Menu

**Choose four problems and solve them.
Explain your methods.**

1 Mrs. Crain spends $8.43 at the grocery store and $9.52 at the drugstore. How much does she spend in all?

2 Hoy has a budget of $10.00 for a birthday present. A book costs $6.95. Wrapping paper costs $1.99. Is he within his budget? Tell why.

3 Estimate prices to complete the problem. Then solve it.

The PTA charges ■ for each cookie and ■ for each cup of apple cider. How much does it cost for 2 cookies and 1 cup of cider?

4 Amber walks 8 blocks to her aunt's house. Together they walk 10 blocks to the bakery. Then they both return to their homes. How far does Amber's aunt walk?

5 Mr. Dixon buys 2 seashell collections. One collection has 209 shells. The other collection has 176 shells. About how many shells are there altogether?

6 Sora buys a notebook that costs $3.59. She pays with four one-dollar bills. What is the least number of coins she could receive in change? What could the coins be?

Choose two problems and solve them. Explain your methods.

7 Use the table to plan two lunches. Keep the total to less than $2.50, but more than $2.00. The lunch should include a sandwich and at least two other items.

Sandwiches	Cost		Item	Cost
Peanut butter and jelly	$1.00		Apple or orange	40¢
Bologna	$1.25		Milk	35¢
Cheese	$1.30		Juice	55¢
Tuna salad	$1.50		Frozen juice bar	65¢

8 Andy is spending the weekend at the Willow Lake campground. He wants to begin and end all of his hikes at this campsite. Plan hikes for Andy that are exactly 6, 7, and 8 miles long.

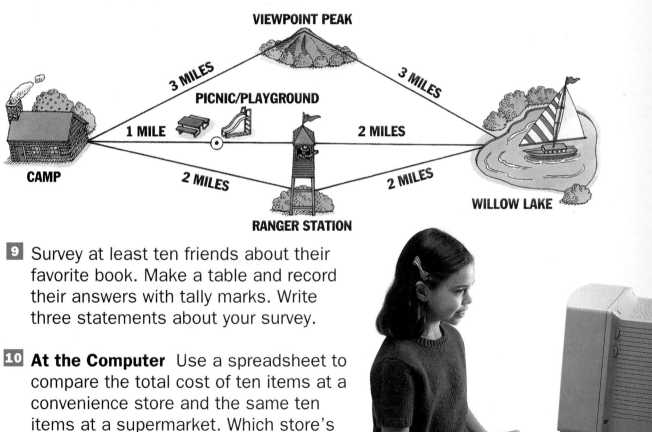

VIEWPOINT PEAK

3 MILES

3 MILES

PICNIC/PLAYGROUND

1 MILE

2 MILES

CAMP

2 MILES

2 MILES

RANGER STATION

WILLOW LAKE

9 Survey at least ten friends about their favorite book. Make a table and record their answers with tally marks. Write three statements about your survey.

10 **At the Computer** Use a spreadsheet to compare the total cost of ten items at a convenience store and the same ten items at a supermarket. Which store's total is less?

Language and Mathematics

Complete the sentence. Use a word in the chart.

1 The ▨ of 51 and 37 is 88.

2 You ▨ to change 17 tens to 1 hundred 7 tens.

3 When an exact answer is not needed you can ▨.

4 To estimate 557 + 873 you can ▨ each number to the nearest hundred.

● ●

Concepts and Skills

Add mentally.

5 33 + 60　　　**6** 10 + 70　　　**7** 300 + 260　　　**8** 700 + 300

Estimate the sum.

9 38 + 44　　　**10** 92 + 125　　　**11** 524 + 273　　　**12** 391 + 825

Add.

13　　64
　　　 + 83

14　　$4.07
　　　 + 2.81

15　　1,353
　　　+ 1,961

16　　593
　　　　951
　　　+ 709

Add.

17 394 + 82 + 13

18 $7.48 + $9.61 + $1.44

Find the amount of change. List the coins and bills you use.

19 Cost: 54¢
You give: 75¢

20 Cost: 35¢
You give: $1.00

21 Cost: $2.53
You give: $5.03

Write in order from greatest to least.

22 $0.36, $0.62, $0.38

23 $7.65, $7.85, $9.86, $8.67

Round to the nearest dollar.

24 $1.95

25 $7.22

Think critically.

26 Analyze. Tell what the error is and correct it.

27 Generalize. Write a rule that tells when to regroup. Give examples.

$$\begin{array}{r} 1 \\ 492 \\ + \ 364 \\ \hline 756 \end{array}$$

MIXED APPLICATIONS

Problem Solving

Pencil & Paper   Calculator   Mental Math

28 Mrs. Vargas got four prices for a radio from three different stores. Which price is the least?
a. $235   b. $205
c. $198   d. $190

29 Paco walks 17 blocks to a music store. He returns home and then walks 5 blocks to the market. How far has he walked when he returns home from the market?

Use the price list for problems 30–33.

30 What is the cost of stickers, a notebook, and a package of pens?

31 Ray has $12.00. Does he have enough to buy 3 notebooks? Tell why.

32 Scott has $5.00. He wants to buy the stickers. What else can he buy?

33 Rita pays for a package of pencils with a $5 bill. What is the least number of coins and bills she could receive as change?

Item	Price
Stickers	$2.98
Pencil case	$1.50
Notebook	$2.90
Ruler	$0.95
Package of pencils	$3.65
Package of pens	$4.99

Add mentally.

1 20 + 50

2 40 + 12

3 500 + 180

4 400 + 600

Estimate the sum.

5 52 + 28

6 124 + 210

7 537 + 388

8 763 + 834

Add.

9
```
  52
+ 34
```

10
```
  3,417
+ 4,256
```

11
```
  $2.95
+  3.09
```

12
```
  456
  238
+ 519
```

13 287 + 28 + 175

14 $5.66 + $1.88 + $3.75

Find the amount of change. List the coins and bills you use.

15 Cost: 88¢
You give: $1.00

16 Cost: 35¢
You give: 50¢

17 Cost: $2.59
You give: $5.00

Write in order from least to greatest.

18 $0.48, $0.19, $0.90

19 $6.58, $8.72, $4.99, $9.50

Round to the nearest dollar.

20 $5.58

21 $3.19

Solve.

22 Vernon buys a pair of socks for $3.98. He gives the clerk $5.03. What is the least number of coins and bills he can receive as change?

23 Cara rode her bike 2 miles to the Mall of America. She rode home and then rode 3 miles each way to the grocery store and back. How far did she ride in all?

24 On a store shelf, the pens are left of the rulers and right of the pencils. Are the pencils to the left or to the right of the rulers?

25 Fran has $13.00. Pens cost $2.75 each. Does he have enough to buy 4 pens? Tell why.

What Did You Learn?

You need to decide how much food allowance you need each week. Write a note to someone that explains how much money you will need for school lunches and snacks. Show all your work.

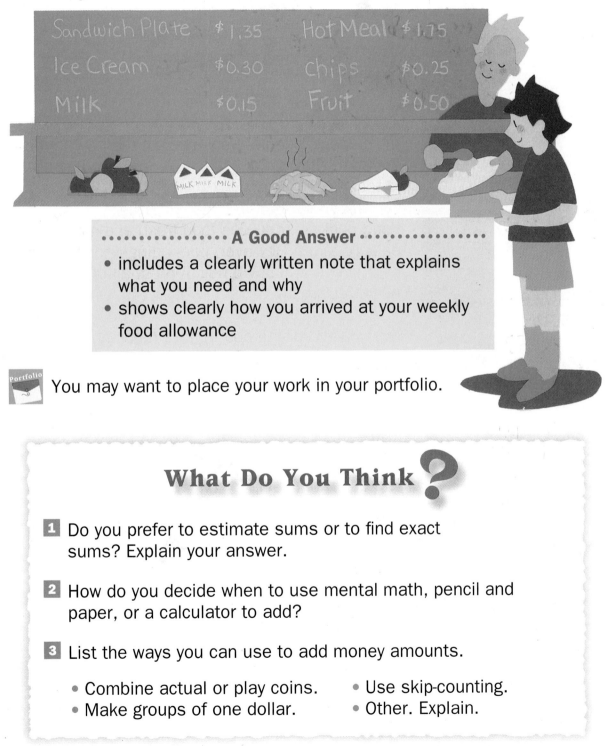

Sandwich Plate $1.35   Hot Meal $1.75

Ice Cream $0.30   Chips $0.25

Milk $0.15   Fruit $0.50

················· **A Good Answer** ·················

- includes a clearly written note that explains what you need and why
- shows clearly how you arrived at your weekly food allowance

Portfolio You may want to place your work in your portfolio.

What Do You Think?

1 Do you prefer to estimate sums or to find exact sums? Explain your answer.

2 How do you decide when to use mental math, pencil and paper, or a calculator to add?

3 List the ways you can use to add money amounts.

- Combine actual or play coins.
- Make groups of one dollar.
- Use skip-counting.
- Other. Explain.

Garbage

> ### Cultural Note
> Modern food packaging started in 1795 with the invention of canning. A French candy maker, Nicolas Appert, heated food in glass bottles.

In the past, people grew more of their own food. The food they did buy was not packaged as it is today.

Food packaging keeps food fresh and makes it easy to store. However, packaging adds to the cost of everything we buy. Almost all of it becomes trash.

Many areas of the country are running out of space for all this garbage.

To help with this problem, you can practice the three Rs.

Reduce Do not buy things that come in unnecessary packaging.

Reuse Use juice containers and other things that can be used more than once.

Recycle Send things made of glass, metal, plastic, and paper to recycling centers for reuse.

▶ Where does the trash in your neighborhood go?

▶ Make a list of ways you can practice the three Rs at home or in school.

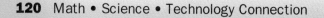

How Much Garbage?

Study the table in order to answer the questions below.

Amount of Solid Waste Produced in the United States	
Year	Pounds of Waste per Person
1970	1,147
1975	1,138
1980	1,217
1985	1,249
1990	1,280
1995	1,319

1 Write a statement about the change in the number of pounds each person wasted per year between 1970 and 1995.

2 If the amount of waste for 1996 was 28 pounds more than 1995, what was the amount of waste for 1996?

3 **What if** it was predicted that by the year 2000 the amount of waste produced by each person would go up 37 pounds. How many pounds would each person waste in 2000?

At the Computer

Amount of Trash			
	Paper	Pencils	Bottles
Monday	6	1	1
Tuesday			
Wednesday			

4 Keep track of what you throw out in your classroom each day for a week. Use a spreadsheet program to find the weekly total for each type of trash.

5 Write three statements using the information in the spreadsheet.

Chapters 1–3

Choose the letter of the correct answer.

1 Find 13 − 5.
- **a.** 8
- **b.** 18
- **c.** 7
- **d.** 9

2 What number comes next?
3, 5, 7, ■
- **a.** 13
- **b.** 10
- **c.** 9
- **d.** not given

3 Add $5.41 + $8.97.
- **a.** $43.38
- **b.** $14.38
- **c.** $1.43
- **d.** $13.38

4 Daniel had $15. He buys fishing bait for $3. What operation would you use to find how much money he has left?
- **a.** rounding
- **b.** addition
- **c.** subtraction
- **d.** not given

5 Ryan buys a poster for $3.71. He pays for it with a five-dollar bill. Which change is incorrect?
- **a.** 4 pennies, 1 quarter, 1 one-dollar bill
- **b.** 4 pennies, 4 nickels, 1 one-dollar bill
- **c.** 4 pennies, 5 nickels, 1 one-dollar bill
- **d.** 9 pennies, 4 nickels, 1 one-dollar bill

6 Find 6 + 8 + 3.
- **a.** 17
- **b.** 16
- **c.** 11
- **d.** 18

7 Find the missing number.
7 + 5 + 3 = 7 + ■ + 5
- **a.** 12
- **b.** 10
- **c.** 8
- **d.** 3

8 Estimate 553 + 291 + 498.
- **a.** 900
- **b.** 1,200
- **c.** 1,300
- **d.** 1,400

9 Choose the number.
nine hundred forty-one thousand, six hundred six
- **a.** 19,416
- **b.** 946
- **c.** 900,416
- **d.** 941,606

10 Order the numbers from greatest to least.
814, 941, 948, 874
- **a.** 948, 941, 874, 814
- **b.** 941, 874, 948, 814
- **c.** 814, 874, 941, 948
- **d.** not given

11 Add 406 + 679 + 92.
- **a.** 1,067
- **b.** 1,167
- **c.** 1,177
- **d.** 2,005

12 Choose the most reasonable number.

Megan borrowed ▨ books from the library.
a. 5
b. 50
c. 500
d. 5,000

13 Which number comes next?
235, 240, 245, ▨
a. 250
b. 230
c. 246
d. 255

14 If one number is removed from each box, the box sums would be equal. Which numbers should be removed?

4
     2
 7   3
	3
	   6 1
	     8

a. 2 and 8
b. 4 and 6
c. 7 and 3
d. 7 and 8

15 What digit is in the tens place of two hundred seventy-five?
a. 275
b. 75
c. 5
d. not given

16 Mrs. Rodriguez buys 40 pounds of dog food and 20 pounds of cat food. How many pounds of pet food does she buy?
a. 6 pounds
b. 20 pounds
c. 60 pounds
d. 100 pounds

17 Suppose you skip-count by twos beginning at 0. Which number would you *not* say?
a. 12
b. 20
c. 18
d. 9

18 Max is next to last. He is nineteenth in the line. How many people are in the line?
a. 18
b. 19
c. 21
d. 20

Use the table for ex. 19–20.

19

Survey of Students' Favorite Vegetables	
Potatoes	⁄⁄⁄⁄ ⁄⁄⁄⁄ ⁄⁄⁄⁄
Corn	⁄⁄⁄⁄ ⁄⁄⁄⁄ ///
Tomatoes	⁄⁄⁄⁄ ///
Carrots	⁄⁄⁄⁄ ⁄⁄⁄⁄ //

Which statement is true?
a. All students like vegetables.
b. No students like tomatoes.
c. More students like potatoes than like carrots.
d. Students like fruit.

20 Which statement is *not* true?
a. 25 students like either corn or carrots.
b. 4 more students like carrots than like tomatoes.
c. 3 fewer students like corn than like potatoes.
d. More than 40 students were surveyed.

SUBTRACTION

Getting from Here to There

People travel all over the world in many different ways. By using subtraction, you can learn how far they travel, how fast they go, and how much it costs.

What Do You Know?

Chantal rides the bus to school. Cooper rides in a car. Lee walks, and Katie rides her bike.

1 How much longer does it take Chantal to get to school than Cooper? Write a number sentence.

2 How much longer does it take Lee than Katie? Explain how you solved this problem.

3 Portfolio Write a question about how long it takes Lee and Cooper to get to school. Then write a question about Lee's and Chantal's times. Explain how to find the answers.

GETTING TO SCHOOL

by bus
18 min

by car
7 min

by walking
23 min

by bicycle
10 min

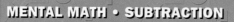

Subtract Whole Numbers

Theresa Cebuhar, a highway maintenance worker

Have you ever been on a highway that never seems to end? Interstate 80 across Nebraska is about 500 miles (mi) long. If you pass mile marker 300, how many more miles are there until the end?

Subtract: 500 − 300

You can use patterns to subtract mentally.

$5 - 3 = 2$
$50 - 30 = 20$
$500 - 300 = 200$

Think:
5 ones − 3 ones = 2 ones
5 tens − 3 tens = 2 tens
5 hundreds − 3 hundreds = 2 hundreds

You will need to drive 200 more miles.

What if you have only 100 miles left to travel. After 50 miles you stop to buy gasoline. How many miles do you still need to go? Explain how you found your answer.

Talk It Over

▶ What is 12 − 5? How can this fact help you find 120 − 50 mentally?

▶ What pattern did you use to find the differences mentally?

Suppose you drive 96 mi on Interstate 80 in Nebraska from Fort Kearney State Historical Park to Buffalo Bill Ranch. You stop in Lexington after going 35 mi. How many miles do you have left?

Subtract: 96 − 35

Sometimes you can subtract mentally by starting with tens.

$$\begin{array}{r} 96 \\ -35 \\ \hline 61 \end{array}$$

Think: Start with tens.
$90 - 30 = 60$
$6 - 5 = 1$

You have 61 more miles to go.

More Examples

A
$$\begin{array}{r} 177 \\ -\ 57 \\ \hline 120 \end{array}$$

Think: Start with hundreds.
$100 - 0 = 100$
$70 - 50 = 20$
$7 - 7 = 0$

B
$$\begin{array}{r} 685 \\ -104 \\ \hline 581 \end{array}$$

Think: Start with hundreds.
$600 - 100 = 500$
$80 - 0 = 80$
$5 - 4 = 1$

Check for Understanding
Copy and complete the pattern.

1 $9 - 2 = $ ■
$90 - 20 = $ ■
$900 - 200 = $ ■

2 $7 - 1 = $ ■
$70 - 10 = $ ■
$700 - 100 = $ ■

3 ■ $- 4 = 6$
■ $- 40 = 60$
■ $- 400 = 600$

Subtract mentally. Explain your method.

4
$$\begin{array}{r} 40 \\ -10 \end{array}$$

5
$$\begin{array}{r} 86 \\ -32 \end{array}$$

6
$$\begin{array}{r} 120 \\ -\ 90 \end{array}$$

7
$$\begin{array}{r} 700 \\ -100 \end{array}$$

8
$$\begin{array}{r} 789 \\ -702 \end{array}$$

THINK CRITICALLY: Generalize Explain your reasoning.

9 When is it easy to subtract mentally?

Turn the page for Practice. ▶

Practice

Copy and complete the pattern.

1
$4 - 2 = \blacksquare$
$40 - 20 = \blacksquare$
$400 - 200 = \blacksquare$

2
$9 - 3 = \blacksquare$
$90 - 30 = \blacksquare$
$900 - 300 = \blacksquare$

3
$6 - \blacksquare = 5$
$60 - \blacksquare = 50$
$600 - \blacksquare = 500$

4
$5 - 3 = \blacksquare$
$50 - \blacksquare = 20$
$\blacksquare - 300 = 200$

5
$\blacksquare - 4 = 3$
$70 - \blacksquare = 30$
$\blacksquare - \blacksquare = 300$

6
$8 - \blacksquare = 1$
$80 - \blacksquare = \blacksquare$
$\blacksquare - 700 = \blacksquare$

Subtract mentally.

7
$\begin{array}{r} 60 \\ -20 \\ \hline \end{array}$

8
$\begin{array}{r} 70 \\ -30 \\ \hline \end{array}$

9
$\begin{array}{r} 90 \\ -70 \\ \hline \end{array}$

10
$\begin{array}{r} 500 \\ -300 \\ \hline \end{array}$

11
$\begin{array}{r} 800 \\ -500 \\ \hline \end{array}$

12
$\begin{array}{r} 57 \\ -21 \\ \hline \end{array}$

13
$\begin{array}{r} 69 \\ -47 \\ \hline \end{array}$

14
$\begin{array}{r} 76 \\ -43 \\ \hline \end{array}$

15
$\begin{array}{r} 367 \\ -104 \\ \hline \end{array}$

16
$\begin{array}{r} 209 \\ -106 \\ \hline \end{array}$

17
$\begin{array}{r} 140 \\ -\ 70 \\ \hline \end{array}$

18
$\begin{array}{r} 694 \\ -\ 90 \\ \hline \end{array}$

19
$\begin{array}{r} 407 \\ -301 \\ \hline \end{array}$

20
$\begin{array}{r} 970 \\ -800 \\ \hline \end{array}$

21
$\begin{array}{r} 566 \\ -140 \\ \hline \end{array}$

22 $90 - 20$

23 $50 - 50$

24 $600 - 300$

25 $150 - 80$

26 $543 - 200$

27 $530 - 420$

28 $502 - 202$

29 $435 - 123$

30 $85 - 70$

31 $120 - 60$

32 $888 - 333$

33 $768 - 754$

Find the missing digit.

34
$\begin{array}{r} 69 \\ -3\blacksquare \\ \hline 37 \end{array}$

35
$\begin{array}{r} 71 \\ -\blacksquare 0 \\ \hline 41 \end{array}$

36
$\begin{array}{r} 25\blacksquare \\ -132 \\ \hline 122 \end{array}$

37
$\begin{array}{r} 326 \\ -1\blacksquare 0 \\ \hline 206 \end{array}$

38
$\begin{array}{r} 92\blacksquare \\ -220 \\ \hline 707 \end{array}$

············· **Make It Right** ·················

39 Robin subtracted mentally.
Tell what the error is and
correct it.

$56 - 3 = 26$

Pencil & Paper   Calculator   Mental Math

40 Logical reasoning Phil wants to do one activity each day on Monday, Wednesday, and Friday. He wants to spend as little money as possible. What should his schedule be?

Activity	Cost
Water Park Mon.–Thurs. Fri.–Sun.	 $16.50 $17.50
Zoo	$5.00 (Wed. free)
Hike	Free

41 The Tamiami Trail in Florida is 88 miles long. If Juan drives 18 miles, how many more miles is it to the end of the trail?

42 Make a decision Mrs. Wilson can usually drive 400 miles on a full tank of gas. She has driven 200 miles since she filled the tank. How many more miles should she drive before buying more gas?

43 How many feet less does it take a car going 40 miles per hour to stop than one going 10 miles per hour faster? See INFOBIT.

INFOBIT
A car going 40 miles per hour needs 123 feet to stop. A car going 50 miles per hour takes 183 feet to stop.

more to explore

Zigzag Subtraction

Here is another method for subtracting mentally.

Subtract: $67 - 35 = 32$ **Think:** $67 - 30 = 37$
$37 - 5 = 32$

Subtract mentally. Explain your method.

1 $84 - 21$	**2** $45 - 32$	**3** $77 - 36$	**4** $97 - 25$
5 $69 - 57$	**6** $56 - 35$	**7** $66 - 46$	**8** $156 - 85$

Estimate Differences

Traveling through France on the TGV, the world's fastest train, is almost like flying! It can go up to 320 miles per hour. Usually it goes 132 miles per hour. How much faster is its top speed than its usual speed?

Estimate: 320 − 132

Round each number to find the difference mentally.

Think: 320 − 132
        ↓   ↓   ←Round to the nearest hundred.
       300 − 100 = 200
So 320 − 132 is about 200.

The train's top speed is about 200 miles per hour faster than its usual speed.

More Examples

A Estimate: 78 − 18   Think: Round to the nearest ten. 80 − 20 = 60

B Estimate: 685 − 315   Think: Round to the nearest hundred. 700 − 300 = 400

C Estimate: 175 − 61   Think: Round to the nearest ten. 180 − 60 = 120

Check for Understanding
Estimate the difference. Tell how you rounded.

1 49 − 12   2 83 − 68   3 42 − 17   4 95 − 87

5 839 − 152   6 401 − 190   7 551 − 194   8 178 − 93

THINK CRITICALLY: Analyze   Explain your reasoning.

9 Journal How else could you round the numbers in ex. 8 to estimate the difference? What would the estimate be?

Practice

Estimate the difference. Round to the nearest ten.

1 85 − 42   **2** 91 − 63   **3** 87 − 33   **4** 52 − 15

5 68 − 36   **6** 76 − 22   **7** 195 − 42   **8** 362 − 48

Estimate the difference. Round to the nearest hundred.

9 585 − 242   **10** 791 − 463   **11** 637 − 423   **12** 752 − 215

13 912 − 377   **14** 876 − 229   **15** 424 − 29   **16** 302 − 64

Algebra Estimate. Write > or < to make a true sentence.

17 89 − 42 ● 40   **18** 71 − 56 ● 20   **19** 137 − 32 ● 100

20 732 − 215 ● 600   **21** 912 − 377 ● 400   **22** 876 − 209 ● 600

23 487 − 193 ● 300   **24** 654 − 212 ● 500   **25** 727 − 359 ● 300

MIXED APPLICATIONS
Problem Solving

Use the table for problems 26–27.

26 About how much farther is a flight to Chicago than a flight to Boston?

Air Miles from New York City			
City	Boston	Chicago	Detroit
Miles	188	711	483

27 **Make a decision** Gail has a ticket for 1,000 miles free travel from New York City. Where should she go? Why?

28 **Data Point** Does the train from Newark to Philadelphia go more or less than 80 miles in 1 hour? Explain your reasoning. See the Databank page 533.

---

mixed review

Estimate the sum.

1 49 + 74   **2** 65 + 38   **3** 19 + 76   **4** 53 + 92

5 410 + 592   **6** 750 + 841   **7** 603 + 269   **8** 253 + 839

Subtract 2-Digit Numbers

You can use what you know about place value to find differences.

Work Together
Work in a small group.

Spin the spinner four times. Use the digits to write two 2-digit numbers.

Model the greater number. Then subtract the lesser number from it. Record your results.

Use the spinner again to make two more 2-digit numbers. Repeat the activity.

Compare your methods with those of others.

Make Connections
Julio's group spun 63 and 26. They used models to find the difference.

> **You will need**
> • *place-value models*
> • *0–9 spinner*

> **KEEP IN MIND**
> Remember to regroup when you can.

Here is how Julio's group found the difference.

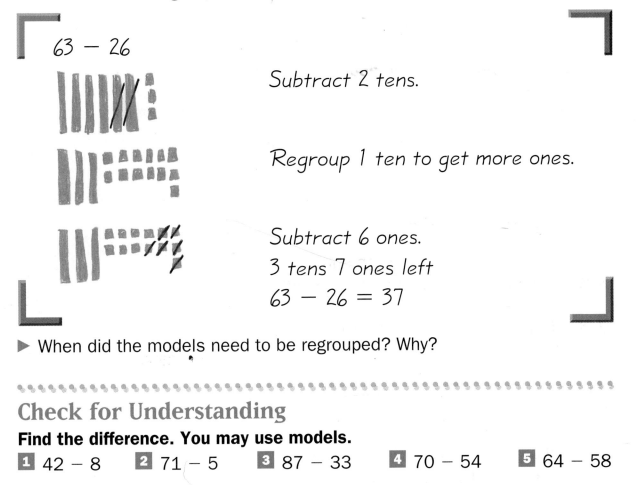

63 − 26

Subtract 2 tens.

Regroup 1 ten to get more ones.

Subtract 6 ones.
3 tens 7 ones left
63 − 26 = 37

▶ When did the models need to be regrouped? Why?

Check for Understanding
Find the difference. You may use models.

1 42 − 8   **2** 71 − 5   **3** 87 − 33   **4** 70 − 54   **5** 64 − 58

THINK CRITICALLY: Generalize

6 Journal   Explain how you tell that you need to regroup when subtracting. Give some examples.

Practice
Find the difference. Explain your method.

| **1** 52 −13 | **2** 71 −39 | **3** 68 −15 | **4** 94 −57 | **5** 88 −22 | **6** 24 − 9 |

| **7** 63 −47 | **8** 96 −85 | **9** 30 −17 | **10** 74 −14 | **11** 36 − 8 | **12** 80 −23 |

13 90 − 40   **14** 56 − 39   **15** 54 − 8   **16** 87 − 32   **17** 25 − 18

18 83 − 57   **19** 48 − 48   **20** 60 − 30   **21** 75 − 25   **22** 40 − 9

Subtract 2-Digit Numbers

In desert areas of Africa and Asia, camels are used to carry people and goods. If the market is 53 miles away and you have gone 19 miles, how much farther do you have to go?

Subtract: 53 − 19

Estimate the difference.

Think: 50 − 20 = 30

In the last lesson you used models to find the exact difference. Here is another method.

Cultural Note
Camels carrying heavy loads should only travel 25 miles a day.

Step 1
Subtract the ones.
Regroup if necessary.

$$
\begin{array}{r}
4\ 13 \\
\cancel{5}\ \cancel{3} \\
-\ 1\ 9 \\
\hline
4
\end{array}
$$

Think: 5 tens 3 ones = 4 tens 13 ones
13 ones − 9 ones = 4 ones

You have 34 miles left to go.

Step 2
Subtract the tens.

$$
\begin{array}{r}
4\ 13 \\
\cancel{5}\ \cancel{3} \\
-\ 1\ 9 \\
\hline
3\ 4
\end{array}
$$

Think: 4 tens − 1 ten = 3 tens

Check for Understanding
Subtract. Estimate to check if your answer is reasonable.

1 25 − 6   **2** 30 − 7   **3** 79 − 19   **4** 91 − 49   **5** 64 − 58

THINK CRITICALLY: Generalize   Explain your reasoning.

6 How many days does it take you to make the trip?

7 How can you estimate to check if your answer is reasonable?

Practice

Subtract. Remember to estimate.

1 45 − 8

2 69 − 29

3 73 − 8

4 76 − 11

5 92 − 39

6 40 − 15

7 31 − 7   **8** 94 − 60   **9** 35 − 17   **10** 87 − 35   **11** 42 − 38

12 23 − 6   **13** 62 − 5   **14** 78 − 56   **15** 70 − 37   **16** 61 − 42

Find the differences that are greater than 30.
Write *under* for the others.

17 79 − 23

18 60 − 46

19 35 − 19

20 56 − 8

21 97 − 28

22 83 − 42

MIXED APPLICATIONS
Problem Solving
Pencil & Paper   Calculator   Mental Math

23 Nakki lives 130 miles from Delhi. Traveling 25 miles a day, could Nakki get there in 4 days? Why or why not?

25 One camel is carrying a load of 270 pounds. A second camel is carrying a load of 318 pounds. How much are they carrying in all?

26 Rama brings 50 pounds of food to feed his camel. After he feeds his camel the first night, about how much food will be left? See INFOBIT.

24 **Write a problem** that can be solved by 75 − 29 = 46. Solve it. Share it with others.

INFOBIT
Camels eat about 8 pounds of food a day.

mixed review

1 26 + 21   **2** 500 + 46   **3** 253 + 259   **4** 896 + 181

5 80 + 59   **6** 124 + 78   **7** 103 + 269   **8** 492 + 451

Solve Multistep Problems

Read   **Two trolley lines run in San Diego. How much longer does the trip from American Plaza to El Cajon take than the one from County Plaza to San Ysidro?**

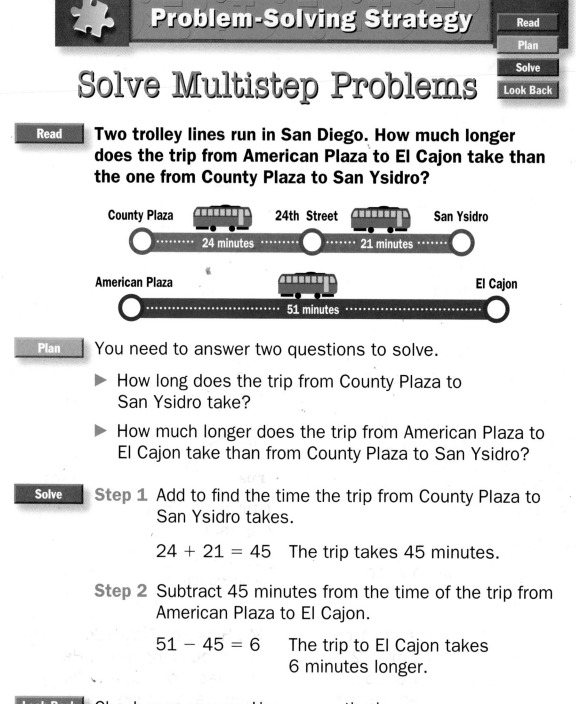

Plan   You need to answer two questions to solve.

▶ How long does the trip from County Plaza to San Ysidro take?

▶ How much longer does the trip from American Plaza to El Cajon take than from County Plaza to San Ysidro?

Solve   **Step 1** Add to find the time the trip from County Plaza to San Ysidro takes.

$24 + 21 = 45$ The trip takes 45 minutes.

Step 2 Subtract 45 minutes from the time of the trip from American Plaza to El Cajon.

$51 - 45 = 6$ The trip to El Cajon takes 6 minutes longer.

Look Back   Check your answer. Use any method.

Check for Understanding

1 **What if** the trolley to San Ysidro is delayed 15 minutes at one stop and 5 minutes at the other. How much longer does its trip take than the trip of the other trolley?

THINK CRITICALLY: Analyze   **Explain your reasoning.**

2 Why do you need to find hidden questions?

Problem Solving

Pencil & Paper · Calculator · Mental Math

Use the map for problems 1–4.

○ ···6 min··· ○ ··5 min·· ○ ·······10 min······· ○ ·········11 min········· ○ 4 min ○

Iris Avenue — H Street — 24th Street — Imperial — American Plaza — County Center

1 How much longer does the trolley trip from Iris Avenue to Imperial take than the trip from Imperial to County Center?

2 Mrs. Ortiz allows 30 minutes to go from Iris Avenue to Imperial. How many extra minutes does she have?

3 Between which two stops does the trip take the most time?

4 An express line makes the complete trip in 25 minutes. How much time does it save?

Use the price list for problems 5–8.

5 Mrs. Weber buys a regular monthly pass and 2 youth passes. About how much does she spend in all?

6 **Write a problem** using the price list. Solve it. Ask others to solve it.

Trolley Ticket Prices	
Fares	**Cost**
Regular monthly pass	$49.00
Youth (6–18) pass	$24.50
One-way fare	$1.75
Round-trip fare	$3.50

7 Megan has 2 quarters and 1 one-dollar bill. Lily has 2 dimes, 2 nickels, 2 quarters, and 1 one-dollar bill. Together can they buy 2 one-way fares? Why or why not?

8 Mr. Hing uses a five-dollar bill to buy a round-trip ticket. He receives 2 one-dollar bills, 3 dimes, and 2 nickels in change. What is wrong with his change?

Use the tally for problems 9–10.

9 Ernesto keeps a record of how often the trolley is late to his stop. How many days has he kept his record?

10 Write a statement describing the information in Ernesto's tally.

8:15 trolley
On time ⊬⊬ //
Late //

Subtract mentally.

1 60 − 30   **2** 74 − 20   **3** 150 − 90   **4** 99 − 52

5 900 − 400   **6** 646 − 200   **7** 709 − 506   **8** 838 − 416

Estimate the difference.

9 46 − 18   **10** 83 − 54   **11** 158 − 92   **12** 335 − 123

13 76 − 32   **14** 89 − 23   **15** 478 − 182   **16** 814 − 504

Subtract.

17 46
  − 8

18 60
  − 11

19 24
  − 9

20 98
  − 17

21 55
  − 49

22 93
  − 17

23 74
  − 23

24 82
  − 9

25 60 − 57   **26** 63 − 19   **27** 70 − 31   **28** 65 − 23

Solve.

29 New York City plans to buy 425 buses in two years. They buy 190 buses in the first year. About how many more do they have to buy?

30 Ryan is on a train traveling 65 miles an hour. The train is 150 miles from Ryan's stop. Will Ryan be there in 2 hours? Why or why not?

31 One yak carries 200 pounds. Another yak carries two bundles. One bundle weighs 156 pounds, and the other weighs 144 pounds. How much more does the second yak carry?

32 There are 23 people on the bus. At the first stop, 6 people get off and 2 people get on. How many people are now on the bus?

33 Journal Explain how you can find 689 − 104 mentally.

Missing Numbers

Did you know that more than 22 million U.S. students ride a bus to school? Suppose you and a friend ride together for 10 minutes. Your ride is 40 minutes altogether. How many minutes are you on the bus before your friend gets on?

You can use either addition or subtraction to solve the problem.

Using Addition
What number plus 10 is 40?

$$\blacksquare + 10 = 40$$
$$\blacksquare = 30$$

Think: 30 + 10 = 40

Using Subtraction
40 minus 10 is what number?

$$40 - 10 = \blacksquare$$
$$\blacksquare = 30$$

Think: 40 − 10 = 30

You are on the bus for 30 minutes before your friend.

These number sentences are related like a fact family.
30 + 10 = 40 and 40 − 10 = 30

▶ What two other number sentences would be in the same family?

Find the missing number. Complete the family of number sentences.

1 40 + 34 = ■
■ − 34 = 40

2 59 + 21 = ■
■ − 59 = 21

3 510 + 60 = ■
■ − 60 = 510

4 700 + 300 = ■
■ − 700 = 300

Solve. Write the addition and subtraction sentences you can use.

5 Phil rides his bike for 25 minutes to get to the park. Jack rides with him the last 12 minutes. How long did Phil ride alone?

6 Mr. Palmer drives 24 miles before buying gasoline. He drives a total of 90 miles. How many miles did he drive after buying the gasoline?

How Far Would You Travel?

Imagine you can visit the relative or friend who lives the farthest from you. How far would you travel? Across the country? Around the world? In this activity, you will work in teams to plan trips to visit people who live far away.

Whom could you visit?

Think about someone you would like to visit who lives far away. Choose a family member, a friend, or a place you would like to see. Talk to your parents to find out exactly where your relatives live.

How could you get there?

Think of ways to get information about location, distance, and transportation.

Planning Your Trip

1 Each team member chooses a person or place to visit. As a team discuss the choices.

2 Decide on one long trip and one short trip the team can take.

3 Plan the trips.

a. Use maps, atlases, or encyclopedias.

b. Call companies such as airlines, railroads, or bus companies.

Report Your Findings

4 Portfolio Prepare a report on what you learned. Include the following:

▶ Make a table to show the distances of the trips.

▶ Compare the long trip with the short trip.

▶ Explain where you found the information you used to plan the trips.

5 Compare your report with the reports of other teams.

Revise your work.

▶ Is your table neat and easy to understand?

▶ Are your calculations correct?

▶ Did you proofread your work?

MORE TO INVESTIGATE

PREDICT how long the trip you planned would take.

EXPLORE the different ways you would travel on your trip.

FIND the shortest route to where you would like to go.

Subtract 3-Digit Numbers

You can use what you know about place value to subtract 3-digit numbers.

Work Together
Work in a small group.

Make two cards for each of the numbers 0 through 9. Mix up the cards. Place them facedown.

Pick six cards. Use the digits to write two 3-digit numbers.

Use place-value models to help you subtract the lesser number from the greater number. Record your results.

Use the cards to write other 2- and 3-digit numbers. Repeat the activity.

Talk It Over
▶ How did you use the models to subtract?

▶ When did you have to regroup? Why?

▶ **What if** you picked 303 − 145. Tell how you use models to find the difference.

You will need
- *place-value models*
- *index cards*

KEEP IN MIND
Remember to regroup when you can.

Make Connections

Kelly's group picked 427 and 234. Here is how they found the difference.

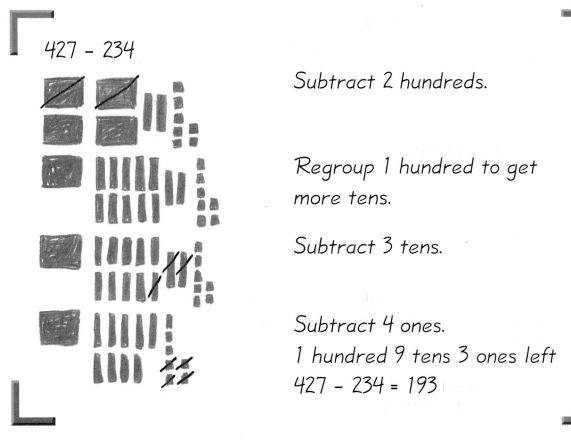

427 – 234

Subtract 2 hundreds.

Regroup 1 hundred to get more tens.

Subtract 3 tens.

Subtract 4 ones.
1 hundred 9 tens 3 ones left
427 – 234 = 193

▶ Why did Kelly need to regroup one hundred?

Check for Understanding
Show how you find the difference.

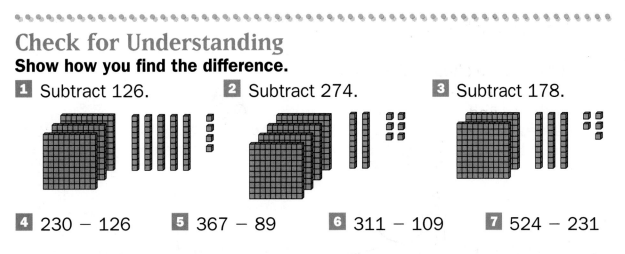

1 Subtract 126.

2 Subtract 274.

3 Subtract 178.

4 230 – 126   **5** 367 – 89   **6** 311 – 109   **7** 524 – 231

THINK CRITICALLY: Generalize   Explain your reasoning.

8 How is subtracting 3-digit numbers like subtracting 2-digit numbers?

Turn the page for Practice. ➡

Practice

Show how you find the difference.

1 Subtract 107.

2 Subtract 238.

3 Subtract 345.

4 Subtract 372.

Find the difference. Explain your method.

5	**6**	**7**	**8**	**9**	**10**
688	445	956	415	273	672
− 427	− 139	− 336	− 375	− 115	− 588

11 231 − 126   **12** 687 − 568   **13** 411 − 209   **14** 724 − 232

Algebra Use + or − to make a true sentence.

15 32 ● 47 = 79   **16** 56 ● 42 = 14   **17** 382 ● 37 = 345

18 859 ● 263 = 1,122   **19** 635 ● 143 = 778   **20** 215 ● 9 = 206

MIXED APPLICATIONS
Problem Solving
Pencil & Paper   Calculator   Mental Math

21 The train Jill rides to work normally takes 25 minutes. This morning it was delayed. The trip took 51 minutes. How long was the train delayed?

22 A regular train ticket costs $8.75. During rush hour there is an extra charge of $3.50. How much does the ticket cost during rush hour?

23 A train normally carries about 175 people. During rush hour it carries about 325 people. About how many more people does the train carry during rush hour?

24 Paul is riding with his two sons. A child's ticket costs $4.25. Paul's ticket costs $6.50. He gives the clerk a $20 bill. How much change does he get?

Race to Zero Game!

Make two cards for each number 0 through 9.

Mix up the cards. Place the deck facedown.

Play the Game

You will need
- index cards
- place-value models

▶ Start with 900 points.

▶ Each player picks three cards. Then each player uses the digits to write a 3-digit number.

▶ Each player subtracts the 3-digit number from 900 points. You may use models.

▶ Mix up the cards. Pick again. Subtract the number you make from the number of points remaining.

▶ Continue until one player reaches or comes closer to zero. After the first number, players may choose to subtract 3-digit, 2-digit, or 1-digit numbers.

more to explore

Make a Ten
You can "make a ten" to subtract mentally.

Subtract: $64 - 39$ **Think:** $64 - 39$
$$+1\downarrow \quad \downarrow +1$$
$$65 - 40 = 25$$

Subtract mentally. Explain your method.

1 $71 - 29$ **2** $44 - 19$ **3** $67 - 39$ **4** $38 - 29$

5 $88 - 69$ **6** $57 - 39$ **7** $83 - 49$ **8** $92 - 58$

Subtract 3-Digit Numbers

Cultural Note

In Alaska people travel along the coasts on ferry boats. Bush pilots fly people and supplies between remote villages.

A ferry boat left Valdez, Alaska, with 324 passengers. At Seward 132 passengers got off. How many passengers were left on the boat?

Subtract: 324 − 132

In the last lesson you used models to find the exact difference. Here is another method.

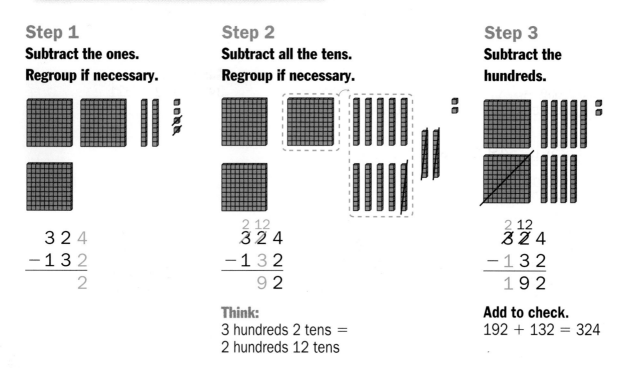

Step 1

Subtract the ones. Regroup if necessary.

```
  3 2 4
− 1 3 2
      2
```

Step 2

Subtract all the tens. Regroup if necessary.

```
  2 12
  3 2 4
− 1 3 2
    9 2
```

Think:
3 hundreds 2 tens =
2 hundreds 12 tens

Step 3

Subtract the hundreds.

```
  2 12
  3 2 4
− 1 3 2
  1 9 2
```

Add to check.
192 + 132 = 324

There are 192 passengers left.

Talk It Over

▶ When did you need to regroup? Why?

▶ How did you record the regrouping?

▶ How can you estimate to see if your answer is reasonable?

Suppose a bush pilot flies from Fairbanks to Stevens Village and then to Barrow. How far is the flight from Stevens Village to Barrow?

Town	Distance from Fairbanks
Stevens Village	172 miles
Barrow	521 miles

Subtract: 521 − 172

Estimate the difference. **Think:** 500 − 200 = 300

Step 1
Subtract the ones. Regroup if necessary.

```
    1 11
  5 2 1
- 1 7 2
      9
```

Think:
2 tens 1 one =
1 ten 11 ones

Step 2
Subtract the tens. Regroup if necessary.

```
     11
  4 1 11
  5 2 1
- 1 7 2
    4 9
```

Think:
5 hundreds 1 ten =
4 hundreds 11 tens

Step 3
Subtract the hundreds.

```
     11
  4 1 11
  5 2 1
- 1 7 2
  3 4 9
```

Add to check.
349 + 172 = 521

The flight is 349 miles.

More Examples

A
```
    15
  3 8 17
  4 8 7
-   7 8
  3 8 9
```

B
```
    16
  4 8 10
  5 7 0
- 4 8 7
    8 3
```

C
```
      4 12
  3 5 2
- 1 3 8
  2 1 4
```

Check for Understanding
Subtract. Estimate to check your answer.

1	**2**	**3**	**4**	**5**	**6**
942 − 731	678 − 387	293 − 9	820 − 328	545 − 381	731 − 64

THINK CRITICALLY: Generalize Explain your reasoning.

7 How is checking that an answer is reasonable different from checking an answer by adding?

Turn the page for Practice. ➡

Practice

Subtract. Remember to estimate.

1 241
   − 61

2 174
   −   7

3 594
   − 162

4 281
   − 79

5 916
   − 850

6 887
   − 668

7 720
   − 151

8 623
   − 86

9 851
   − 303

10 944
    −   8

11 723
    − 694

12 727
    − 608

13 639
    − 49

14 980
    − 814

15 552
    − 85

16 968
    − 937

17 648
    − 189

18 478
    − 389

19 983 − 92

20 269 − 155

21 773 − 6

22 160 − 128

23 343 − 8

24 395 − 79

25 953 − 830

26 926 − 587

Find the differences that are less than 300.
Write *over* for the others.

27 820
    − 39

28 718
    − 522

29 285
    − 15

30 775
    − 308

31 437
    − 194

32 548
    − 389

33 768 − 5

34 931 − 357

35 948 − 723

36 695 − 586

Algebra Use the rule to find the difference.

37

Rule: Subtract 28.	
Input	Output
339	▦
176	▦
436	▦
619	▦

38

Rule: Subtract 7.	
Input	Output
193	▦
482	▦
217	▦
239	▦

39

Rule: Subtract 263.	
Input	Output
837	▦
975	▦
472	▦
658	▦

·················· **Make It Right** ··················

40 Ben subtracted this way.
Tell what the error is and correct it.

$$\begin{array}{r} \overset{16}{4\cancel{6}3} \\ -\ 381 \\ \hline 182 \end{array}$$

Problem Solving

Joan lives 53 miles from Kobuk. She can travel by snowmobile, dogsled, truck, or airplane.

Method of Transportation	Amount of Time to Travel 53 Miles
Dogsled	720 minutes
Truck	70 minutes
Snowmobile	95 minutes
Airplane	30 minutes

41 How much longer does it take to drive a truck than to fly?

42 About how much longer does it take to dogsled than to snowmobile?

43 How much longer does it take to dogsled than to fly?

44 Anchorage and Fairbanks are two of the largest cities in Alaska. They are 361 miles apart. How much farther is it from Anchorage to Fairbanks than from Alaska to Siberia? See INFOBIT.

INFOBIT
The most western point of the mainland of Alaska is 51 miles from Siberia.

more to explore

Using Front Digits to Estimate
Here is another way to estimate a difference.

Subtract the front digits. Write zero for the other digits.

Estimate: 552 − 206   **Think:** 500 − 200 = 300

Use the front digits to estimate the difference.

1	**2**	**3**	**4**	**5**	**6**
337	566	829	958	721	637
− 104	− 236	− 173	− 632	− 281	− 322

7 376 − 228   **8** 918 − 175   **9** 679 − 397   **10** 788 − 169

Subtract Across Zero

Suppose 205 bikers start a tour of Mexico, but only 118 bikers finish. How many bikers do not finish?

Subtract: 205 − 118   Estimate.   **Think:** 200 − 100 = 100

Step 1
Subtract the ones.
No tens to regroup.
Regroup hundreds.

```
  1 10
  2 0̸ 5
− 1 1 8
```

Think: 2 hundreds 0 tens =
1 hundred 10 tens

Step 2
Regroup tens.

```
      9
  1 1̸0 15
  2 0̸ 5̸
− 1 1 8
```

Think: 10 tens 5 ones =
9 tens 15 ones

Step 3
Subtract the ones, tens, and hundreds.

```
      9
  1 1̸0 15
  2 0̸ 5̸
− 1 1 8
      8 7
```

Add to check.
87 + 118 = 205

87 bikers do not finish the race.

More Examples

A
```
      9
  4 1̸0 14
  5̸ 0̸ 4̸
− 1 0 8
  3 9 6
```

B
```
      9
  0 1̸0 10
  1̸ 0̸ 0̸
−     6 1
      3 9
```

C
```
      9
  3 1̸0 10
  4̸ 0̸ 0̸
− 2 8 7
  1 1 3
```

Check for Understanding
Subtract. Estimate to check your answer.

1 408 − 49   **2** 300 − 8   **3** 604 − 299   **4** 708 − 602

THINK CRITICALLY: Analyze

5 Laura solves example C by subtracting 399 − 286.
Does she get the same answer? Why?

Practice

Subtract. Remember to estimate.

1
```
  304
-  27
```

2
```
  502
- 393
```

3
```
  400
- 209
```

4
```
  605
-   6
```

5
```
  707
- 298
```

6
```
  907
- 878
```

7
```
  105
-   9
```

8
```
  600
- 318
```

9
```
  206
-  19
```

10
```
  808
- 422
```

11
```
  900
- 101
```

12
```
  700
- 500
```

13 501 − 46

14 200 − 127

15 103 − 8

16 904 − 671

17 607 − 257

18 406 − 77

19 500 − 302

20 809 − 788

Subtract mentally. Explain your method.

21 400 − 299

22 702 − 399

23 550 − 350

24 407 − 205

MIXED APPLICATIONS
Problem Solving
Pencil & Paper   *Calculator*   *Mental Math*

25 Janell is training for a bicycle race. She bicycles 135 miles each week. Her goal is 300 miles each week. How many more miles to her goal?

26 How much farther is a trip from Ensenada to San Quintín than from Ensenada to Tecate?

27 Pablo wants to travel less than 1,000 miles in all. Can he go from Tijuana to Guerrero Negro and back? Explain your reasoning.

Tijuana
Tecate
70 MILES
71 MILES
Ensenada
121 MILES
San Quintín
253 MILES
Guerrero Negro

mixed review

Round to the nearest ten.

1 46

2 33

3 98

4 257

5 736

6 975

Subtract Greater Numbers

In 1984 Joe Kittinger flew a helium balloon from Maine to Italy. The trip covered nearly 3,543 miles. After 40 hours he had traveled 1,926 miles. How many miles were left?

Subtract: 3,543 − 1,926

Estimate.   **Think:** 4,000 − 2,000 = 2,000

Subtract. Use pencil and paper.

Step 1	**Step 2**	**Step 3**	**Step 4**
Subtract the ones. Regroup if necessary.	Subtract the tens. Regroup if neccessary.	Subtract the hundreds. Regroup if necessary.	Subtract the thousands.

Step 1
Subtract the ones. Regroup if necessary.

```
      3 13
3,5 4̸ 3̸
−1,9 2 6
        7
```
Think:
4 tens 3 ones =
3 tens 13 ones

Step 2
Subtract the tens. Regroup if neccessary.

```
       3 13
3,5 4̸ 3̸
−1,9 2 6
      1 7
```

Step 3
Subtract the hundreds. Regroup if necessary.

```
  2 15 3 13
3̸,5̸ 4̸ 3̸
−1,9 2 6
    6 1 7
```
Think:
3 thousands 5 hundreds =
2 thousands 15 hundreds

Step 4
Subtract the thousands.

```
  2 15 3 13
3̸,5̸ 4̸ 3̸
−1,9 2 6
1,6 1 7
```

You can also use a calculator: 3,543 − 1,926 = *1617.*

There were 1,617 miles left.

More Examples

A
```
  1,486
−   400
  1,086
```

B
```
       12
    3 2̸ 16
  8,4̸ 3̸ 6̸
− 5,3 5 7
  3,0 7 9
```

C
```
        9 9
  3 10 10 15
  4̸,0̸ 0̸ 5̸
− 1,5 2 6
  2,4 7 9
```

Check for Understanding
Subtract. Explain your method.

1 7,451 − 49   **2** 2,361 − 1,000   **3** 6,935 − 423   **4** 2,058 − 1,362

THINK CRITICALLY: Analyze Explain your reasoning.

5 How can you decide whether to use mental math, pencil and paper, or a calculator?

Practice

Subtract. Remember to estimate.

1   5,469
    − 1,400

2   4,429
    − 2,369

3   2,572
    −   69

4   1,700
    −   422

5   8,015
    − 4,228

6   2,874
    −   973

7   8,643
    − 4,014

8   7,008
    − 5,009

9   4,166
    − 2,481

10   7,004
    − 6,829

11 1,246 − 42

12 3,010 − 700

13 7,324 − 1,003

14 4,000 − 2,336

15 4,817 − 3,943

16 9,833 − 520

MIXED APPLICATIONS
Problem Solving
Pencil & Paper   *Calculator*   *Mental Math*

17 Mr. Kittinger's balloon flew 3,543 miles. A plane flying across the United States would cross 3,987 miles. How much farther would the plane fly than the balloon?

18 Mr. Kittinger's trip took 5,020 minutes. A supersonic jet flies from New York to Paris in 210 minutes. How much longer was Mr. Kittinger's trip than the supersonic jet's trip?

Cultural Connection   Abacus

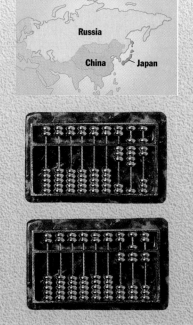

Russia

China   Japan

Different types of **abacuses** are used in China, Japan, and Russia.

Each upper bead on a rod stands for 5. Each lower bead stands for 1. Each rod has a different value. This Chinese abacus shows the number 397.

To subtract 125, move the beads away from the crossbar. The abacus shows the answer 272.

1 Draw a picture of another number on the abacus.

2 Pick yet another number. Explain how you would find the difference of these two numbers. Draw a picture of the difference.

Subtract Money

In Jamaica a bus ride costs Mona $1.78 in U.S. dollars. When she returns home it costs $4.60 to ride the same distance. How much less does the bus ride in Jamaica cost?

Subtract: $4.60 − $1.78

Estimate. Round each number to the nearest dollar.

Think: $5 − $2 = $3

Subtract. Use pencil and paper.

Cultural Note
In Jamaica people use minibuses to travel all over the countryside.

Step 1	Step 2	Step 3
Line up the decimal points.	**Subtract as you would subtract whole numbers.**	**Write the dollar sign and decimal point in the answer.**
$4.60 − 1.78	15 3 ⅔ 10 $4.6 0̸ − 1.7 8 2 8 2	15 3 ⅔ 10 $4.6 0̸ − 1.7 8 $2.8 2

 You can also use a calculator.   4.60 − 1.78 = **2.82**

The bus ride in Jamaica costs $2.82 less.

Check for Understanding
Subtract. Estimate to check your answer.

1 $0.47
− 0.12

2 $0.64
− 0.59

3 $9.47
− 9.29

4 $8.05
− 3.37

5 $6.10
− 2.05

THINK CRITICALLY: Summarize   Explain your reasoning.

6 How is subtracting money like subtracting whole numbers?

Practice

Subtract. Remember to estimate.

1 $0.85
   − 0.14

2 $0.42
   − 0.38

3 $0.71
   − 0.15

4 $4.92
   − 3.60

5 $8.00
   − 7.69

6 $7.03
   − 4.83

7 $5.64
   − 3.00

8 $9.46
   − 5.21

9 $90.00
   − 10.97

10 $79.21
   − 37.98

11 $0.84 − $0.25

12 $7.00 − $3.66

13 $28.59 − $14.00

Subtract mentally. Explain your method.

14 $5.00 − $2.99

15 $6.50 − $2.50

16 $4.67 − $2.67

MIXED APPLICATIONS
Problem Solving

17 The Eurostar train can carry 794 passengers. If 518 passengers are on board, about how many seats are empty?

18 A small pizza costs $5.25. Jordan pays for a small pizza with $10.00. How much change should he receive?

19 The English Channel Tunnel is 32 miles long. The part of the tunnel that is underwater is 24 miles long. How much of the tunnel is *not* underwater?

20 **Make a decision** Should Mrs. Brown buy a first-class Eurostar ticket for $172, or the standard-class ticket for $121? The first-class ticket includes a meal.

21 **Data Point** In your class, what is the favorite way to travel? Make a tally like the one shown. Write a statement based on your results.

Favorite Ways to Travel	
Plane	JHT JHT
Car	JHT JHT JHT IIII
Train	JHT III
Bus	JHT I

mixed review

1 85 + 13

2 69 − 31

3 58 + 29

4 84 − 38

5 73 − 15

6 25 + 60

7 74 − 55

8 67 − 46

Problem Solvers at Work

Read
Plan
Solve
Look Back

Part 1 Finding Missing Information

Kim can take the bus or ride her bike to school. She rides her bike when the weather is sunny. She takes the bus when it is rainy or too cold.

Bus Ticket Choice	Cost
Single Fare	$0.75
Monthly Pass	$15.00
Ticket Book (1 dozen fares for the cost of 10)	$7.50

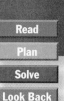

Work Together
Solve. Identify any missing information.

1 Kim buys a ticket book. How much will she save over buying 12 single fares?

2 How many fares are there in a ticket book? How do you know?

3 Does Kim ride the bus to school today?

4 Kim thinks she will ride the bus about 26 times this month. What should she buy? Why?

5 **What if** Kim lived in your community. How could you find out how much a single bus fare costs?

6 **Make a decision** It is December. This month there are only 13 days of school for Kim. The weather is usually rainy and cold. Should Kim buy a monthly pass, a ticket book, or pay single fares? Explain your reasoning.

Part 2 Write and Share Problems

Brian wrote this problem about another bus line.

7 Solve Brian's problem.

8 Explain how to solve Brian's problem using only words.

9 **Write a problem** of your own that is similar to Brian's problem.

10 Solve the new problem. How is your problem like Brian's problem? How is it different?

11 Trade problems. Solve at least three problems written by your classmates.

12 What was the most interesting problem you solved? Why?

Kres paid for a monthly pass with a $20 bill. For change, he got 3 one-dollar bills, 4 quarters, 9 dimes, and 2 nickels. How much did the monthly pass cost?

Brian "Luke" Rhodes
Mandarin Oaks
Elementary School
Jacksonville, FL

Turn the page for Practice Strategies.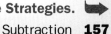

Part 3 Practice Strategies

Menu

Choose four problems and solve them. Explain your methods.

1 Andrew has $25.00. He pays $12.50 to ride the ferry. He buys a sandwich and juice for $4.65. How much money does Andrew have left?

2 Paco takes the train from Tucson to El Paso. The trip is 320 miles long. He buys a magazine for $2.95 and an apple for 75¢. How much money does he spend?

3 Mr. Turner buys gasoline for his truck. It costs $26.55. He gives the clerk $30.00. He receives 1 nickel, 1 dime, 1 quarter, and 3 one-dollar bills in change. Is this correct? Why or why not?

4 Emma wants to buy a backpack for $19.95, jeans for $21.50, and two T-shirts for $12.95 each. She has $50. Does she have enough money? Why or why not?

Use the table for problems 5–6.

5 Which city is about 600 miles from Dallas?

6 Which is the closest city to Dallas? How much farther away from Dallas is Boston than the closest city?

Air Miles	
From Dallas, TX	**Miles**
to Atlanta, GA	795
to Boston, MA	1,748
to Chicago, IL	917
to Tulsa, OK	257
to Omaha, NE	644

**Choose two problems and solve them.
Explain your methods.**

7 Use the table to plan two different trips. Each trip should be between 300 and 400 miles long. Each trip should begin in Little Rock and go through either Memphis or Fort Smith.

From Little Rock, AR	Miles
to Memphis, TN	137
to Fort Smith, AR	160

From Memphis, TN	Miles
to New Orleans, LA	393
to Nashville, TN	210

From Fort Smith, AR	Miles
to Tulsa, OK	116
to Oklahoma City, OK	180

8 Spatial reasoning Trace the shape without taking your pencil off the paper or retracing any lines. Put an X to show where you start. Number the sides and use arrows to show your path. A sample start is shown.

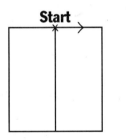

Start

9 Camille asked her classmates how they travel to school. She made this tally of the results. Write 3 statements she could make about the results.

Car	JHT III
Bus	JHT JHT I
Walk	III
Bike	JHT
In-line skate	I

10 At the Computer Use a drawing program to build as many different figures as you can using 4 squares, 5 squares, and 6 squares. Each square in a figure must share at least one side with another square.

Extra Practice, page 497

Language and Mathematics

Complete the sentence. Use a word in the chart.

1 You can estimate or ■ to check your work when you subtract.

2 The ■ between 699 and 143 is 556.

3 To subtract 186 from 307, ■ 3 hundreds 0 tens as 2 hundreds 10 tens.

4 To ■ a difference, round each number to the same place.

5 To subtract money amounts, always line up the ■ points.

Vocabulary
estimate
difference
subtract
regroup
add
round
decimal

Concepts and Skills

Subtract mentally.

6 56 − 31   **7** 47 − 25   **8** 600 − 100   **9** 773 − 271

Estimate the difference.

10 94 − 58   **11** 46 − 13   **12** 529 − 126   **13** 869 − 817

Subtract.

14
$$26 - 19$$

15
$$45 - 27$$

16
$$96 - 82$$

17
$$74 - 27$$

18
$$\$0.83 - 0.55$$

19
$$135 - 19$$

20
$$\$8.38 - 0.53$$

21
$$485 - 62$$

22
$$982 - 573$$

23
$$801 - 587$$

24
$$700 - 321$$

25
$$1{,}023 - 948$$

26
$$\$5.06 - 2.45$$

27
$$2{,}670 - 657$$

28
$$\$8.03 - 2.54$$

29 $10.59 − $7.68   **30** $6.00 − $2.90   **31** $0.91 − $0.29

Think critically.

32 Analyze. Tell what the error is and correct it.

$$
\begin{array}{r}
832 \\
-\ 75 \\
\hline
843
\end{array}
$$

MIXED APPLICATIONS
Problem Solving
Pencil & Paper | Calculator | Mental Math

33 Last month 35 people signed up for the canoe trip down the Suwannee River. On the day of the trip 7 people did not show up. How many people went on the canoe trip?

34 Roy buys 1 full-fare ticket for $5.65 and 2 children's tickets for $1.75 each for their trip to the city. He gives the clerk a $10 bill. How much change does he receive?

35 There are 650 people on the southbound train for the morning commute. After 3 stops, 210 people have gotten off. No one has gotten on. How many people are left on the train?

36 Roy rides 15 miles to the post office in town. He rides 9 miles farther to a park. The route he rides home is 21 miles. How many miles less is his ride home?

Use the table for problems 37–40.

37 Ms. Yee flew from New York to Rio de Janeiro. Mr. Watson flew from New York to Los Angeles. How much longer was Ms. Yee's flight?

From New York	Miles
to Rio de Janeiro	4,801
to Rome	5,707
to Los Angeles	2,451
to Montreal	331
to Mexico City	2,090

38 About how far is it from New York to Mexico City?

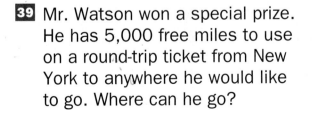

39 Mr. Watson won a special prize. He has 5,000 free miles to use on a round-trip ticket from New York to anywhere he would like to go. Where can he go?

40 Mrs. Strongbow needs to know about how much shorter the trip from New York to Paris is than the trip from New York to Rome. Can you tell? Why or why not?

Subtract mentally.

1 60
     − 40

2 75
     − 32

3 800
     − 400

4 89
     − 63

5 678
     − 462

6 36 − 12   **7** 78 − 53   **8** 500 − 300   **9** 956 − 351

Estimate the difference.

10 57 − 23   **11** 94 − 46   **12** 724 − 382   **13** 982 − 921

14 87 − 56   **15** 63 − 44   **16** 518 − 21

Subtract.

17 54
      − 47

18 26
      − 15

19 154
      − 48

20 95
      − 78

21 $0.76
      − 0.47

22 $7.56
      − 2.48

23 87
      − 43

24 790
      − 354

25 800
      − 565

26 704
      − 476

27 $15.62 − $8.48   **28** $8.00 − $5.20   **29** $0.86 − $0.58

Solve. Use the table for problems 30–32.

30 How many more students walk than bike?

31 About how many more students come by bus than car?

How Our Students Get to School	
Walk	315
Bus	268
Car	174
Bike	76
Other	18

32 How many different ways do students get to school? Can you tell? Why or why not?

33 Kevin has $20. He buys a bus pass for $10.50 and lunch for $4.85. How much does he have left?

What Did You Learn?

The first week Dana's class collected 425 cans. The second week they collected 515 cans. The third week they collected 543 cans.

▶ Explain the results of collecting cans for 3 weeks. Show all your work.

▶ Explain what Dana's class needs to do to reach their $54.75 goal. Show all your work.

·············· **A Good Answer** ··············
- clearly explains how each answer was found
- shows all your work, and is clearly organized, labeled, and accurate

You may want to place your work in your portfolio.

What Do You Think?

1. Are you able to decide when you need to add and when you need to subtract to solve a problem? Explain your answer.

2. List the ways you might use to solve a subtraction problem:
   - Use place-value models.
   - Use mental math.
   - Use pencil and paper.
   - Other. Explain.

3. How do you decide how to round the numbers in a problem when you estimate?

Ball Bearings

Many modern skate wheels are made out of a type of plastic called *urethane.* They also have *ball bearings* inside. These tiny balls lower the amount of friction made by the wheels.

Friction is created when two things slide over one another. It slows them down.

Try this activity to study how ball bearings reduce friction.

1 Place the marbles in a jar lid. Place the lid and the marbles on a piece of cardboard. Slowly lift one end of the cardboard until the lid begins to move. Try this several times.

2 Turn the lid upside down. Again, slowly lift one end of the cardboard until the lid begins to move.

▶ How did the motion of the lid change when the marbles were on the bottom?

▶ Why do you think ball bearings are used in skate wheels?

Which One Rolls Farthest?

Several students hold a contest to see who can build a toy car that can roll the farthest.

Rolling Race	
Name	**Distance (in feet)**
Jim	25
Charlene	32
Kim	34
Ann	29
Flo	41
Jen	22
Abe	33
Ron	19
Ellis	35
Thelma	30

1 Make a table and order the students from first place to tenth place.

2 **What if** Ron had oiled the wheels on his car and it went 12 feet farther. In what place would he have finished?

3 Which car do you think had the least friction? Why?

At the Computer

Ball bearings and oil are ways of lowering the amount of friction. However, we do not always want to lower friction.

People often fall on wet or icy sidewalks because the sidewalks are slippery. The water or ice has lowered the amount of friction too much. In fact, you would not even be able to walk if there was not any friction.

4 Use a word processing program to write a story about how life would be different if there was not any friction!

CHAPTER 5

TIME, DATA, AND GRAPHS

Life After School

There are many different things to do after school. You can use mathematics to plan your time, to find which activities are the most popular, and to display this data.

What Do You Know ?

Adam makes a pictograph to show how much time he spends on his favorite activities each week.

1 How much more time does he spend fishing than reading? How did you use the graph to find the answer?

2 **What if** Adam starts skating at 3:30 and stops at 5:30. On the pictograph, how can you show how long he skated?

3 Explain three things that you know by looking at Adam's pictograph.

Time Spent on Favorite Activities

Fishing

Reading

Softball

Video games

= 1 hr.

Estimate Time

**Have you ever said, "I'll be there in a minute!"?
Find out how long a *minute* really is.**

Work Together

Work with a partner. Write and complete ten addition facts on a sheet of paper. Have your partner time you. How long did it take?

Think of some things that might take less than a minute, about a minute, and more than a minute to do. Make a list.   **Note:** 60 seconds = 1 minute

Try some of the activities from your list. Have your partner time you. Were your estimates close to the actual times?

Make Connections

Here is how Erica and Michael recorded their results.

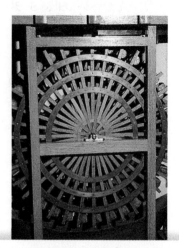

Cultural Note
Historians think that the first mechanical clocks were invented in China about 1,000 years ago.

You will need
• analog clock or watch with a second hand

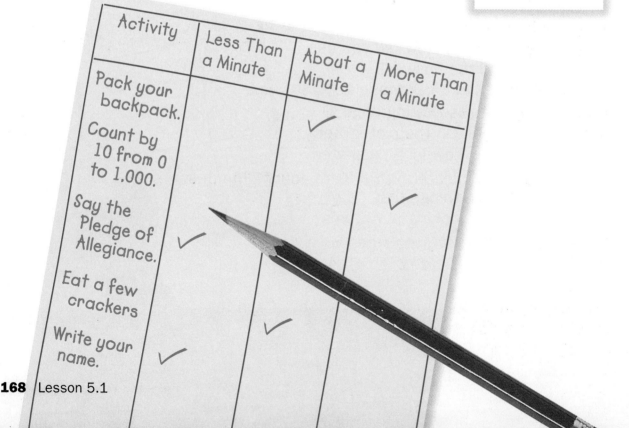

Activity	Less Than a Minute	About a Minute	More Than a Minute
Pack your backpack.		✓	
Count by 10 from 0 to 1,000.			✓
Say the Pledge of Allegiance.	✓		
Eat a few crackers		✓	
Write your name.	✓		

There are 60 minutes in 1 hour. It can take an hour to watch two shows on television.

▶ What else takes about an hour?

Check for Understanding
Choose the more reasonable time.

1 Walk a dog—15 minutes or 15 hours?

2 Watch a movie—2 minutes or 2 hours?

3 Catch a baseball—1 second or 1 minute?

4 Attend a holiday picnic—4 minutes or 4 hours?

5 Eat lunch—15 minutes or 15 hours?

THINK CRITICALLY: Analyze

6 How do you decide if an estimate is a reasonable amount of time for an activity?

Practice

Choose the more reasonable time.

1 Wash your hands—
1 minute or 1 hour?

2 Wash a car—
30 minutes or 30 hours?

Write the letter of the most reasonable answer.

3 It takes about ■ minute(s) to eat an apple.
  a. 5　　**b.** 20　　**c.** 40　　**d.** 60

4 It takes about ■ minute(s) to walk up four flights of stairs.
  a. 2　　**b.** 30　　**c.** 40　　**d.** 20

5 It takes about ■ hour(s) to clean your room.
  a. 8　　**b.** 10　　**c.** 1　　**d.** 24

6 It takes about ■ hour(s) to watch a football game.
  a. 3　　**b.** 20　　**c.** 15　　**d.** 8

Tell Time

You can tell time in different ways. There is schooltime, lunchtime, dinnertime, and bedtime.

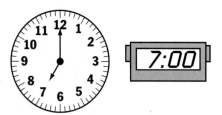

Read: seven o'clock

Write: 7:00

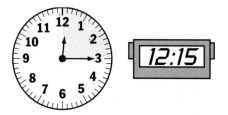

Read: twelve-fifteen, a quarter after twelve, *or* fifteen minutes past twelve

Write: 12:15

Read: five-thirty, half past five, *or* thirty minutes past five

Write: 5:30

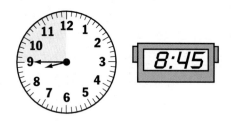

Read: eight forty-five, a quarter to nine, *or* forty-five minutes after eight

Write: 8:45

Talk It Over

▶ How many different ways can you read  ?

You use A.M. to show the time between 12 midnight and 12 noon.

Ben is early for breakfast.

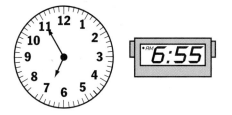 **6:55**

Read: six fifty-five A.M.

Write: 6:55 A.M.

You use P.M. to show the time between 12 noon and 12 midnight.

Taka is late for dinner.

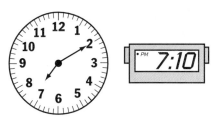 **7:10**

Read: seven-ten P.M.

Write: 7:10 P.M.

Check for Understanding

Write the time using A.M. or P.M. Then show one way to read the time.

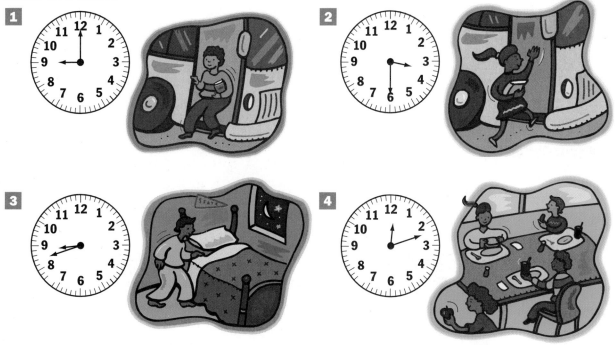

THINK CRITICALLY: Analyze **Explain your reasoning.**

5 Why is it necessary to use A.M. and P.M.?

6 If there were no watches or clocks, how might you know what time it was?

Turn the page for Practice. ➡

Practice

Write the time using A.M. or P.M. Then show one way to read the time.

1

2

3

4

Match. Write the correct letter.

5 3:42 P.M.

6 10:00 A.M.

7 six-thirty

8 a quarter past eight

9 twelve minutes after five

10 7:43

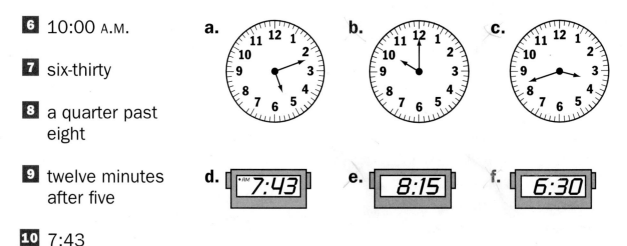

a.

b.

c.

d. •AM 7:43

e. 8:15

f. 6:30

⸱⸱⸱⸱⸱⸱⸱⸱⸱⸱⸱⸱⸱⸱⸱⸱⸱⸱⸱⸱⸱⸱ **Make It Right** ⸱⸱⸱⸱⸱⸱⸱⸱⸱⸱⸱⸱⸱⸱⸱⸱⸱⸱⸱⸱⸱⸱

11 Sarita called to find out when the ferry leaves. The clerk told her 8:00. She went to the dock that evening. The ferry was not there. What was the error?

Problem Solving

12 Silvia has math class at 1:30 P.M. on Monday. James has math class at half past one in the afternoon on Monday. Could they be in the same class? Why or why not?

13 Lincoln School needs $1,000 for a new playground. The school received donations of $350, $425, and $200. Did the school receive enough money? How do you know?

14 Suppose it is Saturday. What might Ben be doing at 7:20 A.M.? at 7:20 P.M.?

15 **Write a problem** about an important time in your day. Solve it. Then share it with others.

16 Find the total amount.

Cultural Connection Iroquois Calendar

The Iroquois Lunar Months	
New Moon	**The Moon of the . . .**
First moon	snow and blizzard
Second moon	winds
Third moon	forming of maple syrup
Fourth moon	planting time
Fifth moon	flowers
Sixth moon	strawberries
Seventh moon	gentle breeze
Eighth moon	hot weather
Ninth moon	harvest
Tenth moon	leaves
Eleventh moon	frost
Twelfth moon	cold weather
Thirteenth moon	snow shoes

Iroquois tradition says that a year has thirteen lunar, or moon, months. A lunar month has 28 days. Each moon is named after something that is special in that month.

Iroquois Nation

1 During which Iroquois moon does your birthday occur?

2 During which Iroquois moon does school end for summer vacation?

Elapsed Time

Ferry Schedule P.M. **Hours**

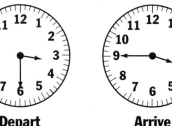

Depart		Arrive	
Ferry Point	3:30	Bubble Beach	3:45
Bubble Beach	4:00	Angel Island	4:30
Angel Island	4:45	Cape Lookout	6:15
Cape Lookout	6:45	Ferry Point	

Many boys and girls help their parents after school. Suppose your family runs the ferry across Sunset Bay. How long does it take to go from Ferry Point to Bubble Beach?

Think: Skip-count by fives:

5   5   5

3:30   3:35   3:40   3:45

From 3:30 P.M. to 3:45 P.M. is 15 minutes.

It takes 15 minutes to get to Bubble Beach.

Depart   **Arrive**

How long does it take the ferry to go from Angel Island to Cape Lookout?

Think: From 4:45 P.M. to 5:45 P.M. is 1 hour. From 5:45 P.M. to 6:15 P.M. is 30 minutes.

It takes 1 hour and 30 minutes to get to Cape Lookout.

Depart   **Arrive**

Check for Understanding

1 How long does it take the ferry to go from Bubble Beach to Angel Island?

2 It takes 2 hours for the ferry to return to Ferry Point from Cape Lookout. At what time will the ferry dock?

THINK CRITICALLY: Generalize **Explain your reasoning.**

3 How does knowing elapsed time help you understand a schedule?

Practice

1 What time will it be in one minute?

2 What time will it be in one hour?

3 What time will it be in 10 minutes?

How much time has passed?

4 Begin: 1:20 A.M.
End: 1:40 A.M.

5 Begin: 9:55 P.M.
End: 11:25 P.M.

6 Begin: 1:30 A.M.
End: 10:30 A.M.

7 Begin: 3:05 P.M.
End: 5:45 P.M.

8 Begin: 6:30 A.M.
End: 11:30 A.M.

9 Begin: 6:25 P.M.
End: 6:45 P.M.

MIXED APPLICATIONS
Problem Solving

10 **Data Point** Lou has from 2:30 P.M. to 4:00 P.M. to go on rides at the park. Use the table on page 534 in the Databank to make a list of rides he could take. Explain why you think your list is reasonable.

11 Paul and his uncle want to go to Bubble Beach Park. Paul earned a reading award good for $10 off the $24.50 children's ticket price. An adult ticket costs $28.75. How much will it cost them to get into the park?

12 Santo goes for football practice at 2:45 P.M. He gets home 3 hours later. What time does Santo get home?

13 **Write a problem** about finding elapsed time. Trade it with a friend and solve.

---

mixed review

1 358
     − 46

2 471
     + 139

3 257
     − 166

4 901
     + 782

5 500
     − 413

6 427 + 648

7 804 − 628

8 347 + 221

9 743 − 697

Use a Calendar

It is November 4. How many days is it before the soccer game?

Look at the calendar. The soccer game is on November 11.

Count the days between November 4 and November 11.

It is 7 days before the soccer game.

More Examples

A What is the date for the fourth Sunday in November?

Think: Count down the Sunday column. The fourth Sunday is November 26.

B On what day of the week is the last piano lesson in the month?

Think: Find the last piano lesson. Look at the top of the column to find the day, Wednesday.

NOVEMBER

S	M	T	W	T	F	S
			1 piano lesson	2	3 Scouts meeting	4
5	6	7 ELECTION DAY	8 piano lesson	9	10	11 Big soccer game VETERAN'S DAY
12	13	14	15 piano lesson	16	17 Scouts meeting	18
19	20	21	22 piano lesson	23 THANKS-GIVING	24	25
26	27	28	29 piano lesson	30		

Time Facts

7 days = 1 week

30 or 31 days = 1 month*

about 4 weeks = 1 month

12 months = 1 year

52 weeks = 1 year

365 days = 1 year

366 days = 1 leap year

*February has 28 days, but in a leap year, it has 29.

Check for Understanding

What is the date for:

1 the first Monday? **2** Thanksgiving? **3** Election Day?

What day of the week is:

4 November 7? **5** the first scout meeting? **6** the soccer game?

THINK CRITICALLY: Generalize

7 Give a reasonable estimate of what can be done in a day, in a week, in a month, and in a year.

Practice

Use the calendar for ex. 1–8. What is the date for:

1 the first Tuesday?   **2** the Friday after Presidents' Day?

3 the fourth Thursday?   **4** Valentine's Day?

What day of the week is:

5 February 28?   **6** February 5?

7 February 17?   **8** March 1?

FEBRUARY

S	M	T	W	T	F	S
			1	2	3	4
5	6	7	8	9	10	11
12	13	14 VALENTINE'S DAY	15	16	17	18
19	20 PRESIDENTS' DAY	21	22	23	24	25
26	27	28				

Choose the letter of the most reasonable estimate.

9 You go to school each year for ▓.
   a. 10 days   **b.** 10 weeks   **c.** 10 months

10 Tom's house was built in ▓.
   a. 6 days   **b.** 6 months   **c.** 6 years

MIXED APPLICATIONS
Problem Solving

Pencil & Paper   *Calculator*   *Mental Math*

11 Joanne and Carla met at a football game on November 2. Today is November 30. For how many weeks have they known each other?

12 **What if** you read for 1 hour each school night. Estimate the number of hours you would spend reading in a month. Explain your method.

more to explore

A Calendar Time Line

Make a calendar time line like the one shown.

1 Write the names of your school and after-school events on your time line.

2 Choose two events. How many weeks or months are there between them? Are there other events between them?

Extra Practice, page 499

Time, Data, and Graphs **177**

Guess, Test, and Revise

Read George bought a backpack and a canteen for $22. He spent $4 more for the backpack than he did for the canteen. How much did each cost?

Plan Guess some prices. Try them out. Revise your guesses if you need to. Record your work.

Solve Try two prices whose total is $22. Find the difference. Is the difference $4? If not, try two different prices.

The backpack cost $13, and the canteen cost $9.

Cost of Backpack	Cost of Canteen	Total	Difference
Try $16.	Try $6.	$22	$10
Try $15.	Try $7.	$22	$8
Try $13.	Try $9.	$22	$4

Look Back How could you have solved the problem using fewer guesses?

Check for Understanding

1 Nancy bought a compass. She received 55 cents in change. There were 8 coins, all nickels and dimes. How many coins were nickels? How many were dimes?

THINK CRITICALLY: Generalize

2 Explain how you made your first guess for problem 1.

3 Why is a table helpful for recording your work?

1. Which number would you leave out to get a sum of 94? Explain your thinking.

| 21 | 62 | 46 | 11 |

Use the sign for problems 3–7.

3. Elaine takes $20 to see the play. She wants to buy a ticket, a souvenir program, and two raffle tickets. Does she have enough money? Explain.

4. Fred uses a $20 bill to pay for 3 tickets. What is his change?

6. **Make a decision** You have $12 to spend at the theater. What can you buy besides a ticket to the play?

8. **Logical reasoning** A mystery even number has three digits. The sum of its digits is 8. The tens digit and ones digit are the same. No digit is zero. What number could it be?

9. The Gershwin Theater in New York has 1,933 seats. How many more seats does the Perth Entertainment Center have? See INFOBIT.

10. **Write a problem** that may be solved using the guess, test, and revise strategy. Solve it. Ask others to solve it.

2. The baseball team left school at 3:15 P.M. They traveled for 45 minutes. At what time did they arrive for the game?

Play Tonight at 8:00 P.M.

Tickets	$5.50
Souvenir Program	$3.25
Raffle ticket	$5.00
Parking	$4.50

5. Delcia spent $19.25 at the play. What could she have bought?

7. Samantha and Wapi arrive 15 minutes early for the play. At what time do they arrive?

INFOBIT
The Perth Entertainment Center in Western Australia has 8,003 seats. It was completed in 1976.

Choose the more reasonable time.

1 Watch a baseball game—
3 minutes or 3 hours?

2 Eat a sandwich—
15 minutes or 15 hours?

Write the time using A.M. **or** P.M.
Then show one way to read the time.

3

4

Use the calendar for ex. 5–7.

5 What day of the week is June 8?

6 What is the date for Flag Day?

7 What is the date for the second Sunday?

JUNE

S	M	T	W	T	F	S
				1	2	3
4	5	6	7	8	9	10
11	12	13	14 FLAG DAY	15	16	17
18	19	20	21	22	23	24
25	26	27	28	29	30	

Solve.

8 Roberto got home from school at
3:30 P.M. He spent 1 hour and
30 minutes doing homework. At
what time did he finish his
homework?

9 At a flea market, hardcover books cost 75¢, and
softcover books cost 50¢. If Sam spent $2.50 and
bought both kinds, how many of each did he buy?

10 Journal Look at any calendar page. Describe as many
patterns as you can.

Analyzing Data

The title of a table helps explain what the data is about. Which of the titles below do you think best explains this data?

Title:?	
Ryan	4 hours
Kristen	2 hours
Gail	1 hour
Ed	2 hours

Titles
Total Time Sleeping
Time Spent Eating Lunch
3rd-Grade Student Heights
Bike-a-thon Riding Distances
Hours Spent Reading
3rd-Grade Student Foot Length

Think:
▶ The table shows amounts of time.
▶ One hour is too short a time for total time sleeping.
▶ 4 hours is too long to spend eating.

The title **Hours Spent Reading** describes the data best.

Match the table with the title that describes it best. Explain your choice.

1

Nikole	8 miles
Jeff	9 miles
Cristina	10 miles
Jim	7 miles
Claire	9 miles

2

Lee	52 inches
Jaime	55 inches
Sol	49 inches
Marie	48 inches
David	50 inches

3

Claudio	20 minutes
Marina	40 minutes
Corrine	35 minutes
Marc	45 minutes
Isabelle	35 minutes

4

Lynn	11 hours
Steven	7 hours
Ann Marie	9 hours
Craig	9 hours
Kerry	8 hours

5 Create a mystery table. Trade with a friend. Write a title that describes the data.

An After-school Schedule

Work together to plan an after-school schedule.

▶ Decide how much time you have after school each day.

▶ Decide how you want to spend the time each day. Write what time you will begin and end each activity.

▶ Decide how you will display your group's schedules.

▶ Compare your schedules with those of other groups.

Making a Schedule

1 How much time do you have after school until bedtime each day?

2 Decide how much time you need for homework.

3 Is there anything you do on the same day each week, such as lessons or practice?

4 Compare your schedule with other schedules in your group. Is there anything in your schedule you would like to change?

Report Your Findings

5 **Portfolio** Prepare a report on what you learned about scheduling your time. Include the following:

▶ Explain how you planned your schedule. How did you decide what you wanted to do? How did you decide the amount of time you wanted to allow for it?

▶ How are your group's schedules alike? How are they different?

▶ Did you change your schedule? Why?

Revise your work.
▶ Are your explanations clear and are your ideas well organized?
▶ Is your schedule accurate?
▶ Did you proofread your work?

MORE TO INVESTIGATE

PREDICT how your schedule will be different at this time next year.

EXPLORE a schedule for Saturday and Sunday.

FIND railroad, bus, and plane schedules. Use them to plan a family trip.

Tallies and Line Plots

Do you take music lessons? The tally below shows which instruments the students in one class want to learn to play.

Work Together

Work with a partner. Copy and complete the tally table and the line plot. Then answer the questions.

Tally

What Would You Like to Play?

Instrument	Tally	Number of Students
Piano	ЖĦ II	7
Flute	IIII	4
Violin	I	1
Guitar	ЖĦ III	▓
Trumpet	II	▓

Line Plot
What Would You Like to Play?

```
X
X
X
X        X
X        X
X        X
X        X        X
Piano  Flute  Violin  Guitar  Trumpet
            INSTRUMENTS
```

▶ How did the tally help you complete the line plot?

▶ What was the most popular instrument? the least popular? How do you know?

▶ How many students are in the class? How do you know?

▶ Do you prefer the tally or the line plot to display data? Why?

Make Connections

To make a tally table:
► write a title for each column.
► list the items.
► show a tally mark for each response.
► write a number to show the total number of tally marks for each item.
► write a title for the table.

To make a line plot:
► draw and label the bottom line.
► show an X for each response.
► write a title for the plot.

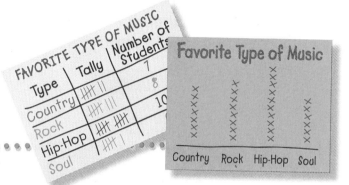

Check for Understanding

1 **What if** two students switch from guitar to flute. How would the line plot on page 184 change? What would remain the same?

THINK CRITICALLY: Analyze

2 How are a tally and a line plot alike? different?

Practice

Use the tally for problems 1–4.

1 Twelve students attended the Art Club meeting in Week 5. Use this data to complete the tally.

2 Use the tally to make a line plot.

3 Use the line plot to tell about the attendance over the five weeks.

Art Club Attendance		
Week	**Tally**	**Number of Students**
Week 1	卌 卌	10
Week 2	卌 卌 IIII	14
Week 3	卌 卌 III	13
Week 4	卌 卌	10
Week 5		■

4 About how many students would you expect at the next meeting? Explain your answer.

5 **Data Point** Survey your class about the instrument they want to play. Use a tally or a line plot to organize your data.

6 What could be a good title for this line plot? Why?

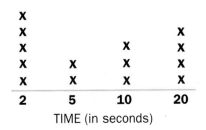

Pictographs

Collecting for a Community Pantry is a great way to help others. This data shows the number of bags of food collected by one pantry.

Bags of Food Collected	
Day	**Number of Bags**
Monday	25
Tuesday	15
Wednesday	20
Thursday	15
Friday	30
Saturday	50

Bags of Food Collected

Monday	🛍🛍🛍🛍🛍
Tuesday	
Wednesday	🛍🛍🛍🛍
Thursday	🛍🛍🛍
Friday	
Saturday	

Key: Each 🛍 stands for 5 bags.

Work Together
Work with a partner. Copy and complete the pictograph. Then answer the questions.

▶ How did you decide how many symbols to draw?

▶ On which day were the greatest number of bags collected? the least number? How do you know?

▶ On which days were the same number of bags collected? How do you know?

Make Connections

To make a pictograph:
▶ list the items.
▶ choose a symbol to represent the responses.
▶ use a key to tell the number each symbol stands for.
▶ draw symbols to show the responses for each item.
▶ write a title for the pictograph.

Check for Understanding

1 **What if** 55 bags were collected on Sunday. How would the pictograph on page 186 change?

THINK CRITICALLY: Analyze **Explain your reasoning.**

2 You want someone to see the day on which the most food was collected. Would you show them the table or the pictograph?

Practice

Use the table and the pictograph for ex. 1–5.

1 Use the data in the table to copy and complete the pictograph.

2 How many more dogs did you draw for October?

3 In which month was the greatest number of dogs adopted? How many symbols did you draw?

4 **What if** you added 🐕🐕🐕🐕🐕 for January. How many dogs do these symbols stand for?

5 How many more dogs were adopted in December than in September?

Dogs Adopted	
Month	**Number of Dogs**
September	4
October	8
November	6
December	12

Dogs Adopted	
September	🐕 🐕
October	🐕
November	
December	

Key: Each 🐕 stands for 2 dogs.

6 **Data Point** Ask your classmates what kind of help they would like to give in their community. Show the data in a pictograph.

Bar Graphs

Dave helps students in school. He needs to know what their interests are and what they think about.

Work Together

Work with a partner. Copy and complete the bar graph. Then answer the questions.

Dave Chin, School
Adjustment Counselor,
Kennedy School,
Franklin, MA

After-School Activities

Activity	Number of Students
Baseball	18
Reading	10
Art	3
Skating	8
Soccer	14
Bicycling	6

After-School Activities

(Bar graph: NUMBER OF STUDENTS vs ACTIVITY — Baseball 18, Reading 10, Art 3, Skating, Soccer, Bicycling)

Talk It Over

▶ How did you show 3 students on the bar graph? **What if** you had to show 9 students?

▶ What is the most popular activity? the least popular? How do you know?

▶ What does the graph tell you about the way students feel about indoor and outdoor activities?

▶ Would you show this data on a line plot? Why or why not?

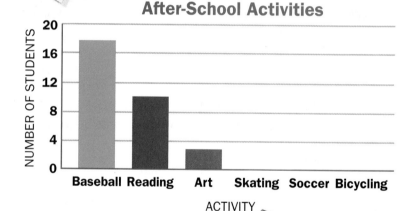

Make Connections

To make a bar graph:

► list the items along one side of the graph.

► starting with 0, write a scale with numbers along the other side of the graph.

► draw a bar to match each of the numbers in the table.

► write a title for the graph and label the sides.

Why is bar graph a useful way to record data?

When you choose a scale for a graph what do you have to think about?

Check for Understanding

1 **What if** art was taken off the list on page 188. How would the results change?

2 **What if** 11 students like reading. How would you show it on the graph on page 188?

THINK CRITICALLY: Analyze **Explain your reasoning.**

3 📓 When is a bar graph more useful than a table? When is a table more useful than a bar graph?

Turn the page for Practice. ➡

Practice

1 Marathon Reading Club members keep track of the number of books they read each week. Use the tally to copy and complete the bar graph. Write titles for each.

Title: ?		
Week	Tally	Number of Books
1	✝✝✝ ✝✝✝	10
2	✝✝✝ ✝✝✝ ✝✝✝ |||	18
3	✝✝✝ ✝✝✝ ✝✝✝ ✝✝✝ ✝✝✝	25
4	✝✝✝ ✝✝✝ ✝✝✝ ✝✝✝	20
5	✝✝✝ ✝✝✝ ✝✝✝ ✝✝✝ ✝✝✝	25

Title: ?

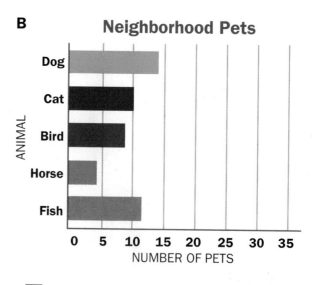

WEEK / NUMBER OF BOOKS

Use the completed bar graph for problems 2–5.

2 Why was skip-counting by threes chosen for the numbers at the bottom of the graph?

3 How did you decide where to end the bar for Week 4?

4 During which week did the members read the fewest number of books? the greatest?

5 Do you think more or fewer books will be read during Week 6? Explain why you think so.

Use graphs A and B for problems 6–7.

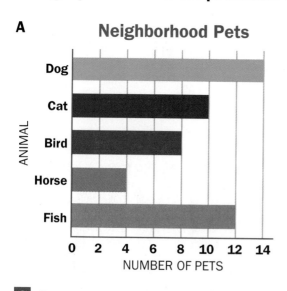

A Neighborhood Pets

ANIMAL / NUMBER OF PETS

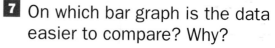

B Neighborhood Pets

ANIMAL / NUMBER OF PETS

6 Do the bar graphs show the same data? How do you know?

7 On which bar graph is the data easier to compare? Why?

Problem Solving

Pencil & Paper | Calculator | Mental Math

Use the data for problems 8–12.

8 Which lets you quickly find the exact number of people who like a certain color bicycle?

9 Which lets you compare the number of bicycles sold in a month?

10 Which would you use to show how the colors compare?

11 How many more people like white than like black?

12 Which color should the company make the most of? Why?

13 Data Point Gather data about the after-school activities of your class. Display the results on a bar graph. Discuss your graph.

Popular Bicycle Colors		
Color	Tally	Number of People
Blue	////	4
Red	////	5
Green	///	3
White	//// //	7
Black	//	2

Popular Bicycle Colors

```
                              x
                              x
                    x         x
          x         x         x
          x         x    x    x
          x         x    x    x    x
          x         x    x    x    x
        Blue      Red  Green White Black
```

Bicycles Sold This Month

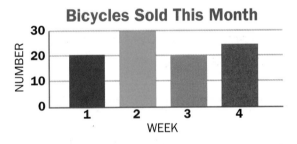

---

more to explore

Range

You can state the **range** of a set of data in two ways.

The number of children ranges from 23 to 35.

Subtract: 35 − 23 = 12

The range in the number of children is 12.

1 In your own words, explain what *range* means.

2 Find the range of the numbers of books in problem 1 on page 190.

Dance Class Size	
Time	Number of Children
11 A.M.	23
Noon	28
1 P.M.	30
2 P.M.	35

Problem Solvers at Work

Part 1   Interpret Data

You can read and interpret data easily when it is displayed in a graph.

Number of Tickets Sold at Drama Club Show

Thursday	🎟️ 🎟️
Friday	🎟️ 🎟️ 🎟️
Saturday	🎟️ 🎟️ 🎟️ 🎟️ 🎟️
Sunday	🎟️ 🎟️ 🎟️ 🎟️

Key: Each 🎟️ stands for 10 tickets.

Amount of Money Raised

NUMBER OF DOLLARS (0, 10, 20, 30, 40, 50, 60, 70)

Thursday: 35, Friday: 49, Saturday: 72, Sunday: 64

NIGHT OF THE SHOW

Work Together

1. What types of graphs are shown? What information does each show?

2. For which night were the most tickets sold? How do you know?

3. For which night was the least money raised? How do you know?

4. **Make a decision** Suppose the Drama Club could only have two shows next year. On which nights should they be? Why?

5. **What if** you change the pictograph key so that each 🎟️ stands for 5 theater tickets. What will happen to the graph?

Part 2 Write and Share Problems

Larry used the data in the bar graph to write the problem.

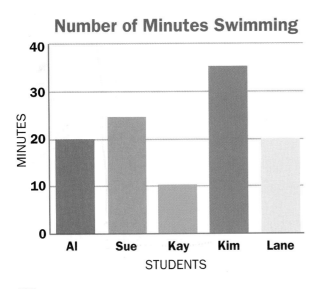

Number of Minutes Swimming

MINUTES

Al Sue Kay Kim Lane

STUDENTS

6 Solve Larry's problem.

7 Rewrite Larry's problem so that the answer is Al and Lane.

8 **Write a problem** of your own that uses the information in the bar graph.

9 Solve the new problem. How is it like Larry's problem? How is it different?

10 Trade problems. Solve at least three problems written by your classmates.

11 Which problem was the hardest to solve? Which was the easiest?

Who swam for the least number of minutes?

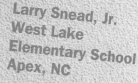

Larry Snead, Jr.
West Lake
Elementary School
Apex, NC

Turn the page for Practice Strategies. ➡

Part 3 Practice Strategies

Menu

Choose four problems and solve them. Explain your methods.

1 Which month had the most rain? Which had the least?

Rainfall

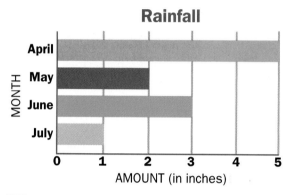

MONTH

April

May

June

July

0 1 2 3 4 5

AMOUNT (in inches)

2 Ruth has $125 saved to buy a bicycle and a helmet. The bicycle she wants costs $99, and the helmet costs $19. Does she have enough money? Explain.

3 Tina graduates on June 1. Her cousin graduates two weeks later. What is the date of her cousin's graduation?

4 Calvin and Margo arrived at the mall at 9:30 A.M. Calvin left at 11:00 A.M. Margo left at 12:15 P.M. Who was at the mall longer? How much longer?

5 A potted tree weighs 25 pounds. The pot weighs 7 pounds more than the tree. How much does the tree weigh without the pot?

6 Look at the pictograph.
a. How many students chose blue as their favorite color?

b. Jake said, "More students chose green than pink." Is he right? Why?

Favorite Color	
Purple	🛢 🛢
Blue	🛢 🛢 🛢 🛢
Green	🛢
Pink	🛢 🛢 🛢

Each 🛢 stands for 10 students.

**Choose two problems and solve them.
Explain your methods.**

7 Use the schedule to plan an afternoon visit to the museum. Plan to arrive at noon and leave before closing time. You should do at least one activity and go on one tour. You should also allow time for seeing the rest of the museum.

Art Museum Schedule of Events

Museum closes at 4:30 P.M.

Tours	Time	Length
Watercolors	12 noon	$1\frac{1}{2}$ hours
Abstract Art	1:00 P.M.	1 hour
Computer Art	2:30 P.M.	$1\frac{1}{2}$ hours

Activities	Time	Length
How to Draw	12 noon 2:30 P.M.	$\frac{1}{2}$ hour
Make a Mask	2:00 P.M. 3:30 P.M.	$\frac{1}{2}$ hour
Work with Clay	1:00 P.M. 3:30 P.M.	$\frac{1}{2}$ hour

8 Survey your class. Ask students which is their favorite food. Then ask which food they like least. Display your data in two line plots, pictographs, or bar graphs. Write a statement describing your results.

9 **Spatial reasoning** Trace the figure at the right. Do not lift the pencil from the paper or retrace any lines. Begin with the first letter you touch and list the letters you touch in order.

10 **At the Computer** Use a graphing program to display your data from problem 8 in three different ways. Write a paragraph telling which graph you think displays the data best and why.

Language and Mathematics

Complete the sentence. Use a word in the chart.

1 A ■ is a graph that uses pictures to display data.

2 You use ■ after the time to show hours between midnight and noon.

3 There are 60 ■ in an hour.

4 A ■ is a graph that uses bars and a scale to display data.

5 A pictograph uses a ■ to show how many things each picture stands for.

Vocabulary
A.M.
P.M.
o'clock
key
pictograph
seconds
minutes
bar graph

Concepts and Skills

Choose the more reasonable time.

6 Roasting a chicken—
2 hours or 2 minutes?

7 Brushing your teeth—
3 minutes or 3 hours?

Choose the letter of the most reasonable answer.

8 It takes about ■ minutes to take a shower.
  a. 1   **b.** 4   **c.** 28   **d.** 60

9 It takes about ■ hours to get a good night's sleep.
  a. 4   **b.** 24   **c.** 8   **d.** 2

Write the time using A.M. or P.M. Then show one way to read the time.

Use the line plot for ex. 12–13.

12 Which drink is most popular? Which drink is least popular?

13 You volunteer to bring drinks for the class trip. What drinks will you bring? Why?

Think critically.

14 Analyze. What is wrong with the scale of this bar graph?

15 Analyze. You are drawing a bar graph to compare people's heights. You begin the heights at zero. What is the greatest reasonable height you would show? Explain your answer.

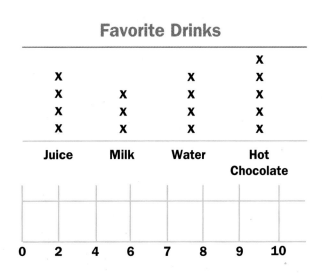

Favorite Drinks

	Juice	Milk	Water	Hot Chocolate
				x
	x		x	x
	x	x	x	x
	x	x	x	x
	x	x	x	x

0 2 4 6 7 8 9 10

MIXED APPLICATIONS

Problem Solving

Pencil & Paper   Calculator   Mental Math

16 You get home from school at 3:00 P.M. You go to bed 6 hours later. What time do you go to bed?

17 You spend $24 for shoes and socks. The shoes cost $18 more than the socks. How much does each cost?

Use the calendar page for problems 18–19.

18 What is the date for Labor Day?

19 School begins 4 days after Labor Day. On which date will school begin?

20 What is the difference in the number of votes for the most popular and the least popular sandwiches?

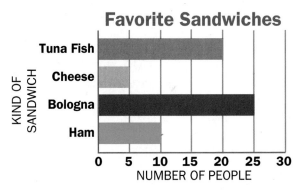

SEPTEMBER

S	M	T	W	T	F	S
					1	2
3	4 LABOR DAY	5	6	7	8	9

Favorite Sandwiches

KIND OF SANDWICH

Tuna Fish
Cheese
Bologna
Ham

0   5   10   15   20   25   30
NUMBER OF PEOPLE

Choose the more reasonable time.

1 Cooking a hamburger on the grill—15 minutes or 15 hours?

2 Playing a game of soccer— 2 minutes or 2 hours?

Write the time using A.M. or P.M. Then show one way to write the time.

3

4

Use the calendar page for ex. 5–6.

5 What is the date of Thanksgiving?

6 Tara goes back to school 4 days after Thanksgiving. On what date does she go back to school?

NOVEMBER

S	M	T	W	T	F	S
			1	2	3	4
5	6	7	8	9	10	11
12	13	14	15	16	17	18
19	20	21	22	23 THANKS- GIVING	24	25
26	27	28	29	30		

Solve.

7 A school play starts at 7 P.M. It lasts 1 hour 30 minutes. When does the play end?

8 Chris spent $18 on a CD and a tape. The CD cost $6 more than the tape. How much did each cost?

Use the bar graph for ex. 9–10.

9 Which sport was less popular than football?

10 How many more people picked hockey than baseball?

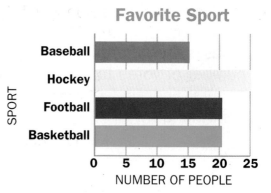

Favorite Sport

SPORT

Baseball
Hockey
Football
Basketball

0   5   10   15   20   25
NUMBER OF PEOPLE

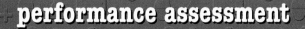

What Did You Learn?

Erin has a dog-walking business after school.

▶ Display Erin's data in at least two other different ways. Which display makes her data easiest to read? Why?

▶ Describe any patterns that might help Erin schedule her time next month.

A Good Answer

- includes a carefully made tally, table, line plot, or graph that shows Erin's data
- tells why one display is better than the others for reading the data
- clearly shows that there is an understanding of what the data means to Erin's schedule

Portfolio   You may want to place your work in your portfolio.

What Do You Think ?

1 Can you look at a simple table or graph and describe what the data is about? Why or why not?

2 How do you decide which type of graph to use to display a particular group of data?

3 What do you need to think about when you make a graph?
- Which kind of graph is best for the data?
- Is a symbol or key needed?
- What scale will you use?
- What is the best title?
- Other. Explain.

MAKE A WATER CLOCK

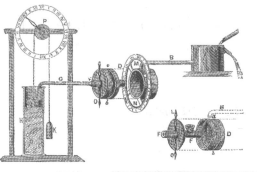

Two early ways to tell time were the sundial and the water clock. A sundial worked well on a sunny day. Water clocks were used to tell time when the sun was not shining or at night.

In this activity, you will construct your own water clock.

You will need
- *foam cup*
- *plastic jar*
- *water*
- *masking tape*

1

Carefully put a very small pinhole in the bottom of the foam cup.

2

Place a piece of masking tape on the side of the jar. Then, put the cup into the jar.

3

Write down the time. Fill the cup with water.

4

Mark the water level on the masking tape every 2 minutes for 10 minutes.

What Time Is It?

1 At what time did you start your water clock? When was the cup empty? How long did it take for the cup to completely empty?

2 How could you measure a time of one minute with your water clock?

3 Use your water clock to time something. Time the same thing with a watch or a clock. Compare the water clock time with the watch or clock.

4 Were all of the marks you placed on the jar the same space apart? Why or why not?

5 What are some of the problems with using a water clock?

At the Computer

Use a word processing program to prepare a report on what you have learned by making the water clock. Include the following points:

▶ an explanation of how it is able to keep time

▶ any problems you had making the water clock

▶ any suggestions you might have for making the water clock better

▶ a diagram of your clock

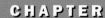

THEME Collections

Do you collect rocks, stamps, or dolls? There are all sorts of collections. Understanding multiplication can help you arrange and count your collection.

What Do You Know ?

Martina collects interesting shells.

1. How many shells are in each box? How many shells does Martina have in all?

2. **What if** Martina has 4 full boxes of shells. How many shells does she have in all? Explain your method.

3. **Portfolio** Ken has 24 shells in his collection. Show different ways he can place them in equal rows. You may use counters or drawings.

Equal Groups

You can use equal groups to help you find totals.

Work Together

Work with a partner. Draw and label a table like the one shown.

Mix up the number cards. Choose a card. Record it as the number in each group.

Number in each group	Number of groups	Total
2	5	10
5	2	10

Choose another card. Record that number as the number of groups.

You will need
- connecting cubes
- number cards 1–9

One partner uses cubes to make equal groups and find the total. Record the total in the table.

The other partner separates the cubes into other equal groups and records the results.

Mix up the number cards and repeat the activity for two other numbers.

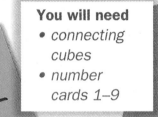

Talk It Over

▶ How did you find the totals?

▶ **What if** you have only 1 in each group. How many groups would you need for any total?

▶ What do you notice about separating a total into several different equal groupings?

Make Connections

Here is what Megan and James recorded.

Number in each group	Number of groups	Total
3	8	24
8	3	24
4	6	24
6	4	24
2	12	24

▶ How many different equal groups did Megan and James find for 24?

▶ **What if** they had 12 in each group. How many groups would they have?

Check for Understanding
Find the total. You may use models.

1 2 groups of 5   2 3 groups of 3   3 5 groups of 2

4 4 groups of 9   5 4 groups of 5   6 2 groups of 8

THINK CRITICALLY: Analyze

7 **What if** you keep the total the same. What happens to the number of groups as the number in each group increases?

Turn the page for Practice. ➡

Practice

Write the letter of the picture that matches the phrase.
Then give the total.

1 6 groups of 2   **2** 2 groups of 6   **3** 3 groups of 4

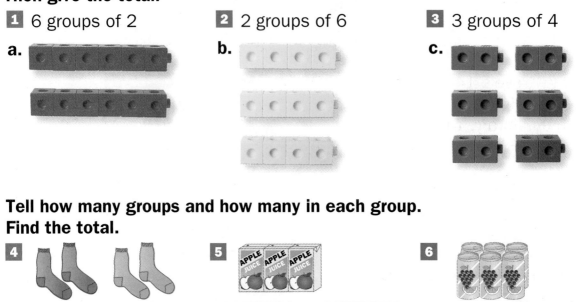

a.   b.   c.

Tell how many groups and how many in each group.
Find the total.

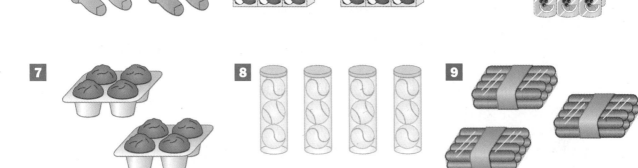

4   **5**   **6**

7   **8**   **9**

Find the total. You may use models.

10 5 groups of 3   **11** 3 groups of 9   **12** 5 groups of 5

13 4 groups of 6   **14** 2 groups of 7   **15** 6 groups of 5

16 3 groups of 5   **17** 7 groups of 5   **18** 4 groups of 8

19 number of fingers on 4 gloves   **20** number of wheels on 6 tricycles

21 number of wings on 3 birds   **22** number of days in 4 weeks

23 number of socks in 8 pairs   **24** number of tires on 5 cars

Problem Solving

25 Kate buys 4 bags of rolls. Each bag holds 4 rolls. How many rolls does Kate buy?

26 Paul makes 6 sandwiches. He uses 2 slices of bread for each. How many slices does he use?

27 Lars travels 14 miles to the store. He travels 3 miles farther to the library. Then he returns home. How far is his trip?

28 Marta buys a photo album for $4.59 and a roll of film for $3.99. She pays $10.00. How much change should she get?

29 Martin displays photos on posters. One poster has 3 rows of 5 photos. Another poster has 2 rows of 6 photos. Which poster has more photos? Why?

30 **Data Point** Survey your classmates about what they collect. Display your data in a bar graph. Use it to write a statement about your class.

Cultural Connection Mayan Numbers

The Maya live in Central America. Their civilization was at its height between A.D. 300 and 900.

In their marketplaces, the Maya traded cotton, honey, sweet potatoes, baskets, metals, and many other things. Instead of writing numbers, they sometimes used sticks and stones to calculate.

NORTH AMERICA

Maya Empire

SOUTH AMERICA

Each stone stood for 1. A stick stood for 5 stones.

For example: ⬭⬭⬭ showed 13.

What number is shown by the sticks and stones?

1 **2** **3** **4**

Draw sticks and stones to show the number.

5 3   **6** 9   **7** 15   **8** 12

Addition and Multiplication

Yoshi keeps his collection of temari balls on 3 shelves. Each shelf holds 4 balls.

Kiko also uses 3 shelves for her collection. She has 3 balls on the top shelf, 4 balls on the middle shelf, and 5 balls on the bottom shelf.

How many balls does each of them have?

Cultural Note
Handmade temari balls were originally used in games in Japan, but now they are used mostly for decoration.

Work Together
Work with a partner. Use cubes to model the groups in each collection.

Find the total number of temari balls in each collection.

Change the numbers in the problem to other numbers less than or equal to 9. Repeat the activity.

You will need
- *connecting cubes*

Talk It Over
▶ How did you find the total in Yoshi's collection the first time? the second time?

▶ How did you find the total in Kiko's collection the first time? the second time?

▶ Could you use skip-counting to find either total? Why or why not?

Make Connections

There are several ways to find the total in Yoshi's collection.

You can skip-count.

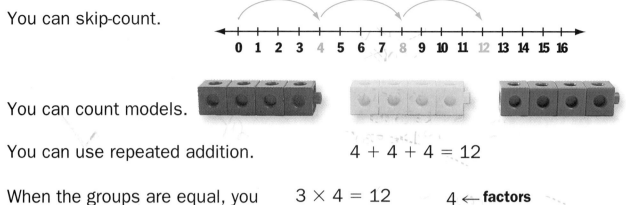

You can count models.

You can use repeated addition.

$$4 + 4 + 4 = 12$$

When the groups are equal, you can also write a **multiplication sentence.**

$$3 \times 4 = 12 \qquad 4 \leftarrow \text{factors}$$
$$\uparrow \quad \uparrow \quad \uparrow \qquad \underline{\times 3}$$
$$\text{factors} \quad \text{product} \rightarrow \quad 12$$

Read: 3 times 4 is equal to 12.

▶ Can you multiply to find the total of Kiko's collection in the first problem? Why or why not?

• •

Check for Understanding

Find the total. Write an addition or multiplication sentence.

1

2

3

4 4 groups of 2

5 6 and 3 more

THINK CRITICALLY: Generalize

6 *Journal* Explain why some problems can be solved by addition or multiplication and why others can only be solved by addition.

Turn the page for Practice. ➡

Practice

Find the total. Write an addition or multiplication sentence.

1

2

3

4

5

6

7 4 times 6

8 a group of 3 plus a group of 8

9 6 and 7 more

10 5 groups of 5

Find the product. You may use models.

11	**12**	**13**	**14**	**15**	**16**
7	7	6	5	2	3
$\times 5$	$\times 1$	$\times 5$	$\times 3$	$\times 4$	$\times 3$

17 9×2 **18** 4×9 **19** 1×8 **20** 3×6 **21** 3×8

22 2×7 **23** 2×2 **24** 5×9 **25** 5×8 **26** 4×7

Algebra Write + or x to make a true number sentence.

27 $2 \bullet 7 = 14$ **28** $8 \bullet 8 = 16$ **29** $5 \bullet 6 = 11$

30 $4 \bullet 5 = 20$ **31** $3 \bullet 2 = 6$ **32** $7 \bullet 5 = 12$

• • • • • • • • • • • • • • • • • • **Make It Right** • • • • • • • • • • • • • • • • •

33 Marissa multiplied this way. Tell what the error is and correct it.

$$\begin{array}{r} 4 \\ \times 3 \\ \hline 7 \end{array}$$

Concentrate on the Facts Game!

Play with a partner.

Make two cards for each of eight multiplication facts. One card has the factors, the second card has the product.

Play the Game

▶ Mix up the cards and lay them facedown in four rows of four cards.

▶ One partner turns over two cards.

If the cards make a multiplication fact, keep the cards and choose again.

If the two cards do not make a fact, turn the cards facedown. Then it is the other partner's turn.

▶ The game is over when all pairs of cards have been collected.

▶ The player with more cards wins.

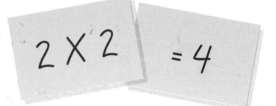

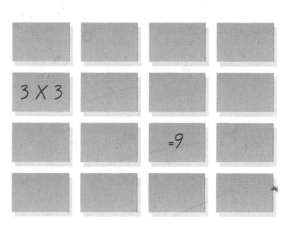

---

more to explore

Crisscross Model

You can use lines to model multiplication facts. The product is the number of places the lines intersect or cross.

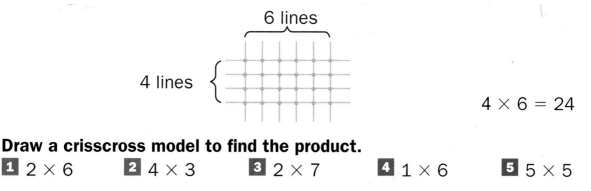

6 lines

4 lines

$4 \times 6 = 24$

Draw a crisscross model to find the product.

1 2×6 **2** 4×3 **3** 2×7 **4** 1×6 **5** 5×5

Multiplication Properties/ Facts for 0 and 1

A stamp with a mistake on it was sold to a collector for more than $1,000,000! Look at this album. How many stamps are in each part of the album?

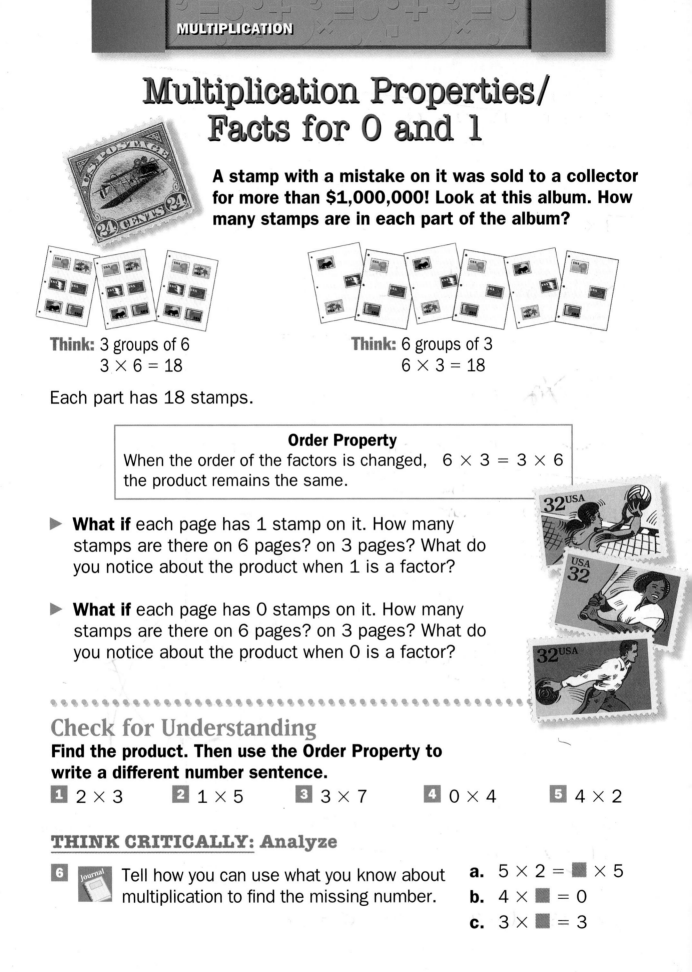

Think: 3 groups of 6
$3 \times 6 = 18$

Think: 6 groups of 3
$6 \times 3 = 18$

Each part has 18 stamps.

Order Property
When the order of the factors is changed, $6 \times 3 = 3 \times 6$
the product remains the same.

▶ **What if** each page has 1 stamp on it. How many stamps are there on 6 pages? on 3 pages? What do you notice about the product when 1 is a factor?

▶ **What if** each page has 0 stamps on it. How many stamps are there on 6 pages? on 3 pages? What do you notice about the product when 0 is a factor?

Check for Understanding
Find the product. Then use the Order Property to write a different number sentence.

1 2×3 **2** 1×5 **3** 3×7 **4** 0×4 **5** 4×2

THINK CRITICALLY: Analyze

6 *Journal* Tell how you can use what you know about multiplication to find the missing number.

a. $5 \times 2 = \blacksquare \times 5$

b. $4 \times \blacksquare = 0$

c. $3 \times \blacksquare = 3$

Practice

Find the product. Then use the Order Property to write a different number sentence.

1 2×7 **2** 3×5 **3** 1×9 **4** 4×1 **5** 0×8

6 4×7 **7** 5×6 **8** 1×7 **9** 2×6 **10** 5×8

11 3×4 **12** 0×3 **13** 2×8 **14** 5×4 **15** 0×7

Algebra Find the missing number.

16 $\blacksquare \times 5 = 0$ **17** $4 \times \blacksquare = 4$ **18** $3 \times 5 = \blacksquare \times 3$

19 $\blacksquare \times 13 = 13 \times 9$ **20** $1{,}236 \times \blacksquare = 0$ **21** $\blacksquare \times 287 = 287$

MIXED APPLICATIONS
Problem Solving

Pencil & Paper   Calculator   Mental Math

22 Sharon has 355 stamps in her collection. This month, she gets 10 more stamps. How many stamps does she have now?

23 Taylor is making a poster with 3 rows of 8 stamps. What is another way he could arrange the same number of stamps?

24 In 1847, how much would it cost for 6 of the Ben Franklin stamps? See INFOBIT.

> **INFOBIT**
> In 1847, the first official U.S. postage stamp cost 5¢. Today one of those unused stamps is worth about $2,800.

mixed review

Find the missing number.

1 $5 + \blacksquare = 3 + 5$ **2** $7 + 8 = 8 + \blacksquare$ **3** $\blacksquare + 7 = 7 + 1$

4 $24 + 13 = \blacksquare + 24$ **5** $21 + \blacksquare = 7 + 21$ **6** $19 + 0 = 0 + \blacksquare$

Find the total. Write an addition or multiplication sentence.

1 *(shells, 3 rows)* **2** *(shells, 4 rows)* **3** *(buttons)*

4 5 groups of 2

5 7 groups of 4

6 5 times 8

7 a group of 6 plus a group of 7

Find the product. You may use models.

8 5
   ×1

9 6
   ×2

10 0
    ×5

11 2
    ×2

12 7
    ×3

13 3
    ×4

14 4 × 5   **15** 2 × 9   **16** 1 × 8   **17** 7 × 0   **18** 5 × 9

Find the product. Then use the Order Property to write a different number sentence.

19 3 × 4   **20** 2 × 7   **21** 1 × 7   **22** 3 × 6

Find the missing number.

23 ■ × 2 = 0   **24** 6 × ■ = 6   **25** 5 × 9 = ■ × 5

26 9 × ■ = 0   **27** 4 × ■ = 2 × 4   **28** ■ × 8 = 8

Solve.

29 Orville has 3 pairs of shoes. How many shoes does Orville have in all?

30 Taylor gives one postcard to each of 8 friends. How many postcards does he give away?

31 Jessica has 5 plate blocks of stamps. Each plate block has 4 stamps. Jeffrey has 18 stamps. Who has more stamps?

32 Ashley puts 2 dolls on each of 5 shelves. How many dolls would she need to put on each shelf to get all the dolls on 2 shelves?

33 Journal How are the Order Properties of addition and multiplication alike? Give examples.

Use Counters and a Table

Quit

Activities

Projects

Print

Graphs

Tables

Geometry

Fractions

Money

Base 10

Counters

Coin Toss

Spinner

Tumble Drum

Notes

Calculator

You can use a computer to build a model to help you multiply. A table linked to the models can automatically record your work.

TABLE		
Number of Groups	Number in Each Group	Total
4	5	20
	6	
	5	

Use the counter tool to stamp out sets of objects.

The table will record the number of groups, the number of items in each group, and the total.

▶ If you change the number of ✹, the numbers in the table change. What would the table show if you added one ✹ to each group?

▶ What would the table show if you added one group of ✹ ✹ ✹ ✹ ✹ to the original groups?

Use stamps or counters and a table to solve.

1 3×4	**2** 9×6	**3** 5×2	**4** 4×7
5 3×8	**6** 1×3	**7** 6×5	**8** 4×4

THINK CRITICALLY: Generalize

9 When do you think it is better to use a computer to solve a problem? When do you think it is better to use another method?

real-life investigation

APPLYING MULTIPLICATION

Group Search

Many things are sold in groups. Buying things in groups can save money. In this activity you will work in teams to investigate what kinds of things are sold in groups.

▶ Think of a store you can visit to look for things sold in groups.

▶ Decide how you will organize your search and record your data.

▶ Visit the store and carry out your search.

Visiting the Store

1 Visit a local store. Look for items that are sold in packages of more than one.

2 Write down the name of each item. Also write down the number in each package.

3 Make an organized list. List items that are sold in groups of 2, 3, 4, and so on.

4 Choose one item that comes in more than one type of package. Tell how many different ways you can buy 24 of that item.

Report Your Findings

5 [Portfolio] Prepare a report on the data you gathered at the store. Include the following:

▶ a list of items sold in packages organized by the number of items in a group

▶ a display comparing the number of items sold in 2s, 3s, 4s, and so on

▶ a description of the different ways you can buy 24 of one of the items

6 Share your findings. Compare them with the findings of other groups.

Revise your work.
▶ Is the data you collected accurate and clearly displayed?
▶ Is your report neat and organized?
▶ Did you proofread your work?

PREDICT which size group is most common.

EXPLORE why items are packaged in groups.

FIND why some items come in packages with different-size groups.

2 and 5 as Factors

Have you ever seen travel decals on a car window? Suppose you collect and mount 2 decals on each of 4 frames. How many decals are there?

You can skip-count to find the total.

There are 8 travel decals in the frames.

You can also multiply.

$4 \times 2 = 8$

What if you mount 5 travel decals in each frame. How many travel decals would be in 7 frames?

You can skip-count on the calculator.
Enter 5 + 5 =, then keep pressing =.

Number of Skips (=)	1	2	3	4	5	6	7
Number of Decals	5	10	15	20	25	30	35

You would have 35 travel decals in 7 frames.

Check for Understanding
Find the product.

1 $\begin{array}{r} 2 \\ \times 5 \end{array}$ **2** $\begin{array}{r} 2 \\ \times 3 \end{array}$ **3** $\begin{array}{r} 5 \\ \times 1 \end{array}$ **4** $\begin{array}{r} 6 \\ \times 2 \end{array}$ **5** $\begin{array}{r} 4 \\ \times 5 \end{array}$ **6** $\begin{array}{r} 2 \\ \times 4 \end{array}$ **7** $\begin{array}{r} 2 \\ \times 2 \end{array}$

8 8×5 **9** 3×5 **10** 8×2 **11** 9×2 **12** 2×5

THINK CRITICALLY: Analyze   **Explain your reasoning.**

13 How are skip-counting and multiplication alike?

Practice

Find the product.

1 2
×2

2 6
×2

3 5
×8

4 2
×3

5 7
×5

6 8
×2

7 9×5

8 2×4

9 4×5

10 2×0

11 5×6

12 3×5

13 9×2

14 2×7

15 5×5

16 2×5

Describe and complete the pattern.

17 ■, 4, 6, 8, ■, ■, ■, ■, 18

18 ■, 10, 15, 20, ■, ■, ■, 40, ■

Use the table to answer. Explain your method.

19 How many people are in 4 cars? in 6 cars?

Cars	1	2	3
People	5	10	15

20 How many wheels are on 4 bicycles? on 6 bicycles?

Bicycle	1	2	3
Wheels	2	4	6

MIXED APPLICATIONS
Problem Solving
Pencil & Paper Calculator Mental Math

21 Sara buys one decal for $2.75 and another decal for $1.75. She gives the clerk a $5 bill. How much change does she receive?

22 Vlad buys 2 boxes of film on sale. Each box holds 5 rolls of film. How many rolls of film does Vlad buy?

23 Rocco buys 12 muffins. There are twice as many corn muffins as bran muffins. How many corn muffins does he buy?

24 **Write a problem** that could be solved using the multiplication sentence $5 \times 2 = 10$. Then give it to others to solve.

mixed review

How much time has passed?

1 Begin: 3:15 A.M.
End: 3:55 A.M.

2 Begin: 8:30 P.M.
End: 10:45 P.M.

3 Begin: 2:50 P.M.
End: 9:00 P.M.

Problem-Solving Strategy

Read
Plan
Solve
Look Back

Use Alternate Methods

Read **Many collectors protect their cards in plastic sleeves. Each sleeve holds four cards. How many cards are in 8 sleeves?**

Plan Many problems can be solved in more than one way. To solve the problem, you can:
▶ draw a picture, or
▶ choose an operation.

Cultural Note
The first sports cards were made in 1887. Today the most popular sports cards are baseball and football.

Solve **Draw a picture.** Show 8 sleeves with 4 cards on each. Then count to find the total.

Choose an operation. Since each sleeve has the same number of cards, you can multiply.

Think: 8 groups of 4 $8 \times 4 = 32$

There are 32 cards in 8 sleeves.

Look Back How could you solve this problem in a different way?

Check for Understanding

1 Nina gives 2 cartoon-character cards to each of 6 friends. How many cards does she give away?

THINK CRITICALLY: Analyze

2 Describe different ways you can solve problem 1.

1. Ben surveyed the students in his class. He made a tally of their favorite types of sports cards. How many students did he survey?

Baseball	‖‖‖ ‖‖‖ ‖‖‖
Football	‖‖‖
Basketball	‖‖
Hockey	‖‖‖

2. **Write a problem** that uses the information in the tally.

3. Vernon's two most valuable baseball cards are worth $22.50 and $18.50. About how much are the two cards worth in all?

4. For his birthday Paul receives 4 packs of sports cards. Each pack has 5 cards. How many cards does he receive in all?

5. Miliama trades 5 sports cards with each of 5 friends. How many sports cards does she trade in all?

6. At a trading-card store, Rita buys a set with 3 cards, a set with 5 cards, and a set with 6 cards. How many cards does she buy?

7. Twelve of the 25 stores in the mall sold clothes. Five of the clothes stores closed. How many clothes stores are left? What information did you *not* need to solve this problem?

8. Mr. Hall pays his bills in order from least to greatest. Which bill will he pay first?

$245 $18 $85 $178 $205

9. Mark buys 6 cards from Alan and 5 cards from Sue. He sells 15 cards to Rex. Does he have more or fewer cards than he started with? Explain your thinking.

10. Emma has 125 hockey cards. She has 2 boxes of baseball cards, one with 200 cards and one with 158 cards. How many more baseball cards does she have than hockey cards?

11. Vera arrives at a trading-card fair at 9:45 A.M. She spends 1 hour looking at displays. Then she talks to a trader for 30 minutes. How much time is left until noon?

12. **Data Point** How much more valuable is a 1972 Kellogg's All-Time Greats Babe Ruth card than the Lou Gehrig card? See the Databank on page 535.

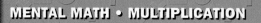

3 as a Factor

Would you believe that since 1959, Barbie dolls have been among the most popular toys in the United States? How many dolls are in a display with 3 rows of 4 dolls?

Think: 3 rows of 4 dolls   Multiply: 3×4

You can add on to a known fact to find a new fact.

Ruth Handler designed two famous dolls. She named the dolls after her two children, Barbie and Ken.

3 groups of 4 = 2 groups of 4 plus 4

$$3 \times 4 \;=\; \underbrace{2 \times 4}_{8} \qquad + 4$$
$$ + 4 = 12$$

There are 12 dolls on display.

▶ **What if** the display has 4 rows of 3 dolls. How many dolls are there? How do you know?

Check for Understanding
Multiply.

1 $\begin{array}{r} 2 \\ \times 3 \\ \hline \end{array}$ **2** $\begin{array}{r} 3 \\ \times 4 \\ \hline \end{array}$ **3** $\begin{array}{r} 5 \\ \times 3 \\ \hline \end{array}$ **4** $\begin{array}{r} 8 \\ \times 3 \\ \hline \end{array}$ **5** $\begin{array}{r} 6 \\ \times 3 \\ \hline \end{array}$ **6** $\begin{array}{r} 7 \\ \times 3 \\ \hline \end{array}$ **7** $\begin{array}{r} 2 \\ \times 2 \\ \hline \end{array}$

8 1×3 **9** 2×3 **10** 3×3 **11** 9×2 **12** 9×3

THINK CRITICALLY: Generalize

13 Look at the facts with 3 as a factor. What patterns do you notice?

Practice

Write the multiplication sentence.

1

2

3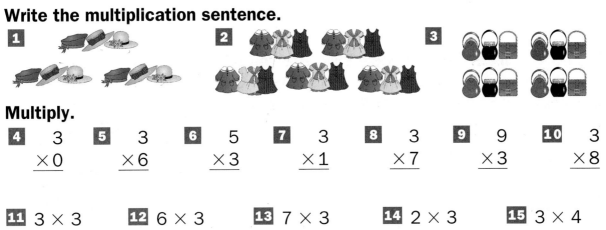

Multiply.

4 3
    ×0

5 3
    ×6

6 5
    ×3

7 3
    ×1

8 3
    ×7

9 9
    ×3

10 3
     ×8

11 3 × 3

12 6 × 3

13 7 × 3

14 2 × 3

15 3 × 4

Algebra Complete the table.

16

Rule: Multiply by 3				
Input	3	4	5	6
Output	■	■	■	■

17

Rule: ■				
Input	4	5	6	7
Output	1	2	3	4

MIXED APPLICATIONS
Problem Solving
Pencil & Paper · Calculator · Mental Math

18 Make a decision Rosa has her dolls in 4 rows with 3 dolls in each row. Choose another way to arrange them. Decide on the number of rows and the number of dolls in each row.

19 An early 1900s baseball card of Honus Wagner was sold at auction for $451,000. About how much more valuable is this card than the one found in the can? See INFOBIT.

> **INFOBIT**
> A faded copy of a Honus Wagner card found in a can is worth between $15,000 and $40,000.

mixed review

Estimate.

1   122
    + 65

2   402
    + 81

3   756
    +103

4   577
    +269

5 1,172
    +4,091

4 as a Factor

Do you think bugs are creepy, or do you think they are cool to collect? If you have 6 bugs in each jar, how many are in 4 jars?

Think: 4 jars with 6 bugs   **Multiply:** 4 × 6

You can double a known fact to find a new fact.

4 groups of 6 =	2 groups of 6	plus	2 groups of 6
4 × 6 =	2 × 6	+	2 × 6
	12	+	12 = 24

There are 24 bugs.

▶ **What if** there are 4 bugs on each of 6 jars. How many bugs are there? How do you know?

Check for Understanding
Multiply.

1. $\begin{array}{r} 7 \\ \times 4 \end{array}$
2. $\begin{array}{r} 4 \\ \times 8 \end{array}$
3. $\begin{array}{r} 2 \\ \times 4 \end{array}$
4. $\begin{array}{r} 4 \\ \times 4 \end{array}$
5. $\begin{array}{r} 2 \\ \times 9 \end{array}$
6. $\begin{array}{r} 4 \\ \times 9 \end{array}$
7. $\begin{array}{r} 4 \\ \times 0 \end{array}$

8. 6 × 2
9. 6 × 4
10. 3 × 2
11. 4 × 3
12. 4 × 5

THINK CRITICALLY: Generalize   Explain your reasoning.

13. Journal How can doubling a fact help you find other facts?

Practice

Multiply.

1 6
×4

2 4
×7

3 1
×4

4 8
×4

5 3
×4

6 5
×4

7 2
×4

8 4 × 3 **9** 0 × 4 **10** 4 × 4 **11** 6 × 4 **12** 9 × 4

Solve.

13 If each box holds 4 bugs, how many bugs are in these boxes?

14 If each box holds 3 bugs, how many bugs are in these boxes?

MIXED APPLICATIONS
Problem Solving

15 **Logical reasoning** Lon, Jamie, and Rosie each collect something different: comic books, shells, or marbles. Lon's collection can roll. Jamie cannot read her collection. What does Rosie collect?

16 Shelby puts all the fireflies she collects in jars. She puts them 4 to a jar. Do all the fireflies fit in 5 jars? Explain your reasoning.

17 Does Shelby have over 170 bugs in her collection? How do you know?

18 How many more ants are there than fireflies and spiders?

SHELBY'S BUG COLLECTION	
Type of Bug	Number of Bugs
Ant	116
Firefly	26
Spider	7

mixed review

Write the time using numbers.

1

2

3

4

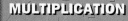
Use a Multiplication Table

You can use the patterns you find in the multiplication table to help you remember multiplication facts.

To find the product of 4 × 2, look where the 4s row and the 2s column meet.

$$4 \times 2 = 8$$

Columns

x	0	1	2	3	4	5
0	0	0	0	0	0	0
1	0	1	2	3	4	5
2	0	2	4	6	8	10
3	0	3	6	9	12	15
4	0	4	8	12	16	20
5	0	5	10	15	20	25
6						
7						
8						
9						

Rows

▶ **What if** you used the 2s row and the 4s column. What do you notice about the product?

▶ Copy and complete the table.

▶ What patterns do you see in the 2s column? in the 5s row?

Check for Understanding
Multiply.

1. 2
×7

2. 3
×2

3. 5
×6

4. 0
×4

5. 1
×8

6. 2
×2

7. 5
×7

8. 6 × 3   **9.** 8 × 5   **10.** 9 × 1   **11.** 4 × 3   **12.** 5 × 5

13. 4 × 5   **14.** 6 × 2   **15.** 3 × 8   **16.** 9 × 3   **17.** 0 × 1

THINK CRITICALLY: Analyze

18. What other patterns do you see in the table?

Practice

Multiply.

1 5
×7

2 4
×6

3 0
×5

4 2
×4

5 1
×6

6 5
×3

7 5
×5

8 2
×5

9 3
×8

10 2
×9

11 5
×2

12 3
×1

13 0
×9

14 9
×4

15 1×4

16 6×5

17 7×3

18 6×0

19 8×2

20 5×4

21 2×1

22 9×5

23 8×4

24 4×4

Algebra **Write >, <, or = to complete the number sentence.**

25 $2 \times 4 \bullet 2 \times 5$

26 $6 \times 3 \bullet 3 \times 6$

27 $1 \times 1 \bullet 9 \times 0$

28 $3 \times 4 \bullet 2 \times 5$

29 $3 \times 8 \bullet 6 \times 2$

30 $8 + 8 \bullet 2 \times 8$

MIXED APPLICATIONS
Problem Solving
Pencil & Paper *Calculator* *Mental Math*

31 Shannon wants to buy a book about collecting dolls. The book costs $8.31 on sale. She has 1 five-dollar bill, 2 one-dollar bills, 3 quarters, and 2 dimes. How much more money does she need?

32 Zack plans to display part of his rock collection at the science fair. He plans to put 4 rocks on each of 5 shelves. He has 80 rocks in his collection. How many rocks does he plan to leave home?

33 Leah brings 2 packs of juice to a party. Each pack has 6 cans in it. How many cans of juice does Leah bring?

34 **Make a list** of things that come in groups. Choose one item. Write a problem that could be solved using multiplication.

mixed review

1 352
−247

2 664
−200

3 790
−279

4 841
−384

5 687
−254

Part 1 Solving Multistep Problems

A meeting room at the sports convention has 3 groups of seats. On either side, there are 5 rows with 2 seats in each row. The middle group has 4 rows with 5 seats in each row. How many seats are there in the meeting room?

Work Together

Solve. Be prepared to explain your methods.

1 What do you need to find before you can find the total number of seats?

2 How can you find this information?

3 How can you find this information in a different way?

4 What steps can you follow to solve the rest of the problem?

5 **Make a decision** Tell which way of solving the problem you prefer and why.

6 **What if** there had been 5 rows of seats with 5 seats in each row in the middle group. How can you solve this problem in a different way?

Part 2 Write and Share Problems

Katy used the data in the pictograph to write the problem.

Preston's Autograph Collection	
Type of Autograph	**Number of Autographs**
Men athletes	🏃🏃🏃
Women athletes	🏃🦵
Men writers	🏃
Women writers	🏃🦵

Key: Each 🏃 stands for 10 autographs.
        Each 🦵 stands for 5 autographs.

Preston has 15 women athletes' autographs and 15 women writers' autographs. What if he had 20 more women writers' autographs. How many women's autographs would he have?

7 Solve Katy's problem.

8 Change Katy's problem so that it is either easier or harder to solve. Do not change any of the data.

9 Solve the new problem and explain why it is easier or harder to solve.

10 Write a problem of your own that uses the information from the pictograph.

11 Trade problems. Solve at least three problems written by your classmates.

12 What was the most interesting problem you solved? Why?

Katy Branston
Snowden Elementary School
Memphis, TN

Turn the page for Practice Strategies.

Menu

Choose five problems and solve them. Explain your methods.

1 Amber displays her spoon collection in a rack. The rack has 4 rows with 4 spoons in each row. How many spoons does she have?

2 Cody buys a comic book for $5.50 and a pack of sport trading cards for $1.95. He pays with 2 five-dollar bills. How much change should he receive?

3 Alex has 567 sports stickers. Tom has 228 sports stickers. About how many do they have altogether?

4 Ramona wants to buy an abalone shell for $2.85. She has 2 one-dollar bills, 1 quarter, and 3 dimes. How much more money does she need?

5 Ming leaves home at 8:15 A.M. He arrives at the Collectors Club meeting at 8:55 A.M. How long did he take to get there?

6 Mrs. Washington has 3 shelves with 5 clocks each and 2 shelves with 4 clocks each. How many clocks does she have in all?

7 Mr. Hawkins wants to have 500 antique bottles in his collection. He has 145 bottles. How many more does he need to reach his goal?

8 Jim Bob walks 9 blocks to school. After school he walks 7 blocks to a store. Then he gets a ride most of the way home, but he walks the last 3 blocks. How many blocks does he walk in all?

Choose two problems and solve them.
Explain your methods.

9 Write three statements about the pictograph.

Type of Cards Collected by Local Collectors	
Type of Cards	**Number of Collectors**
Star Trek	⌐
Star Wars	𝆏 ⌐
Jurassic Park	𝆏 𝆏
Dixie	𝆏 𝆏 𝆏 𝆏 𝆏 𝆏 𝆏

Key: 𝆏 stands for 10 collectors. ⌐ stands for 5 collectors.

10 There are three different ways to score exactly 15 points by throwing two darts. What are the ways?

How many different ways are there to score exactly 15 points by throwing three darts? What are they?

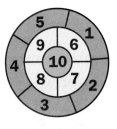

11 **Spatial reasoning** Make three squares by changing two toothpicks.

12 **At the Computer** Use a spreadsheet to find the current total value of a set of trading cards. Then find the value in five years if the value doubles every year.

Note: For current values you can use the values listed in the Databank on page 535 or call a trading-card store.

Language and Mathematics

Complete the sentence. Use a word in the chart.

1 You ■ to find the product.

2 The ■ of 6 and 4 is 24.

3 When you multiply 7 times 2, you think of 7 ■ of 2.

4 In the multiplication sentence 5 × 2 = 10, the 5 and the 2 are ■.

Vocabulary
groups
difference
multiply
regroup
factors
product

Concepts and Skills

Find the total.

5 8 groups of 3

6 7 groups of 5

7 the number of wheels on 6 bicycles

8 the number of horseshoes needed for 5 horses

Write the number sentence and find the product.

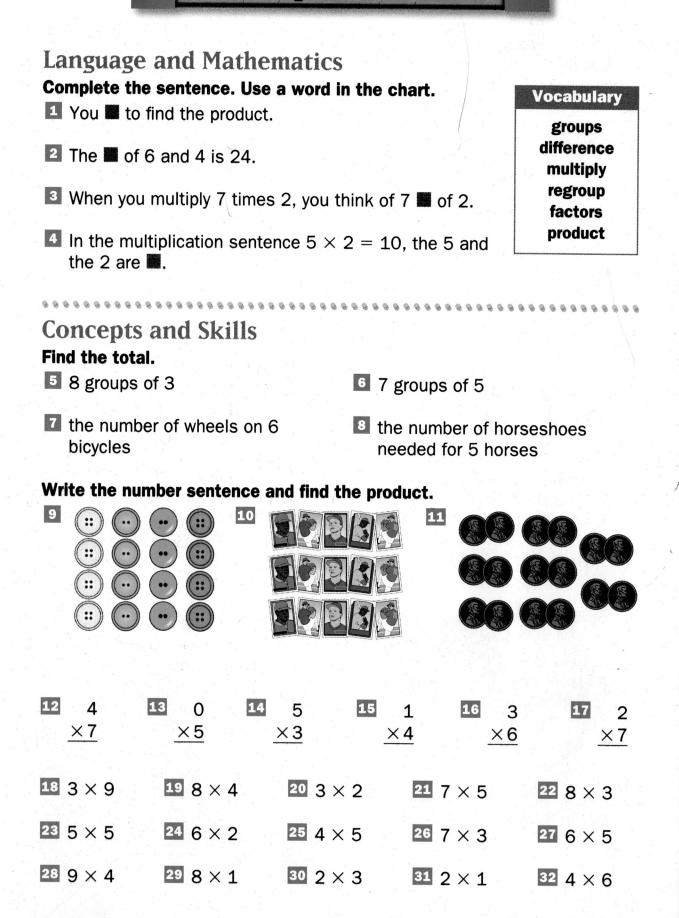

12
$\begin{array}{r} 4 \\ \times 7 \\ \hline \end{array}$

13
$\begin{array}{r} 0 \\ \times 5 \\ \hline \end{array}$

14
$\begin{array}{r} 5 \\ \times 3 \\ \hline \end{array}$

15
$\begin{array}{r} 1 \\ \times 4 \\ \hline \end{array}$

16
$\begin{array}{r} 3 \\ \times 6 \\ \hline \end{array}$

17
$\begin{array}{r} 2 \\ \times 7 \\ \hline \end{array}$

18 3 × 9

19 8 × 4

20 3 × 2

21 7 × 5

22 8 × 3

23 5 × 5

24 6 × 2

25 4 × 5

26 7 × 3

27 6 × 5

28 9 × 4

29 8 × 1

30 2 × 3

31 2 × 1

32 4 × 6

Think critically.

33 Analyze. Joel added on to find a new fact. Tell what the error is and correct it.

$3 \times 6 = 2 \times 6 + 3$

34 Generalize. Write *always, sometimes,* or *never.* Give an example to support your answer.

a. When 0 is a factor, the product is 0.

b. The sum of two numbers is less than their product.

MIXED APPLICATIONS

Problem Solving   Pencil & Paper   Calculator   Mental Math

35 Baxter buys 6 packs with 5 trading cards each. Ron buys 9 packs with 4 trading cards each. Who buys more cards?

36 Reba gave 1 postcard to each of 6 friends. How many postcards did she give to her friends?

37 Su Ming makes spring rolls for some friends. She packs the rolls in 4 boxes. She places 4 spring rolls in each box. How many spring rolls does Su Ming pack for her friends?

38 Tomás has 15 arrowheads. His display case has 4 shelves. He wants to put 5 arrowheads on each shelf. How many more arrowheads does he need to fill his display case?

39 Olga collects Olympic coins. She has 5 cases that hold 4 coins each. She has 3 other cases that hold 6 coins each. How many Olympic coins does Olga have in her collection?

40 At the Juice Bar juice boxes are sold in 3-packs and in 6-packs. Beth buys 21 juice boxes. She has 3 times as many 6-packs as 3-packs. How many 3-packs does she buy?

Find the total.

1 6 groups of 4

2 the number of wheels for 7 tricycles

3 5 groups of 3

4 the number of legs on 5 sea gulls

Write the number sentence.

5

6

7

Multiply.

8 $\begin{array}{r} 3 \\ \times 6 \\ \hline \end{array}$

9 $\begin{array}{r} 2 \\ \times 4 \\ \hline \end{array}$

10 $\begin{array}{r} 5 \\ \times 3 \\ \hline \end{array}$

11 $\begin{array}{r} 9 \\ \times 4 \\ \hline \end{array}$

12 $\begin{array}{r} 6 \\ \times 5 \\ \hline \end{array}$

13 $\begin{array}{r} 8 \\ \times 2 \\ \hline \end{array}$

14 5×5

15 3×8

16 5×9

17 4×4

Write the missing number.

18 $4 \times 9 = \blacksquare \times 4$

19 $5 \times \blacksquare = 0$

20 $1 \times \blacksquare = 2$

21 $\blacksquare \times 5 = 5 \times 3$

Solve.

22 Mario is packing 6 jars of jam to a box. He has 21 jars of jam. How many more jars will he need to fill 5 boxes?

23 Tami buys 2 balloons of each of 8 colors for a party. How many balloons does she buy?

24 Suke buys 3 packs of invitations. There are 5 invitations in each pack. Does she have enough invitations to invite 20 people?

25 J.D. has $20. He spends $8.95 on a cap and $5.88 on supplies. What is the least number of coins and bills he could receive in change?

What Did You Learn?

Play the game **Take Four** with a partner. Play at least two times. Then write about:

▶ how you usually find products.

▶ the strategies you used to try to win.

How to play:

▶ Choose a factor from 1 through 5. Spin to get the second factor. Find the product. Put a counter on it.

▶ Take turns. Two counters can be on the same product.

▶ The winner is the first person to place four counters in a row or in a column.

10	9	1	2	3
1	3	4	5	9
5	6	20	8	4
8	9	15	16	20
25	10	12	6	16

You will need
- *15 counters*
- *1–5 spinner*

················· **A Good Answer** ·················
- describes how you multiply two numbers
- clearly explains what decisions you made to try to win

You may want to place your work in your portfolio.

What Do You Think ?

1 How do you know when to multiply and when to add? Explain. Give an example.

2 List some methods you might use to multiply.

3 Which method do you prefer? Why?

Collecting Leaves

Throughout the world people use the leaves, twigs, bark, and other parts of trees in a wide variety of ways. Scientists collect leaves from many trees so they can study and compare them.

It is fun and easy to make a collection of leaves.

▶ Collect leaves from trees or other plants.

▶ Use field guides and other books to sort the leaves and name the trees or plants they came from.

▶ Dry the leaves so they will last.

1 Place the leaves between sheets of newspaper.

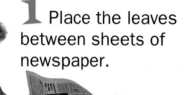

2 Place a heavy book or other weight on top of the newspaper. Leave the leaves alone for at least a week so they dry completely.

3 Glue equal numbers of leaves to pieces of paper. Then glue each paper to a piece of heavy cardboard.

4 Cover the cardboard with clear plastic wrap.

How Many Leaves?

1. How many of each type of leaf do you have? How many leaves do you have in all?

2. Which type of leaf did you collect the most of?

3. Compare your collection with those of other students. How are they the same? different?

4. Combine your collections. How many of each type of leaf does your class have? How many leaves does your class have in all?

5. Arrange your class collection in equal rows. How many rows did you make? How many leaves are in each row? How can you arrange them another way?

At the Computer

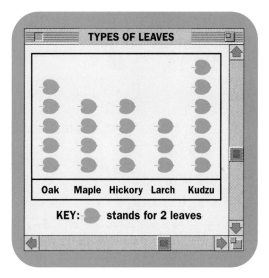

6. Use a graphing program to display how many of each type of leaf you have.

7. Write two statements about your collection based on the graph.

Chapters 1–6

Choose the letter of the correct answer.

1 What number comes next?
10, 14, 18, 22, ■
  a. 4   **b.** 30
  c. 26   **d.** 22

2 Find 5×4.
  a. 2   **b.** 10
  c. 20   **d.** 24

3 The school band concert is
about 50 ■ long.
  a. seconds   **b.** minutes
  c. hours   **d.** days

4 Choose the symbol to make a
true statement.
4×3 ● $25 - 10$
  a. <   **b.** >
  c. =   **d.** not given

5 Estimate $28.14 - 12.79$.
  a. \$1.00   **b.** \$2.00
  c. \$10.00   **d.** \$20.00

6 Mildred has \$5, and Ralph has
\$13. Which operation do you
use to find how much money
they have altogether?
  a. addition   **b.** subtraction
  c. rounding   **d.** not given

7 Find $1,730 + 1,924 + 6,625$.
  a. 9,179   **b.** 9,269
  c. 8,279   **d.** 10,279

8 Felix buys a sandwich for \$1.05
and juice for 50¢. He gives the
clerk 1 one-dollar bill. Which
coins should he also give the
clerk?
  a. 2 quarters, 1 dime
  b. 5 dimes, 1 nickel
  c. 1 quarter, 5 nickels
  d. 1 quarter, 5 dimes

9 Becky puts 3 photos on each
page of her photo album. She
has 6 blank pages left. How
many photos can she put on
the blank pages?
  a. 9 photos   **b.** 18 photos
  c. 12 photos   **d.** 3 photos

10 Jaime says he saved about
\$100. Which amount of money
do you think he has?
  a. \$175   **b.** \$45
  c. \$151   **d.** \$98

11 Delaney leaves her home at
2:30 P.M. She goes to the
library for 30 minutes. She
visits a friend for 1 hour and
returns home. She spends 40
minutes traveling altogether.
When does she get home?
  a. 4:40 P.M.   **b.** 3:40 P.M.
  c. 5:20 P.M.   **d.** 4:20 P.M.

12 Subtract 406 − 181.
a. 85
b. 225
c. 385
d. 325

13 Jean has 6 quarters, 2 dimes, and 1 nickel. Which item can she buy?

Price List	
pen	$1.80
crayons	$1.65
notebook	$1.85
ruler	$2.25

a. pen
b. notebook
c. ruler
d. crayons

14 Find the rule.

Input	Output
3	8
4	9
9	14
10	15

a. Add 5.
b. Add 3.
c. Subtract 5.
d. Subtract 3.

15 Find the missing number.
6 × ▓ = 6
a. 0
b. 1
c. 6
d. not given

16 Estimate 689 − 305.
a. 100
b. 200
c. 400
d. 500

17 Subtract $5.02 − $0.98.
a. $1.00
b. $4.04
c. $4.06
d. $6.00

18 Which statement is *not* true?

OCTOBER						
SUN	MON	TUE	WED	THU	FRI	SAT
1	2	3	4	5	6	7
8	9	10	11	12	13	14
15	16	17	18	19	20	21
22	23	24	25	26	27	28
29	30	31				

a. The last Tuesday of the month is October 31.
b. October has 31 days.
c. The sixth day of October is Friday.
d. October 12 is a Saturday.

Use the graph to answer ex. 19–20.

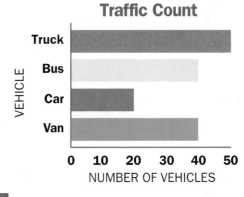

19 Which statement is true?
a. There were more cars then buses.
b. There were fewer trucks than vans.
c. 30 trucks were counted.
d. There were the same number of vans as buses.

20 The numbers on the graph were rounded to the nearest 10. Which count could actually be 19?
a. truck
b. bus
c. car
d. van

Let's Go to the Park!

Amusement parks and national parks are fun to visit. Using multiplication facts can help you when you buy admission and ride tickets, food, and souvenirs.

What Do You Know?

Sarah and her 5 friends visit a local amusement park.

1 Sarah and her friends want to ride the Crazy Cups. How many tickets do they need in all?

2 Six people can ride in a Wet 'n' Wild log. Seven logs go through the ride at the same time. How many people can ride the Wet 'n' Wild at the same time?

3 Portfolio Choose 3 rides that need different amounts of tickets. Tell how many tickets you and a group of 7 friends would need for each ride. Explain how you found your answers.

ALL TICKETS — **50¢ each**

ADMIT ONE

CRAZY CUPS	2 Tickets
WET n' WILD	3 Tickets
SPEED COASTER	6 Tickets
WILD WHEEL	1 Ticket
SLIP & SLIDE	7 Tickets
JUNGLE SAFARI	5 Tickets

6 and 7 as Factors

Many people ride horses on the trails in the Black Hills. Suppose there are 6 groups on a trail ride. Each group has 4 riders. How many people are on the trail ride?

Think: 6 groups of 4 riders
6 × 4

You can double a known fact to find a new fact.

Cultural Note
This statue of the Oglala Sioux hero Crazy Horse is being carved from a mountain in the Black Hills of South Dakota.

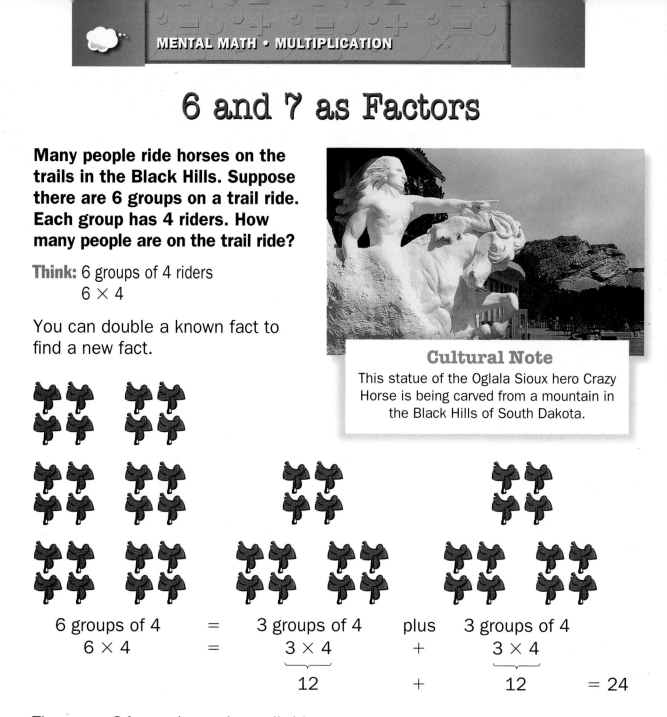

6 groups of 4	=	3 groups of 4	plus	3 groups of 4
6 × 4	=	3 × 4	+	3 × 4
		12	+	12	= 24

There are 24 people on the trail ride.

Talk It Over

▶ **What if** there are 4 groups of 6 riders. How many people are on the trail? How do you know?

▶ How can you find 6 × 9 by doubling a multiplication fact with 3 as a factor?

▶ What is 3 × 8? Double the fact. Write a multiplication sentence for the new fact.

Other people tour the Black Hills in large buses. On this bus the tour guide has 7 boxes of lunches. Each box holds 5 lunches. How many lunches are there?

Think: 7 boxes of 5 lunches
7×5

You can add on to a known fact to find a new fact.

7 groups of 5   =   6 groups of 5   plus   5
7×5 6×5
                              30   +   5   = 35

There are 35 lunches.

▶ What other multiplication fact has the same product as 7×5? How do you know?

▶ What is 6×8? Add on 8. Write a multiplication sentence for the new fact.

Check for Understanding
Find the product.

1 5	**2** 4	**3** 7	**4** 2	**5** 6	**6** 3	**7** 4
$\times 6$	$\times 7$	$\times 3$	$\times 6$	$\times 7$	$\times 6$	$\times 6$

8 7×7 **9** 1×6 **10** 5×7 **11** 6×6 **12** 2×7

THINK CRITICALLY: Analyze

13 [Journal] Write two examples of how you can add on to a known fact to find another fact.

Turn the page for Practice. ➡

Practice

Write the multiplication sentence.

1 〔row of bag shapes〕

2 ○○○○○○
○○○○○○
○○○○○○
○○○○○○

3

Multiply. Explain your method.

4 $3 \times 5 = ▪$
$6 \times 5 = ▪$

5 $2 \times 6 = ▪$
$4 \times 6 = ▪$

6 $2 \times 5 = ▪$
$4 \times 5 = ▪$

7 $2 \times 7 = ▪$
$3 \times 7 = ▪$

8 $6 \times 4 = ▪$
$7 \times 4 = ▪$

9 $6 \times 6 = ▪$
$7 \times 6 = ▪$

Find the product.

10 $\begin{array}{r} 0 \\ \times 6 \\ \hline \end{array}$
11 $\begin{array}{r} 7 \\ \times 3 \\ \hline \end{array}$
12 $\begin{array}{r} 7 \\ \times 8 \\ \hline \end{array}$
13 $\begin{array}{r} 8 \\ \times 6 \\ \hline \end{array}$
14 $\begin{array}{r} 5 \\ \times 6 \\ \hline \end{array}$
15 $\begin{array}{r} 1 \\ \times 7 \\ \hline \end{array}$
16 $\begin{array}{r} 6 \\ \times 9 \\ \hline \end{array}$

17 $\begin{array}{r} 9 \\ \times 7 \\ \hline \end{array}$
18 $\begin{array}{r} 7 \\ \times 7 \\ \hline \end{array}$
19 $\begin{array}{r} 4 \\ \times 8 \\ \hline \end{array}$
20 $\begin{array}{r} 5 \\ \times 7 \\ \hline \end{array}$
21 $\begin{array}{r} 3 \\ \times 6 \\ \hline \end{array}$
22 $\begin{array}{r} 7 \\ \times 0 \\ \hline \end{array}$
23 $\begin{array}{r} 7 \\ \times 6 \\ \hline \end{array}$

24 7×2
25 4×7
26 3×6
27 9×5
28 0×7

29 6×4
30 5×4
31 6×1
32 5×3
33 4×9

Algebra Complete the table.

34

Rule: Multiply by 7.					
Input	5	6	7	8	9
Output	▪	▪	▪	▪	▪

35

Rule: ▪					
Input	2	3	4	5	6
Output	12	18	24	30	36

······················· **Make It Right** ·······················

36 Van multiplied 6×3 mentally. Tell what the error is and correct it.

> 6 x 3 is 6 x 2, or 12, add 2 more; so the product is 14.

Sit in a circle with three other players. Work as a team to count to 30 without making a mistake.

Play the Game

▶ The first player starts by saying "One." Each player in turn says the next number.

▶ When the count reaches a number that has 4 as a factor, the player says "Bing" instead. If 6 is a factor, players say "Bang." Players say "Boom" if both 4 and 6 are factors.

▶ Players must start counting from 1 again if a player forgets to say "Bing," "Bang," or "Boom," or says any of them for the wrong number.

▶ Replay the game using different factors.

Sample Play:	
Number Said	
One	
Two	
Three	
Bing	Think:
Five	$4 \times 1 = 4$
Bang	Think:
Seven	$6 \times 1 = 6$
Bing	Think:
Nine	$4 \times 2 = 8$
Ten	
Eleven	
Boom	Think:
	$4 \times 3 = 12$ and
	$6 \times 2 = 12$

Cultural Connection
Native American Sign Language

Great Plains

The Kiowa were skillful users of sign language among the Native Americans living on the Great Plains. Here are the hand signs for the numbers from 1 to 5.

1 What is the rule for adding 1 to each number in this sign language?

2 Work with a partner to develop signs to show multiplication facts. Describe your method.

8 and 9 as Factors

Clair's company builds wooden roller coasters like those built in the 1920s and 1930s. A plan for small roller coasters has 6 seats in each train. If the company builds 8 trains for the new rides, how many seats are there in all?

Think: 8 groups of 6 seats
8 × 6

In the last lesson you learned you can double a known fact to find a new fact.

Clair Hain, Jr., president of Great Coasters Int., Inc., in Northumberland, PA

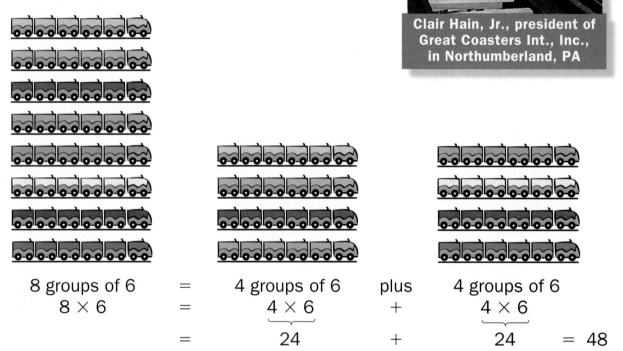

8 groups of 6	=	4 groups of 6	plus	4 groups of 6	
8 × 6	=	4 × 6	+	4 × 6	
	=	24	+	24	= 48

There are 48 seats in all.

Talk It Over

▶ **What if** there are 6 cars on the tracks with 8 seats in a car. How many seats are there? How do you know?

▶ Kerstin likes to use facts for 2 to help her remember her facts for 8. Use her method to find 8 x 9.

Think:
2 × 3 = 6
Double the fact. → 4 × 3 = 12
Double the new fact. → 8 × 3 = 24

A looping roller-coaster ride costs 6 tickets a person. If 9 friends want to ride it, how many tickets do they need in all?

Think: 9 groups of 6 tickets
9×6

You can multiply by 10 and subtract to find facts for 9.

Think: $10 \times 6 = 6$ tens $= 60$

$9 \times 6 = \underbrace{10 \times 6}$ subtract 6

$60 - 6 = 54$

$9 \times 6 = 54$

They need 54 tickets in all.

▶ **What if** the same 9 friends go on a ride that costs 8 tickets a person. How could you use multiplying by 10 to find the total number of tickets they use?

Check for Understanding

Find the product.

1	8	**2**	9	**3**	8	**4**	7	**5**	5	**6**	7	**7**	8
	$\times 8$		$\times 8$		$\times 6$		$\times 8$		$\times 9$		$\times 9$		$\times 5$

8 6×9 **9** 9×8 **10** 8×2 **11** 9×9 **12** 9×3

THINK CRITICALLY: Analyze

13 How can you use adding to help find multiplication facts? Give examples.

14 Greg uses subtraction to find other facts. To find 4 x 8, he thinks "5 x 8 subtract 8; so 40 − 8 = 32." Explain why this works.

Turn the page for Practice. ➡

Practice

Write the multiplication sentence.

1

2

3

Multiply.

| **4** 6
×8 | **5** 7
×9 | **6** 8
×4 | **7** 9
×8 | **8** 9
×3 | **9** 7
×8 | **10** 6
×9 |

| **11** 0
×8 | **12** 4
×9 | **13** 5
×8 | **14** 9
×5 | **15** 2
×8 | **16** 1
×9 | **17** 8
×8 |

| **18** 3
×7 | **19** 2
×5 | **20** 4
×6 | **21** 5
×7 | **22** 3
×6 | **23** 0
×7 | **24** 6
×2 |

25 7 × 6　　**26** 7 × 8　　**27** 3 × 6　　**28** 6 × 5　　**29** 0 × 3

30 7 × 2　　**31** 9 × 9　　**32** 5 × 6　　**33** 1 × 8　　**34** 3 × 7

Describe and complete the pattern.

35 16, 24, 32, ■, ■　　　　　　　　**36** 0, ■, 18, ■, 36, ■

Solve.

37 Each box holds 8 mugs. How many mugs in all?

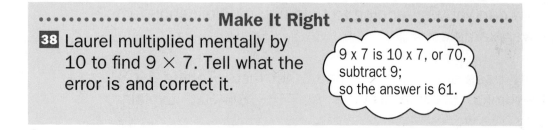

···················· **Make It Right** ····················

38 Laurel multiplied mentally by 10 to find 9 × 7. Tell what the error is and correct it.

9 x 7 is 10 x 7, or 70, subtract 9; so the answer is 61.

Pencil & Paper Calculator Mental Math

Use the table for problems 39–42.

39 If 8 friends go in the fun house, how many tickets do they use?

40 Margaret and 7 friends ride the monorail and the Ferris wheel. How many tickets do they use?

41 **Make a decision** You have 36 tickets. Which rides will you go on?

42 **Write a problem** about amusement park rides. Use the information about the number of tickets needed for each ride.

43 The passenger cab on the first Ferris wheel was about as big as ■. See INFOBIT.
a. a car   **b.** an elevator
c. a train car   **d.** a house

Number of Tickets for Rides	
Rides	**Tickets**
Monorail	4
Roller coaster	5
Bumper cars	6
Fun house	6
Ferris wheel	3

INFOBIT
The first Ferris wheel was built for the 1893 World's Fair in Chicago. Each passenger cab could carry 60 people.

more to explore

Odd or Even Multiplying

If one factor is odd and one factor is even, what will the product be?

Look at these examples.

$3 \times 2 = 6$ $2 \times 3 = 6$ **Think:** odd $\times$ even = even
$5 \times 4 = 20$ $4 \times 5 = 20$ even $\times$ odd = even
$7 \times 6 = 42$ $6 \times 7 = 42$

Find what the product will be. Give examples.

1 Both factors are even.

2 Both factors are odd.

Make an Organized List

Read | Tisa plans to buy an outfit at Hershey Park. She wants shorts, a T-shirt, and a hat. She picks red shorts. She can choose either a pink or orange T-shirt, and either a red or blue hat. How many different outfits does she have to choose from?

Plan | You can make an organized list of all the different outfits that are possible. Then you can count the number of outfits in your list to answer the question.

Solve | List the possible outfits. Then count the number of choices.

1. red shorts, orange T-shirt, red hat
2. red shorts, orange T-shirt, blue hat
3. red shorts, pink T-shirt, red hat
4. red shorts, pink T-shirt, blue hat

Tisa has four different outfits to choose from.

Look Back | How could you solve this problem in a different way?

Check for Understanding

1 **What if** Tisa can choose either red or blue shorts. How many different outfits would she have to choose from then?

THINK CRITICALLY: Analyze

2 How did you organize your list to answer problem 1?

MIXED APPLICATIONS

Problem Solving

Pencil & Paper Calculator Mental Math

Use the sign for problems 1–5.

1 The snack bar offers a lunch special with a choice of sandwich, salad, and beverage. How many different lunches without dessert are possible?

2 How many different lunches with dessert are possible?

3 How much more would 4 lunches cost with dessert than without dessert?

4 **Write a problem** using the information from the snack-bar sign. Ask others to solve it.

5 Neil and 2 friends buy the lunch special without dessert. About how much do they spend in all for lunch?

SNACK BAR

LUNCH SPECIAL $4.95
Includes Sandwich, Salad and Beverage

Sandwiches
Tuna or Chicken

Salads
Green Salad or Potato Salad

Beverages
Milk or Juice

Desserts ($1.00 extra)
Brownie or 2 Cookies

6 **Make a decision** You may buy a bag of 4 snacks for 6¢ each. Another bag holds 8 snacks for 3¢ each. Which bag of snacks would you buy? Why?

7 **Data Point** A new ride will have 4 cars. Each car can hold 7 people. Which of the other rides in the park carries the same number of people? Use the Databank on page 536 to find the answer.

8 Emilio wants to buy a sweatshirt and a pair of sweatpants in the souvenir shop. He can choose among 3 designs of sweatshirts. Sweatpants come in 2 styles. How many different outfits can Emilio choose from?

mixed review

1 345 + 257 **2** 502 − 368 **3** 456 + 135 **4** 700 − 399

5 621 + 729 **6** 439 − 358 **7** 713 + 333 **8** 846 − 686

Write the multiplication sentence.

1 ❋ ❋ ❋ ❋ ❋ ❋ ❋
❋ ❋ ❋ ❋ ❋ ❋ ❋
❋ ❋ ❋ ❋ ❋ ❋ ❋
❋ ❋ ❋ ❋ ❋ ❋ ❋

2 (mugs, 8 columns × 6 rows)

3 (caps, 6 columns × 6 rows)

Find the product.

4	8 ×7	**5**	8 ×9	**6**	7 ×8	**7**	6 ×3	**8**	6 ×9	**9**	8 ×6	**10**	7 ×0

11	4 ×8	**12**	9 ×5	**13**	6 ×6	**14**	3 ×7	**15**	6 ×5	**16**	9 ×4	**17**	8 ×3

18 9×9 **19** 2×6 **20** 3×9 **21** 7×7 **22** 8×1

23 6×1 **24** 7×5 **25** 7×9 **26** 8×5 **27** 9×2

Solve. Use the sign for problems 28–31.

28 Marty spends $5 on tickets. How many tickets does she get?

29 Rita and 5 friends ride the Octopus twice. How many tickets do they use in all?

30 Millie rides the Super Slide 6 times. How many tickets does she use?

31 How many more tickets are needed to ride the Super Slide twice than are needed to ride the Roundabout three times?

32 Lars wants to buy a cap. Caps come in red, blue, or green. They also come with either of 2 pictures. How many caps does Lars have to chose from?

33 Journal Explain how to find 9×6 in as many different ways as you can.

FUNLAND AMUSEMENT PARK

6 Tickets for $1.00

Ride	Tickets
Roundabout	3
Octopus	4
Runaway Train	6
Super Slide	9

Area Model of Multiplication

You can arrange 24 square tiles into different rectangles. One rectangle has 3 rows of 8 tiles.

$3 \times 8 = 24$

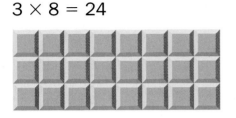

Another rectangle has 4 rows of 6 tiles.

$4 \times 6 = 24$

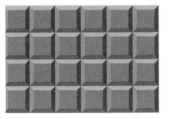

▶ What other ways could you arrange 24 tiles into a rectangle?

Draw as many rectangles as you can.

1 Use 10 tiles.

2 Use 36 tiles.

3 Use 18 tiles.

4 Use 7 tiles.

5 Use 12 tiles.

6 Use 30 tiles.

7 Use any number of tiles.

8 Why can you make more than 1 rectangle with 24 tiles, but only 1 rectangle with 7 tiles?

The Cost of Admission

Amusement parks have different kinds of price plans. Some charge a set fee for admission. For one price you can ride as many rides as you want.

The parks often offer many different discounts off the full admission price.

FUNLAND

ANNUAL PASSPORTS

Premium	$199
Deluxe	$129
Regular	$99

DAILY PASSPORTS

	1 Day	2 Day	3 Day
Regular	$34	$59	$82
Child (Age 3-11)	$26	$45	$63

ADVENTURE PARK

ADMISSION

GENERAL ADMISSION INCLUDES UNLIMITED USE OF ALL RIDES, SHOWS AND ATTRACTIONS

ADULTS	$29.95
CHILDREN (Ages 3 Through 11 years)	$19.95
SENIORS	$19.95

ANNUAL PASS

ADULT	$99.95
CHILDREN	$69.95

BUY YOUR TICKETS HERE

36 Ticket Book	$17.00
24 Ticket Book	$13.00
12 Ticket Book	$7.50
Individual Ticket	each .70

Other parks do not charge an admission fee. You buy tickets and use them to pay for each ride. These parks offer discounts on books of tickets. The more you buy, the more you save.

► Which do you think is a better deal, paying a set fee or paying for rides one at a time? Why?

► **What if** you can spend only two hours in the park. Does the amount of time you have change your choice?

Make Your Own Price Plan

1 Work as a team. Each member makes up a name for his or her own amusement park and writes a price plan for the park.

2 Discuss all of the team members' plans.

3 Decide which plan you prefer if:
  a. your team wants to go for a full day.
  b. you go with your family.
  c. all of the students from your school go on a class trip.

Report Your Findings

4 **Portfolio** Prepare a report on your price plans. Include the following:

▶ Prepare an advertisement that promotes your price plan.

▶ Explain how you decided on the prices and discounts.

▶ Explain why different plans work better than others in different situations.

5 Share your findings with the class. How do your team's decisions compare with those of other teams?

Revise your work.
▶ Is your advertisement clear and creative?
▶ Is your information accurate, and is it displayed correctly?
▶ Did you proofread your work?

PREDICT which price plans are the most popular.

EXPLORE the other choices amusement parks offer: discounts, promotions, and so forth.

FIND the history of your favorite amusement park.

Square Numbers

What is a square number? You can use crayons and graph paper to find out.

Work Together
Work with a partner.

Draw a square on graph paper.

▶ How many rows are in the square?

▶ How many ☐ are in each row?

▶ How many ☐ in all?

Record your work in a table.

You will need
- *graph paper*
- *crayons or markers*

KEEP IN MIND
A square has the same number of ☐ on each side.

Number of Rows	X	Number in Each Row	=	Number in All
	X		=	

Draw other squares. Record your work in a table.

Make Connections
Here is what Yoshi and Rebecca recorded for one square.

Number of Rows	X	Number in Each Row	=	Number in All
3	X	3	=	9

3 rows of 3 is equal to 9.
9 is a square number.

▶ What other square numbers did you find? Make a class list.

▶ What do you notice about the factors of a square number?

▶ What would be the next square number after 81? How do you know?

Check for Understanding
Draw the model and find the product.

1 5 × 5   **2** 6 × 6   **3** 7 × 7

THINK CRITICALLY: Analyze
4 Explain how you can use square numbers to find other multiplication facts. Give an example.

Practice
Write the multiplication sentence.

1   **2**

Draw the model and find the product.

3 2 × 2   **4** 8 × 8   **5** 9 × 9

Describe and complete the pattern.

6 1, 4, 9, 16, ■, 36, ■, 64, ■   **7** 2, 4, 6, ■, 10, ■, 14, ■

Find the product.

8 0 ×0	**9** 1 ×1	**10** 2 ×2	**11** 4 ×4	**12** 6 ×6	**13** 8 ×8	**14** 7 ×7

15 7 × 6   **16** 6 × 5   **17** 8 × 7   **18** 9 × 8   **19** 5 × 4

20 9 × 2   **21** 4 × 3   **22** 3 × 3   **23** 4 × 6   **24** 5 × 5

25 3 × 6   **26** 5 × 8   **27** 2 × 9   **28** 7 × 2   **29** 3 × 9

Use a Multiplication Table

You can use patterns that you see on a multiplication table to help you remember multiplication facts.

Work Together

Work with a partner.

Copy and complete the multiplication table.

Look for patterns in the table.

Color in the rows and columns to show the patterns you find.

Columns

x	0	1	2	3	4	5	6	7	8	9
0	0	0	0	0	0	0				
1	0	1	2	3	4	5				
2	0	2	4	6	8	10				
3	0	3	6	9	12	15				
4	0	4	8	12	16	20				
5	0	5	10	15	20	25				
6										
7										
8										
9										

Rows

Make Connections

Paula and Francisco recorded these patterns they found in the multiplication table.

The 5s row shows skip-counting by fives.

x	0	1	2	3	4	5	6	7	8	9
5	0	5	10	15	20	25	30	35	40	45

In the 9s row, 9 is always the sum of the digits in the product, except for zero.

x	0	1	2	3	4	5	6	7	8	9
9	0	9	18	27	36	45	54	63	72	81

▶ How does knowing the pattern in the 9s row help you learn the multiplication facts for 9?

▶ What other patterns do you see in the multiplication table?

Check for Understanding

Multiply. You may use the multiplication table.

1 6	**2** 8	**3** 2	**4** 0	**5** 7	**6** 5	**7** 2
×9	×5	×8	×7	×9	×5	×4

THINK CRITICALLY: Analyze

8 Beth looks at the numbers that have 3 as a factor and the numbers that have 6 as a factor and sees a pattern. What pattern does she see?

Practice

Find the product. You may use the multiplication table.

1 8	**2** 9	**3** 5	**4** 4	**5** 9	**6** 0	**7** 9
×2	×7	×3	×4	×5	×3	×1

8 9	**9** 8	**10** 7	**11** 5	**12** 6	**13** 7	**14** 4
×9	×6	×7	×2	×3	×8	×6

15 3 × 8 **16** 2 × 3 **17** 6 × 9 **18** 7 × 3 **19** 7 × 5

20 5 × 9 **21** 8 × 3 **22** 4 × 0 **23** 7 × 8 **24** 5 × 8

Algebra Write >, <, or = to complete the number sentence.

25 6 × 7 ● 45   **26** 32 ● 4 × 8   **27** 8 ● 8 × 0

28 16 ● 3 × 4   **29** 8 × 6 ● 50   **30** 21 ● 3 × 7

31 How many people are in 4 vans? in 6 vans?

Vans	1	2	3
People	7	14	21

32 How many wheels are on 5 trucks? on 7 trucks?

Trucks	1	2	3
Wheels	8	16	24

Three or More Factors

Each boat on the Platte River tour has 4 boards for seats. Two people can fit on each board. There are 3 boats on each tour. How many people can go on a tour?

Work Together
Work in a group.

Use connecting cubes to model the problem.
You need to see:

▶ the number of boards in each boat.

▶ the number of people on each board.

▶ the number of boats.

Write the number sentence that shows the model.

Write a problem that uses three factors.
Then model the problem with connecting cubes to solve it.

> **You will need**
> • *connecting cubes*

> **KEEP IN MIND**
> You can multiply only two numbers at a time. Use parentheses ( ) to group them.

Make Connections
Here's how Cole's group modeled the problem.

Number of people in boats	Number of boats	Number of people in all
4 X 2	X 3	= 24
8	X 3	= 24

There can be 24 people on the tour.

▶ What did Cole's group multiply to find the number of people in each boat?

▶ What other multiplication sentence could you write using the three factors in this problem? (Hint: Group the factors differently.)

▶ Does the product change when you change the grouping of the factors? Why or why not?

Check for Understanding
Find the product. You may use models.

1 $(2 \times 3) \times 3$ **2** $7 \times (2 \times 2)$ **3** $(5 \times 0) \times 3$ **4** $8 \times (4 \times 2)$

THINK CRITICALLY: Analyze

5 Journal **What if** you wanted to multiply 3 x 5 x 3. How could you group the factors to be easy to multiply mentally?

Practice
Find the product.

1 $(3 \times 2) \times 2$ **2** $7 \times (1 \times 6)$ **3** $(2 \times 4) \times 5$ **4** $7 \times (0 \times 7)$

5 $(1 \times 5) \times 9$ **6** $9 \times (2 \times 3)$ **7** $(2 \times 3) \times 6$ **8** $(4 \times 2) \times 9$

9 $7 \times (2 \times 4)$ **10** $(3 \times 3) \times 4$ **11** $4 \times (4 \times 2)$ **12** $(2 \times 3) \times 8$

13 $(2 \times 2) \times 8$ **14** $7 \times (3 \times 3)$ **15** $(6 \times 1) \times 9$ **16** $9 \times (0 \times 7)$

17 $(2 \times 3) \times (2 \times 3)$ **18** $(3 \times 3) \times (3 \times 3)$ **19** $(6 \times 1) \times (2 \times 4)$

20 $(2 \times 2) \times (2 \times 2)$ **21** $(3 \times 2) \times (3 \times 3)$ **22** $(4 \times 2) \times (2 \times 2)$

mixed review

1 5×7 **2** 4×6 **3** 3×3 **4** 2×8 **5** 1×5

6 4×3 **7** 2×2 **8** 4×5 **9** 2×5 **10** 3×6

Part 1 Choose the Operation

Work Together

Solve. Explain your methods.

1 How many people can ride the Roller Coaster? the Wild Mouse?

2 Which ride of these two rides holds more people? How many more?

3 **What if** another car is attached to the Wild Mouse. How many people can ride it now?

4 **Analyze a solution** Gail wrote this plan for solving problem 3. Explain what she did wrong. Write a correct plan.

Multiply the total found for the Wild Mouse in problem 1 by 4.

5 Tell how you know when to add, subtract, or multiply to solve problems 1–4.

Number of People on a Ride		
Ride	Number of Cars	Number in Each Car
Roller Coaster	8	4
Wild Mouse	4	4
Snake	8	3
Tilt-A-Whirl	6	6
Log Ride	6	4

Part 2 Write and Share Problems

Katy used the data in the table on page 262 to write these problems.

6 Solve Katy's problems. What operations did you use?

7 Change Katy's problem so that it uses another operation. Explain how you would solve it.

8 **Write a problem** of your own that uses multiplication, addition, or subtraction.

9 Trade problems. Solve at least three problems written by your classmates.

10 What was the most interesting problem you solved? Why?

How many people can ride the Snake? Try to find out how many could ride it if you put 1 more car on.

Katy Ayer
Mandarin Oaks
Elementary School
Jacksonville, FL

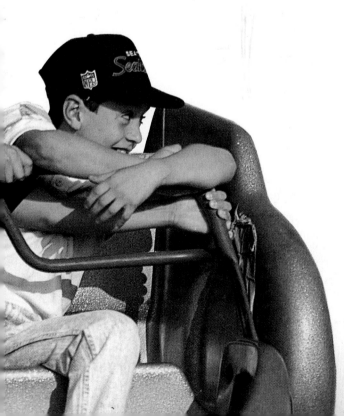

Turn the page for Practice Strategies. ➡

Menu

Choose five problems and solve them.

Explain your methods.

1 Brooke had $40.00 when she arrived at the amusement park. When she went home, she had $15.35. How much money did she spend during the day?

2 Caps for the park come in 2 fabrics and 3 colors. You can choose between 2 logos. How many types of caps do you have to choose from?

3 The Bright Angel Trail goes down into the Grand Canyon. It takes twice as long to hike up as it does to hike down. If it takes 2 hours to hike down, how long does it take to hike back up?

4 Eighty people stay overnight at Duke's Ranch in the cabins and bunkhouses. Each cabin holds 4 people, and 8 of the cabins are full. How many people are in the bunkhouses?

5 For the Spaceship ride, the wait is 3 minutes for every group of people in line. If 6 groups are in line in front of Kathryn, how long does she have to wait?

6 Daniel buys a lunch special for $4.95, a drink for $1.75, and a dessert for $2.25. About how much does he spend in all?

7 Lono and Suke got to Adventure Land at 12:30 P.M. Lono had to leave at 3:00 P.M. Suke stayed until 5:45. Who stayed longer? How much longer?

8 Melissa saw 4 times as many elk as bison in Yellowstone National Park. She saw 6 bison. How many elk did she see?

Choose two problems and solve them. Explain your methods.

9 Logical reasoning For their last ride, Annie, Rachel, Weston, and Eric each chose a different ride. Use these clues to decide who went on each ride.

Clue 1 Rachel used the fewest tickets.

Clue 2 Weston used an odd number of tickets.

Clue 3 Annie's ride cost more than $1.

Ride Tickets 4 for $1

Ride	Tickets
Scrambler	6
Flying scooter	3
Sidewinder	5
Spider	4

10 You have 20 ride tickets to use. Make a plan to ride at least four different rides and use up your tickets.

Ride	Tickets
Sky Ride	2
Train	2
Twister	3
Fun Factory	3
Himalaya Coaster	4
Pirate Ship	4
Hurricane	5

11 Spatial reasoning Move three toothpicks to create two squares. (Hint: One square is inside the other square.)

12 At the Computer Use a drawing program to divide a 4-by-4 array into two parts, each having the same shape. All of the square units should be complete. How many different shapes can you find?

Language and Mathematics

Complete the sentence. Use a word in the chart.

1 Both factors of a ■ are the same.

2 You can ■ a known fact to find a new fact.

3 In the multiplication sentence 6 x (2 x 4) = 48, 6 is a ■.

4 In the multiplication sentence 5 x (2 x 3) = 30, 30 is the ■.

5 Changing the ■ of the factors does not change the product.

Vocabulary
sum
product
square number
order
factor
double

Concepts and Skills

Write the number sentence.

6   **7**   **8**

Multiply.

9   5   **10**   6   **11**   4   **12**   8   **13**   9   **14**   8   **15**   9
$\times 6$ $\times 1$ $\times 7$ $\times 2$ $\times 0$ $\times 1$ $\times 7$

16   9   **17**   7   **18**   8   **19**   3   **20**   6   **21**   9   **22**   8
$\times 5$ $\times 2$ $\times 9$ $\times 7$ $\times 8$ $\times 4$ $\times 8$

23 5×7 **24** 7×8 **25** 7×6 **26** 3×8 **27** 6×6

28 9×6 **29** 4×7 **30** 5×8 **31** 4×6 **32** 8×9

33 $(2 \times 3) \times 4$ **34** $(3 \times 2) \times 8$ **35** $7 \times (1 \times 7)$

36 $9 \times (1 \times 3)$ **37** $(3 \times 5) \times 1$ **38** $8 \times (4 \times 2)$

39 $4 \times (2 \times 4)$ **40** $(9 \times 0) \times 9$ **41** $2 \times (3 \times 3)$

Think critically.

42 Analyze. Tell what the error is and correct it.

43 Generalize. Does it matter in what order you multiply factors? Give examples.

$(3 \times 2) \times 5 = 5 \times 5 = 25$

MIXED APPLICATIONS
Problem Solving

Pencil & Paper   Calculator   Mental Math

44 The roller coaster has 9 cars. Each car can hold 6 people. How many people can the roller coaster hold at one time?

45 At the snack bar, individual pizzas cost $4 each. Mrs. Wright buys 8 pizzas. How much does she spend?

46 The sign at the snack bar shows the toppings and the types of crust you can get. How many kinds of pizza can you get?

Pizza Any topping with any type of crust	
Topping	**Type of Crust**
Cheese	Regular
Olive	Thin
Pepperoni	Thick
Sausage	

47 Rebecca spends $9 on ride tickets at the park. Eight tickets cost $1. How many tickets does Rebecca buy?

48 A tour guide has 7 boxes, each with 5 lunches. She hands out 23 lunches. How many lunches does she have left?

49 The souvenir shop sells 7 different colors of T-shirts in sizes small, medium, large, and extra large. How many different T-shirts does the shop sell in all?

50 Suppose your whole class goes to the park. You separate into 3 groups. If there are 2 groups of 8 students and 1 of 7 students, how many students are in your class?

Write the number sentence.

1.

2.

3.

Multiply.

4	9	5	7	6	9	7	9	8	6	9	5
	×1		×8		×3		×9		×7		×8

10	2	11	1	12	8	13	5	14	7	15	6
	×7		×8		×6		×9		×0		×6

16. $(2 \times 4) \times 4$

17. $(2 \times 3) \times (9 \times 1)$

18. $6 \times (1 \times 8)$

19. $6 \times (2 \times 4)$

20. $8 \times (0 \times 5)$

21. $(2 \times 3) \times 9$

Solve.

22. Tesha wants to take 3 rides, one outdoor, one indoor, and one water. In how many different orders can she go on the rides?

Rides—3 for $1		
Water	**Indoor**	**Outdoor**
Log Jam	Mine Tunnel	Carousel
Raft City	Bumper Cars	Train
	Haunted House	

23. If Tesha wants to take 9 rides, how much will it cost?

24. Kim buys a snack and a drink. He can buy popcorn, peanuts, or chips and soft drink, juice, or lemonade. How many choices does he have?

25. Kareem spent $6.88 on lunch and $9.00 on souvenirs. He took 3 rides. How much did he have left from $20?

What Did You Learn?

Flashlight batteries come in packages of 2, 4, 6, and 8. Tell how many batteries you would get if you bought 5 packages of each size. How many batteries would you have in all?

▶ Explain at least two different methods you can use to solve this problem.

·············· **A Good Answer** ··············
• correctly identifies how many batteries are in 5 packages of each size and how many batteries there are in all
• clearly and completely shows at least two methods for finding these answers

You may want to place your work in your portfolio.

What Do You Think ?

1 Which facts do you find the easiest? How do you use them to find harder facts?

2 List some methods you might use to multiply.

3 How do your methods change when there are three or more factors?

What a Roller Coaster

Cultural Note

The first roller coasters were built in Russia in the 1700s. The first looping roller coaster was built in France in 1846.

The thrill of a roller coaster comes from gravity. First the cars are pulled to the top of a large hill. The force of gravity pulls the coaster down at a great enough speed to get the coaster through all of the twists, turns, hills, and loops.

Have you ever wondered why people do not fall out of a looping roller coaster?

Look at the girl in the photo. The force of the string pulling in on the ball is balanced by another force pushing out.

As long as a roller coaster is moving fast enough the same kind of force holds people onto their seats.

▶ When does a roller coaster go faster? When does it slow down? Why do you think this happens?

▶ Look at the picture of the roller coaster. Which hill is the highest? Why do you think it was built this way?

▶ Why do you think all roller coasters come with seat belts, bars, and harnesses?

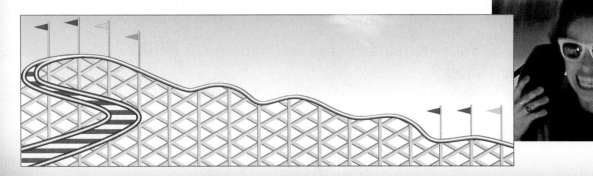

How Many Ride?

1 Each train on a roller coaster called the Looper has 6 cars. Each car holds 4 riders. How many people can fit on the train at one time?

2 The Looper has twin tracks. Two trains can run at the same time. How many people can ride the Looper at the same time?

3 For safety, the cars on looping roller coasters have 4 wheels on the inside and 4 wheels on the outside of the tracks. How many wheels are there on the Looper?

4 One ride on the Looper costs $2. How much do 7 rides cost?

5 The ride on the Looper takes 3 minutes. How long does it take for 9 rides in a row?

At the Computer

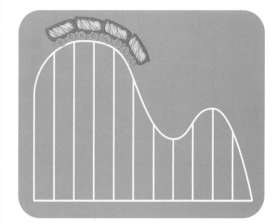

6 Use drawing software to design and draw your own roller coaster.

7 Write an advertisement that could be used on a poster or in a newspaper to encourage people to try your roller coaster. Be sure to give it a name that makes people want to ride it.

8 DIVISION FACTS

Pets

People love their pets. In this chapter you will see how people use division in pet stores, when caring for pets, and when buying pet food and other supplies.

What Do You Know ?

1 One of the easiest pets to care for is a turtle. There are 18 turtles in a large tank. If you put the same number of turtles in each of 6 smaller tanks, how many turtles would you put in each?

2 Suppose the turtles need more room, so only 2 can fit in a tank. How many tanks would they need?

3 **Portfolio** Another tank holds 12 goldfish. In how many different ways can you place the goldfish equally into smaller tanks? Use counters or drawings to help explain your method.

The Meaning of Division

Have you ever thought of going into business for yourself? Suppose you and a friend earn $18 by walking neighbors' dogs. If you share the money equally, how much will you get?

You will need
- *play money— dollars*

Work Together

Work with a partner. Use play dollars to model each problem. Draw a picture of your model. Record your results in a table.

Problem A

Find how many in each group.

Count out $18. Share them equally with your partner.

How many dollars do you each get?

Model the problem several times using different even numbers of dollars.

Total Number of Dollars	Number of People	Number of Dollars for Each Person
18	2	

Problem B

Find how many groups.

Start with the same total number of dollars as you modeled in Problem A.

You want to give 2 dollars to each friend who walked a dog for you.

How many friends can you pay?

Total Number of Dollars	Number of Dollars for Each Person	Number of People
18	2	

Talk It Over

▶ Explain how you found each answer.

▶ How are your answers to the two problems alike? different?

Make Connections

Here is how Shanna and Gail solved Problem A.

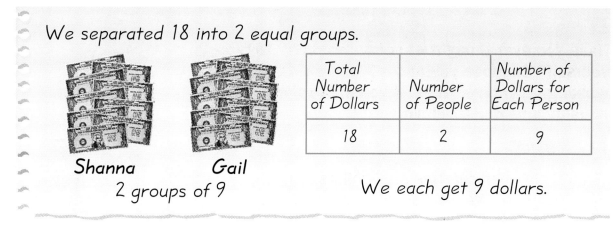

We separated 18 into 2 equal groups.

Shanna   Gail

2 groups of 9

Total Number of Dollars	Number of People	Number of Dollars for Each Person
18	2	9

We each get 9 dollars.

Here is how Shanna and Gail solved Problem B.

We kept subtracting 2 until there was nothing left.
We subtracted 9 times.

Total Number of Dollars	Number of Dollars for Each Person	Number of People
18	2	9

$18 - 2 = 16$ $12 - 2 = 10$ $6 - 2 = 4$
$16 - 2 = 14$ $10 - 2 = 8$ $4 - 2 = 2$
$14 - 2 = 12$ $8 - 2 = 6$ $2 - 2 = 0$

9 dog walkers can each
get 2 dollars.

9 groups of 2

Check for Understanding

Complete. Explain your methods. You may use models.

1

■ groups of 3

2 3 groups of ■

3 2 groups of ■

THINK CRITICALLY: Analyze

4 Start with 16 dollars. Can you share them equally with 2 people? 3 people? 4 people? Tell why or why not.

Turn the page for Practice.

Practice

Complete. Explain your methods. You may use models.

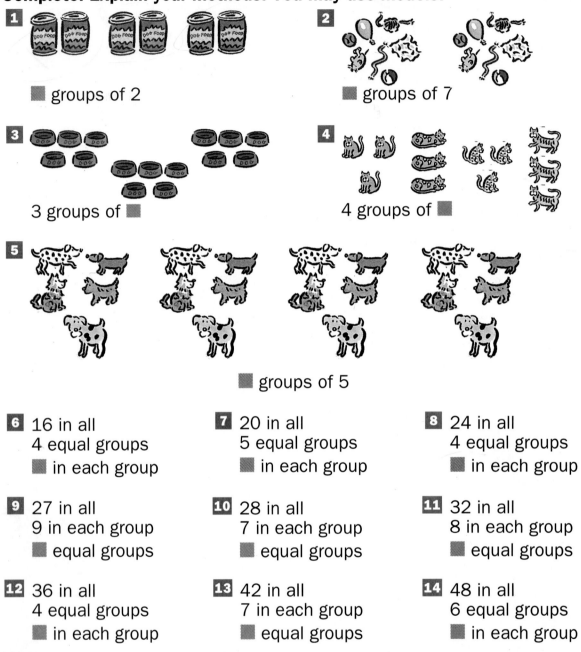

1 ▮ groups of 2

2 ▮ groups of 7

3 3 groups of ▮

4 4 groups of ▮

5 ▮ groups of 5

6 16 in all
4 equal groups
▮ in each group

7 20 in all
5 equal groups
▮ in each group

8 24 in all
4 equal groups
▮ in each group

9 27 in all
9 in each group
▮ equal groups

10 28 in all
7 in each group
▮ equal groups

11 32 in all
8 in each group
▮ equal groups

12 36 in all
4 equal groups
▮ in each group

13 42 in all
7 in each group
▮ equal groups

14 48 in all
6 equal groups
▮ in each group

Copy and complete the table. You may use models.

	Total Number	Number of Equal Groups	Number in Each Group
15	18	3	▮
16	24	▮	6
17	25	5	▮
18	32	▮	8

19 Tomás uses 3 leashes for 9 dogs. He puts the same number of dogs on each. How many are on each leash?

20 Dina raises 24 poodles. She puts 4 poodles in each pen. How many pens are there?

21 Pam buys 5 boxes of dog food. Each box holds 8 cans. How many cans does she buy?

22 Claire's Puppy Shop has 5 dogs and 15 cats for sale. How many more cats than dogs are there?

23 Last month, the Riverdale Animal Hospital treated 78 dogs, 56 cats, 4 rabbits, and 1 gerbil. How many animals were cared for at the hospital last month?

24 **Data Point** There are 24 dogs in a show. The same number of dogs from each group are entered. Use the Databank on page 537 to find how many dogs from each group are entered.

Cultural Connection The Division Symbol

Mathematicians have not always used the same symbol to show division.

$\frac{8}{4}$ Around 1200 in Arabia, al-Hazzar would have written a fraction to find how many groups of 4 there are in 8.

4)8 In 1544, Michael Stifel introduced this symbol in Germany.

$8 \div 4$ In 1659, J. H. Rahn, a Swiss mathematician, used this symbol.

4|8 This symbol is still used in Cuba and South America.

8/4 In many computer programs, this symbol is used to show division.

Map showing SWITZERLAND, GERMANY, CUBA, SAUDI ARABIA

Write the division sentence another way. You may use models to find the answer.

1 $4 \div 2$ **2** 2|8 **3** 12/6 **4** 3)6

Relate Multiplication and Division

You can use counters to learn how multiplication and division are related.

Work Together

Work with a partner.

Separate 18 counters into equal groups. Draw a picture of your model.

Write a multiplication sentence about your model. Record your sentence in a table.

Number of Groups	x	Number in Each Group	=	Number in All
■	×	■	=	18

You can also write a **division sentence** about your model.

Number in All	÷	Number of Groups	=	Number in Each Group
18	÷	■	=	■

↑ dividend   ↑ divisor   ↑ quotient

Repeat the activity by separating 18 counters into other equal groups.

▶ Compare the number sentences. What do you notice?

▶ Repeat the activity. Try 12 counters, 16 counters, 24 counters. Compare your results to those of others.

Make Connections

Sam and Ella share their work with the class.

Number of Groups	x	Number in Each Group	=	Number in All
3	x	6	=	18

Number in All	÷	Number of Groups	=	Number in Each Group
18	÷	3	=	6

▶ What other multiplication and division sentences can you write using the same numbers as Sam?

▶ Explain how your number sentences show that multiplication and division are opposite operations.

Check for Understanding

Write a pair of related multiplication and division sentences.

1 **2** **3**

4 3, 4, 12 **5** 2, 7, 14 **6** 1, 2, 2 **7** 3, 5, 15 **8** 2, 8, 16

THINK CRITICALLY: Summarize

9 How are multiplication and division related?

Practice

Write a pair of related multiplication and division sentences.

1 **2** **3**

4 3, 8, 24 **5** 4, 4, 16 **6** 5, 6, 30 **7** 1, 9, 9 **8** 4, 5, 20

9 Each box holds 6 bags of birdseed. How many bags are in 5 boxes?

10 Four boxes hold 32 cans of dog food. How many cans are in 1 box?

Divide by 2 and 5

A small dog, like a Westie, eats 2 pounds of dog food a week. How many weeks will a 10-pound bag last?

You can skip-count backward.

Think: How many groups of 2 are in 10?
There are 5 groups of 2 in 10.

You can also divide.

$10 \div 2 = 5$ or $2)\overline{10}$ ← quotient / ← dividend
↑ divisor

Think: What number times 2 is equal to 10?
■ $\times 2 = 10$
$5 \times 2 = 10$

A 10-pound bag of dog food will last 5 weeks.

For a larger dog, like a springer spaniel, a 25-pound bag of dog food would last 5 weeks. How many pounds does the dog eat each week?

You can skip-count backward on a calculator.

Enter $25 - 5$, then keep pressing $=$ until it reads 0.

Number of Skips (=)	0	1	2	3	4	5
Number in Display	25	20	15	10	5	0

Think: There are 5 groups of 5 in 25.
$25 \div 5 = 5$

The dog eats 5 pounds of dog food a week.

Check for Understanding
Divide.

1 $6 \div 2$ **2** $15 \div 5$ **3** $4 \div 2$ **4** $5)\overline{30}$ **5** $2)\overline{14}$

THINK CRITICALLY: Analyze

6 Describe patterns you see when you skip-count by twos and by fives.

Practice

Divide.

1 20 ÷ 5   **2** 10 ÷ 2   **3** 30 ÷ 5   **4** 16 ÷ 2   **5** 40 ÷ 5

6 2)$\overline{8}$ **7** 5)$\overline{45}$ **8** 2)$\overline{12}$ **9** 5)$\overline{35}$ **10** 2)$\overline{18}$

11 How many groups of 5 are in 40?   **12** How many groups of 2 are in 14?

13 Divide 12 by 2.   **14** Divide 20 by 4.

15 How much does one can weigh?   **16** One can weighs 9 pounds. How many cans are under the cloth?

Describe and complete the pattern.

17 35, 30, 25, ■, ■, ■   **18** 14, 12, 10, ■, ■, ■

MIXED APPLICATIONS
Problem Solving
Pencil & Paper   Calculator   Mental Math

19 Marla sells homemade dog treats. Today, she baked 20 dog treats. She packed 2 treats in each bag. How many bags of treats will she have to sell?

20 **Make a decision** Carol has 15 photographs. If she wants the same number on each page of an album, should she put 2 or 5 on a page? Why?

21 Dog licenses cost $6 each. Jaime paid $24 for dog licenses. How many dogs does he have?

22 **Write a problem** that can be solved using the division sentence 10 ÷ 2 = 5. Ask others to solve it.

mixed review

1 9 × 0   **2** 9 × 5   **3** 1 × 7   **4** 8 × 8   **5** 3 × 2 × 5

6 6 × 7   **7** 4 × 8   **8** 3 × 9   **9** 5 × 5   **10** 2 × 4 × 5

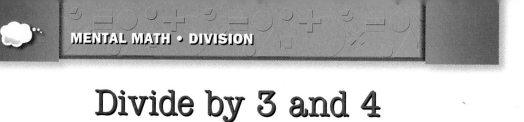

Divide by 3 and 4

Suddenly, you have 24 more gerbils than you can handle. You have 3 friends who want them. How can you share them equally?

Divide to find the number in each group.
Divide: 24 ÷ 3

You can use a related multiplication fact.

Think: 3 times what number is 24?
$3 \times \blacksquare = 24$
$3 \times 8 = 24$
So $24 \div 3 = 8$.

Each friend gets 8 gerbils.

There are 3 groups of 8 in 24.

What if you decide instead to give 4 gerbils each to some of your friends. How many friends can you give gerbils to?

Divide to find the number of groups.
Divide: 24 ÷ 4

You can use a related multiplication fact.

Think: What number times 4 is 24?
$\blacksquare \times 4 = 24$
$6 \times 4 = 24$
So $24 \div 4 = 6$.

Six friends can have gerbils.

There are 6 groups of 4 in 24.

Check for Understanding
Divide.

1 9 ÷ 3   **2** 36 ÷ 4   **3** 3)$\overline{27}$ **4** 21 ÷ 3   **5** 4)$\overline{28}$

THINK CRITICALLY: Generalize

6 Give an example of how dividing by 4 is like dividing by 2 twice.

Practice

Write a division sentence.

1 [mice illustration] **2** [gerbils illustration] **3** [dogs illustration]

Divide.

4 8 ÷ 4   **5** 18 ÷ 3   **6** 12 ÷ 4   **7** 27 ÷ 3   **8** 32 ÷ 4

9 3)‾12   **10** 4)‾28   **11** 3)‾9   **12** 4)‾36   **13** 3)‾24

14 How many groups of 4 are in 16?   **15** How many groups of 3 are in 15?

Algebra Complete the table.

16

Rule: Divide by 4.				
Input	36	32	28	24
Output	9	■	■	■

17

Rule: ■				
Input	24	21	18	15
Output	8	7	6	5

MIXED APPLICATIONS
Problem Solving

[Pencil & Paper] [Calculator] [Mental Math]

18 Kathy has 14 mice. She wants to share them equally with José. How many mice will each of them have?

19 **Write a problem** that could be solved using division. Its answer should be "2 gerbils each." Ask others to solve it.

20 **Spatial reasoning** How many boxes are in the stack?

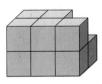

21 Mr. Carl buys 9 goldfish at the pet shop. Can he separate the goldfish equally into 4 fishbowls? Why or why not?

mixed review

How much time has passed?

1 Begin: 1:20 P.M.
End: 1:50 P.M.

2 Begin: 5:30 A.M.
End: 6:45 A.M.

3 Begin: 10:05 P.M.
End: 10:30 P.M.

Divide by 6 and 7

Gardeners raise earthworms in "worm boxes" to improve the soil. Each box holds 6 pounds of soil. If there are 18 pounds of soil, how many boxes can be made?

Divide to find the number of boxes. $18 \div 6 = \blacksquare$

You can use a related multiplication fact.

Think: What number times 6 is 18?

$\blacksquare \times 6 = 18$

$3 \times 6 = 18$

So $18 \div 6 = 3$.

Three worm boxes can be made.

There are 3 groups of 6 in 18.

A gardener separates 42 earthworms into equal groups. She puts a group in each of 7 worm boxes. How many earthworms are in each worm box?

Divide to find the number in each box. $42 \div 7 = \blacksquare$

You can use a related multiplication fact.

Think: 7 times what number is 42?

$7 \times \blacksquare = 42$

$7 \times 6 = 42$

So $42 \div 7 = 6$.

There are 6 earthworms in each box.

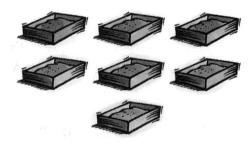

There are 7 groups of 6 in 42.

Check for Understanding
Divide.

1 $21 \div 7$ **2** $12 \div 6$ **3** $7 \div 7$ **4** $7\overline{)49}$ **5** $6\overline{)48}$

THINK CRITICALLY: Analyze **Explain your reasoning.**

6 journal Choose some numbers you can divide by 3. Choose some numbers you can divide by 6. Write about the patterns you see.

Practice

Divide.

1 12 ÷ 6   **2** 14 ÷ 7   **3** 56 ÷ 7   **4** 54 ÷ 6   **5** 28 ÷ 7

6 18 ÷ 2   **7** 27 ÷ 3   **8** 16 ÷ 4   **9** 45 ÷ 5   **10** 32 ÷ 4

11 6)18   **12** 6)30   **13** 2)12   **14** 6)42   **15** 7)63

16 4)24   **17** 5)35   **18** 3)21   **19** 5)30   **20** 4)28

21 How many groups of 7 are in 49?   **22** How many groups of 3 are in 18?

23 Divide 14 by 2.   **24** Divide 36 by 6.

Algebra Complete the table.

25

Rule: Divide by 7.				
Input	14	21	28	35
Output	2	▨	▨	▨

26

Rule: ▨				
Input	24	30	36	42
Output	4	5	6	7

MIXED APPLICATIONS
Problem Solving

Pencil & Paper   Calculator   Mental Math

27 Mr. Boylan uses 42 inches of nylon rope to make 6 handles for the worm boxes. How long is each handle?

28 Jim buys 36 tulip bulbs. He plants them in groups of 6 bulbs. How many groups of 6 does he have?

29 The amount of soil earthworms turn over was rounded to the nearest ten tons. What could be the least number of tons? the greatest number? See INFOBIT.

INFOBIT
Earthworms burrow, mix, fertilize, and loosen soil. They have been known to turn over about 40 tons of topsoil in each acre of land.

mixed review

1 498 − 70   **2** 657 + 48   **3** 452 − 354   **4** 900 + 245

Divide by 8 and 9

Does your class pet go home during vacations?
A school is closed 16 weeks a year. If
8 students can take home the class rabbit,
for how long should each one have it?

Divide to find the number of weeks. $16 \div 8 = \blacksquare$

You can use a related multiplication fact.

Think: 8 times what number is 16?

$8 \times \blacksquare = 16$
$8 \times 2 = 16$
So $16 \div 8 = 2$.

Each student should have it for 2 weeks.

A large bag of rabbit food can last about
9 weeks. If there are 36 weeks when school
is open, how many bags of food will be needed
for the school year?

Divide to find the number of food bags. $36 \div 9 = \blacksquare$

You can use a related multiplication fact.

Think: What number times 9 is 36?

$\blacksquare \times 9 = 36$
$4 \times 9 = 36$
So $36 \div 9 = 4$.

4 bags of food are needed for the school year.

Check for Understanding
Divide.

1 $24 \div 8$ **2** $54 \div 9$ **3** $32 \div 8$ **4** $9\overline{)63}$ **5** $9\overline{)45}$ **6** $8\overline{)24}$

THINK CRITICALLY: Generalize

7 When you know $36 \div 9 = 4$, you also know $36 \div 4 = 9$.
Explain why this is true.

Practice

Divide.

1 $16 \div 8$ **2** $18 \div 9$ **3** $56 \div 8$ **4** $54 \div 9$ **5** $72 \div 8$

6 $81 \div 9$ **7** $48 \div 8$ **8** $27 \div 9$ **9** $45 \div 5$ **10** $56 \div 7$

11 $8\overline{)24}$ **12** $9\overline{)72}$ **13** $8\overline{)64}$ **14** $8\overline{)32}$ **15** $9\overline{)63}$

16 $5\overline{)40}$ **17** $6\overline{)54}$ **18** $3\overline{)24}$ **19** $7\overline{)63}$ **20** $6\overline{)48}$

21 How many cages do you need if you want to put 3 rabbits in each cage?

22 How many rabbits would be in each cage if you put the same number in each of 9 cages?

Algebra Write +, −, x, or ÷ to complete the number sentence.

23 $45 \bullet 9 = 5$

24 $3 \bullet 8 = 24$

25 $24 \bullet 8 = 16$

26 $18 \bullet 9 = 9$

27 $48 \bullet 8 = 6$

28 $32 \bullet 8 = 40$

MIXED APPLICATIONS
Problem Solving

Pencil & Paper | Calculator | Mental Math

29 You observe that after 7 days a rabbit's food bag is 21 ounces lighter. About how much did the rabbit eat each day?

30 Dermot pays $36 for water bottles for his rabbits. Each bottle costs $9. How many water bottles does he buy?

31 **Logical reasoning** Write at least three things these numbers have in common.   12   24   36

32 **Write a problem** that can be solved by finding a quotient of 8. Give it to others to solve.

mixed review

Round to the nearest hundred.

1 145 **2** 671 **3** 61 **4** 327 **5** 989

Write a pair of related multiplication and division sentences.

1

2

3 5, 5, 25

4 7, 8, 56

Find the quotient.

5 12 ÷ 2

6 24 ÷ 3

7 16 ÷ 2

8 28 ÷ 4

9 8 ÷ 4

10 30 ÷ 5

11 42 ÷ 7

12 72 ÷ 9

13 21 ÷ 3

14 30 ÷ 6

15 36 ÷ 4

16 40 ÷ 5

17 $5\overline{)20}$

18 $9\overline{)81}$

19 $3\overline{)15}$

20 $8\overline{)48}$

21 $8\overline{)72}$

22 $7\overline{)49}$

23 $9\overline{)27}$

24 $8\overline{)64}$

25 How many groups of 7 are in 35?

26 How many groups of 8 are in 40?

27 Divide 36 by 6.

28 Divide 63 by 9.

Solve.

29 Kirby, the dog, eats 5 pounds of dog food a week. For how many weeks will a 10-pound bag of dog food last?

30 Anna gives each of her dogs 3 dog biscuits. If she takes 12 biscuits out of the box, how many dogs does she have?

31 Lionel shares 30 animal crackers equally with 5 friends. How many crackers does each person get?

32 Toni places 9 crickets in each cage. She has 54 crickets. How many cricket cages does she use?

33 Journal Explain as many different ways to find 45 ÷ 9 as you can.

Different Names for the Same Number

What do 1 + 3, 5 − 1, 2 × 2, and 12 ÷ 3 have in common?

They are all ways to name the number 4.

Here are some other ways to name the number 4.

$$(2 \times 5) - 6 \qquad (16 \div 8) + 2 \qquad (72 \div 9) - 5 + 1$$

$$\underbrace{10 - 6} \qquad \underbrace{2 + 2} \qquad \underbrace{8 - 5 + 1}$$

$$4 \qquad\qquad 4 \qquad\qquad 3 + 1$$

$$\underbrace{}$$

$$4$$

All whole numbers can be named in a variety of ways.

▶ What other ways can you think of to name the number 4? Which operations did you use?

Write the number in at least three different ways.

1 8   **2** 12   **3** 5   **4** 36   **5** 56

6 Work with a partner. Write a number from 2 through 60 on a piece of paper. Exchange papers. Write as many names for the number as you can. Time yourselves for 5 minutes.

Set Up an Aquarium

Fish are common and practical pets. Aquariums are often used as homes for these special pets. Do you know what it takes to care for fish?

How would you set up your own 20-gallon aquarium?

▶ Use the information to get started.

▶ Decide where you can find out what you would need to set up an aquarium.

▶ Make a list of what you would need and what each item on your list would cost.

▶ Decide how you will report your findings to the class.

Type of Fish	Type of Fish Food	Water Temperature	Grouping	Adult Size
Angelfish	All-Purpose	75° to 86°F	1 or more	5 inches
Black molly	All-Purpose or Vegetable	75° to 86°F	pair	2 inches
Goldfish	Goldfish	65° to 75°F	1 or more	4 inches
Guppy	All-Purpose or Vegetable	75°F	pair	2 inches
Keep No More Than 1 Inch of Fish for Each Gallon of Water				

Researching Fish Care

1. What types of fish would you include in your aquarium? How many of each type?

2. What else would you need to set up the aquarium? What items might you have available?

3. How would your group share the work of keeping the aquarium?

Report Your Findings

4. **Portfolio** Prepare a report on the information you've gathered. Include the following:

   ▶ Describe how you would set up the aquarium. Include what you would buy and why. List the cost of each item and the total cost.

   ▶ Write a brief summary of the care and costs to keep the aquarium.

5. Share your report with your classmates. How does your report compare with those of other teams?

Revise your work.
   ▶ Is the information you gathered accurate and easy to understand?
   ▶ Are your drawing and report organized and clear?
   ▶ Did you proofread your work?

MORE TO INVESTIGATE

PREDICT which type of fish would be chosen most often.

EXPLORE what types of fish survive the longest in an aquarium.

FIND what it takes to run a large aquarium such as Sea World or Coney Island.

Divide with 0 and 1

Horses sleep 1 to a stall. If 6 horses are boarded at a horse farm, how many stalls are needed?

Divide 6 by 1.

> When you divide any number by 1, the quotient is that number.

6 stalls are needed.

There are six 1s in 6.
$6 \div 1 = 6$

What if no one is boarding horses at the farm. There are 0 horses in 6 stalls. How many are in each stall?

Divide 0 by 6.

> When you divide 0 by any number, the quotient is 0.

There are 0 horses in each stall.

There are zero 6s in 0.
$0 \div 6 = 0$

If a stable has 6 stalls, how many stables do you need for 6 horses?

Divide 6 by 6.

> When you divide any number by itself, the quotient is 1.

You need 1 stable.

There is one 6 in 6.
$6 \div 6 = 1$

Check for Understanding

1 $4 \div 1$ **2** $2 \div 2$ **3** $8 \div 1$ **4** $5\overline{)0}$ **5** $1\overline{)7}$

THINK CRITICALLY: Analyze

6 Can you draw a picture for the sentence $3 \div 0 = \blacksquare$? Why or why not?

Think: Can any number complete $0 \times \blacksquare = 3$?

Practice

Find the quotient.

1 $7 \div 1$ **2** $0 \div 2$ **3** $4 \div 4$ **4** $8 \div 1$ **5** $0 \div 9$

6 $3\overline{)0}$ **7** $3\overline{)3}$ **8** $1\overline{)5}$ **9** $1\overline{)0}$ **10** $1\overline{)1}$

11 $4\overline{)0}$ **12** $7\overline{)7}$ **13** $1\overline{)6}$ **14** $7\overline{)0}$ **15** $6\overline{)6}$

16 How many 9s are in 9?   **17** How many 1s are in 4?

18 Divide 5 by 5.   **19** Divide 8 by 8.   **20** Divide 0 by 6.

Algebra Find the missing number.

21 $5 \div \blacksquare = 1$ **22** $\blacksquare \times 9 = 0$ **23** $4 \div \blacksquare = 4$ **24** $\blacksquare + 2 = 2$

25 $\blacksquare - 6 = 0$ **26** $\blacksquare \div 1 = 7$ **27** $\blacksquare - 8 = 0$ **28** $\blacksquare \div 1 = 3$

MIXED APPLICATIONS
Problem Solving

29 Apples are good treats for horses. If you share 8 apples equally among 8 horses, how many apples will each horse get?

30 David spent $40 on bales of hay for his horse. He bought 8 bales each at the same price. How much did each bale cost?

31 **Spatial reasoning** This is one half of a figure. Trace it. Then draw the bottom half. What figure did you draw?

32 **Make a decision** You can buy 3 cans of saddle soap for $9 at one store or 4 cans for $8 at another store. Which would you buy? Why?

mixed review

1 3×3 **2** 6×7 **3** 3×4 **4** 8×0 **5** 4×8

6 0×7 **7** 9×1 **8** 5×4 **9** 8×9 **10** 8×8

Use a Multiplication Table to Divide

Animal shelters need help from volunteers. Suppose 24 students want to volunteer. The shelter wants smaller groups. How many groups of 4 helpers can you make?

Divide: 24 ÷ 4

You can use a multiplication table to divide.

Think: What number times 4 is 24?

■ × 4 = 24

Use the table to find the **missing factor.**

▶ Find the product, 24, in the row for the factor you know, 4.

▶ The missing factor is at the top of that column.
6 × 4 = 24   So 24 ÷ 4 = 6.

You can make 6 groups of 4 helpers.

Columns

x	0	1	2	3	4	5	6	7	8	9
0	0	0	0	0	0	0	0	0	0	0
1	0	1	2	3	4	5	6	7	8	9
2	0	2	4	6	8	10	12	14	16	18
3	0	3	6	9	12	15	18	21	24	27
4	0	4	8	12	16	20	24	28	32	36
5	0	5	10	15	20	25	30	35	40	45
6	0	6	12	18	24	30	36	42	48	54
7	0	7	14	21	28	35	42	49	56	63
8	0	8	16	24	32	40	48	56	64	72
9	0	9	18	27	36	45	54	63	72	81

Rows

Check for Understanding

Find the missing number. Use the multiplication table.

1 32 ÷ 8 = ■
8 × ■ = 32

2 21 ÷ 3 = ■
3 × ■ = 21

3 45 ÷ 9 = ■
■ × 9 = 45

4 54 ÷ 6 = ■
■ × 6 = 54

THINK CRITICALLY: Analyze

5 **What if** you find the product in the column for a known factor. Where would you find the missing factor? How do you know?

Practice

Divide.

1 $63 \div 9$ **2** $16 \div 2$ **3** $56 \div 8$ **4** $16 \div 4$ **5** $18 \div 9$

6 $48 \div 6$ **7** $35 \div 7$ **8** $15 \div 5$ **9** $27 \div 3$ **10** $64 \div 8$

11 $28 \div 7$ **12** $18 \div 6$ **13** $32 \div 4$ **14** $30 \div 6$ **15** $36 \div 6$

16 $45 \div 5$ **17** $49 \div 7$ **18** $40 \div 8$ **19** $54 \div 9$ **20** $56 \div 7$

Algebra **Write the letter of the missing number.**

21 $9 \times \blacksquare = 36$ **a.** 3   **b.** 4   **c.** 27   **d.** 28

22 $72 \div \blacksquare = 8$ **a.** 7   **b.** 8   **c.** 9   **d.** 64

23 $\blacksquare \times 7 = 42$ **a.** 5   **b.** 6   **c.** 7   **d.** 35

MIXED APPLICATIONS
Problem Solving

Pencil & Paper   Calculator   Mental Math

24 Michael has 8 kittens. If he puts 1 kitten in each cage, how many cages will he use?

25 If 7 students chip in $4 each to buy a hamster cage, how much does the cage cost?

26 A cat's scratching post weighs 15 pounds. The base weighs 5 more pounds than the post. How much does the post weigh without the base?

27 A swimming pool has 6 lanes. The boys swim in lanes 2, 4, and 6. The girls swim in the other lanes. In which lanes do the girls swim?

28 Marie walked 24 miles in 4 days. She walked the same amount each day. How many miles did she walk each day?

29 **Data Point** Survey your friends about the pets they have. Make a bar graph or pictograph to show the results.

mixed review

1   365
       $+ 134$

2   209
       $- 151$

3   451
       $+ 149$

4   503
       $- 408$

5   960
       $+ 267$

Work Backward

Read Jeremy's class wants to adopt a whale at the local aquarium. They have already raised $18. This is twice as much as they still need to have the adoption fee. How much is the adoption fee?

Plan Begin at the end of the story and work backward to find the amount of the adoption fee.

Solve Start by finding how much they still need to raise.

$$\blacksquare \times 2 = \$18$$
$$\$18 \div 2 = \$9$$

← The amount they have raised is twice the amount they still need.

Then add the amount they need and the amount they raised.

$$\$18 + \$9 = \$27$$ ← The total is the amount of the adoption fee.

The adoption fee is $27.

Look Back Does the answer make sense?
Check by working forward.

$$\$27 - \$18 = \$9$$ ← They raised $18 and still need $9.

$$\$9 \times 2 = \$18$$ ← The amount raised is twice the amount needed.

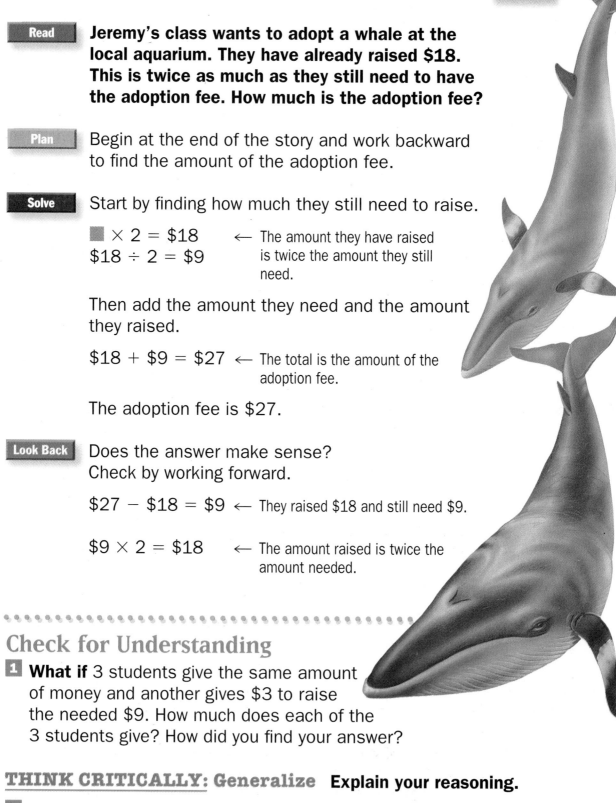

Check for Understanding

1 **What if** 3 students give the same amount of money and another gives $3 to raise the needed $9. How much does each of the 3 students give? How did you find your answer?

THINK CRITICALLY: Generalize **Explain your reasoning.**

2 When do you need to work backward to solve a problem?

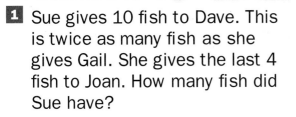
1 Sue gives 10 fish to Dave. This is twice as many fish as she gives Gail. She gives the last 4 fish to Joan. How many fish did Sue have?

2 Mr. Albee plants 8 rows of tomato plants. In each row, there are 5 plants. How many tomato plants are there altogether?

3 **Spatial reasoning** How can you remove 4 sticks and leave 2 squares?

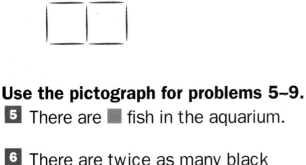

4 Kathy gives away some baseball cards. She gives 4 to Lisa, 5 to Mei, 4 to Thomas, and 7 to Asa. Do you add or multiply to find how many cards she gave away? Why?

Use the pictograph for problems 5–9.

5 There are ■ fish in the aquarium.

6 There are twice as many black mollies as there are ■.

7 How many more zebra clanios are there than neon tetras?

8 Jason buys 6 more tiger barbs. He needs to draw ■ more 🐟 in the pictograph.

9 **What if** the pictograph's key showed that each 🐟 stands for 4 fish. How many fish would Jason have? How did you find the answer?

10 Jason spends $36 on a tank and a filter. The tank costs twice as much as the filter. How much does the tank cost? How much does the filter cost?

11 Jason has $4 left. He spent $12 to buy the tiger barbs. How much money did he have before he bought the fish?

12 **Write a problem** about money that can be solved using the work-backward strategy. Solve it. Ask others to solve it.

Fact Families

Nicole brings 12 birds to the nursing home. She puts them into 4 cages. She puts the same number in each cage. How many birds are in each cage?

Divide to find the number in each group.

There are four 3s in 12.

$12 \div 4 = 3$

There are 3 birds in each cage.

You can also use a related multiplication fact.

Think: 4 times what number is 12?
$4 \times \blacksquare = 12$
$4 \times 3 = 12$
So $12 \div 4 = 3$.

You can also write two other related sentences using these numbers.

$12 \div 4 = 3$ $4 \times 3 = 12$ $12 \div 3 = 4$ $3 \times 4 = 12$

Together, these four related facts are called a **fact family.**

Talk It Over

▶ Why do we say that number sentences in a fact family are related?

▶ Do all fact families have the same number of multiplication and division sentences in them? Give examples to prove your answer.

Nicole has 12 canaries. She places them in cages in groups of 6. How many cages does she use?

You can use related facts in different ways to find the number of groups.

$12 \div 6 = \blacksquare$ $\blacksquare \times 6 = 12$

Think: If $12 \div 2 = 6$, then $12 \div 6 = 2$.   **Think:** If $6 \times 2 = 12$, then $2 \times 6 = 12$.
So $\blacksquare = 2$.   So $\blacksquare = 2$.

Nicole uses 2 cages.

More Examples

A $32 \div \blacksquare = 4$ **B** $7 \times \blacksquare = 42$ **C** $\blacksquare \div 5 = 6$

Think: If $8 \times 4 = 32$,   **Think:** If $42 \div 7 = 6$,   **Think:** If $5 \times 6 = 30$,
   then $32 \div 8 = 4$.   then $7 \times 6 = 42$.   then $30 \div 5 = 6$.
   So $\blacksquare = 8$.   So $\blacksquare = 6$.   So $\blacksquare = 30$.

Check for Understanding

Write a fact family for the group of numbers.

1 3, 6, 18   **2** 4, 5, 20   **3** 7, 5, 35   **4** 9, 9, 81

THINK CRITICALLY: Analyze **Explain your reasoning.**

5 Tell how you can use a multiplication fact to check the answer to $36 \div 4 = \blacksquare$.

6 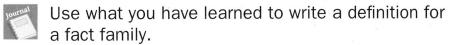 Use what you have learned to write a definition for a fact family.

Turn the page for Practice. ➡

Practice

Write a fact family.

1

2 4, 6, 24　　**3** 3, 3, 9　　**4** 5, 9, 45　　**5** 8, 9, 72

6 7, 8, 56　　**7** 7, 3, 21　　**8** 6, 6, 36　　**9** 3, 8, 24

Find the product. Then write a related division fact.

10 5×4　　**11** 6×7　　**12** 7×4　　**13** 9×9　　**14** 8×2

15 3×5　　**16** 8×6　　**17** 7×7　　**18** 5×1　　**19** 3×9

20 6×9　　**21** 4×9　　**22** 2×6　　**23** 5×8　　**24** 4×3

Find the quotient. Then write a related multiplication fact.

25 $12 \div 6$　　**26** $25 \div 5$　　**27** $28 \div 4$　　**28** $9 \div 3$　　**29** $63 \div 7$

30 $14 \div 2$　　**31** $72 \div 9$　　**32** $35 \div 5$　　**33** $32 \div 8$　　**34** $9 \div 9$

35 $36 \div 6$　　**36** $27 \div 3$　　**37** $48 \div 8$　　**38** $24 \div 4$　　**39** $42 \div 6$

Algebra Find the missing number.

40 $36 \div \blacksquare = 4$　　**41** $3 \times \blacksquare = 24$　　**42** $30 \div \blacksquare = 6$　　**43** $4 \times \blacksquare = 4$

44 $\blacksquare \div 6 = 9$　　**45** $\blacksquare \times 8 = 64$　　**46** $\blacksquare \div 9 = 1$　　**47** $\blacksquare \times 3 = 0$

···················· **Make It Right** ····················
48 Cristina found the missing number this way.
Tell what the error is and correct it.

$\blacksquare \times 7 = 21$　　　$14 \times 7 = 21$　　　$\blacksquare = 14$

Go Fish for Facts Game!

First, write the number sentences for ten fact families on index cards. Put one fact on each card.

Play the Game

▶ Play in groups of three. Mix up the cards. Deal five cards to each player. Place the rest of the stack facedown.

▶ The dealer asks the player on the left for a fact the dealer needs to complete a fact family. If the second player has that card, it goes to the dealer. The dealer asks until the second player does not have a fact asked for.

▶ The second player then says, "Go fish." The dealer picks a card from the top of the stack. Then the second player asks the third player for cards, and so on.

▶ When a fact family is completed, the player puts those cards facedown in his or her pile.

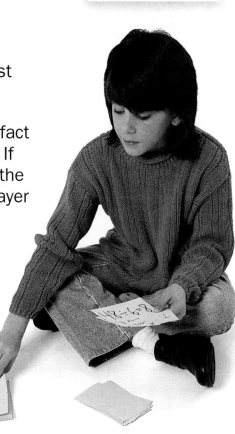

▶ The game ends when there are no more cards in the stack or to be asked for. The player with the most fact families wins.

more to explore

Odd or Even Dividing

If both the dividend and the divisor are odd, what will the quotient be?

You can use examples to find out.

$63 \div 9 = 7 \qquad 15 \div 5 = 3$
$35 \div 7 = 5 \qquad 27 \div 3 = 9$

Think: odd $\div$ odd = odd

Find what the quotient will be. Give examples.

1 The dividend is even and the divisor is odd.

2 The dividend and the divisor are even.

Divide with a Remainder

Suppose the veterinarian has 15 nonemergency patients. She would like to see these animals in about 7 hours. How many animals should La Tondra schedule each hour?

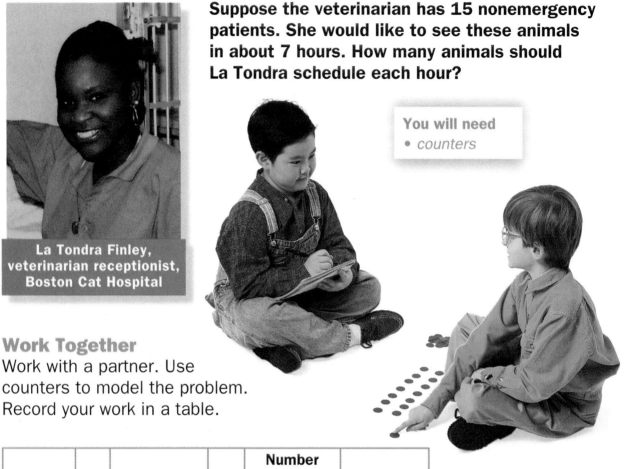

La Tondra Finley, veterinarian receptionist, Boston Cat Hospital

You will need
• *counters*

Work Together

Work with a partner. Use counters to model the problem. Record your work in a table.

Number in All	÷	Number of Hours	=	Number in Each Hour	Number Left
15	÷	7	=	2	1

Note:
The number left is called the **remainder.**

▶ **What if** there are more animals? Repeat the activity for each number up to 23 animals.

Talk It Over

▶ Look at your table. What pattern do you see in the number sentences? in the remainders?

▶ When you divide by 7, why is 6 the greatest remainder you can have?

▶ How does 21 ÷ 7 help you find 22 ÷ 7?

Make Connections

Here is how Joan uses a division fact to find the quotient and remainder.

$23 \div 7 = 3 \text{ R}2$

Think: There are three 7s in 23.
$21 \div 7 = 3$
23 is 2 more than 21.
So the quotient is 3 with 2 left over.

Here is how Joey found the quotient and remainder.

$$
\begin{array}{r}
3 \text{ R}2 \\
7\overline{)23} \\
-21 \\
\hline
2
\end{array}
$$

Think: Find a multiplication fact close to, but not greater than, the problem.
$3 \times 7 = 21 \leftarrow$ close
$4 \times 7 = 28 \leftarrow$ greater than
Subtract 21 from 23 to find the remainder 2.

▶ How are their methods different? How are they the same?

▶ In what ways could Joey's method be more useful than Joan's for other division problems?

Check for Understanding

Find the quotient and the remainder. You may use models.

1 $10 \div 3$ **2** $34 \div 4$ **3** $26 \div 5$ **4** $11 \div 4$ **5** $40 \div 8$

6 $4\overline{)13}$ **7** $7\overline{)42}$ **8** $3\overline{)28}$ **9** $5\overline{)34}$ **10** $6\overline{)52}$

THINK CRITICALLY: Analyze

11 What is the greatest remainder possible if you are dividing by 4? by 5? Explain.

Turn the page for Practice. ▶

Practice

Complete.

1 ◯◯◯ ◯◯◯ ◯◯◯ ◯◯
◯◯ ◯◯ ◯◯
◯◯ ◯◯

16 ÷ 7 = ▨

2 ◯◯◯ ◯◯◯ ◯◯◯ ◯◯
◯◯ ◯◯ ◯◯ ◯◯
◯◯ ◯◯ ◯◯ ◯◯

22 ÷ 6 = ▨

3 ◯◯ ◯◯ ◯◯ ◯◯
◯◯ ◯◯ ◯◯ ◯
◯ ◯ ◯

18 ÷ 5 = ▨

4 ◯◯◯ ◯◯◯ ◯◯
◯◯◯ ◯◯◯ ◯◯
◯◯◯ ◯◯◯ ◯◯

24 ÷ 9 = ▨

Find the quotient and the remainder.
You may use models.

5 15 ÷ 8   **6** 22 ÷ 3   **7** 8 ÷ 8   **8** 30 ÷ 7   **9** 46 ÷ 6

10 11 ÷ 2   **11** 19 ÷ 5   **12** 32 ÷ 5   **13** 24 ÷ 8   **14** 85 ÷ 9

15 4)‾14   **16** 7)‾38   **17** 5)‾35   **18** 2)‾9   **19** 8)‾48   **20** 7)‾17

21 8)‾64   **22** 6)‾29   **23** 4)‾38   **24** 1)‾9   **25** 3)‾29   **26** 9)‾76

27 Divide 43 by 6.   **28** Divide 21 by 4.   **29** Divide 23 by 7.

30 Divide 81 by 9.   **31** Divide 48 by 6.   **32** Divide 29 by 3.

How many pages in a photo album can you fill?
How many photos will be left over?

33 if you put 2 on a page

34 if you put 3 on a page

35 if you put 4 on a page

36 if you put 5 on a page

37 if you put 6 on a page

MIXED APPLICATIONS

Problem Solving

Pencil & Paper | Calculator | Mental Math

38 There are 36 appointments for Tuesday. About how many animals should the veterinarian schedule to see over 7 hours?

39 Les gives his 3 children 6 photos each. He keeps the remaining 18 photos. How many photos did he start with?

40 Mickey got a shipment of dog food. There were 6 boxes. Each box had 8 cans. How many cans were in the shipment?

41 Kit has a 72-inch board. How many 9-inch shelves can she cut?

42 Mrs. Sofia pays $11.75 for 3 rolls of film. She gives the clerk a $20 bill. How much is her change?

43 If you buy a pet turtle this year, in what year would it set a new record for oldest turtle ever? See INFOBIT.

INFOBIT
Many types of turtles live to be over 50 years old. One lived to be 152.

more to explore

Dividing on a Calculator

When you divide on a calculator, you may not recognize the remainder in the quotient.

$37 \div 4 = \blacksquare$ Press [3] [7] [÷] [4] [=] 9.25

Multiply the quotient 9 by the divisor 4.

$9 \times 4 = \blacksquare$ Press [9] [×] [4] [=] 36.

Subtract 36 from 37 to get the remainder.

$37 - 36 = \blacksquare$ Press [3] [7] [−] [3] [6] [=] 1.

The quotient and remainder are 9 R1.

Use a calculator to divide.

1 $47 \div 5$ **2** $36 \div 6$ **3** $29 \div 4$ **4** $74 \div 8$ **5** $54 \div 7$

Part 1 Write a number sentence

Did you know that most people who own cats have 2 cats? Suppose a third-grade class takes a survey of what types of pets the students own. They tally the total numbers for the class.

Pets We Own	Number of Each Pet
Cats	JHT JHT JHT III
Dogs	JHT JHT
Hamsters	JHT III
Birds	II
Fish	JHT JHT JHT JHT IIII

Work Together

Work with your partner to solve the problem. Write a number sentence to record your work.

1 Suppose each cat owner has 2 cats. How many students own cats?

2 Do the students own more cats or dogs? How many more?

3 If the hamsters and birds all live in cages, how many of the students' pets altogether live in this type of home?

4 **What if** you learn that students own 5 times as many gerbils as birds. How many gerbils are there?

5 Suppose only one person owns birds. How many birds does he or she own?

6 **Take a stand** Paul says, "You can only write one correct number sentence to solve a problem." Tell whether you agree or disagree with Paul's statement. Give examples.

Part 2   Write and Share Problems

Kayla used the data in the chart to write a problem.

Animal Adoption Costs	
Dogs	$25
Cats	$10
Other animals	$7

7 Write a number sentence that will help you solve Kayla's problem. Then solve it.

8 Rewrite the problem to involve a different operation. Explain how you solve it.

9 **Write a problem** of your own using the data in the chart.

10 Trade problems. Solve at least three problems written by your classmates.

11 Which problem was the most interesting? Why?

Lisa has $25 to spend. She does not want a dog or a cat. She has to choose among a lizard, a rabbit, or a porcupine. She decides to buy some rabbits. How many rabbits can she buy?

Kayla Harrow
West Lake
Elementary School
Apex, NC

Turn the page for Practice Strategies.

Menu
**Choose five problems and solve them.
Explain your methods.**

1 Casey bought a new leash and collar for $21. The collar cost twice as much as the leash. How much did each cost?

2 Maris can choose from 3 tops and 3 pairs of pants to wear today. How many different outfits can she make?

3 Sue got back $3.01 in change. She bought a water bowl for $4.75 and a grooming comb for $6.36. She gave the clerk $15. How much was the tax?

4 A small box holds 4 books. A large box holds 8 books. A bookstore gets a shipment of 8 small boxes and 9 large boxes. How many books are in the shipment?

5 Four friends give $18 to the Animal League. One gives $6. Each of the others gives the same amount of money. How much does each of the others give?

6 Daisy's birthday comes 1 day before Juno's. Selina's comes 3 days before Daisy's. Ping's comes 2 days before Selina's. Whose birthday comes first?

Diane bought the postage stamps at the right.

7 Write two number sentences that tell how many stamps she bought.

8 Write two number sentences that show how she can share the stamps.

Choose two problems and solve them. Explain your methods.

9 Use the data in the pictograph.

 a. Write a multiplication problem. Then write a number sentence to solve it.

 b. Write another problem that can be solved using another operation. Write a number sentence to solve it.

Most Popular Dogs Survey	
German shepherd	🐾 🐾 🐾 🐾 🐾 🐾 🐾
Cocker spaniel	🐾 🐾 🐾 🐾
Collie	🐾
Poodle	🐾 🐾
Mixed breed	🐾 🐾 🐾 🐾 🐾

Each 🐾 stands for 3 dogs.

10 How many houses are on Elm Street? (Hint: The houses all have the same three digits in their addresses.)

11 Halley's comet was seen in the sky in the years 1456, 1531, 1607, and 1682. Edmund Halley saw a pattern in these dates and correctly predicted it would reappear in 1758. In what year will this comet return next?

12 **At the Computer** You can use the computer to explore multiplication and division with arrays.

Use the drawing program to model the number 48 in as many ways as you can. Write a fact family for each way. Repeat the activity using numbers of your choice.

Language and Mathematics

Complete the sentence. Use a word in the chart.

1 You ■ to find how many equal groups or how many in each equal group.

2 12 ÷ 4 = 3 and 3 × 4 = 12 are ■ facts.

3 The number left over after separating things into equal groups is called a ■.

4 The ■ is the result of a division.

5 The number used to divide another number is a ■.

Vocabulary
divide
divisor
factor
remainder
related
product
quotient

Concepts and Skills

Write a pair of related multiplication and division sentences.

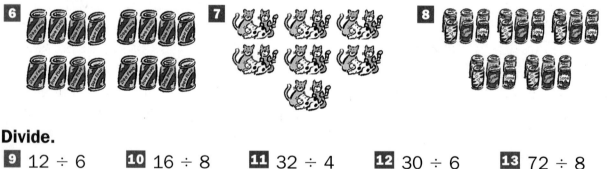

6 **7** **8**

Divide.

9 12 ÷ 6 **10** 16 ÷ 8 **11** 32 ÷ 4 **12** 30 ÷ 6 **13** 72 ÷ 8

14 4 ÷ 4 **15** 7 ÷ 1 **16** 45 ÷ 5 **17** 54 ÷ 6 **18** 18 ÷ 3

19 3)24 **20** 5)27 **21** 9)45 **22** 8)0 **23** 7)35

24 2)14 **25** 6)42 **26** 4)36 **27** 7)42 **28** 8)32

Find the missing number.

29 ■ ÷ 3 = 8 **30** 4 × ■ = 20 **31** ■ ÷ 9 = 1 **32** ■ × 7 = 49

33 28 ÷ ■ = 4 **34** ■ × 8 = 64 **35** ■ ÷ 5 = 6 **36** 9 × ■ = 63

Write a fact family for the group of numbers.

37 4, 6, 24   **38** 3, 6, 18   **39** 7, 7, 49   **40** 7, 8, 56

Think critically.

41 Analyze. Carla divided 32 by 5. Tell what the error is and correct it.

$$5\overline{)32}$$ with 6 above

42 Summarize. Explain how you can use multiplication facts to find division facts. Give an example.

MIXED APPLICATIONS
Problem Solving

Pencil & Paper   Calculator   Mental Math

43 Mr. Fine got a shipment of 12 tangs and 24 butterfly fish. He separates them equally into 4 fishbowls. How many fish are in each fishbowl?

44 Janet sells 9 gerbils to Dave. This is 3 times as many as she sells to Uma. She sells the last 6 to Mona. How many gerbils did Janet have?

45 You can choose short-haired or long-haired guinea pigs. They come in 4 different colors. How many different kinds of guinea pigs do you have to choose from?

46 The fish tanks in the Aqualand pet store are set up in 5 rows. There are 6 tanks in each row. There are about 25 fish in each tank. How many tanks are there in the pet store?

47 Gary had some books. He bought 2 more books, returned 1 to the library, and gave 3 to Mary. Now he has 10. With how many books did he start?

48 There are 24 members in the school band. They travel with 4 members in each car. Write a number sentence to find how many cars they use.

49 Mrs. Wolf buys 38 red buttons. She sews 5 buttons on each dress. How many dresses can she sew them on? Will she have any buttons left over?

50 Dolores earns $32 a month pet-sitting and walking dogs. She makes the same amount each week. How much does she earn each week? (Hint: There are about 4 weeks in a month.)

Write a division sentence and a related multiplication sentence.

1 **2** **3**

Divide.

4 15 ÷ 3   **5** 63 ÷ 9   **6** 25 ÷ 5   **7** 10 ÷ 5

8 48 ÷ 6   **9** 27 ÷ 3   **10** 20 ÷ 4   **11** 18 ÷ 2

12 6)18   **13** 4)28   **14** 8)40   **15** 7)0

Find the missing number.

16 ■ ÷ 4 = 9   **17** 7 × ■ = 42   **18** ■ ÷ 6 = 1

Write a fact family for the group of numbers.

19 5, 6, 30   **20** 4, 8, 32   **21** 9, 9, 81

Solve.

22 Uri buys 14 neon tetras and 13 wrasses. He separates them equally into 3 fishbowls. How many fish are in each fishbowl?

23 Janet gives 3 kittens to Hazel. This is 3 times as many as she gives to Jim. She gives the last 2 kittens to Zoë. How many kittens did Janet have to start?

24 Li buys 25 patches. She sews 6 patches on each pair of jeans. How many pairs can she sew them on? Will she have any patches left over?

25 There are 35 members in the choir. They travel with 7 members in each van. Write a number sentence to find how many vans they use.

What Did You Learn?

▶ How are the numbers alike in Section A? in Section B? in Section C? Explain your thinking. You may use drawings or counters.

▶ Choose new numbers that would go into each section. Tell why they belong.

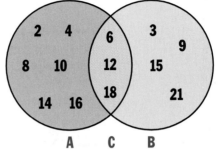

A   C   B

················ **A Good Answer** ················
- clearly explains one or more ways that the numbers in each section are alike
- clearly explains how the numbers in Section C relate to the numbers in A and B
- includes new numbers that would go into each section

 You may want to place your work in your portfolio.

What Do You Think❓

1 How do you know when to multiply and when to divide to solve a problem? Explain.

2 How do you know when a factor is missing from a problem?

3 List some methods you might use to find a quotient.
- Use models to divide a group equally.
- Use a related multiplication fact.
- Use a related division fact.
- Other. Explain.

SMART DOG? — Dog IQ

Dogs are thought to be the first animals that humans tamed, or domesticated. Scientists believe that dogs were living with people as long as 14,000 years ago.

People test dogs to find how smart different breeds are. In the test, a dog treat is hidden under something while the dog is watching. Then the dog is released.

Its intelligence is ranked on whether or not it can remember where the treat is and how long it takes to find it. This may sound simple, but it is not an easy task for a dog.

Compared to most animals, dogs are quite smart. They do understand words—about as many as a two-year-old child. Some well-trained dogs have learned over 65 words or commands.

Cultural Note

The formal training of Seeing Eye or guide dogs began in Germany in 1916.

▶ Why do you think people want to know how smart different kinds of dogs are?

▶ What other animals do you think are smart? Why?

Which Types of Dogs Are the Smartest?

The ratings in the table are based on an 8-point scale where 8 is the smartest and 1 is the least smart.

Trainers rated the intelligence of the dogs according to how easily they could be trained.

1 How many different dog breeds are included in the table?

2 Into how many different ratings are the breeds divided?

3 If the dogs were divided evenly among the ratings, how many breeds would get each rating?

4 Why do you think German shepherds, Labrador retrievers, and golden retrievers are most commonly used as guide dogs?

At the Computer

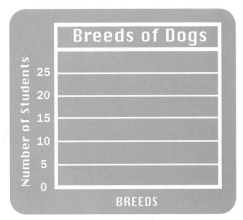

5 Survey your classmates to find how many own dogs.

Find out which types of dogs they own.

Use a graphing program to present the results of your survey.

6 What conclusions can you make based on your results?

Intelligence of Dog Breeds	
Intelligence Rating	**Dog Breed**
8	German shepherd, Collie, Labrador retriever, Golden retriever
7	Schnauzer, Springer spaniel, Cocker spaniel
6	Weimaraner, Airedale, Welsh corgi, Pomeranian
5	Samoyed, Irish setter, Dalmatian, Fox terrier
4	Pointer, Boxer, Great Dane, Siberian husky, Greyhound
3	Whippet, Pug, Boston terrier
2	English sheepdog, Shih tzu, Saint Bernard, Chihuahua
1	Afghan, Basset hound, Beagle, Pekingese

ADAPTED FROM COREN, *THE INTELLIGENCE OF DOGS*, 1994, PAGES 182–183.

CHAPTER 9

MEASUREMENT

Sports and Recreation

How far? How high? How heavy? The answers to questions like these are very important in many sports. In this chapter you will learn how measurement is used in sports and games.

What Do You Know ?

1 What tool can you use to measure the distance from home plate to first base on a softball field? What unit can you use?

2 What tool can you use to measure the weight of a softball? What unit can you use?

3 *Portfolio* Choose two or more items shown in the photographs. For each item, tell:
  ▶ what you can measure about it.
  ▶ what tool you can use and why.
  ▶ what unit of measurement you can use and why.

Length in Customary Units

You use measurement to describe things all the time.

An **inch (in.)** is a customary unit of length. It is used to measure short lengths.

To the nearest inch, a hockey puck is 1 in. thick and 3 in. wide.

Work Together

Work with a partner to help you improve your measurement skills. Estimate. Then measure the length of five objects in your classroom.

Record your estimates and measurements in a table.

Object	Estimate	Measurement

You will need
• *inch ruler or measuring tape*

KEEP IN MIND
▶ Line up one end of the object with the 0 mark on the ruler.
▶ Look for the closest inch mark at the other end.

Talk It Over

▶ How did you estimate the length of each object? How do your estimates compare with your measurements?

▶ How can you make better estimates the next time you measure?

▶ When you measure an object, how do you determine which is the nearer inch?

Make Connections

Here is what Ramon and Eva recorded to show their measurements.

Object	Estimate	Measurement
Chalk	2 in.	3 in.
Pen	6 in.	5 in.
Plant	10 in.	12 in.
Flagpole	45 in.	36 in.
Table (length)	45 in.	38 in.

You can also use the units **foot (ft)** and **yard (yd)** to measure longer objects.

The plant Ramon measured is 12 inches, or 1 foot, tall. The flagpole is 1 yard, or 3 feet, long.

12 inches (in.)	= 1 foot (ft)
3 feet (ft)	= 1 yard (yd)
36 inches (in.)	= 1 yard (yd)

▶ Look at your list of measurements. Which objects are about 1 foot long? 1 yard long?

Check for Understanding

Estimate. Then measure to the nearest inch.

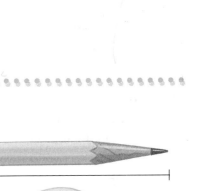

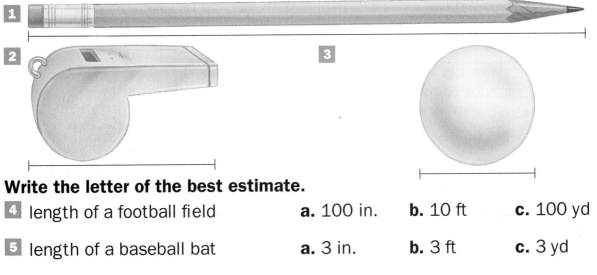

Write the letter of the best estimate.

4 length of a football field   **a.** 100 in.   **b.** 10 ft   **c.** 100 yd

5 length of a baseball bat   **a.** 3 in.   **b.** 3 ft   **c.** 3 yd

THINK CRITICALLY: Generalize

6 Why do you think we usually use a ruler to measure length in feet rather than a person's foot?

Turn the page for Practice. ➡

Practice

Estimate. Then measure to the nearest inch.

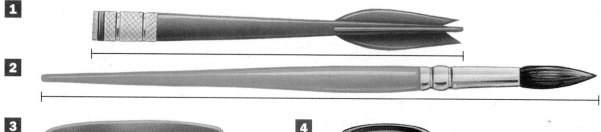

1

2

3 **4**

Write the letter of the best estimate.

5 length of an eraser   **a.** 2 in.   **b.** 2 ft   **c.** 2 yd

6 width of a door   **a.** 1 in.   **b.** 1 ft   **c.** 1 yd

7 height of a basketball hoop   **a.** 10 in.   **b.** 10 ft   **c.** 10 yd

8 your height   **a.** 4 in.   **b.** 4 ft   **c.** 4 yd

Measure to the nearest inch. Compare your measurements to those of others.

9 your arm from the tips of your fingers to your elbow

10 your stride—the distance from the heel of the front foot to the heel of the back foot

Name an object that makes a true sentence.

11 My math book is thicker than ■.   **12** My notebook is thinner than ■.

13 My desk is higher than ■.   **14** I am taller than ■.

· · · · · · · · · · · · · · · · · · ·**Make It Right**· · · · · · · · · · · · · · · · · · · ·
15 Flo says the straw is 6 in. long. Tell her how to measure the straw correctly.

```
0       1       2       3       4       5       6
inches
```

Guess and Cut Game!

Play with a group of four. Give each player eight straws.

Play the Game

You will need
- *straws*
- *rulers*
- *scissors*
- *1–5 spinner*

▶ The first player spins to find the number of inches each player needs to cut from a straw.

▶ Each player estimates how much to cut. Then each cuts a straw.

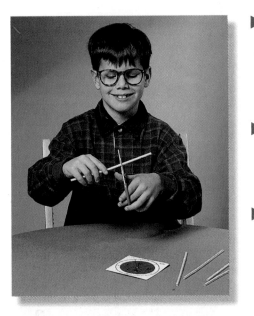

▶ Measure and compare the lengths of the cut pieces to the length on the spinner. The player with a piece closest to the length on the spinner takes all the pieces.

▶ Repeat the activity so that each player spins the spinner twice. The player with the most pieces wins.

▶ **Challenge** All players lay their straw pieces end-to-end. Estimate the total length. Then measure. See whose estimate is best.

more to explore

Mile

A **mile (mi)** is 5,280 ft, or 1,760 yd.

It takes a third grader about 20 minutes to walk 1 mi.

1 **What if** you were to walk a mile from your school. About where would you be?

2 Give examples of when a mile is used as a unit of measurement.

Length in Metric Units

Most of the world uses metric units to measure length.

The **centimeter (cm)** is a small unit of length in the metric system.

To the nearest centimeter, this crayon is 1 cm wide and 10 cm long.

Work Together

Work with a partner. Estimate. Then measure five objects in your classroom.

Record your estimates and measurements in a table.

You will need
• *centimeter ruler or measuring tape*

Object	Estimate	Measurement

Talk It Over

▶ How did you estimate the length of each object? How did your estimates compare with your measurements?

▶ How can you make better estimates the next time you measure?

▶ How does a centimeter compare with an inch?

Making Connections

Here is what Betty and Sam recorded to show their measurements.

Object	Estimate	Measurement
Door	235 cm	200 cm
Teacher's desk	85 cm	100 cm
My desk	50 cm	40 cm
Pencil holder	12 cm	10 cm
Eraser	5 cm	6 cm

You can also use the units **decimeter (dm)** or **meter (m)** to measure longer objects.

The pencil holder is 10 centimeters, or 1 decimeter, tall. The teacher's desk is 100 centimeters, or 1 meter, wide.

> 10 centimeters (cm) = 1 decimeter (dm)
> 10 decimeters (dm) = 1 meter (m)
> 100 centimeters (cm) = 1 meter (m)

▶ Does it take more centimeters or more decimeters to measure the same object? Why?

Check for Understanding

Estimate. Then measure to the nearest centimeter.

1

2

Write the letter of the best estimate.

3 width of your finger   **a.** 1 cm   **b.** 10 cm   **c.** 1 m

4 length of a new pencil   **a.** 2 cm   **b.** 20 cm   **c.** 2 m

5 depth of a diving pool   **a.** 3 cm   **b.** 30 cm   **c.** 3 m

THINK CRITICALLY: Analyze   **Explain your reasoning.**

6 How do you decide which unit to use when you measure?

Turn the page for Practice.

Practice

Estimate. Then measure to the nearest centimeter.

1

2

3

4

Write the letter of the best estimate.

5 width of a sneaker   **a.** 1 cm   **b.** 1 dm   **c.** 1 m

6 length of a straw   **a.** 15 cm   **b.** 60 cm **c.** 15 m

7 length of your ear   **a.** 6 cm   **b.** 60 cm **c.** 6 m

8 height of a football goalpost   **a.** 6 cm   **b.** 6 m   **c.** 60 m

Measure to the nearest centimeter. Compare your measurements to those of others.

9 the width of your thumb   **10** your hand span

11 the height of your desk   **12** the length of a book

13 the width of your foot   **14** the length of your hand

Name an object that makes a true sentence.

15 My desktop is thicker than ▓.   **16** My pencil is thinner than ▓.

17 My chair is lower than ▓.   **18** I am shorter than ▓.

19 **What if** each letter of your last name is 1 cm wide. How long is your last name? Draw a line of this length. Name an object with a length close to that length.

W

Use the graph for problems 20–21.

Egg and Spoon Race

RACER

James
Harry
Letty
Myra

0   10   20   30   40
DISTANCE (in meters)

20 What was the longest distance a racer covered? the shortest distance? Who are these two racers?

21 How many meters difference are there between the longest and shortest distances?

22 Data Point Which is the longest playing field? How much longer is it than the shortest playing field? See the Databank on page 538.

23 In the Olympics, women discus throwers hurl a disc that measures 18 cm across. Which disc is wider, the Frisbee or the discus? How much wider? See INFOBIT.

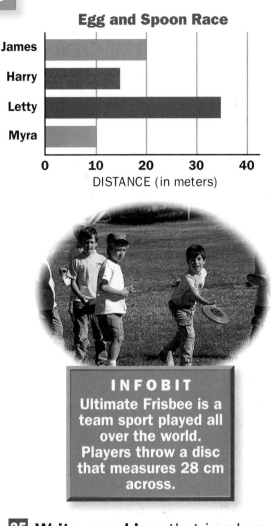

I N F O B I T
Ultimate Frisbee is a team sport played all over the world. Players throw a disc that measures 28 cm across.

24 Emil says a football is about 3 dm long. Jordan says the length is about 30 cm. Who is right? How do you know?

25 Write a problem that involves metric units and addition. Solve your problem. Ask others to solve it.

more to explore

Kilometer
A **kilometer (km)** is 1,000 m.

It takes a third grader about 12 min to walk 1 km.

1 About how many kilometers long is your trip to school?

2 Give examples of distances in your area about 1 km.

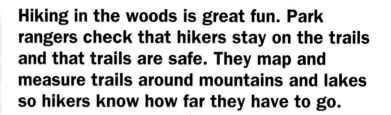

Perimeter

Park ranger posting a trail notice

You will need
- *centimeter ruler*
- *inch ruler*
- *geoboard*
- *dot paper*

Hiking in the woods is great fun. Park rangers check that hikers stay on the trails and that trails are safe. They map and measure trails around mountains and lakes so hikers know how far they have to go.

Perimeter is the distance around an object or shape.

Work Together

Work with a partner to explore perimeter. Use a geoboard or dot paper to make a shape of your choice.

Estimate and then measure to find the perimeter of your shape. Measure to the nearest unit.

Repeat the activity several times. Try different kinds of shapes.

Talk It Over

▶ How did you find the perimeter of each shape?

▶ What unit did you use for each shape? Why?

Make Connections

Kaitlin and Justin found the perimeter of these shapes.

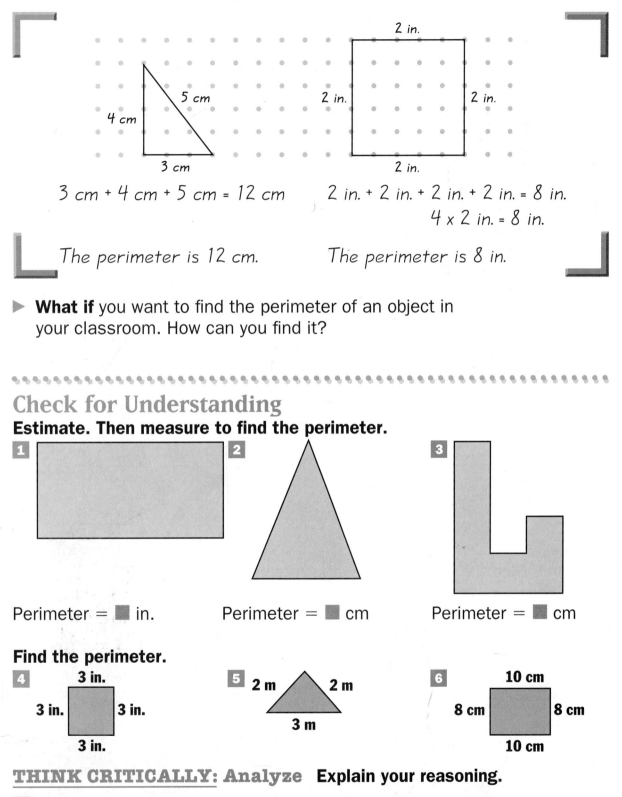

3 cm + 4 cm + 5 cm = 12 cm

2 in. + 2 in. + 2 in. + 2 in. = 8 in.

4 x 2 in. = 8 in.

The perimeter is 12 cm.

The perimeter is 8 in.

▶ **What if** you want to find the perimeter of an object in your classroom. How can you find it?

Check for Understanding

Estimate. Then measure to find the perimeter.

1

Perimeter = ▇ in.

2

Perimeter = ▇ cm

3

Perimeter = ▇ cm

Find the perimeter.

4
3 in.
3 in. 3 in.
3 in.

5
2 m 2 m
3 m

6
10 cm
8 cm 8 cm
10 cm

THINK CRITICALLY: Analyze Explain your reasoning.

7 Paul says you only need to measure 2 sides of a rectangle to find its perimeter. Do you agree or disagree? Why?

Turn the page for Practice.

Practice

Estimate. Then measure to find the perimeter.

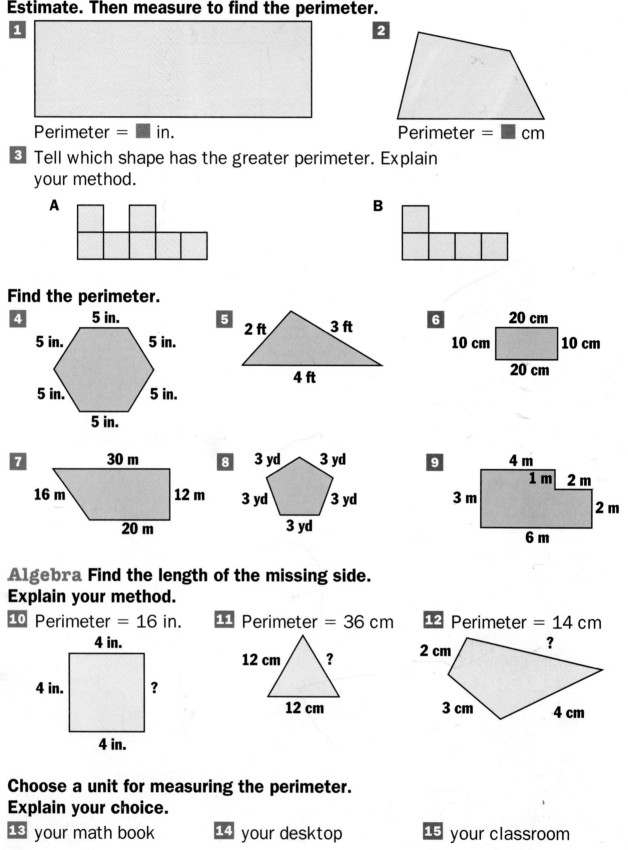

1

Perimeter = ▮ in.

2

Perimeter = ▮ cm

3 Tell which shape has the greater perimeter. Explain your method.

A

B

Find the perimeter.

4
5 in.
5 in.   5 in.
5 in.   5 in.
5 in.

5
2 ft   3 ft
4 ft

6
20 cm
10 cm   10 cm
20 cm

7
30 m
16 m   12 m
20 m

8
3 yd   3 yd
3 yd   3 yd
3 yd

9
4 m
1 m   2 m
3 m
2 m
6 m

Algebra Find the length of the missing side. Explain your method.

10 Perimeter = 16 in.
4 in.
4 in.   ?
4 in.

11 Perimeter = 36 cm
12 cm   ?
12 cm

12 Perimeter = 14 cm
2 cm   ?
3 cm   4 cm

Choose a unit for measuring the perimeter. Explain your choice.

13 your math book   **14** your desktop   **15** your classroom

Problem Solving

16 A rectangular ice rink measures 60 m long and 30 m wide. How long is the safety fence built along the edge of the rink?

17 Each side of a professional baseball diamond is 90 ft. What is its perimeter? Write a number sentence to solve.

18 The height of a horse is measured in "hands." A hand is 4 in. If a Shetland pony is 9 hands tall, how many inches tall is the pony?

19 **Spatial reasoning** Which line looks longer? Measure to check your answer.

20 What distance do you run after hitting a home run in Little League? See INFOBIT.

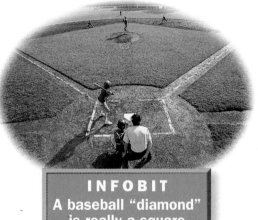

INFOBIT
A baseball "diamond" is really a square shape. The distance between each base on a Little League diamond is 60 ft.

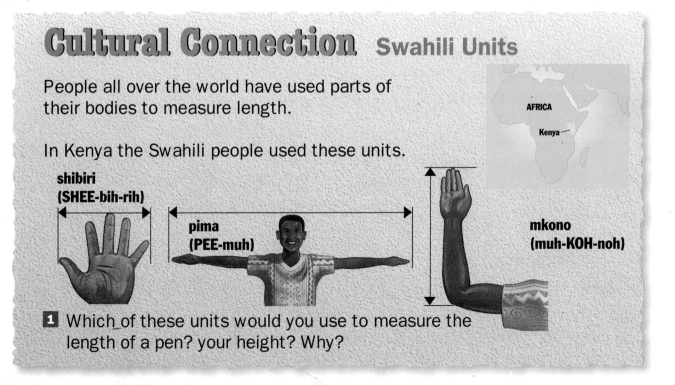

Cultural Connection Swahili Units

People all over the world have used parts of their bodies to measure length.

In Kenya the Swahili people used these units.

AFRICA

Kenya

shibiri
(SHEE-bih-rih)

pima
(PEE-muh)

mkono
(muh-KOH-noh)

1 Which of these units would you use to measure the length of a pen? your height? Why?

Area

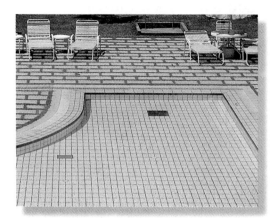

Many tile floors are made from individual square tiles. Tile floors are often used in kitchens, bathrooms, and pools.

Area is the number of **square units** needed to cover the surface of an object.

You can use graph paper to explore area.

Work Together

Work with a partner to design a tile floor.

Plan your design. Draw its perimeter on graph paper. Use crayons to color the squares.

Find the number of squares of each color.

Find the total area of the floor.

> **You will need**
> • *centimeter graph paper*
> • *crayons*

▶ How did you find the area of your floor design?

Make Connections

Shelli and David drew this floor design and described how they found the area.

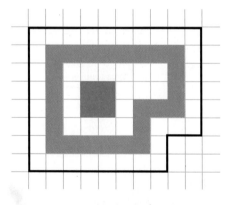

We counted the squares of each color. Added to find the total.
48 white + 24 purple + 4 red = 76 squares
The area of the floor is 76 square units.

▶ How can you use multiplication to find the area of the shape at the right?

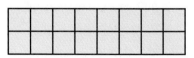

Check for Understanding

Find the area in square units.

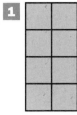

1

2

3

THINK CRITICALLY: Analyze

4 Josh says the area of this figure is 4 square units.
Do you agree or disagree? Why?

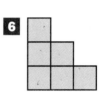

Practice

Find the area in square units.

1

2

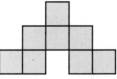

3

4

5

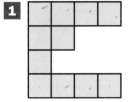

6

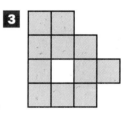

7

8

9

Draw a shape with the given area. Use graph paper.

10 10 square units   **11** 7 square units   **12** 14 square units

13 16 square units   **14** 9 square units   **15** 25 square units

Volume

You already know what a cube is. You can use cubes to measure the volume of an object.

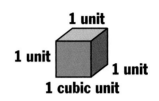

1 unit

1 unit

1 unit

1 cubic unit

Volume is the amount of space an object takes up. You can measure volume using **cubic units.**

You can use connecting cubes to build 3-dimensional figures and explore volume.

Work Together

Work with a partner.

Build a 3-dimensional shape out of 12 cubes.

Draw a picture to record your shape.

Try to rearrange the cubes into other shapes.

You will need
- *connecting cubes*

▶ What is the volume of each of the shapes you made?

Repeat the activity using a different number of cubes.

▶ How did you find the volume of the shapes you made?

Make Connections

Rosina and Peter took a photograph of one of their shapes and wrote about how they found the volume.

> *There are 2 rows of cubes with 2 cubes in each row in the first layer.*
> *There are 3 layers.*
> *There are 12 cubes in all.*
> *The volume of our prism is 12 cubic units.*

▶ What happens to the volume of a rectangular prism when you rearrange its cubes?

Check for Understanding

Find the volume in cubic units.

1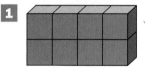

2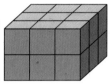

3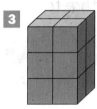

THINK CRITICALLY: Analyze

4 Two rectangular prisms have the same volume. Must they have the same shape? Give an example.

Practice

Find the volume in cubic units.

1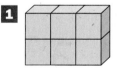

2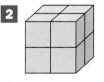

3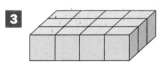

4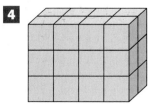

5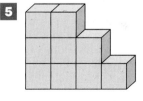

6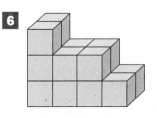

Problem-Solving Strategy

Read
Plan
Solve
Look Back

Using Logical Reasoning

Read As captain of a team, have you ever had to tell your friends what positions to play? Suppose Kim, Zack, and Tia play for your soccer team. You need a forward, a goalie, and a defender. Kim and Zack do not want to be goalie. Kim cannot play forward. Who is the goalie?

Plan Use a table to help you organize the data. Use logical reasoning to complete the table.

Solve Draw a table. Use the data in the problem to write *yes* or *no* in each space.

> **Think:** There can only be one yes in each row or column.

If neither Kim nor Zack play goalie, then Tia must be the goalie.

	Goalie	Forward	Defender
Kim	No		
Tia	Yes		
Zack	No		

Look Back Does your answer make sense? Why?

Check for Understanding

1 Who is the defender? Who is the forward? Complete the table to find out.

THINK CRITICALLY: Analyze

2 Why is it important to fill in all the spaces in a table?

Pencil & Paper · Calculator · Mental Math

1 Mr. Scionti, the gym teacher, has $600 to buy new equipment for the gym. What can he buy at the sale? Find at least five combinations of items. You can use an item more than once.

GYM EQUIPMENT SALE!

Table tennis table	PPT	$185
Trampoline	TP	$65
Exercise bike	EB	$230
Treadmill	TM	$345

2 Pia, Fred, and Ian go out to eat. One eats chicken soup, another has a ham sandwich, and the third has a salad. Pia and Fred do not eat soup. Fred does not eat meat. Who eats the salad?

3 A playroom is shaped like a rectangle. It is 8 ft long and 6 ft wide. Mike is putting down 1-ft-square tiles on the floor. How many tiles does he need to cover the floor?

4 Louie went to the Sports Show. During the day, he went up 5 floors and then down 1 floor. Later, he went down 4 floors and up 3. If he is on the 9th floor now, on which floor did he start?

5 Angie is putting a fence around her garden. The perimeter of the garden is 24 ft. If she puts a fence post every 3 ft, how many fence posts does she need? Draw a picture to find the answer.

6 Jesse and Seth were each 45 in. tall last year. Seth grew 1 in. more than Jesse. Seth is 47 in. tall this year. How tall is Jesse?

7 **Write a problem** that can be solved by using logical reasoning to sort a group of people. Solve it. Ask others to solve it.

8 **Spatial reasoning** Suppose you have a strip of paper 12 in. long. How many times do you have to fold it in half so that it measures 3 in.?

9 Jill, Dan, and Lyle play a different sport each. One plays soccer and one plays football. Jill does not play a sport with a ball. Whose sport is swimming?

Estimate. Then measure to the nearest inch.

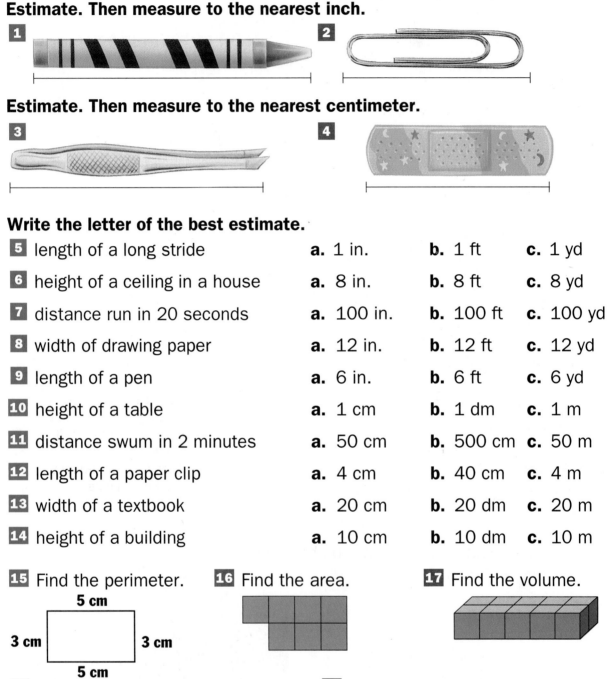

1

2

Estimate. Then measure to the nearest centimeter.

3

4

Write the letter of the best estimate.

5 length of a long stride   **a.** 1 in.   **b.** 1 ft   **c.** 1 yd

6 height of a ceiling in a house   **a.** 8 in.   **b.** 8 ft   **c.** 8 yd

7 distance run in 20 seconds   **a.** 100 in.   **b.** 100 ft   **c.** 100 yd

8 width of drawing paper   **a.** 12 in.   **b.** 12 ft   **c.** 12 yd

9 length of a pen   **a.** 6 in.   **b.** 6 ft   **c.** 6 yd

10 height of a table   **a.** 1 cm   **b.** 1 dm   **c.** 1 m

11 distance swum in 2 minutes   **a.** 50 cm   **b.** 500 cm   **c.** 50 m

12 length of a paper clip   **a.** 4 cm   **b.** 40 cm   **c.** 4 m

13 width of a textbook   **a.** 20 cm   **b.** 20 dm   **c.** 20 m

14 height of a building   **a.** 10 cm   **b.** 10 dm   **c.** 10 m

15 Find the perimeter.   **16** Find the area.   **17** Find the volume.

5 cm

3 cm   3 cm

5 cm

18 The length of a table tennis table is 9 ft. The width is 5 ft. What is the length of the stripe around the edge of the table?

19 Jo, Ana, and Flo plant one kind of flower each. Jo plants mums. Ana does not plant roses. Who plants daisies?

20 Journal   Explain how you decide which customary unit of length to use to measure an object.

Using Benchmarks

People often use common objects or parts of their bodies as **benchmarks** to help them estimate the length of other things.

Choose an object or part of your body as a benchmark and measure it to the nearest inch.

Use it as a benchmark to measure several large and small items in your classroom.

Then use a ruler to measure the same objects.

Record both measurements.

1 Compare your measurements. How close are they?

2 Give an example of something you can use as a benchmark to measure small things; to measure long things.

3 When can using a benchmark be helpful?

Cultural Note

A Roman *passus* (PAS-uhs) was the length of two steps, or about 5 ft. In English, it is called a "pace." 1,000 paces were equal to 1 Roman mile.

Silly Sports

Think about having some sports events at your school. Create some silly sports like the Bubble-Blow event or the Paper Airplane Fly and show what you know about measurement.

You can use what you know about measurement to create a silly sport. Work in teams.

You will need
• *measuring tools*

Step 1 List real sports that use measurement.

Step 2 Create a silly sport event in which you need to use measurement.

Step 3 Choose the measuring tools you will use and the unit you will measure with.

Step 4 Decide what the rules of the sport will be. Record them.
(Hint: Keep the rules and materials simple.)

Step 5 Collect the materials you will need.

Playing the Sport

1 How do you use measurement in your sport? What unit of measure do you use? What tools do you need?

2 Take turns playing your sport.

3 Do the rules you made work or do you need to change some of them?

4 Teach your event to another group.

Report Your Findings

5 Portfolio Prepare a report on the silly sport created. Include the following:

► Describe the rules of the sport.

► Explain why you chose the units you did and how you made your measurements.

► Give examples of the results of playing your sport.

► Tell what you liked about your sport.

6 Compare your silly sport to those of other groups.

Revise your work.
► Is your report clear and organized?
► Did you proofread your work?

MORE TO INVESTIGATE

PREDICT the largest measurement someone can achieve playing your sport.

EXPLORE creating a sport that uses many different kinds of measurements.

FIND the origins of some of your favorite sports.

Capacity in Customary Units

The next time you go to a game, look at the drink containers people are using. Notice the different amounts they hold.

Capacity is the amount of liquid a container can hold.

1 cup (c)

1 pint (pt)

1 quart (qt)

1 gallon (gal)

▶ Which would hold more juice—3 pint containers or 3 quart containers? How do you know?

▶ Collect various containers of your favorite type of drink and compare their capacities. What unit is used to measure their capacities?

> 2 cups (c) = 1 pint (pt)
> 2 pints (pt) = 1 quart (qt)
> 4 quarts (qt) = 1 gallon (gal)

Check for Understanding
Write the letter of the best estimate.

1 a. 1 gal
b. 1 qt
c. 1 c

2 a. 1 pt
b. 1 gal
c. 1 c

3 a. 10 c
b. 10 qt
c. 10 gal

THINK CRITICALLY: Analyze **Explain your reasoning.**

4 Will it take more quarts or gallons to measure the capacity of a container? Why?

Practice

Write the letter of the best estimate.

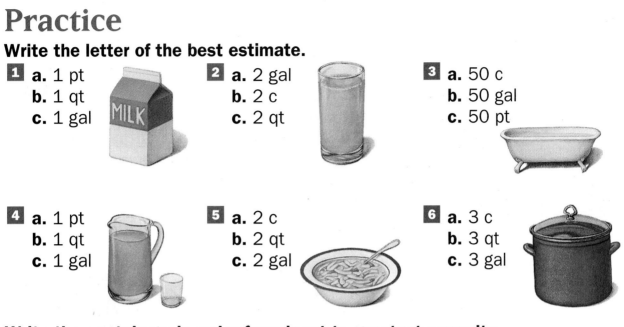

1 **a.** 1 pt
  b. 1 qt
  c. 1 gal

2 **a.** 2 gal
  b. 2 c
  c. 2 qt

3 **a.** 50 c
  b. 50 gal
  c. 50 pt

4 **a.** 1 pt
  b. 1 qt
  c. 1 gal

5 **a.** 2 c
  b. 2 qt
  c. 2 gal

6 **a.** 3 c
  b. 3 qt
  c. 3 gal

Write the containers in order from least to greatest capacity.

7 a glass, a kitchen sink, a bucket

8 a swimming pool, a washing machine, a teakettle

MIXED APPLICATIONS
Problem Solving

9 Gerard fills a thermos with lemonade. Does the thermos hold 8 cups or 8 gallons of lemonade?

10 **Write a problem** using customary units of capacity. Solve it. Then ask others to solve it.

11 Last week, the supermarket sold 235 gallons of regular milk and 176 gallons of low-fat milk. How many gallons is that altogether?

12 **Make a decision** At the market, 2 pints of cream cost $3.50. At Joe's grocery store, 1 quart of cream costs $3. Which is the better buy? Explain your answer.

mixed review

1 $12 \div 2$

2 $20 \div 4$

3 $21 \div 7$

4 $45 \div 5$

5 $6\overline{)48}$

6 $4\overline{)36}$

7 $8\overline{)32}$

8 $7\overline{)49}$

Capacity in Metric Units

Cultural Note

The 2,312-mi Tour de France is the world's most famous bicycle race.

When you compete in any long race, it is important to drink liquids to stay healthy. Many racing bicycles come with containers that hold 1 liter.

1 mL

1 L

Very small amounts of liquid are measured in **milliliters (mL).** Larger amounts of liquid are measured in **liters (L).**

1,000 milliliters (mL) = 1 liter (L)

▶ Name two things that can be measured in milliliters.

▶ Name two things that can be measured in liters.

Check for Understanding

Write the letter of the better estimate.

1 **a.** 240 mL
b. 240 L

2 **a.** 2 mL
b. 2 L

3 **a.** 6 mL
b. 6 L

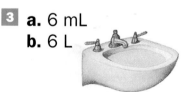

THINK CRITICALLY: Analyze

4 If two containers have the same capacity, must they have the same shape? Why or why not?

Practice

Write the letter of the better estimate.

1 **a.** 100 mL
b. 100 L

2 **a.** 100 mL
b. 100 L

3 **a.** 200 mL
b. 200 L

Estimate. Tell if the container holds more than 1 L, less than 1 L, or about the same as 1 L.

4

5

6

Complete. Choose a reasonable estimate.

7 Hal takes ■ mL of cough medicine.　　**a.** 1　　**b.** 10　　**c.** 1,000

8 A bottle holds ■ L of water.　　**a.** 2　　**b.** 20　　**c.** 200

MIXED APPLICATIONS
Problem Solving

Pencil & Paper　　Calculator　　Mental Math

9 Ken makes 7 L of apple juice for the picnic. There are 6 glasses in each liter. How many glasses can Ken serve?

10 Jen made 18 L of chicken soup. If she pours the soup into 2-liter containers, how many containers will she have?

11 **Logical reasoning** What numbers do A, B, and C stand for?

$$\begin{array}{r} A \\ + B \\ \hline BC \end{array}$$

12 **Data Point** Do a survey of your home. List items and containers where metric units of capacity are used. Share your list with others.

mixed review

Describe and complete the pattern.

1 12, 15, 18, ■, ■

2 18, 24, ■, ■, 42

3 ■, ■, 35, 30, 25

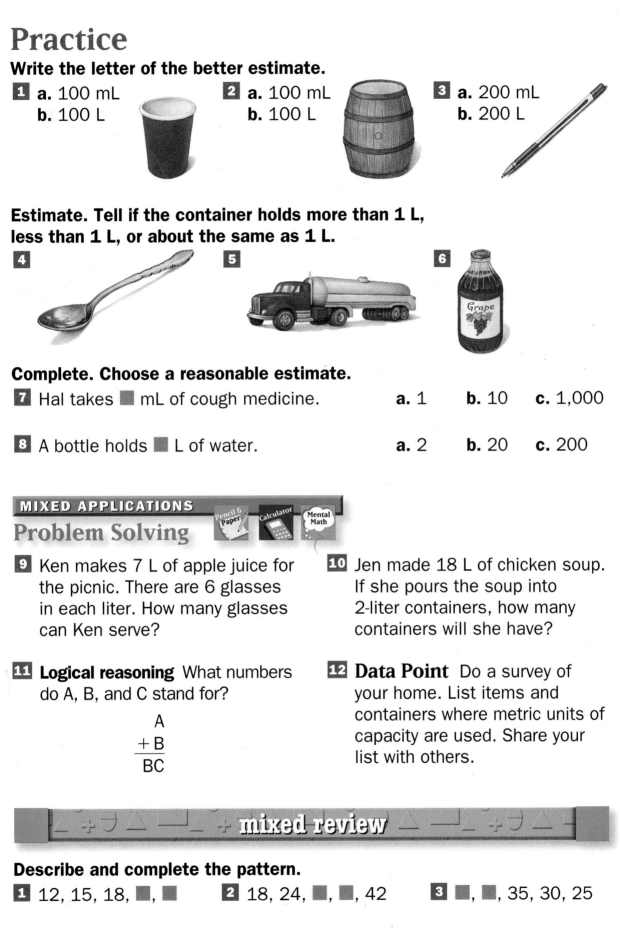

Weight in Customary Units

Have you ever noticed how light your feet feel when you take off your skates? Skates weigh more than shoes.

Weight is the amount of heaviness of an object.

In the customary system, the weights of light objects are measured in **ounces (oz).** The weights of heavier objects are measured in **pounds (lb).**

1 ounce

16 ounces (oz) = 1 pound (lb)

| low sneaker
8 oz | high-top sneaker
15 oz | figure skate
16 oz, or 1 lb | in-line skate
24 oz | leather roller skate
32 oz, or 2 lb | ice-hockey skate
40 oz |

▶ Which skate weighs the most? the least?

▶ Which skate weighs about the same as a high-top sneaker?

Check for Understanding
Write the letter of the better estimate.

1   **a.** 6 oz   **b.** 6 lb

2   **a.** 50 oz   **b.** 50 lb

3   **a.** 265 oz   **b.** 265 lb

THINK CRITICALLY: Analyze   **Explain your reasoning.**

4 How could you find the weight of a pet that will not stay on the scale?

Practice

Write the letter of the better estimate.

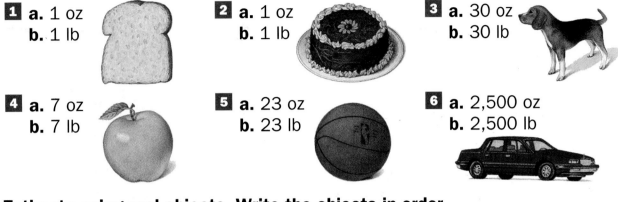

1 a. 1 oz
   b. 1 lb

2 a. 1 oz
   b. 1 lb

3 a. 30 oz
   b. 30 lb

4 a. 7 oz
   b. 7 lb

5 a. 23 oz
   b. 23 lb

6 a. 2,500 oz
   b. 2,500 lb

Estimate using real objects. Write the objects in order from lightest to heaviest.

7 eraser, paper clip, pencil

8 straw, 12-inch ruler, crayon

9 chalk, scissors, rubber band

10 math book, sandwich, pen

11 pen, chair, shoe

12 meterstick, globe, chalk

MIXED APPLICATIONS
Problem Solving
Pencil & Paper | Calculator | Mental Math

13 A dress shoe weighs about 10 oz. Which sneaker on page 344 is it heavier than?

14 A 16-oz box of dry pasta makes 8 servings. How much does each serving weigh dry?

15 Angelina weighs 68 lb. Philip weighs 85 lb. How much more does Philip weigh than Angelina?

16 **Make a decision** Would you buy 1 lb of Swiss cheese for $5 or 16 oz of Swiss cheese for $4.25?

mixed review

1 6 × 4

2 5 × 7

3 8 × 3

4 9 × 8

5 4 × 0

6 1 × 7

7 6 × 6

8 7 × 9

9 5 × 5

10 6 × 8

11 3 × 5

12 8 × 8

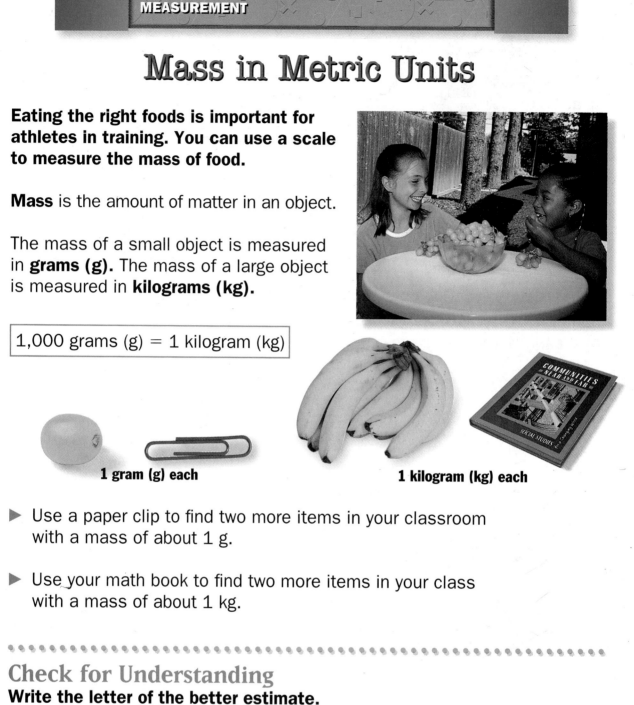

Mass in Metric Units

Eating the right foods is important for athletes in training. You can use a scale to measure the mass of food.

Mass is the amount of matter in an object.

The mass of a small object is measured in **grams (g).** The mass of a large object is measured in **kilograms (kg).**

1,000 grams (g) = 1 kilogram (kg)

1 gram (g) each

1 kilogram (kg) each

▶ Use a paper clip to find two more items in your classroom with a mass of about 1 g.

▶ Use your math book to find two more items in your class with a mass of about 1 kg.

Check for Understanding
Write the letter of the better estimate.

1
a. 100 g
b. 100 kg

2
a. 60 g
b. 60 kg

3
a. 2 g
b. 2 kg

THINK CRITICALLY: Analyze Explain your reasoning.

4 Does a larger object always have more mass than a smaller object? Give an example.

Practice

Write the letter of the better estimate.

1 a. 15 g
   b. 15 kg
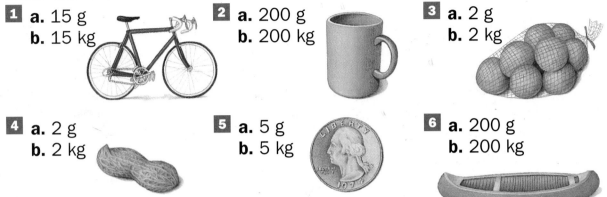

2 a. 200 g
   b. 200 kg

3 a. 2 g
   b. 2 kg

4 a. 2 g
   b. 2 kg

5 a. 5 g
   b. 5 kg

6 a. 200 g
   b. 200 kg

Estimate. Tell if the mass of the object is greater than 1 kg, less than 1 kg, or about the same as 1 kg.

7

8

9

MIXED APPLICATIONS
Problem Solving

10 David bought 1 kg of cheese and a 750-g box of brown rice. How many grams of food did he buy?

11 A mango has a mass of 650 g. An apple has a mass of 98 g. Which has the greater mass? How much greater is its mass?

12 Each cookie has 3 g of fat. How many grams of fat are in 9 cookies?

13 **Write a problem** on comparing metric units of mass. Solve it. Ask others to solve it.

mixed review

Write the money amount.

1 3 quarters, 5 dimes, 2 nickels, 3 pennies

2 1 dollar, 2 quarters, 1 nickel, 5 pennies

3 4 dollars, 8 dimes, 3 nickels, 9 pennies

Part 1   Check If an Answer Is Reasonable

If the thermometer reads 32° Fahrenheit, what should you wear to go outside to a football game?

A **thermometer** is a tool for measuring temperature. Temperature is measured in degrees **Fahrenheit (°F)** in the customary system and degrees **Celsius (°C)** in the metric system.

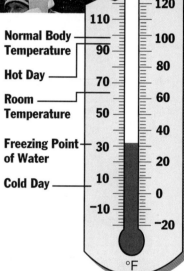

Work Together

Solve. Be prepared to explain your methods.

1 **What if** you decided to wear a winter coat and a hat to the game. Is this reasonable? Why?

2 **What if** the thermometer read 32°C. Would it be reasonable for you to wear a winter coat? Why?

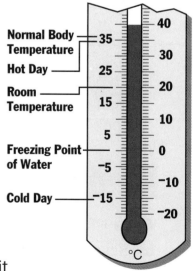

3 On cold days, people like to drink hot cocoa. What is a reasonable temperature for this drink in degrees Fahrenheit?

4 The football coach always keeps an ice pack ready in case someone is injured. What is a reasonable temperature for the ice pack in degrees Celsius?

5 **Make a decision** A thermometer reads ⁻4°C. Would it be reasonable to go ice skating or to go picnicking?

Sonny uses the Fahrenheit thermometer and the table below to write a problem.

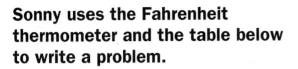

Sonny went to Lima in the summer. He brought mostly light clothes. Is this reasonable? Why or why not?

Record Temperatures in Degrees Fahrenheit		
City	Highest	Lowest
Tokyo, Japan	101°F	17°F
Jerusalem, Israel	107°F	26°F
Montreal, Canada	97°F	⁻35°F
Reykjavik, Iceland	74°F	⁻4°F
Tripoli, Libya	114°F	33°F
Lima, Peru	93°F	49°F

6 Solve Sonny's problem.

7 Rewrite Sonny's problem to change the reasonableness of his choice of clothes. Solve it.

8 **Write a problem** of your own that uses the table and thermometer to solve.

9 Trade problems. Solve at least three problems written by your classmates.

10 What was the most interesting problem you solved? Why?

Sonny Sanavonxay
Luis Munoz Marin School
Bridgeport, CT

Turn the page for Practice Strategies.

Menu

**Choose five problems and solve them.
Explain your methods.**

1 Jackie is comfortable wearing a short-sleeved shirt. The thermometer reads 30°. Is it a Celsius or a Fahrenheit thermometer? How do you know?

2 Mabel, Dennis, and Joan like soccer teams from different cities. Mabel likes the team from Chicago. Dennis does not like the New York team. Who likes the team from Seattle?

3 Ryan wants to build a fence to make a dog-run. How many feet of fencing does he need?

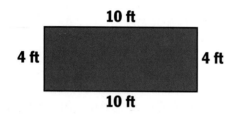

10 ft

4 ft   4 ft

10 ft

4 Martin finished the race in front of Vlad and behind Erin. Abby finished in front of Chris and behind Vlad. Write the names of the racers in the order they finished the race.

5 Nate has 48 sports cards. He puts them on 10 pages of his album. Some pages hold 6 cards each. The rest hold 4 cards each. How many pages hold 6 cards?

6 Jen wants to buy a hockey puck for $3.50 and a pennant for $3.00. She has a 5-dollar bill, 5 quarters, 4 dimes, and 2 nickels. Does she have enough money?

7 Han cuts a 2-ft piece from an extra long sandwich. He cuts a piece 3 times as long for a large family. There is 2 ft left. How long was the sandwich to start with?

8 Team bags come in 2 sizes and 2 fabrics. You can choose between 2 logos. How many different types of bags do you have to choose from?

Choose two problems and solve them. Explain your methods.

9 Choose two statements below. Write *capacity, length, mass,* or *temperature* to tell what should be measured in each situation. Tell what tool and what unit you would use and why.

▶ You need to know if a desk will fit in your room.

▶ You want to know if you can wear shorts and a T-shirt today.

▶ You need to know how much juice to make to fill a large bowl.

▶ You want to order some cheese from a deli.

10 Fence sections come in lengths of 2 ft, 4 ft, 6 ft, 8 ft, or 10 ft. Draw at least two rectangle-shaped fences each with a perimeter of 24 ft that you can make with these sections.

11 **Spatial reasoning** You are placing tiles on a floor to create this design.

You have the tiles below. How many of each kind of tile do you need? If each tile is 1 square unit, what is the area of the floor?

12 **At the Computer** Use square units to make rectangles with a perimeter of 16 units. How many rectangles can you make? What are their areas? Which shape has the greatest area?

Language and Mathematics

Complete the sentence. Use a word in the chart.

1 In the metric system, grams and kilograms are used to measure the ■ of an object.

2 A ■ is a unit of capacity in the metric system.

3 The width of a book is about 8 ■.

4 Temperature is measured in ■.

5 The distance around an object is its ■.

Vocabulary
inches
liter
mass
area
perimeter
degrees

Concepts and Skills

Write the letter of the best estimate.

6 length of a baseball bat   **a.** 1 in.   **b.** 1 ft   **c.** 1 yd

7 height of a student   **a.** 50 in.   **b.** 50 ft   **c.** 50 yd

8 length of a race   **a.** 5 cm   **b.** 50 cm   **c.** 50 m

9 width of a desk   **a.** 7 cm   **b.** 70 cm   **c.** 7 m

10 **a.** 1 c   **b.** 1 pt   **c.** 1 qt

11 **a.** 2 c   **b.** 2 pt   **c.** 2 gal

12 **a.** 20 oz   **b.** 20 lb

13 **a.** 5 oz   **b.** 5 lb

Write the letter of the better estimate.

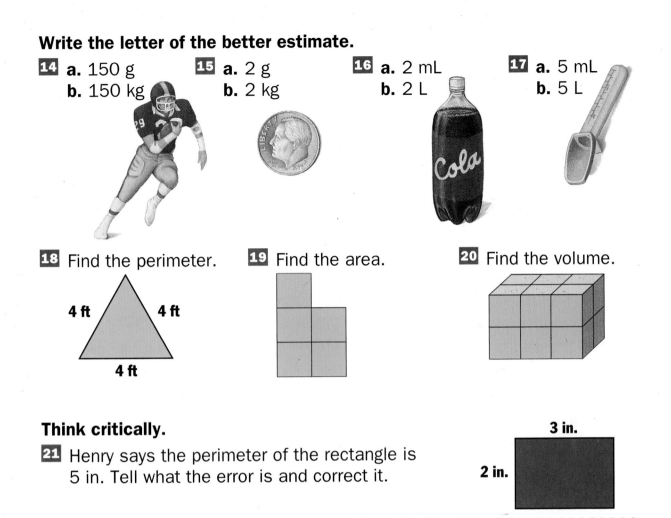

14 a. 150 g
b. 150 kg

15 a. 2 g
b. 2 kg

16 a. 2 mL
b. 2 L

17 a. 5 mL
b. 5 L

18 Find the perimeter.

4 ft   4 ft

4 ft

19 Find the area.

20 Find the volume.

Think critically.

21 Henry says the perimeter of the rectangle is 5 in. Tell what the error is and correct it.

3 in.

2 in.

MIXED APPLICATIONS
Problem Solving

Pencil & Paper   Calculator   Mental Math

22 Liam, Mia, Tamla, and Bruce are all about the same height. Their heights are 47 in., 48 in., 49 in., and 50 in. Liam is not the shortest. Mia's height is an odd number. Bruce is 49 in. tall. Who is the shortest?

23 Alan's team scored 1 field goal and 3 touchdowns. A field goal is worth 3 points. A touchdown is worth 6 points. They kicked all 3 extra points. How many points did Alan's team score?

Use the thermometer for problems 24–25.

24 How many degrees above freezing is the temperature shown?

25 Fritz decides to go to the beach. Is this reasonable? Why?

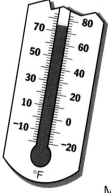

Write the letter of the best estimate.

1 height of a car   **a.** 60 in.   **b.** 60 ft   **c.** 60 yd

2 width of a book   **a.** 2 cm   **b.** 20 cm   **c.** 2 m

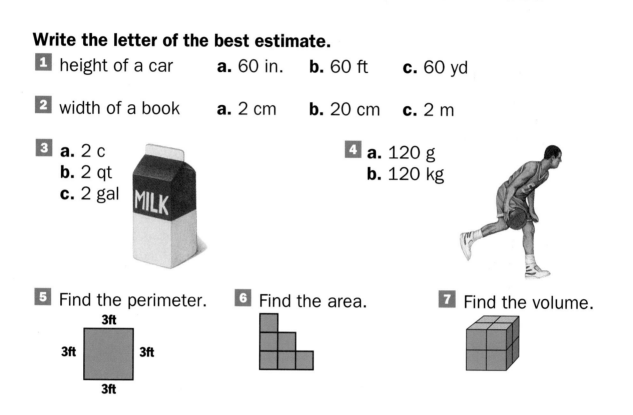

3 **a.** 2 c
   b. 2 qt
   c. 2 gal

4 **a.** 120 g
   b. 120 kg

5 Find the perimeter.

3ft
3ft 3ft
3ft

6 Find the area.

7 Find the volume.

Solve.

8 Mel, Belle, Tanya, and Olive all finish the race. Their times are 45 s, 46 s, 47 s, and 48 s. Mel is not the fastest. Belle's time is an even number. Olive's time is 48 s. Who is the fastest?

Use the thermometer for problems 9–10.

9 What temperature is shown?

10 Lainee wants to wear shorts today. Is this reasonable? Why?

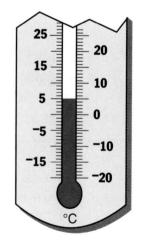

°C

What Did You Learn?

Choose an object in your classroom. Write a description of that object. Measure as many attributes of the object as you can.

Some Ways to Describe Something

Shape	Weight or Mass
Color	Capacity
Length	Perimeter
Width	Area
Depth	Volume
Height	Temperature
Purpose	Smoothness

······· **A Good Answer** ·················

- clearly describes an object
- includes many measurements using the proper units

You may want to place your work in your portfolio.

What Do You Think?

1. Which measurements do you find the easiest to take? Why?

2. What kind of measurements do you make most often? Why?

3. List some things you think about while measuring length, capacity, or weight.
   - how you estimate
   - how you use a measurement tool
   - what unit you use for a given measurement

Lung Capacity

Cultural Note

The Tarahumara (ther-uh-hoo-MAHR-uh) of Mexico are among the best runners in the world. In a race known as a *rarahipa* (rah-ruh-EP-uh), runners may cover over 200 mi in 3 days.

When you run hard or play sports, you can get out of breath. Your muscles need more oxygen to work harder. To get this oxygen, you breathe deeper and faster.

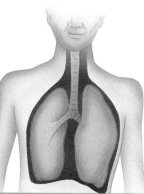

Have you ever wondered how much air you take in when you breathe? In this activity, you will measure the capacity of your lungs. Doctors and nurses usually measure lung capacity in milliliters.

1. Remove all of the air from a large plastic bag. Then blow as much air into it as possible using only one breath. Close the bag tightly.

2. Push down to force all of the air into the bottom of the bag. Then mark how full the bag is.

3. Hold the bag over a large bowl or a sink. Use a measuring cup to fill the bag with water up to the mark. The amount of water it takes is equal to the amount of air you blew into the bag.

▶ What is your lung capacity?

▶ Why do athletes train to try to increase their lung capacity?

Who Has the Greatest Capacity?

Some students wondered if taller people have larger lungs. They measured the height of five people. Then they measured their lung capacities.

Here are the results.

Use the table for problems 1–3.

Height and Lung Capacity	
Height (in.)	**Lung Capacity (mL)**
45	1,550
52	1,900
48	1,700
56	2,300
53	2,100

1 Order the data to show the lung capacities from least to greatest.

2 How many inches taller is the tallest student than the shortest student?

3 How much greater is the greatest capacity than the least?

4 Do the lung capacities of these students seem to be related to their heights?

At the Computer

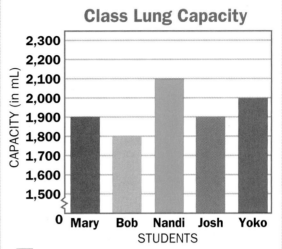

Class Lung Capacity

5 Use graphing software to make a table and bar graph of the lung capacities for your entire class.

6 Write two statements about your class based on the graph.

Chapters 1–9

Choose the letter of the correct answer.

1 Find 568 + 609.
a. 1,177　　b. 1,167
c. 1,161　　d. not given

2 Find 970 − 863.
a. 117　　b. 113
c. 107　　d. 1,833

3 Kevin practices the piano for 45 minutes each day. If he starts at 4:30 P.M., what time will he finish?
a. 4:45 P.M.　　b. 5:00 P.M.
c. 3:15 P.M.　　d. 5:15 P.M.

4 The quotient is 7 R2. Find the division example.
a. $5\overline{)25}$　　b. $4\overline{)30}$
c. $7\overline{)30}$　　d. $8\overline{)41}$

5 Find a related multiplication fact for 56 ÷ 8 = 7.
a. 56 ÷ 7 = 8
b. 7 × 8 = 56
c. 56 × 8 = 7
d. not given

6 What is the value of the digit 3 in 19,384?
a. 3　　b. 30
c. 300　　d. 3,000

7 Jeri spent 6¢ for an eraser. Which one did she buy?
a. Dinosaur　　b. Race car
c. Fish　　d. Bear

Eraser Sale	
Dinosaur	3 for 27¢
Race car	6 for 48¢
Fish	7 for 42¢
Bear	5 for 25¢

8 Find the perimeter.
a. 24 ft　　b. 22 ft
c. 19 ft　　d. not given

3 ft

8 ft　　8 ft

3 ft

9 Jim had some eggs. He ate 3 eggs and gave 5 eggs to Chris. Then, his chicken layed 2 more eggs. Now, he has 7 eggs. How many eggs did he have to start?
a. 13　　b. 7
c. 17　　d. not given

10 Which multiplication fact makes the sentence true?
7 × 6 < ■
a. 9 × 4　　b. 6 × 6
c. 4 × 8　　d. 5 × 9

11 Multiply 7×8.
   a. 15   **b.** 54
   c. 56   **d.** not given

12 It is 2:45 P.M. The bus leaves in 25 minutes. At what time does the bus leave?
   a. 3:10 P.M.   **b.** 2:20 P.M.
   c. 3:15 P.M.   **d.** 3:30 P.M.

13 Mr. Ross buys 3 drinks for $1 each and 3 sandwiches for $2 each. He can pay the bill with about ▪.
   a. $10   **b.** $5
   c. $20   **d.** $3

14 Complete the fact family.
   $6 \times 4 = 24$ $4 \times 6 = 24$
   $24 \div 4 = 6$

   a. $24 = 4 \times 6$
   b. $24 \div 6 = 4$
   c. $24 = 4 + 6$
   d. not given

15 Fran has saved $105.87 for a trip to Wonder World. She earns $14.50 baby-sitting. How much does she have now?
   a. $91.37   **b.** $120.37
   c. $119.37   **d.** $111.37

16 Find $8\overline{)25}$.
   a. 3   **b.** 3 R2
   c. 3 R1   **d.** 2 R9

17 Which difference is between 200 and 300?
   a. $587 - 136$
   b. $1,304 - 691$
   c. $873 - 598$
   d. $2,439 - 2,275$

18 Find the area in square units.

   a. 9   **b.** 12
   c. 16   **d.** not given

19 Chris needs to save $435 to buy a bicycle. He has $290. How much more must he save to buy the bicycle?
   a. $145   **b.** $265
   c. $245   **d.** not given

20 Which statement describes the graph?

Alice's Rides

a. Alice rode each ride once.
b. Alice rode the Twister the least.
c. Alice rode a total of 8 times.
d. Alice rode the Giant Slide the most.

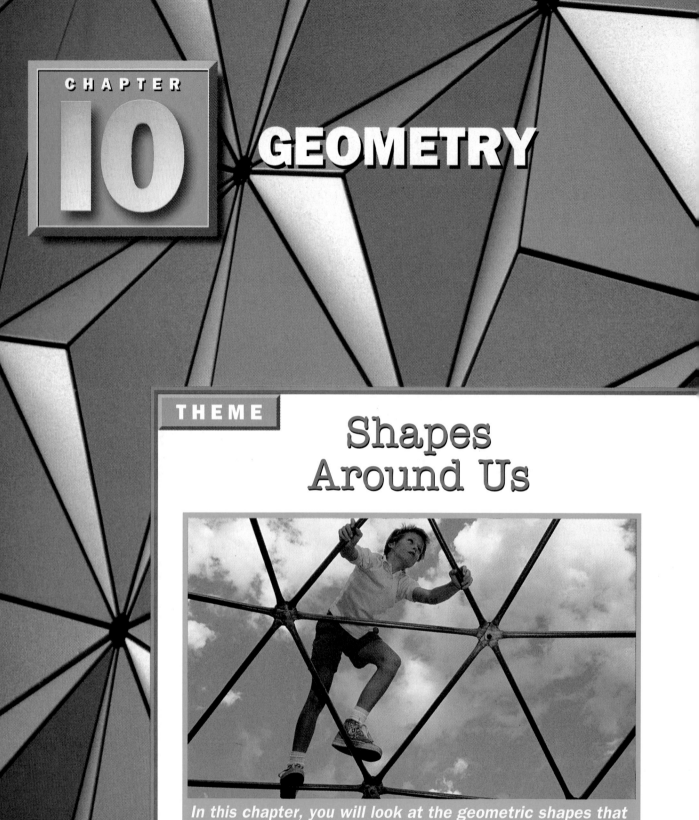

THEME

Shapes Around Us

In this chapter, you will look at the geometric shapes that are around you. You will see how people use geometry in such things as buildings, clothing, and art.

What Do You Know ?

Here is a group of geometric figures you commonly see.

1 Name as many of these figures as you can.

2 Sort these figures into two groups. Tell how you did it.

3 Sort each of your groups into smaller groups. Tell how you did it.

4 Portfolio Choose one of your groups. Give examples of where you can find these shapes in the real world.

3-Dimensional Figures

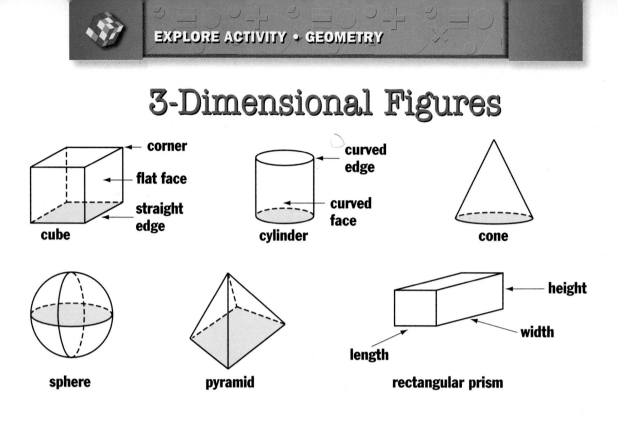

corner

flat face

straight edge

cube

curved edge

curved face

cylinder

cone

sphere

pyramid

height

width

length

rectangular prism

Figures with 3 dimensions are all around you. They all have length, width, and height. Look around and see what you can find.

Work Together

Work in a group to explore 3-dimensional figures. Collect examples of as many figures as you can.

Make a list of the different characteristics of the objects. Then sort the objects by the characteristics.

Talk It Over

▶ What examples of 3-dimensional figures did you find?

▶ Where do you think you can find examples of other 3-dimensional figures?

▶ How did you sort the figures?

Make Connections

Anna's group sorted their examples.

Stackers

Rollers

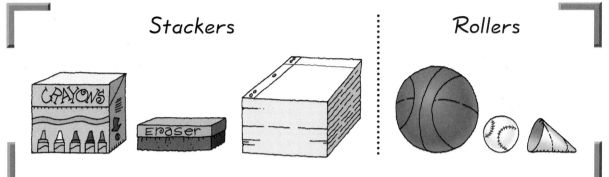

Gary's group counted the faces and edges of the figures.

Example	Geometric figure	Number of Curved Faces	Number of Flat Faces	Number of Edges	Number of Corners
Box of chalk	Rectangular prism	0	6	12	8
Mailing package	Triangular prism	0	5	9	6
Jar of paint	Cylinder	1	2	2	0

▶ **What if** Anna found a jar of paste shaped like a cylinder. Is it a stacker or a roller? Why?

▶ Complete the table to show how many faces and edges the other geometric figures have.

▶ How else can you sort 3-dimensional figures?

Check for Understanding
Name the figure the object looks like.

1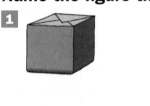

2

3

4

THINK CRITICALLY: Generalize

5 Which geometric objects do you see most often on store shelves? Why do you think these shapes are used?

Turn the page for Practice. ➡

Practice

Name the figure the object looks like.

1  CRACKERS

2

3

4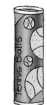

5

6

7 JUICE!

8 Tennis Balls

9 It has 1 flat face and
1 curved face.

10 It has no edges and no corners.

11 All the faces are the same size
and shape.

12 It has 2 curved edges and a
curved face.

13 It has 4 flat faces that are
triangles and 1 flat face that
is a square.

14 It has 4 flat faces that are
rectangles. Opposite faces are
the same size.

Name an example of each.

15 cube

16 cylinder

17 sphere

18 rectangular
prism

19 Choose a 3-dimensional figure. Write a description of
it without naming it. Show your description to other
students. Have them name the figure.

••••••••••••••••••••••••••••• **Make It Right** •••••••••••••••••••••••••••

20 Ryan drew and labeled this figure.
Tell what error was made. Then
correct it.

triangular prism

21 Ella buys a can of soup and a box of crackers. Name the 3-dimensional figures they look like.

22 There are 3 shelves of cereal each with 9 boxes of cereal. How many boxes of cereal in all?

23 **Spatial reasoning** What geometric object would cast this shadow?

24 Robert buys a loaf of bread for $1.29 and a pound of cheese for $3.29. About how much does he spend?

25 For a treat, Mrs. Kostos buys a single-scoop ice cream cone. What 3-dimensional figures does it look like?

26 A 1-lb can of peaches serves four 4-oz portions. How many 1-lb cans are needed to make as many servings as a number 10 can of peaches? See INFOBIT.

INFOBIT
Restaurants usually buy canned fruit in large cans called number 10 cans. Each one serves twenty-five 4-oz portions.

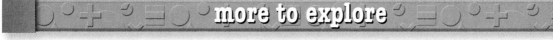
more to explore

Nets

Flat patterns called **nets** can be folded to make 3-dimensional figures.

Tell which 3-dimensional figure can be made from folding the net.

1
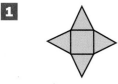

2
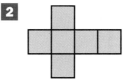

3
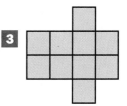

2-Dimensional Figures

What shape do you see when you look at the side of a box?

What shape is at either end of a cylinder?

You can use 3-dimensional figures to explore 2-dimensional figures.

Work Together
Work with a partner.

Place one of your objects on a piece of paper. Trace around the edges of the object on the paper. Remove the object and label the shape you traced.

Turn the object a different way and trace around the edges. Label this shape.

Repeat the activity for each of your objects. Try to find as many different shapes as possible.

> **You will need**
> * *cans, boxes, cones, and other objects*

Make Connections
Here are the shapes that Mariko and Carla traced.

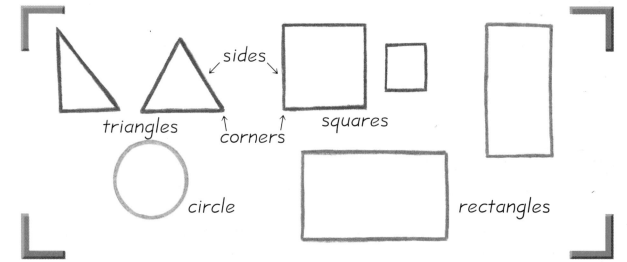

triangles   sides   corners   squares

circle   rectangles

- What shapes have the same number of sides?

- What object could you use to trace a triangle?

- How many corners does a triangle have?

- What shape could you trace from the flat face of a cone?

- **What if** you are standing above a pyramid and look straight down. What shape do you see?

Check for Understanding
Draw the shape and name it.

1 It has 4 sides that are all the same length.

2 It has 3 sides.

3 It is the face of a cylinder.

THINK CRITICALLY: Analyze

4 **What if** you cut a cylinder, pyramid, and sphere down the middle. What shapes would you see on the inside? What if you cut them the other way?

Practice
Write the name of the shape.

1 **2** **3** **4**

5 **6** **7** **8**

Draw the shape and name it.

9 It has no corners.

10 It has 3 corners.

11 It has 4 corners. The opposite sides are all the same length.

12 It has 4 sides and 4 corners.

Polygons

Stained-glass artists find straight-sided shapes easier to cut than circles. What shapes are in the window?

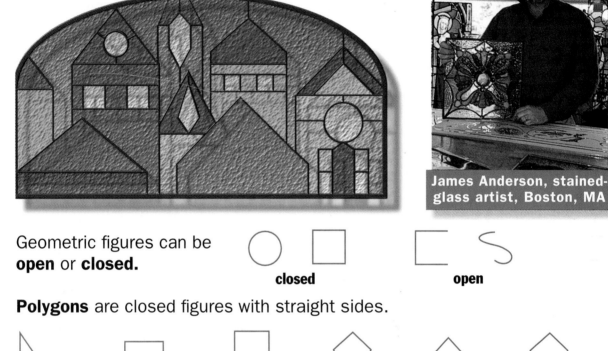

James Anderson, stained-glass artist, Boston, MA

Geometric figures can be **open** or **closed**.

closed   open

Polygons are closed figures with straight sides.

triangle   square   rectangle   kite   pentagon   hexagon

The stained-glass window has triangles, squares, rectangles, pentagons, a kite, and a hexagon.

Check for Understanding

Write *yes* or *no* to tell whether the shape is a polygon. If it is a polygon, name it.

1.   2.   3.   4.

THINK CRITICALLY: Analyze

5. Vince says a circle is not a polygon. Do you agree or disagree? Why?

Practice

**Write *yes* or *no* to tell whether the shape is a polygon.
If it is a polygon, name it.**

1

2

3

4

Draw and identify the polygon.

5 It has 5 sides.

6 It has 4 equal sides.

7 It has 6 sides.

8 It has 2 pairs of equal sides.

**Name the polygon you could make by putting the
polygons together.**

9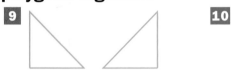

10

11

MIXED APPLICATIONS
Problem Solving

12 A sun catcher has 4 sides. The
sides are not all the same
length. What shape could it be?

13 Mr. Jenkins sells 8 sun catchers
for $9 each. How much money
does he receive from the sale?

14 **Spatial reasoning** How
many triangles are in
this sun catcher?

15 Jim cuts 24 glass squares. He
stacks them in groups of 4. How
many stacks does he make?

16 Chee spends $13.50 for wood
and $2.95 for nails. How much
change does he get from
$20.00?

17 Chloë designs a window with 6
straight sides. Name the shape
of the window.

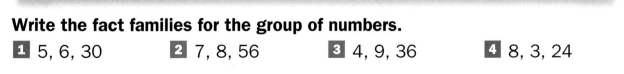
mixed review

Write the fact families for the group of numbers.

1 5, 6, 30

2 7, 8, 56

3 4, 9, 36

4 8, 3, 24

Lines, Line Segments, Rays, and Angles

You can use geometric ideas to describe the parts of 2-dimensional figures and real-world objects.

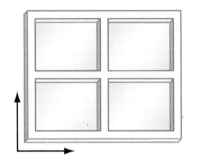

An **angle** is formed when two rays or line segments meet at an **endpoint.**

A **line segment** is part of a line. It is straight and has two endpoints.

A **line** is a straight figure without endpoints. It goes on forever in both directions.

A **ray** is also part of a line. It has one endpoint and goes on forever in one direction.

Work Together

Work with a partner. Fold a piece of paper at least 3 times in different directions.

Open it. Mark each fold with a pencil. Label the figures in the drawings you have made.

Repeat the activity with other pieces of paper folded in different ways. Compare your drawings with those of others.

Make Connections

This drawing shows line segments and angles. The angles are not all the same.

The folds made line segments, angles, and a square.

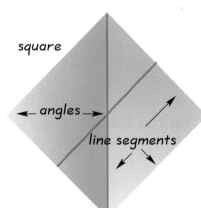

square

← angles →

line segments

Right angles form square corners. Angles can be greater than, equal to, or less than right angles.

Greater Than a Right Angle

Right Angle

Less Than a Right Angle

▶ Look at the drawing on page 370.
How many line segments are there?
How many angles?
How do the angles compare to a right angle?

Check for Understanding
Write *line*, *line segment*, *ray*, or *angle*.

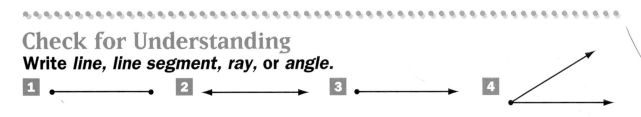

THINK CRITICALLY: Analyze **Explain your reasoning.**

5 **Copy and complete the table. What patterns do you notice?**

Polygon	Number of Line Segments	Number of Angles
Triangle		
Rectangle		
Pentagon		
Hexagon		

Practice
Tell if the angle is *less than*, *equal to*, or *greater than* a right angle.

Write *line*, *line segment*, *ray*, or *angle*.

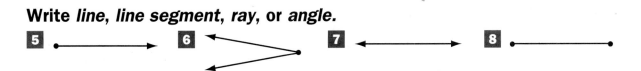

Problem-Solving Strategy

Finding a Pattern

Read You need to finish the belt below. There are enough beads for 3 more shapes. If you continued the pattern, what shapes would you make?

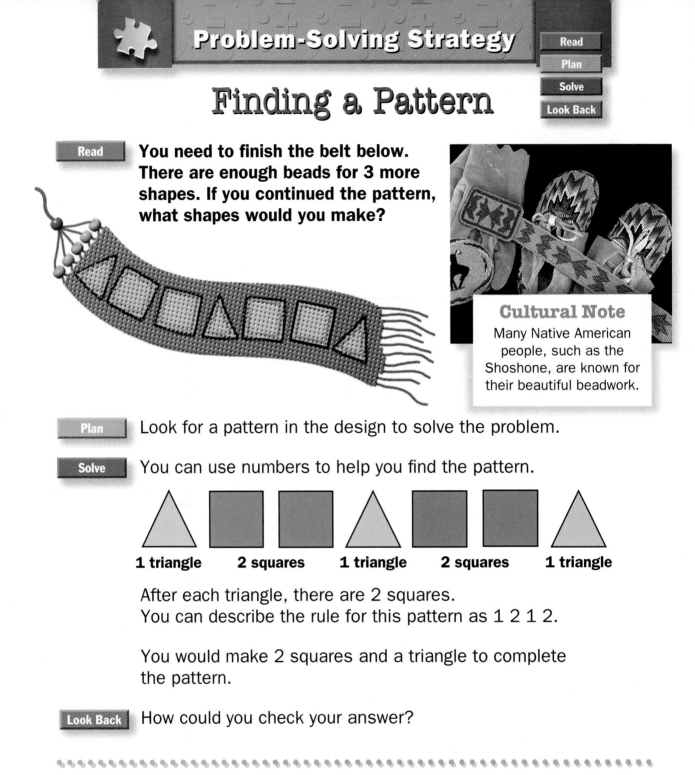

Cultural Note
Many Native American people, such as the Shoshone, are known for their beautiful beadwork.

Plan Look for a pattern in the design to solve the problem.

Solve You can use numbers to help you find the pattern.

| 1 triangle | 2 squares | 1 triangle | 2 squares | 1 triangle |

After each triangle, there are 2 squares.
You can describe the rule for this pattern as 1 2 1 2.

You would make 2 squares and a triangle to complete the pattern.

Look Back How could you check your answer?

Check for Understanding

1 What if you used 3 squares instead of 2 in the pattern. What would the pattern look like?

THINK CRITICALLY: Generalize

2 How do you use numbers to describe patterns? Give an example.

Problem Solving

1 Alan spends 2 hours a day working on his beadwork. If he works every day in March and April, how many hours does he spend on the beadwork?

2 Lee uses 48 red and black beads in a necklace. He uses 3 times as many red beads as he does black beads. How many of each color bead does he use?

3 **Write a problem** that can be solved by finding a pattern. Solve it. Then give it to others to solve.

4 Nina sells 4 pairs of beadwork earrings for a total of $36. What is the cost of each pair?

5 **Data Point** Compare the pattern in this Apache storage basket with the pattern on the flat Pima basket. See Databank on page 539.

6 Skye covers the top of a box with beaded squares. There are 4 squares in each of 4 rows. How many squares are there?

7 How can you describe the rule for this pattern using numbers? What would be the next shape in the pattern?

8 Tama wants to use this pattern on a bag she is decorating. She has space for 24 figures. How many complete patterns will she use?

9 **What if** Tama changed her pattern to include a moon between the stars. How many complete patterns would she use and what could be the last shape?

Name the figure the object looks like.

1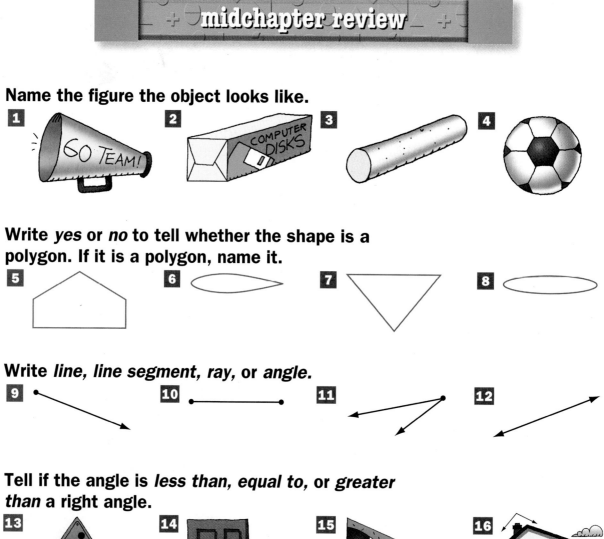

2

3

4

Write *yes* or *no* to tell whether the shape is a polygon. If it is a polygon, name it.

5

6

7

8

Write *line, line segment, ray,* or *angle.*

9

10

11

12

Tell if the angle is *less than, equal to,* or *greater than* a right angle.

13

14

15

16

Solve.

17 Paul is making a belt. He uses this pattern to decorate it. Complete the pattern.

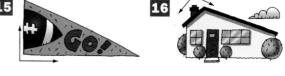 ___ ___

18 How could Paul translate the pattern into numbers.

19 Emmi buys a can of pineapple juice and a box of animal crackers. What geometric figures do they look like?

20  Explain how you can tell whether an angle is a right angle or less than or greater than a right angle.

Use a Geometry Tool

You can use a computer to draw and measure geometric shapes. A table linked to the figures will list the measurements you make.

You can use these tools to draw plans for projects.

Draw the shapes to make a birdhouse.

Measure the lengths of the sides of each shape.

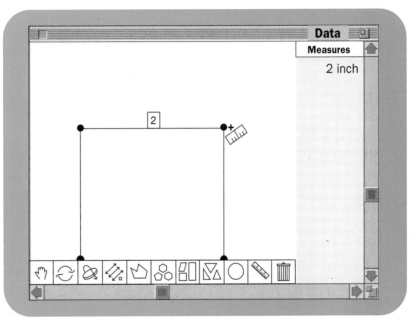

▶ **What if** you wanted the birdhouse to be larger? Change the length of the sides of one of the shapes. What happened to the measures in the table?

1 Use the Geometry and Measuring tools to design your own building. Give the measurements of each shape used.

THINK CRITICALLY: Generalize

2 Why do you think architects like to use computers to help them draw plans for buildings?

Build It Yourself!

If you could design and build a building, what kind would it be? A castle? A log cabin? A tepee? A skyscraper? In this activity, you will work in a group to design and build a model of a building.

What to build

▶ Look for ideas on what to build in magazines, encyclopedias, and other reference books.

▶ Think about the various geometric shapes that make up the building.

How to build it

▶ What materials will you use to make your model?

You could make paper models of geometric shapes.

You could use other materials such as clay, straws, sticks, foam shapes, connecting cubes, milk cartons, and so on.

DECISION MAKING

Making the Model

1 Work as a group to decide on a type of building to model and on a type of building material.

2 Sketch the design for your building. List the different geometric shapes used.

3 Gather the materials and assemble your model. It must be able to stand without support.

Report Your Findings

4 *Portfolio* Prepare a report on what you learned. Include the following:

▶ A sketch of the model you planned to make. You may wish to include a photo of the completed model.

▶ Make a table that lists the materials you used and all of the geometric shapes that are in your model.

5 Compare your model and report with those of other teams.

Revise your work.
▶ Are your table and sketch neat and easy to read?
▶ Is the information in the table complete?
▶ Did you proofread your work?

MORE TO INVESTIGATE

PREDICT the type of building most groups will build.

EXPLORE the kinds of shapes you can make with toy building materials such as Legos.

FIND what architects do to design a building.

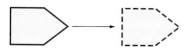
Motion and Congruence

You can make patterns by moving 2-dimensional figures.

You can **slide** a figure.

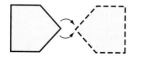

You can **flip** a figure.

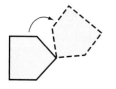

You can **turn** a figure.

Work Together
Work with a partner to explore slides, flips, and turns.

Draw a geometric figure. Trace it, then cut it out. Create a design by sliding, flipping, or turning your figure. Trace the figure after each move.

Write directions for how to make your design.

Repeat the activity using another geometric figure.

Talk It Over
▶ Do the figures change their size or shape when they are moved? How do you know?

You will need
- *tracing paper*
- *graph paper*
- *scissors*

Make Connections

Jacob and Fran created these designs.

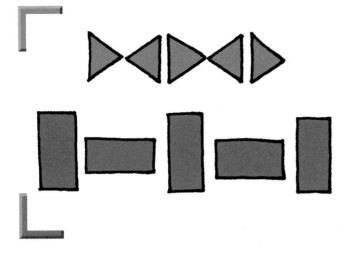

We flipped a triangle 4 times.

We turned a rectangle to the right 4 times.

Figures that are the same shape and size are **congruent figures.**

▶ Are the figures in each of Jacob's and Fran's patterns congruent? How do you know?

Check for Understanding

Write *slide, flip,* or *turn* to tell how the figure was moved.

1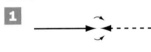

2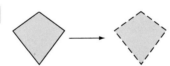

3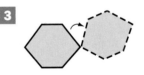

Tell if the two figures are congruent.

4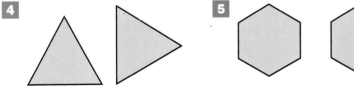

5

6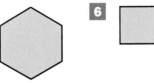

THINK CRITICALLY: Generalize

7 If two figures are the same shape, must they be congruent? Why or why not?

8 How can you use slides, flips, and turns to prove that two figures are congruent?

Turn the page for Practice. ➡

Practice

Write *slide*, *flip*, or *turn* to tell how the figure was moved.

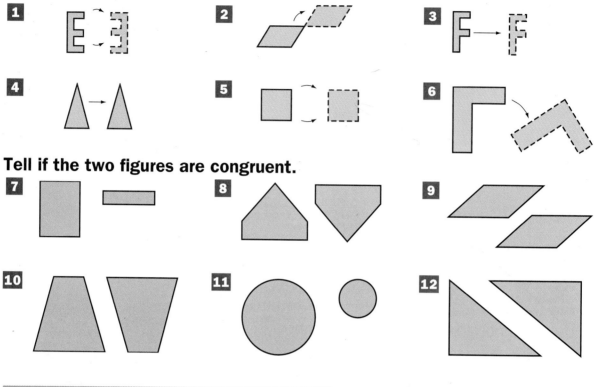

1

2

3

4

5

6

Tell if the two figures are congruent.

7

8

9

10

11

12

MIXED APPLICATIONS

Problem Solving

Pencil & Paper   Calculator   Mental Math

13 Lita is making note cards using rubber stamps. She plans to use this pattern. Describe the pattern.

14 Lita has started this pattern on one card. Complete the pattern.

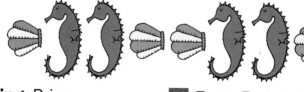

15 Spatial reasoning Brian suggests that Lita stamp a pattern of pairs of sea horses facing each other. Can Lita make this pattern with her rubber stamp? Why or why not?

16 Data Point Make a list of objects in your home that are congruent. Compare your list to those of others. Why do you think they are made that way?

Slide into Home Game!

First, draw a triangle in the center square of a piece of graph paper. Trace it and cut it out 2 times.

Next, make 12 motion cards. Label 4 cards *slide,* 4 cards *flip,* and 4 cards *turn.*

Play the Game

▶ Play with a partner. Mix up the cards. Place them facedown.

▶ Take turns. Each player places a triangle over the triangle on the paper, picks a card, and follows the directions. The player can choose the direction to move in.

▶ You cannot move your triangle to cover the other player's triangle.

▶ The first player to make each type of move at least once and return to the starting position wins.

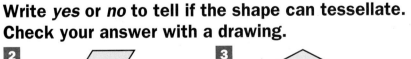

more to explore

Tessellations

Shapes that can **tessellate** cover a flat surface without leaving any gaps.

1 Can squares tessellate? Can circles?

Write *yes* or *no* to tell if the shape can tessellate. Check your answer with a drawing.

2

3

4

Symmetry

People who sew will often cut shapes from folded cloth. When they unfold the cloth, the two parts match exactly.

They have made a **symmetric** figure. The fold line is a **line of symmetry.**

Work Together

Work with a partner to make a symmetric figure. Here is how to make a paper dashiki.

Fold a piece of paper in half and then in half again.

Cultural Note
A dashiki (duh-SHEE-kee) is a West African shirt. It is usually made out of brightly colored fabric.

Cut out a neck opening and cut out side pieces to make the sleeves.

You will need
- *graph paper*
- *scissors*

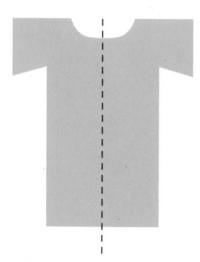

Unfold your dashiki. Mark any lines of symmetry.

Fold and cut other pieces of paper. Unfold them and mark any lines of symmetry.

Talk It Over

▶ Is your dashiki symmetrical? If so, how many lines of symmetry are there?

▶ How are the shapes on opposite sides of the folds alike?

Make Connections

Many figures have lines of symmetry.

▶ How many lines of symmetry does each figure have?

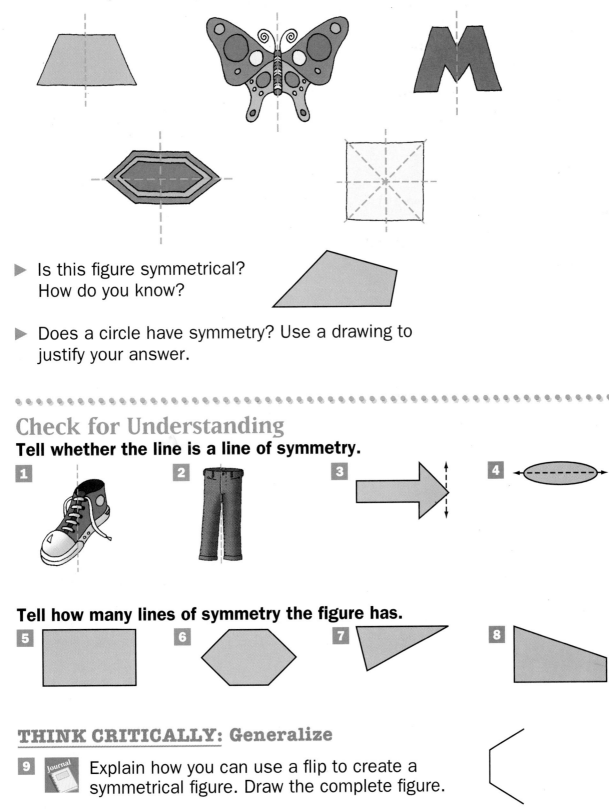

▶ Is this figure symmetrical?
How do you know?

▶ Does a circle have symmetry? Use a drawing to justify your answer.

Check for Understanding

Tell whether the line is a line of symmetry.

1 **2** **3** **4**

Tell how many lines of symmetry the figure has.

5 **6** **7** **8**

THINK CRITICALLY: Generalize

9 Journal Explain how you can use a flip to create a symmetrical figure. Draw the complete figure.

Practice

Tell whether the line is a line of symmetry.

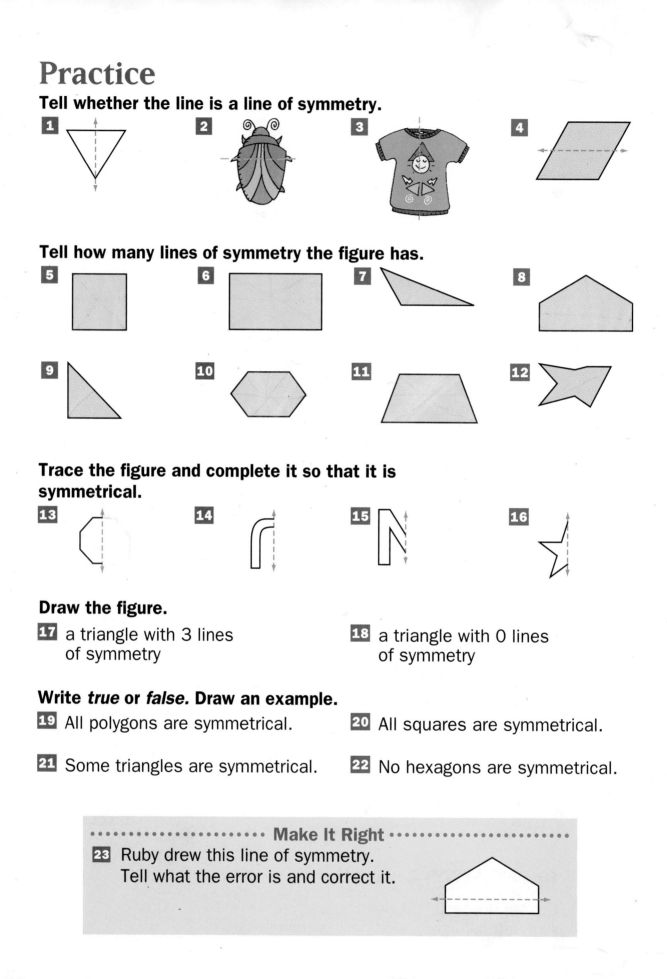

1 **2** **3** **4**

Tell how many lines of symmetry the figure has.

5 **6** **7** **8**

9 **10** **11** **12**

Trace the figure and complete it so that it is symmetrical.

13 **14** **15** **16**

Draw the figure.

17 a triangle with 3 lines of symmetry

18 a triangle with 0 lines of symmetry

Write *true* or *false*. Draw an example.

19 All polygons are symmetrical.

20 All squares are symmetrical.

21 Some triangles are symmetrical.

22 No hexagons are symmetrical.

·· **Make It Right** ··
23 Ruby drew this line of symmetry.
Tell what the error is and correct it.

24 **Make a decision** You can buy 6 bags of beads for $12 at one store or 5 bags for $15 at another store. Which would you buy? Why?

25 **Data Point** Write a list of objects you can see in your classroom that are symmetrical. Compare your list to those of others.

26 Kenesha buys 8 yards of fabric for $40. How much does each yard cost?

27 Draw a real-world object that has exactly one line of symmetry.

28 Kenesha decorated a dashiki with this design. How many lines of symmetry does the design have?

29 **Spatial reasoning** How many ways can this piece be put in the figure without flipping it?

Cultural Connection Symmetry in Kuba Art

The Kuba people live in Zaire, a country in Central Africa. They are famous weavers and embroiderers of raffia cloth.

1 Suppose this is the beginning of a Kuba pattern. Trace the figure and draw the line of symmetry.

2 **What if** the pattern continues like this. What will the next shape look like?

3 Make a pattern using symmetrical shapes. Describe it to another student. See if he or she can draw your pattern.

Ordered Pairs

Has anyone ever drawn you a map so you could find his or her house? Where on the map is Nick's house?

You can name locations on a map by using **ordered pairs.**

Start at (0, 0). The first number tells you how many spaces to count to the right.

The second number tells you how many spaces to count up.

Nick's house is at (3, 0).

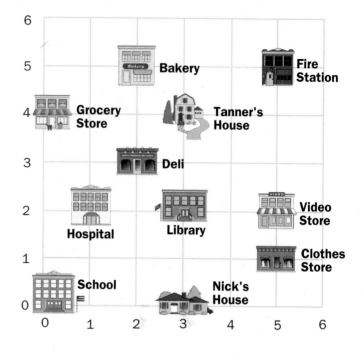

▶ **What if** Tanner goes to (5, 2) on the map. Where is he?

More Examples

A The grocery store is at (0, 4).

B (3, 4) is the location of Tanner's house.

Check for Understanding

Write the ordered pair that tells the location of the building on the map.

1 bakery   **2** deli   **3** fire station   **4** hospital

Tell what is at the point on the map.

5 (3, 2)   **6** (0, 0)   **7** (3, 0)   **8** (5, 1)

THINK CRITICALLY: Analyze **Explain your reasoning.**

9 Journal   Why do the numbers in an ordered pair need to be ordered?

Practice

Write the ordered pair that tells the location of the building on the map.

1 pet shop

2 Sue's house

3 post office

4 barbershop

Tell what is at the point on the map.

5 (1, 0)

6 (3, 6)

7 (1, 5)

8 (3, 1)

MIXED APPLICATIONS
Problem Solving

Use the map of downtown Central City.

9 How many blocks is the doughnut shop from the barbershop?

10 **Write a problem** about a place on the map. Solve it. Ask others to solve it.

11 Emily walks a block in 2 minutes. How long will it take her to walk all the way from the travel agency to Marta's Cafe?

12 Joshua leaves his house at 3:30 P.M. He visits the pet shop and the hardware store. He returns home at 4:45 P.M. How long was he gone?

13 **Make a decision** Start at (0, 0). Pick 3 points to visit in Central City. Decide on the shortest route to take to visit them. **Check student's routes.**

14 As part of her fitness program, Hillary rides her bicycle 8 miles each day. How many miles will she ride in a week?

mixed review

Complete. Write *inches, feet, yards,* or *miles*.

1 Mary's cat is about 2 ■ long.

2 Paul ran 2 ■ in 20 minutes.

3 The door to Brett's room is just over 2 ■ tall.

4 Mrs. Williams's necklace is 18 ■ long.

Part 1   Drawing a Diagram

Ranchers and other people who keep horses need to build corrals. Plan a corral that is 24 ft by 30 ft. There will be a fence post at every corner and every 6 ft. There will be 3 rails between each fence post. A 6-ft gate adds 2 extra fence posts.

Work Together
Solve. Be prepared to explain your methods.

1 Make a diagram of the corral and include all the needed fence posts.

2 How many fence posts are needed for the corral?

3 How many rails are needed for the corral?

4 **What if** the corral were 12 feet longer in each dimension. How many more fence posts would be needed?

5 **What if** a friend offers you 24 fence posts. There still will be a fence post every 6 feet and at every corner. What size square corral could you build with exactly 24 fence posts?

6 **Make a prediction** What would be the next largest square corral you could build? How many fence posts would you need?

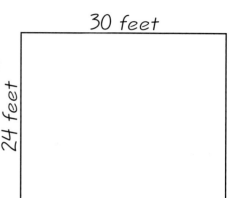

30 feet

24 feet

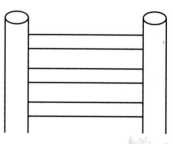

Part 2   Write and Share Problems

Celine used the information in the diagram to write a problem.

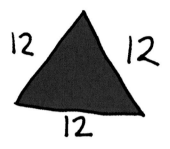

12   12

12

There is a fence post in each corner and every 3 feet. Each post cost $10. How many fence posts are there in all?

7 Solve Celine's problem.

8 What extra information is in Celine's problem?

9 Write Celine's problem without the extra information.

10 **Write a problem** that could be solved using a diagram.

11 Trade problems. Solve at least three problems written by your classmates.

12 Which is the most interesting problem that you solved? Why?

Celine Leung
P.S. 144
Forest Hills, NY

Turn the page for Practice Strategies. ▶

Part 3 Practice Strategies

Menu

Choose five problems and solve them. Explain your methods.

1 Marie decorates a place mat. She wants the opposite edge to have hearts across from the stars and stars across from the hearts. How many hearts does she need in all?

2 Eula gave 10 baskets she wove to her friends. She sold twice as many to a store. She kept the remaining 5. How many baskets did she weave?

3 Mr. Hiro is putting a fence around his garden. The garden is 50 feet by 30 feet. If he has a fence post at each corner and every 5 feet, how many fence posts does he need?

4 Lonato sells 2 silver bracelets and a pair of earrings for $100. The bracelets cost $39.50 and $48.75. What is the cost of the earrings?

5 Bobbie has a library book that is 16 days overdue and one that is 3 days overdue. The library charged 10¢ per day for each overdue book. How much does she owe the library?

6 Estimate to complete the prices and solve. Chet bought a T-shirt for ■ and 3 pairs of socks for ■ each. About how much did he spend in all?

7 Mrs. Hudson plans to take her class on a field trip to the aquarium. They need to be back by 2:45 P.M. What time should they leave the school?

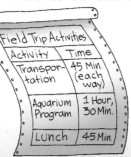

Field Trip Activities

Activity	Time
Transportation	45 Min. (each way)
Aquarium Program	1 Hour, 30 Min.
Lunch	45 Min.

8 Mateo bought a card. He got 65 cents in change. There were 9 coins, all nickels and dimes. How many coins were nickels? How many were dimes?

Choose two problems and solve them.
Explain your methods.

9 **Logical reasoning** Lori, Henry, Amy, Carlo, and Mira are each holding a cylinder, a sphere, a cube, a cone, or a pyramid. Use the clues to tell which shape each person is holding. Write your own puzzle using geometric figures. Give it to others to solve.

a. Lori is holding a figure with no curved faces.

b. Henry is holding a figure with 6 congruent faces.

c. Carlo is holding a figure with no flat faces.

d. Amy is holding a figure with 2 circular faces.

10 Design and draw a symmetrical pattern using polygons. The pattern should have a total of at least 12 figures in it and use at least 3 different polygons.

11 **Spatial reasoning** Trace and cut out the 4 polygons. Fit them together to make a larger polygon. Which one can you make? Can you make another?

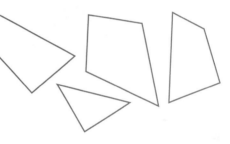

12 **At the Computer** Use a drawing or geometry program to play "Make My Shape Challenge." Draw a geometric figure. Then use the slide, flip, and turn tools to change your figure. Challenge other students to show how you changed the original figure.

Language and Mathematics

Complete the sentence. Use a word in the chart.

1 A figure with 5 angles and 5 sides is a ■.

2 An ■ is 2 rays with the same endpoint.

3 A figure is ■ if the two parts are alike when you fold it along a line.

4 Two figures are ■ if they are the same size and shape.

Vocabulary
angle
square
pentagon
symmetric
congruent
sphere
flip

Concepts and Skills

Name the figure.

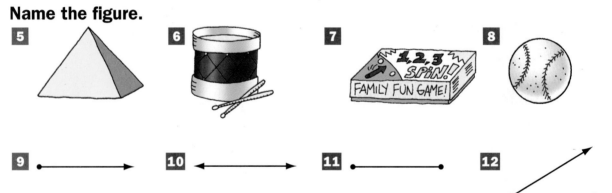

5 **6** **7** **8**

9 **10** **11** **12**

Write *yes* or *no* to tell whether the shape is a polygon. If it is a polygon, name it.

13 P **14** **15** **16** D

Write *slide, flip,* or *turn* to tell how the figure was moved.

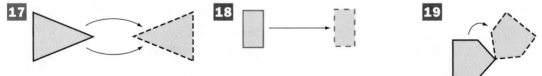

17 **18** **19**

Tell if the two figures are congruent.

20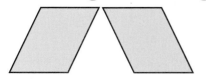

21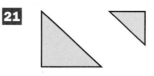

Tell how many lines of symmetry the figure has.

22

23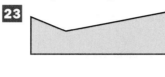

24

Write the ordered pair that tells the location on the map.

25 petting zoo

26 Ferris wheel

Tell what is at the point on the map.

27 (7, 6)

28 (1, 2)

Think critically.

29 Analyze. Maxwell says that all squares are congruent. Do you agree or disagree? Why? Draw an example.

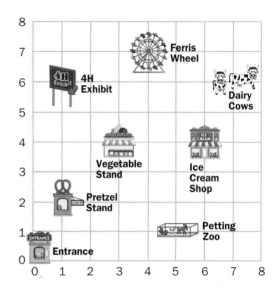

Problem Solving

30 The perimeter of the town wading pool is 36 ft. The wading pool is shaped like a square. What is the length of each side?

31 The main pool is shaped like a rectangle. It is 60 m long and 30 m wide. There are ladders at each corner and every 15 m. How many ladders are there?

32 Molly knits a sweater. She uses a border pattern of leaf, leaf, acorn, leaf, leaf, acorn. What are the next four shapes in the pattern?

33 A quilt sells for $155. The materials cost $67.98. About how much more than the cost of the materials does the quilt sell for?

Name the figure.

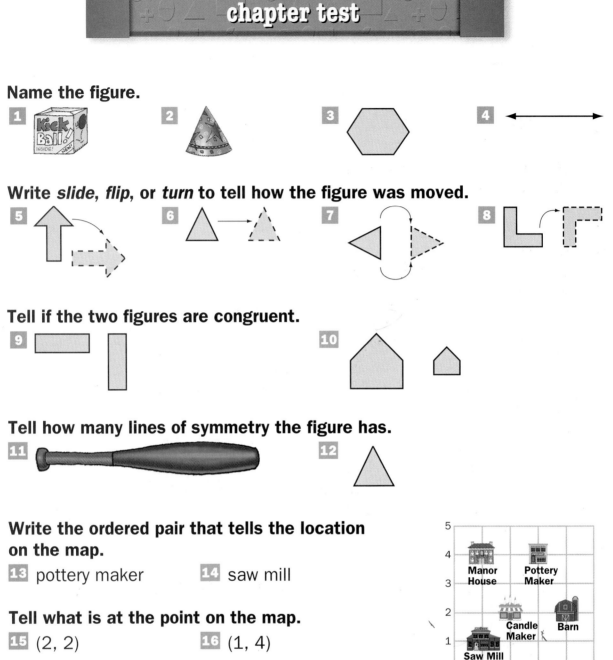

1. Kick Ball

2.

3.

4.

Write slide, flip, or turn to tell how the figure was moved.

5.

6.

7.

8.

Tell if the two figures are congruent.

9.

10.

Tell how many lines of symmetry the figure has.

11.

12.

Write the ordered pair that tells the location on the map.

13. pottery maker

14. saw mill

Tell what is at the point on the map.

15. (2, 2)

16. (1, 4)

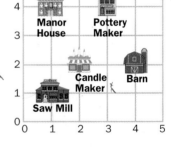

Solve.

17. A painting sells for $258. The materials cost $89. About how much more than the cost of the materials does the painting sell for?

18. The garden is shaped like a pentagon. Each side is 6 m long. There are fence posts at each corner and every 2 m. How many fence posts are there?

19. Gary starts to paint a tie with a pattern made of two circles, a triangle, and a diamond. If the pattern continues like that, what is the tenth figure in the pattern?

20. The perimeter of the fence around the dog's house is 32 ft. The fence is shaped like a square. How long is each side?

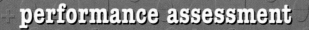
What Did You Learn?

Draw a polygon on dot paper. Name it.

Describe it in as many ways as you can, including the number of lines of symmetry it has.

Tell how your polygon is different from a circle. Flip your figure. Show what it looks like on the dot paper.

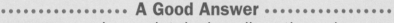

················ **A Good Answer** ··················
- names and completely describes the polygon
- clearly shows what the polygon looks like after it has been flipped

You may want to place your work in your portfolio.

What Do You Think ?

1 How do you sort geometric shapes?

2 Which shapes do you find most interesting? Why?

3 List some features you might use to compare geometric figures.
- number of flat or curved sides
- number and size of angles
- number of lines of symmetry

Geodesic Domes

Cultural Note

The earliest use of domes for stone or brick buildings was in Mesopotamia around 2000 B.C. Domes need the least amount of material for the greatest amount of space inside.

Dr. R. Buckminster Fuller (1895–1983) invented the geodesic dome in the early 1950s. Its strength and light weight come from the shapes used in its design.

▶ What shapes do you see?

In this activity, you will explore the strength of different geometric shapes.

1 Make a rectangle out of four straws. Squeeze the end of one straw and insert it into the end of another. Bend them into a rectangle and tape all of the connections.

2 Use the same method to make a pentagon and a triangle out of straws. Push on a corner of each shape.

▶ Which shape resists bending the most?

▶ Use straws to make a crosspiece on the rectangle. What shapes are formed? Try bending it again. What do you notice?

How Many Triangles?

1 How many triangles were formed when you added the crosspiece to the rectangle?

2 Draw lines from one corner of a pentagon to the opposite corners. How many triangles can you separate the pentagon into?

3 Draw a hexagon. Draw lines from one corner to the opposite corners. How many triangles can you separate the hexagon into?

4 Make a list of buildings or other structures you know that use triangular shapes.

At the Computer

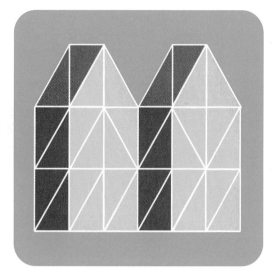

5 Use a drawing or geometry program to design a building. Make a list of the shapes you use.

6 Write a paragraph telling why you chose the shapes you used in the design of the building.

FRACTIONS, DECIMALS, AND PROBABILITY

Arts & Crafts

*Long ago, people made toys, clothes, even games by hand.
Many artists still do. They use fractions and decimals to
measure and describe their work.*

What Do You Know ?

1 What fraction of the painting is red? green? blue?

2 What fraction of the paintbrushes are in the cleaning jar?

3 Portfolio Look around your classroom. What objects or groups can be described using fractions? Describe them.

Meaning of Fractions

In quilting bees, each person sews together parts to make one square. These squares are sewn together to make a whole quilt.

Work Together

Work in a group to design your own quilt square with 4 equal parts.

Color the squares on your grid.

► How can you check that each part is equal?

Compare your design to those of others.

► How are they the same? different?

Repeat the activity to make a design with more equal parts.

Make Connections

Lori and her group describe their square.

► How would you name the parts of the first design you made?

► How many equal parts are in the second design you made? How would you name them?

You will need
- *8-by-8 grids*
- *colored markers or crayons*

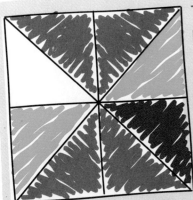

There are 8 equal parts in this design.
One eighth of the square is white.
One eighth of the square is black.
Two eighths of the square is blue.
Four eighths of the square is red.

Fractions name equal parts of a whole.

▶ Which of these designs shows thirds? Tell why.

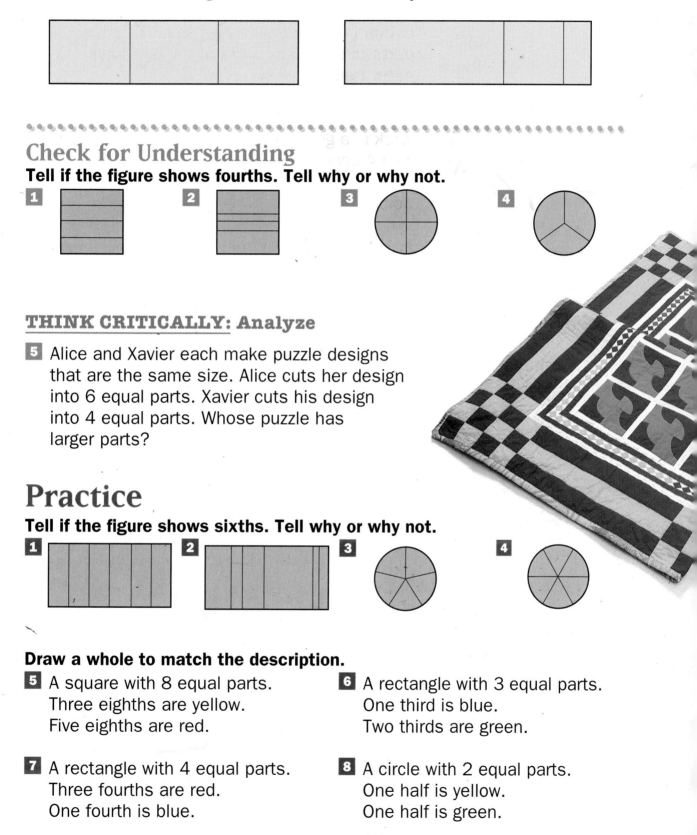

●●

Check for Understanding
Tell if the figure shows fourths. Tell why or why not.

1   **2**   **3**   **4**

THINK CRITICALLY: Analyze

5 Alice and Xavier each make puzzle designs that are the same size. Alice cuts her design into 6 equal parts. Xavier cuts his design into 4 equal parts. Whose puzzle has larger parts?

Practice

Tell if the figure shows sixths. Tell why or why not.

1   **2**   **3**   **4**

Draw a whole to match the description.

5 A square with 8 equal parts.
Three eighths are yellow.
Five eighths are red.

6 A rectangle with 3 equal parts.
One third is blue.
Two thirds are green.

7 A rectangle with 4 equal parts.
Three fourths are red.
One fourth is blue.

8 A circle with 2 equal parts.
One half is yellow.
One half is green.

Parts of a Whole

Leather carver Robert Beard, Bloomfield, NM

Leather carvers use stamps to make fancy designs. How many parts of the belt have roadrunner stamps?

You can write a description of the belt.

3 out of 8 parts have roadrunner stamps on them.

You can also write a fraction.

parts with roadrunner stamps →**3** ←**numerator**
total number of parts →**8** ←**denominator**

Three eighths of the belt has roadrunner stamps on it.

More Examples

A

$\frac{5}{8}$ ← blue parts
← total number of parts

5 out of 8 parts or five eighths of the rectangle is blue.

B

$\frac{1}{6}$ ← blue parts
← total number of parts

1 out of 6 parts or one sixth of the circle is blue.

Check for Understanding
Write a fraction for the part that is blue.

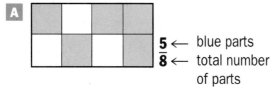

1   **2**   **3**   **4**

THINK CRITICALLY: Analyze Explain your reasoning.

5 What if $\frac{1}{5}$ of the square was shaded. Is $\frac{1}{5}$ of the square larger than or smaller than $\frac{1}{4}$?

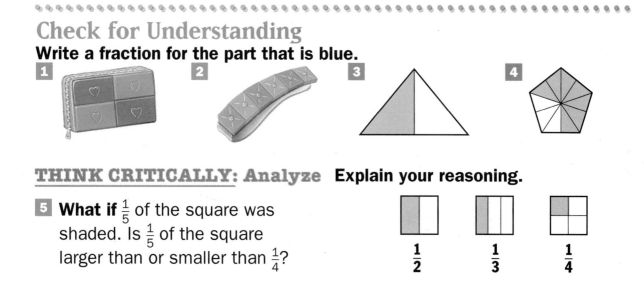

$\frac{1}{2}$ $\frac{1}{3}$ $\frac{1}{4}$

Practice

Write a fraction for the part that is blue.

1

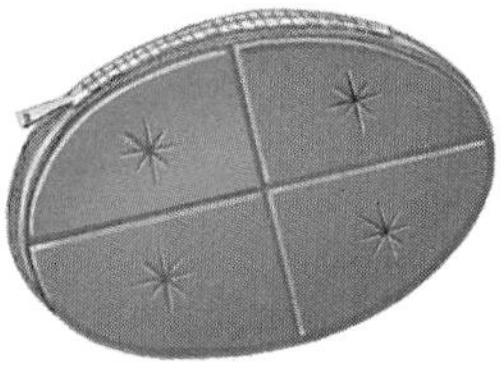

2

3

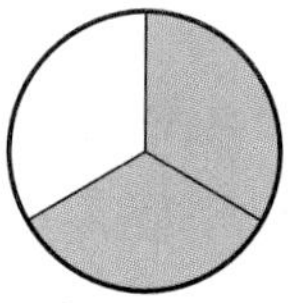

4

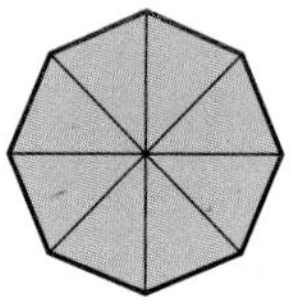

Write a fraction for the word name.

5 one ninth

6 three tenths

7 one half

8 five sixths

Use the fraction to draw the whole.

9 one half

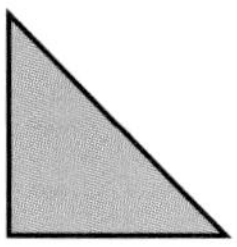

10 one third

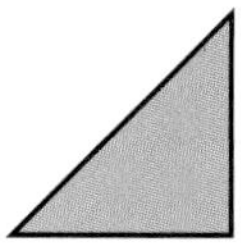

11 one fourth

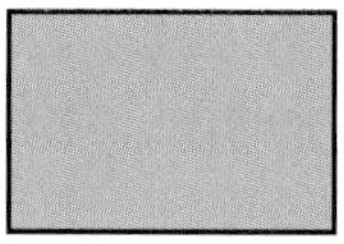

12 one eighth

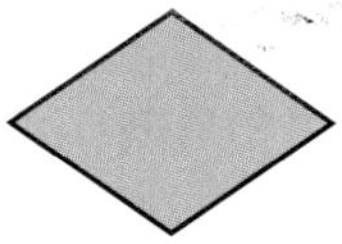

MIXED APPLICATIONS
Problem Solving

Pencil & Paper   Calculator   Mental Math

13 Franco designs a belt with 10 equal pieces. He colors 4 of the pieces blue and 2 of the pieces green. How many pieces does he have left to color?

14 Lara divides a piece of leather into 6 equal parts. She stamps a design on 4 of the parts. What fraction of the whole is stamped?

15 **Spatial reasoning** Tell if the figure shows fourths. Tell why or why not.

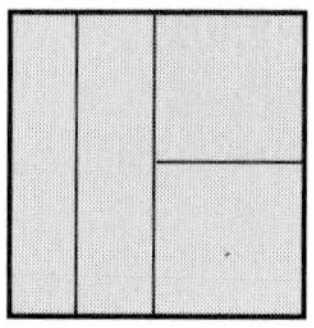

16 Kyle uses 36 red or green pieces in his puzzle. There are twice as many green pieces as there are red pieces. How many green pieces are there?

mixed review

Write the letter of the better estimate.

1 length of a pen
  a. 6 in.
  b. 6 ft

2 height of a person
  a. 4 in.
  b. 4 ft

3 distance run in 1 min
  a. 400 cm
  b. 400 m

4 width of a book
  a. 20 cm
  b. 20 m

Parts of a Group

In a bead store, there are so many choices. Suppose you buy these beads. What part of this group of beads is red?

Work Together

Work with a partner to explore parts of a group. You can use 2-color counters to model the problem.

Show how many of each color bead there are. Write a fraction to name the part of the group that is red.

number of red beads → ■ ← numerator
total number of beads → ■ ← denominator

Draw a picture of your model.

Repeat the activity using a different number of each color bead and a different total number of beads.

Make Connections

Here is how Yasmine and Steve recorded their work.

> You will need
> • 2-color counters

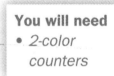

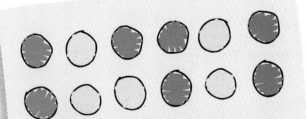

7 out of 12 beads are red.
Seven twelfths, $\frac{7}{12}$, of the beads are red.

▶ What fraction of the beads are yellow?

▶ What fraction of the beads are brown?

▶ What fraction of the beads are leaf-shaped?

Check for Understanding
Write a fraction for the part that is blue.

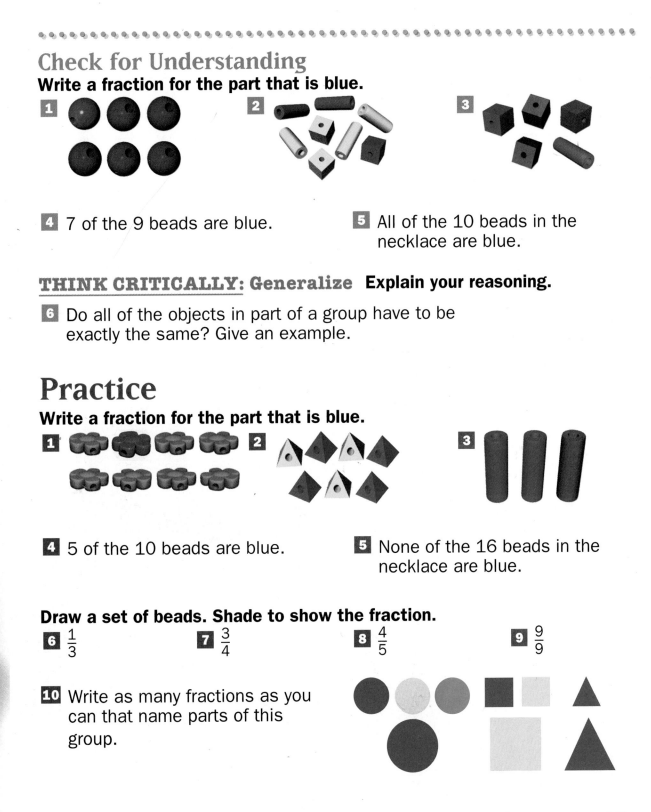

1

2

3

4 7 of the 9 beads are blue.

5 All of the 10 beads in the necklace are blue.

THINK CRITICALLY: Generalize **Explain your reasoning.**

6 Do all of the objects in part of a group have to be exactly the same? Give an example.

Practice
Write a fraction for the part that is blue.

1

2

3

4 5 of the 10 beads are blue.

5 None of the 16 beads in the necklace are blue.

Draw a set of beads. Shade to show the fraction.

6 $\frac{1}{3}$

7 $\frac{3}{4}$

8 $\frac{4}{5}$

9 $\frac{9}{9}$

10 Write as many fractions as you can that name parts of this group.

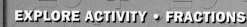
Equivalent Fractions

You can make candles by pouring melted wax into molds. There is $\frac{1}{2}$ cup of melted wax in one cup and $\frac{2}{4}$ cups in the other cup. How do the amounts in each cup compare?

Work Together

Work with a partner. Use fraction strips to model the problem.

Find the strip that shows $\frac{1}{2}$.

Combine two $\frac{1}{4}$ strips to show $\frac{2}{4}$.

Compare.

▶ Do the strips show the same amount?

You will need
• *fraction strips*

Fractions that name the same amount are called **equivalent fractions.** $\frac{1}{2}$ and $\frac{2}{4}$ are equivalent.

Use fraction strips to find other fractions equivalent to $\frac{1}{2}$. Make a list of the fractions you find.

Use fraction strips to find an equivalent fraction.

a. $\frac{1}{3}$ **b.** $\frac{1}{5}$ **c.** $\frac{3}{4}$ **d.** $\frac{4}{6}$

Talk It Over

▶ How can you tell if two fractions are equivalent?

Making Connections

Joseph and Ana found these equivalent fractions for $\frac{1}{2}$.

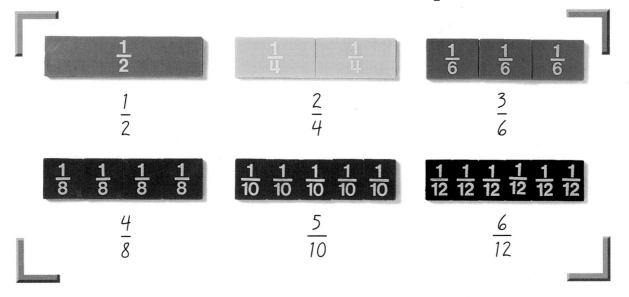

$\frac{1}{2}$

$\frac{2}{4}$

$\frac{3}{6}$

$\frac{4}{8}$

$\frac{5}{10}$

$\frac{6}{12}$

▶ Look at the fractions that are equivalent to $\frac{1}{2}$.
What pattern do you see?

▶ Look at numerators and denominators in the other
groups of equivalent fractions you found. What patterns
do you see?

Check for Understanding

Complete to name the equivalent fraction.

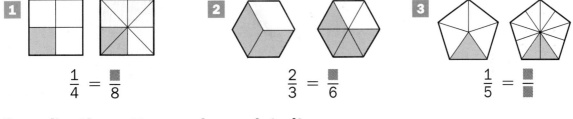

1 $\frac{1}{4} = \frac{\blacksquare}{8}$

2 $\frac{2}{3} = \frac{\blacksquare}{6}$

3 $\frac{1}{5} = \frac{\blacksquare}{\blacksquare}$

Describe the pattern and complete it.

4 $\frac{1}{3}, \frac{2}{6}, \frac{\blacksquare}{9}, \frac{\blacksquare}{12}$

5 $\frac{2}{2}, \frac{3}{3}, \frac{\blacksquare}{4}, \frac{\blacksquare}{\blacksquare}$

THINK CRITICALLY: Generalize   Explain your reasoning.

6 Are $\frac{1}{4}$ and $\frac{2}{6}$ equivalent fractions? Why or why not?
Draw a picture to support your answer.

Turn the page for Practice. ➡

Practice

Complete to name the equivalent fraction. You may use fraction strips.

1 $\frac{1}{3} = \frac{\blacksquare}{12}$ **2** $\frac{3}{4} = \frac{\blacksquare}{8}$ **3** $\frac{6}{10} = \frac{\blacksquare}{5}$ **4** $\frac{2}{4} = \frac{3}{\blacksquare}$ **5** $\frac{8}{12} = \frac{\blacksquare}{\blacksquare}$

Complete to name the equivalent fraction.

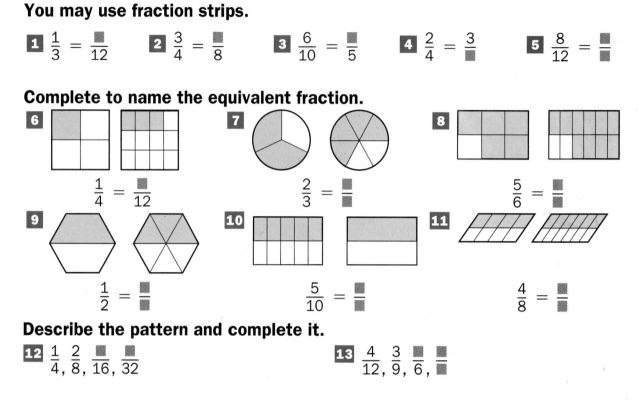

6 $\frac{1}{4} = \frac{\blacksquare}{12}$ **7** $\frac{2}{3} = \frac{\blacksquare}{\blacksquare}$ **8** $\frac{5}{6} = \frac{\blacksquare}{\blacksquare}$

9 $\frac{1}{2} = \frac{\blacksquare}{\blacksquare}$ **10** $\frac{5}{10} = \frac{\blacksquare}{\blacksquare}$ **11** $\frac{4}{8} = \frac{\blacksquare}{\blacksquare}$

Describe the pattern and complete it.

12 $\frac{1}{4}, \frac{2}{8}, \frac{\blacksquare}{16}, \frac{\blacksquare}{32}$ **13** $\frac{4}{12}, \frac{3}{9}, \frac{\blacksquare}{6}, \frac{\blacksquare}{\blacksquare}$

Use the ruler to answer ex. 14–16.

14 How many equal parts is this inch ruler divided into? Write a fraction to name one of these parts.

15 How many quarter inches are in 1 inch?

16 How many eighth inches are in $\frac{1}{2}$ inch?

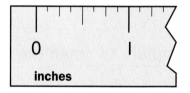

0   I

inches

·······················**Make It Right**·····················

17 Julie said these fractions are equivalent. Find the error and correct it.

$\frac{1}{2} = \frac{2}{5}$

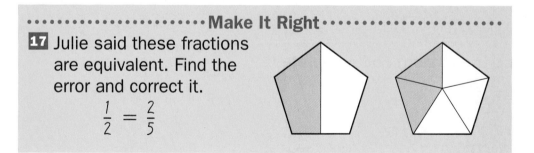

408 Lesson 11.4

Find a Fraction Game!

First, cut 12 index cards in half. Write each fraction shown at the right on one half of a card. Write an equivalent fraction on the other half. Do this for all of the cards.

Next, turn the cards facedown and mix them up. Then spread the cards out on the table.

Play the Game

Play with a partner. Choose who goes first. Pick two cards.

If you pick equivalent fractions, keep the cards. Take another turn.

If you do not find equivalent fractions, put the cards back facedown without mixing them up. Now it is your partner's turn.

The partner with the most pairs of equivalent fractions wins.

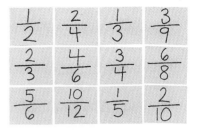

You will need
- *12 index cards*
- *scissors*

---

mixed review

Name the figure.

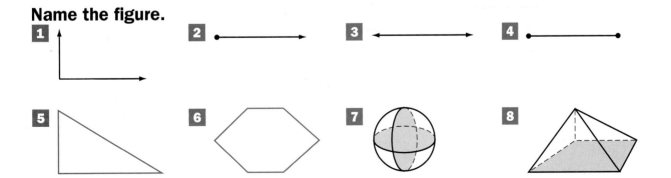

Compare Fractions

The Hopi Indians of Arizona paint bowls with geometric patterns.

$\frac{1}{4}$ of this pattern is painted.

$\frac{3}{4}$ of this pattern is painted.

Which pattern has the greater part painted?

Work Together

Work with a partner. Use fraction strips to compare fractions.

Model the fractions $\frac{1}{4}$ and $\frac{3}{4}$. Compare the models.

You will need
• *fraction strips*

▶ Which fraction is greater?

▶ Use >, <, or = to write two comparison sentences.

▶ Which pattern has the greater part painted?

Note:
< means "is less than."
> means "is greater than."

Work with your partner to model and compare the fractions.

Write a comparison sentence.

a. $\frac{1}{3}$ and $\frac{2}{3}$ **b.** $\frac{2}{5}$ and $\frac{4}{5}$ **c.** $\frac{2}{3}$ and $\frac{3}{8}$ **d.** $\frac{3}{6}$ and $\frac{3}{4}$ **e.** $\frac{6}{8}$ and $\frac{9}{12}$

Choose other fractions to compare. Write a comparison sentence for each.

Talk It Over

▶ Is it easier to compare $\frac{1}{3}$ and $\frac{2}{3}$, or $\frac{3}{6}$ and $\frac{3}{4}$? Why?

Make Connections

Cara and Kyle took a picture of their models.

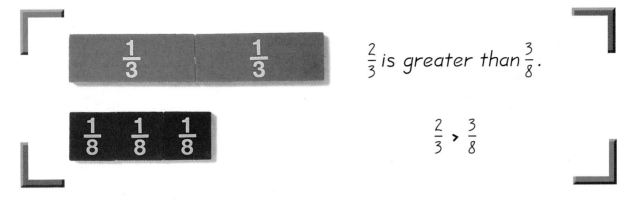

$\frac{2}{3}$ is greater than $\frac{3}{8}$.

$$\frac{2}{3} > \frac{3}{8}$$

There are other ways to compare fractions.

You can draw pictures.

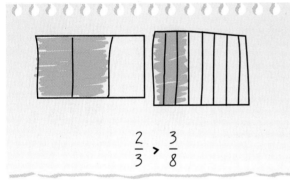

$$\frac{2}{3} > \frac{3}{8}$$

You can use number lines.

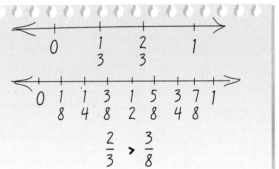

$$\frac{2}{3} > \frac{3}{8}$$

Check for Understanding

Compare the fractions. Write >, <, or =.

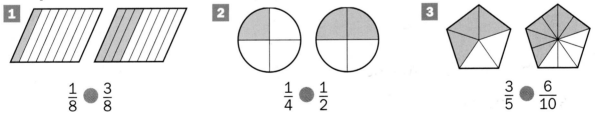

1. $\frac{1}{8}$ ● $\frac{3}{8}$

2. $\frac{1}{4}$ ● $\frac{1}{2}$

3. $\frac{3}{5}$ ● $\frac{6}{10}$

THINK CRITICALLY: Analyze   Explain your reasoning.

4. When the denominators of two fractions are the same, which fraction is greater?

5. When the numerators of two fractions are the same, which fraction is greater?

Turn the page for Practice. ➡️

Practice

Compare the fractions. Write >, <, or =.

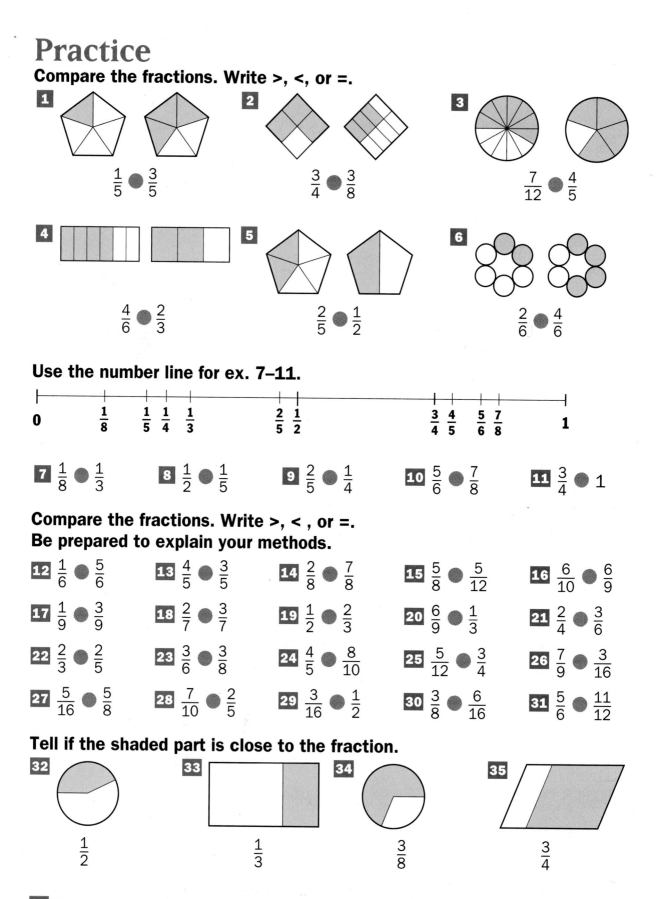

1 $\dfrac{1}{5}$ ⬤ $\dfrac{3}{5}$

2 $\dfrac{3}{4}$ ⬤ $\dfrac{3}{8}$

3 $\dfrac{7}{12}$ ⬤ $\dfrac{4}{5}$

4 $\dfrac{4}{6}$ ⬤ $\dfrac{2}{3}$

5 $\dfrac{2}{5}$ ⬤ $\dfrac{1}{2}$

6 $\dfrac{2}{6}$ ⬤ $\dfrac{4}{6}$

Use the number line for ex. 7–11.

0    $\dfrac{1}{8}$ $\dfrac{1}{5}$ $\dfrac{1}{4}$ $\dfrac{1}{3}$ $\dfrac{2}{5}$ $\dfrac{1}{2}$ $\dfrac{3}{4}$ $\dfrac{4}{5}$ $\dfrac{5}{6}$ $\dfrac{7}{8}$ 1

7 $\dfrac{1}{8}$ ⬤ $\dfrac{1}{3}$

8 $\dfrac{1}{2}$ ⬤ $\dfrac{1}{5}$

9 $\dfrac{2}{5}$ ⬤ $\dfrac{1}{4}$

10 $\dfrac{5}{6}$ ⬤ $\dfrac{7}{8}$

11 $\dfrac{3}{4}$ ⬤ 1

Compare the fractions. Write >, < , or =.
Be prepared to explain your methods.

12 $\dfrac{1}{6}$ ⬤ $\dfrac{5}{6}$

13 $\dfrac{4}{5}$ ⬤ $\dfrac{3}{5}$

14 $\dfrac{2}{8}$ ⬤ $\dfrac{7}{8}$

15 $\dfrac{5}{8}$ ⬤ $\dfrac{5}{12}$

16 $\dfrac{6}{10}$ ⬤ $\dfrac{6}{9}$

17 $\dfrac{1}{9}$ ⬤ $\dfrac{3}{9}$

18 $\dfrac{2}{7}$ ⬤ $\dfrac{3}{7}$

19 $\dfrac{1}{2}$ ⬤ $\dfrac{2}{3}$

20 $\dfrac{6}{9}$ ⬤ $\dfrac{1}{3}$

21 $\dfrac{2}{4}$ ⬤ $\dfrac{3}{6}$

22 $\dfrac{2}{3}$ ⬤ $\dfrac{2}{5}$

23 $\dfrac{3}{6}$ ⬤ $\dfrac{3}{8}$

24 $\dfrac{4}{5}$ ⬤ $\dfrac{8}{10}$

25 $\dfrac{5}{12}$ ⬤ $\dfrac{3}{4}$

26 $\dfrac{7}{9}$ ⬤ $\dfrac{3}{16}$

27 $\dfrac{5}{16}$ ⬤ $\dfrac{5}{8}$

28 $\dfrac{7}{10}$ ⬤ $\dfrac{2}{5}$

29 $\dfrac{3}{16}$ ⬤ $\dfrac{1}{2}$

30 $\dfrac{3}{8}$ ⬤ $\dfrac{6}{16}$

31 $\dfrac{5}{6}$ ⬤ $\dfrac{11}{12}$

Tell if the shaded part is close to the fraction.

32 $\dfrac{1}{2}$

33 $\dfrac{1}{3}$

34 $\dfrac{3}{8}$

35 $\dfrac{3}{4}$

36 Redraw each incorrect figure to show the fraction.

Problem Solving

37 What fraction of the letters in your last name are vowels? consonants?

38 There are 9 boys and 7 girls in Mr. Elkhorn's art class. What fraction of the class are girls?

39 There are 6 boys and 8 girls in the craft class. How many fewer boys are there than girls.

40 Don decorated his bowl for $\frac{3}{4}$ hour. Irma decorated her bowl for $\frac{1}{2}$ hour. Who worked longer?

41 Marva starts to make a beadwork belt. She puts 4 white beads and 4 red beads on each thread on the loom. How many beads are on the loom? See INFOBIT.

INFOBIT
Woven beadwork is created on hand looms. Beads are placed on eight threads at a time.

more to explore

Estimating Fractions

You can use a number line to help estimate if a fraction is closer to 0 or 1.

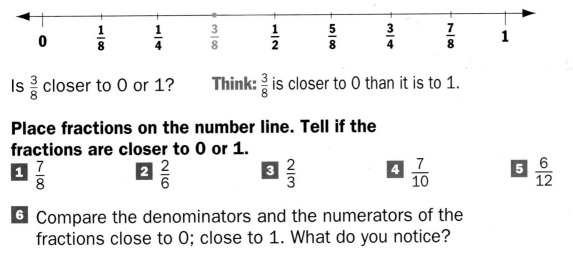

Is $\frac{3}{8}$ closer to 0 or 1?   **Think:** $\frac{3}{8}$ is closer to 0 than it is to 1.

Place fractions on the number line. Tell if the fractions are closer to 0 or 1.

1 $\frac{7}{8}$ **2** $\frac{2}{6}$ **3** $\frac{2}{3}$ **4** $\frac{7}{10}$ **5** $\frac{6}{12}$

6 Compare the denominators and the numerators of the fractions close to 0; close to 1. What do you notice?

Mixed Numbers

You can use things you collect on a nature walk to weave a tapestry. If you complete 2 of them and $\frac{3}{4}$ of another, what number shows how many tapestries you have made?

You can write this amount as a fraction or as a **mixed number.** A mixed number is made up of a whole number and a fraction.

Write: $\frac{11}{4}$ **Read:** eleven fourths

$2\frac{3}{4}$ two and three fourths

You have made $2\frac{3}{4}$ tapestries.

More Examples

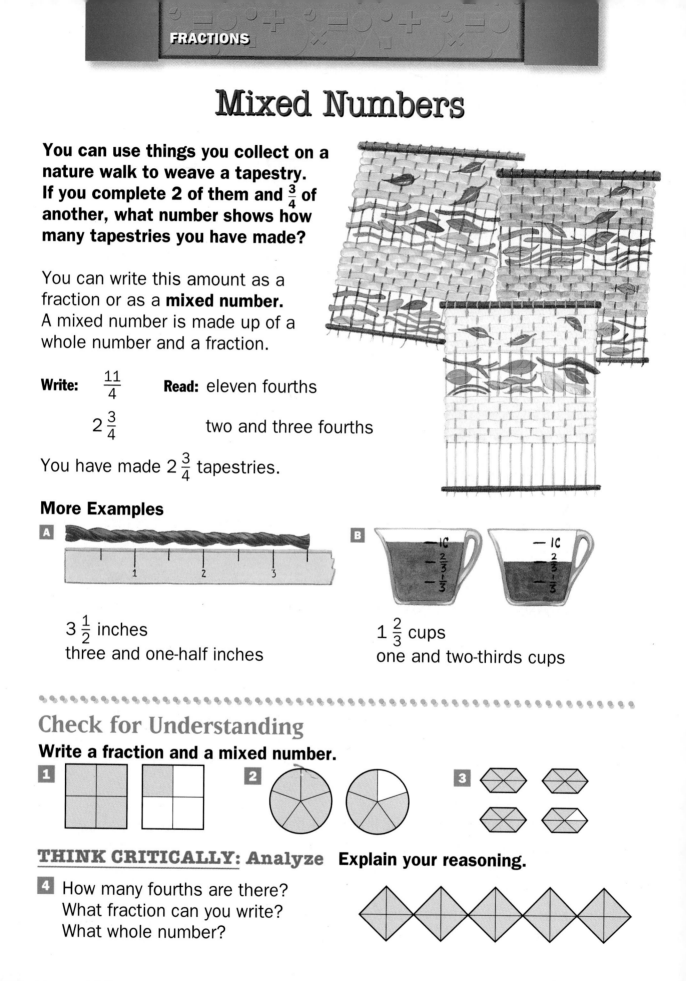

A

$3\frac{1}{2}$ inches
three and one-half inches

B

$1\frac{2}{3}$ cups
one and two-thirds cups

Check for Understanding
Write a fraction and a mixed number.

1

2

3

THINK CRITICALLY: Analyze   Explain your reasoning.

4 How many fourths are there?
What fraction can you write?
What whole number?

Practice

Write a fraction and a mixed number.

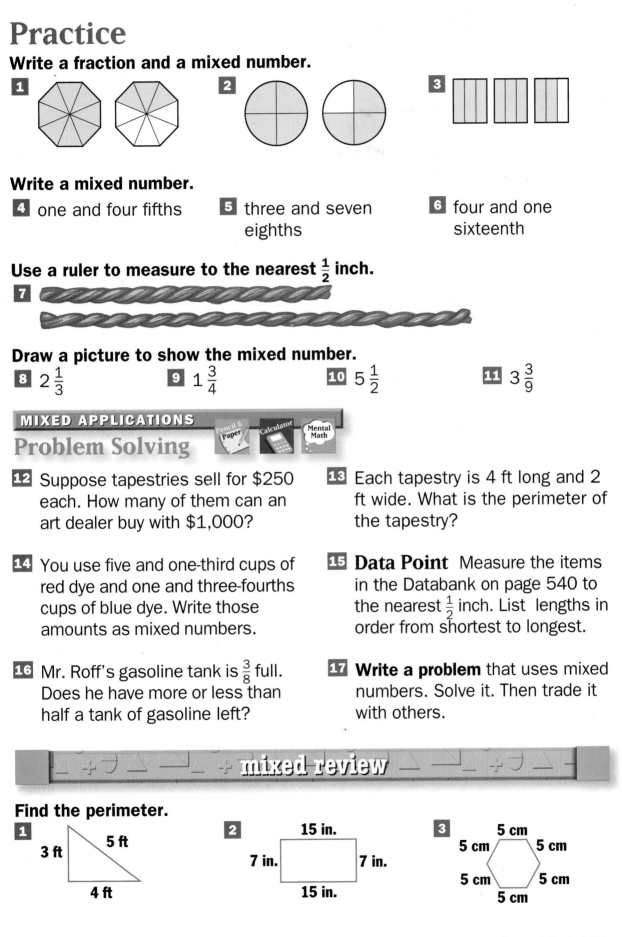

1

2

3

Write a mixed number.

4 one and four fifths

5 three and seven eighths

6 four and one sixteenth

Use a ruler to measure to the nearest $\frac{1}{2}$ inch.

7

Draw a picture to show the mixed number.

8 $2\frac{1}{3}$

9 $1\frac{3}{4}$

10 $5\frac{1}{2}$

11 $3\frac{3}{9}$

MIXED APPLICATIONS
Problem Solving

Pencil & Paper   Calculator   Mental Math

12 Suppose tapestries sell for $250 each. How many of them can an art dealer buy with $1,000?

13 Each tapestry is 4 ft long and 2 ft wide. What is the perimeter of the tapestry?

14 You use five and one-third cups of red dye and one and three-fourths cups of blue dye. Write those amounts as mixed numbers.

15 **Data Point** Measure the items in the Databank on page 540 to the nearest $\frac{1}{2}$ inch. List lengths in order from shortest to longest.

16 Mr. Roff's gasoline tank is $\frac{3}{8}$ full. Does he have more or less than half a tank of gasoline left?

17 **Write a problem** that uses mixed numbers. Solve it. Then trade it with others.

mixed review

Find the perimeter.

1
3 ft
5 ft
4 ft

2
15 in.
7 in.   7 in.
15 in.

3
5 cm
5 cm   5 cm
5 cm   5 cm
5 cm

Write a fraction or mixed number for the part that is shaded.

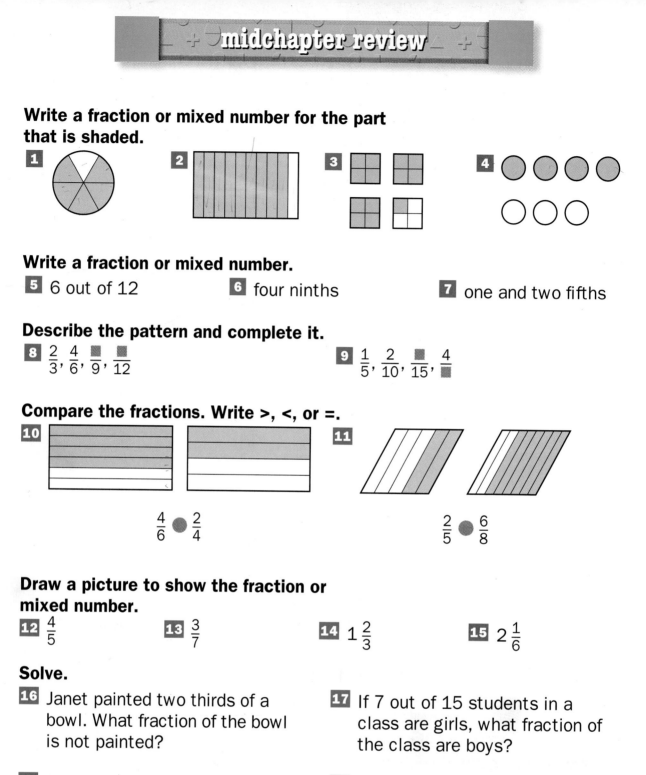

1 ⬛

2 ⬛

3 ⬛

4 ⬛

Write a fraction or mixed number.

5 6 out of 12

6 four ninths

7 one and two fifths

Describe the pattern and complete it.

8 $\frac{2}{3}, \frac{4}{6}, \frac{\blacksquare}{9}, \frac{\blacksquare}{12}$

9 $\frac{1}{5}, \frac{2}{10}, \frac{\blacksquare}{15}, \frac{4}{\blacksquare}$

Compare the fractions. Write >, <, or =.

10 $\frac{4}{6} \bullet \frac{2}{4}$

11 $\frac{2}{5} \bullet \frac{6}{8}$

Draw a picture to show the fraction or mixed number.

12 $\frac{4}{5}$

13 $\frac{3}{7}$

14 $1\frac{2}{3}$

15 $2\frac{1}{6}$

Solve.

16 Janet painted two thirds of a bowl. What fraction of the bowl is not painted?

17 If 7 out of 15 students in a class are girls, what fraction of the class are boys?

18 Don and his friends buy 2 pizzas. Each pie is cut into 6 slices. So far, they have eaten 5 slices. What mixed number tells how much they have left?

19 Joseph pours a full glass of milk. He finishes $\frac{4}{8}$ of a glass of milk. Has he finished more than $\frac{1}{2}$ of the glass?

20 _Journal_ Explain how you compare fractions.

MATH CONNECTION

Find a Fraction of a Number

You have carved 12 figures. If $\frac{1}{3}$ of the figures are animals, how many figures are animals?

You can find $\frac{1}{3}$ of 12 using models.

Think: You are given the total number and the number of groups. You need to find the number in each group.

Separate 12 into 3 equal parts.

There are 4 counters in each equal part.

$\frac{1}{3}$ of 12 is 4.

4 of the figures are animals.

Use counters to find the part.

1 $\frac{1}{2}$ of 12   **2** $\frac{1}{4}$ of 8   **3** $\frac{1}{3}$ of 6   **4** $\frac{1}{10}$ of 10

Solve.

5 There are 9 seats in a van. If $\frac{1}{3}$ of the seats are empty, how many seats are empty?

6 There are 24 muffins. If $\frac{1}{2}$ are blueberry muffins, how many blueberry muffins are there?

7 There are 15 wooden toys. If you sell $\frac{1}{5}$ of them, how many do you sell?

8 The entrance fee for a flea market is $4. If $\frac{1}{4}$ of the fee goes to charity, how much of each entrance fee goes to charity?

9 Can you model $\frac{1}{3}$ of 8? Why or why not?

10 What operation can you use to find the fraction of a number? Give an example.

DESIGNS FROM NATURE

Many designs made on fabric use repeated images of plants or animals.

Choose a Design

▶ Work in a group. Choose an object to use in a design. Collect samples of the object.

▶ Think of the pattern you want to create with the object.

> **You will need**
> - *drawing paper*
> - *newspaper*
> - *paint*
> - *paintbrush*
> - *leaves, plants, or flat objects*
> - *rolling pin or can*

Make a Design

▶ Use a paintbrush to paint the underside of the object you chose. Apply a thin layer of paint.

▶ Place the painted side of the object down on the drawing paper.

▶ For thin objects, place a sheet of newspaper on top. Then, roll a can or rolling pin over the newspaper to press the paint into the drawing paper.

▶ Repeat the steps above for each color you use.

Describing a Design

1 How many images did you use in your design?

2 What colors did you use? How many of each color are there?

3 Write fractions that describe your design.

Report Your Findings

4 **Portfolio** Prepare a report on what you learned. Include the following:

▶ Describe the image you chose to print. Why did you choose it?

▶ Describe your design. Use fractions as much as possible.

5 Compare your report with the reports of other groups.

Revise your work.

▶ Does your report explain your thoughts clearly?

▶ Did you proofread your work?

MORE TO INVESTIGATE

PREDICT what objects will be most commonly used in designs.

EXPLORE the different ways designs are made on fabric.

FIND designs you can describe using fractions.

Decimals Less Than 1

If you know how to knit, it is easy to make a blanket. Two of the 10 stripes in this knitted blanket are blue.

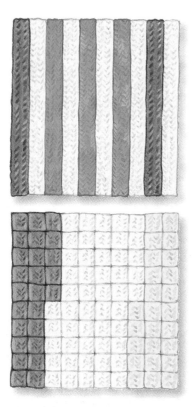

You can use a fraction or a **decimal** to name the part of the blanket that is blue.

Fraction
Write: $\frac{2}{10}$

Read: two tenths

Decimal
Write: 0.2
⌐ decimal point

Read: two tenths

In this blanket, 25 out of the 100 small knitted squares are blue.

You can use a fraction or a decimal to name the part of the blanket that is blue.

Fraction
Write: $\frac{25}{100}$

Read: twenty-five hundredths

Decimal
Write: 0.25

Read: twenty-five hundredths

Work Together

Work with a partner. Use graph paper to explore decimals. Outline 10-by-10 grids on graph paper. Color in columns to show tenths and small squares to show hundredths.

You will need
- graph paper
- crayons, colored pencils, or markers

Model these decimals.

a. 0.5 **b.** 0.7 **c.** 0.9 **d.** 0.10 **e.** 0.65 **f.** 0.09

▶ Design your own blanket by coloring a grid.

Talk It Over

▶ How are fractions and decimals alike? different?

▶ How many hundredths are in a tenth?

Make Connections
Harry and Sara describe the blanket they drew.

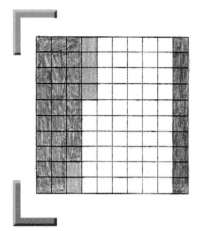

blue: twenty-eight hundredths $\frac{28}{100}$ 0.28

green: six hundredths $\frac{6}{100}$ 0.06

white: fifty-six hundredths $\frac{56}{100}$ 0.56

red: ten hundredths $\frac{10}{100}$ 0.10

▶ What does the zero mean in the decimal 0.28?

▶ What do the zeros mean in the decimal 0.06?

▶ How many tenths are in 0.10?

Check for Understanding
Write a decimal for the part that is shaded.

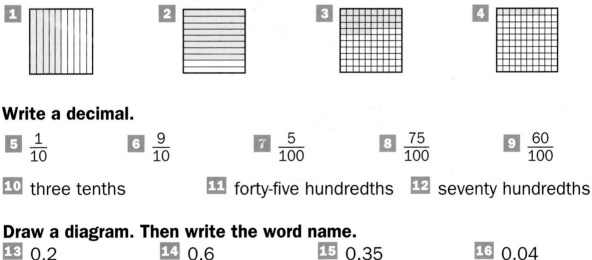

Write a decimal.

5 $\frac{1}{10}$ **6** $\frac{9}{10}$ **7** $\frac{5}{100}$ **8** $\frac{75}{100}$ **9** $\frac{60}{100}$

10 three tenths   **11** forty-five hundredths   **12** seventy hundredths

Draw a diagram. Then write the word name.

13 0.2   **14** 0.6   **15** 0.35   **16** 0.04

THINK CRITICALLY: Analyze

17 Think about how tens and hundreds are related.
Then explain how tenths and hundredths are related.

Practice

Write a decimal for the part that is shaded.

1.

2.

3.

4.

5.

6.

7.

8.

Write a decimal.

9. $\frac{5}{10}$

10. $\frac{2}{10}$

11. $\frac{9}{100}$

12. $\frac{57}{100}$

13. $\frac{83}{100}$

14. eight tenths

15. sixty-two hundredths

16. ninety hundredths

Draw a diagram. Then write the word name.

17. 0.7

18. 0.9

19. 0.42

20. 0.07

Use the number line. Write a decimal for the point.
Tell if it is close to 0, $\frac{1}{2}$, or 1.

21. A

22. B

23. C

24. D

Describe and complete the pattern.

25. 0.15, 0.25, ■, ■, ■, 0.65

26. 0.30, 0.25, ■, ■, ■, 0.05

27. 0.04, 0.08, ■, 0.16, ■, ■

28. 0.92, 0.91, ■, ■, 0.88, ■

•••••••••••••••••• **Make It Right** ••••••••••••••••••

29. Miko wrote this decimal for the diagram.
Find the error and correct it.

nine hundredths 0.9

422 Lesson 11.7

Problem Solving

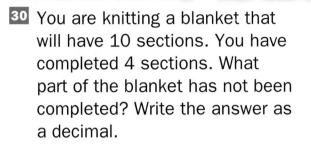

30 You are knitting a blanket that will have 10 sections. You have completed 4 sections. What part of the blanket has not been completed? Write the answer as a decimal.

31 Make a decision Suppose your friend bought a pizza. He asks you if you would like to eat $\frac{3}{8}$ of the pizza or $\frac{1}{2}$. You are very hungry, so which would you choose? Why?

32 It takes 100 pennies to make a dollar. What fraction of a dollar is a nickel? a dime? Write each amount as a decimal.

33 Hank uses 8 rolls of yarn to make a blanket. He has 24 rolls of yarn. How many blankets can he make?

34 Data Point Look through magazines and newspapers. How many different uses can you find for decimals?

35 Spatial reasoning Look at the crazy quilt below. Estimate what part of the square is shaded.

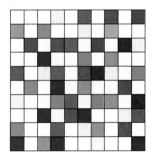

36 Inga has 3 nickels, 4 dimes, 3 quarters, and 2 one-dollar bills. How much money does she have?

more to explore

Fractions on a Calculator

You can use a calculator to help you write fractions as decimals. What decimal is equivalent to $\frac{3}{4}$?

Divide the top number by the bottom number.

Press: 3 ÷ 4 = 0.75

Use a calculator. Find the decimal equivalent for the fraction.

1 $\frac{9}{10}$ **2** $\frac{2}{5}$ **3** $\frac{1}{2}$ **4** $\frac{5}{100}$ **5** $\frac{1}{4}$

Decimals Greater Than 1

If you collect things like rocks and shells, you can show them in display boxes. What part of the two boxes has been filled?

Think: one whole box and 4 out of 10 parts of the second box

You can write a mixed number or a decimal.

Mixed Number

Write: $1\frac{4}{10}$

Read: one and four tenths

Decimal

Write: 1.4

Read: one and four tenths

One and four tenths of the boxes are filled.

More Examples

A

Write: 2.8
Read: two and eight tenths

B

Write: 1.06
Read: one and six hundredths

Check for Understanding
Write the decimal.

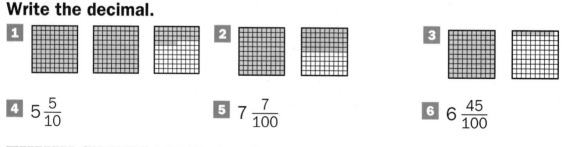

4 $5\frac{5}{10}$

5 $7\frac{7}{100}$

6 $6\frac{45}{100}$

THINK CRITICALLY: Analyze

7 Between which two whole numbers does 3.7 belong? Which whole number is 3.7 closer to? How do you know?

Practice

Write a decimal.

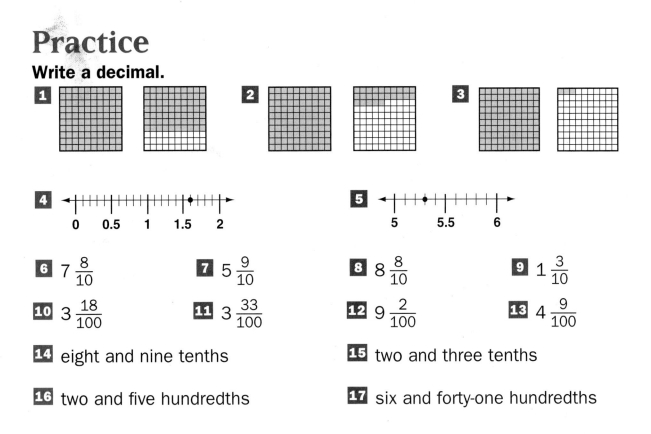

6 $7\frac{8}{10}$ **7** $5\frac{9}{10}$ **8** $8\frac{8}{10}$ **9** $1\frac{3}{10}$

10 $3\frac{18}{100}$ **11** $3\frac{33}{100}$ **12** $9\frac{2}{100}$ **13** $4\frac{9}{100}$

14 eight and nine tenths **15** two and three tenths

16 two and five hundredths **17** six and forty-one hundredths

MIXED APPLICATIONS
Problem Solving

18 Ken and Sal made their own collage boxes. Ken filled 2.7 boxes. Sal filled 2.4 boxes. Who filled more of the boxes? How do you know?

19 The same number of shells are placed in each of 4 sections. If there are 24 shells in all, how many shells are in each section?

20 Ian made a square collage box. If one side measures 10 in., what is the perimeter of the box?

21 **Write a problem** that uses a decimal greater than 1. Solve it. Give it to others to solve.

mixed review

Write *yes* or *no* to tell whether the shape is a polygon. If it is a polygon, name it.

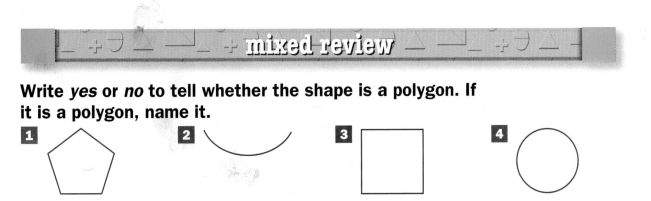

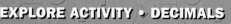

Add and Subtract Decimals

You can use graph paper grids to explore adding and subtracting decimals.

Work Together
Work with a partner.

Spin the spinner four times. Use the digits to write an addition sentence such as the following.

$$2.5 + 1.7$$

Color graph-paper grids to model the problem. Record your results.

Use your model to find the difference between the two numbers. Record your results.

$$2.5 - 1.7$$

Repeat the activity four times. Then spin the spinner six times to create decimals to the hundredths. Use models to find these sums and differences, such as the following.

a. $1.47 + 2.03$ **b.** $1.15 + 2.34$ **c.** $1.67 + 2.33$

d. $2.03 - 1.47$ **e.** $2.34 - 1.15$ **f.** $2.33 - 1.67$

Talk It Over
▶ How do you use your decimal models to add? to subtract?

You will need
- *10-by-10 grids on graph paper*
- *crayons*
- *scissors*
- *0–9 spinner*

Make Connections

Here is how Ben and Mei use models to add and subtract
2.45 and 1.27.

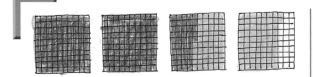

2.45 + 1.27

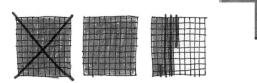

2.45 - 1.27

We added the hundredths.
  72 hundredths
Then, we added the ones.
  3 ones
So the total is 3.72.

We subtracted the hundredths.
  18 hundredths
Then, we subtracted the ones.
  1 one
So the difference is 1.18.

You can use place value to help you add and subtract
without models. Line up the decimal points. Then add or
subtract each place.

Add: 4.56 + 2.29

$$\begin{array}{r} {\scriptstyle 1} \\ 4.56 \\ +\ 2.29 \\ \hline 6.85 \end{array}$$

Subtract: 4.56 – 2.29

$$\begin{array}{r} {\scriptstyle 4\ 16} \\ 4.\cancel{5}\cancel{6} \\ -\ 2.29 \\ \hline 2.27 \end{array}$$

▶ Why do you need to line up the decimal points?

Check for Understanding

Add or subtract. You may use models.

1	**2**	**3**	**4**	**5**	**6**
0.5	0.8	2.5	5.3	3.34	4.72
+ 0.2	− 0.3	+ 4.3	− 3.5	+ 2.46	− 3.87

THINK CRITICALLY: Generalize

7 How is adding and subtracting with decimals the same
as adding and subtracting money?

Turn the page for Practice. ➡

Practice

Use models to show how you find the sum.

1

Add 2.37.

2

Add 2.56.

Use models to show how you find the difference.

3

Subtract 1.63.

4

Subtract 1.38.

Add or subtract. You may use models.

5 $\begin{array}{r} 0.4 \\ + 0.1 \end{array}$ **6** $\begin{array}{r} 0.7 \\ - 0.2 \end{array}$ **7** $\begin{array}{r} 0.5 \\ + 0.5 \end{array}$ **8** $\begin{array}{r} 0.9 \\ - 0.3 \end{array}$ **9** $\begin{array}{r} 1.6 \\ + 3.2 \end{array}$ **10** $\begin{array}{r} 4.6 \\ - 2.5 \end{array}$

11 $\begin{array}{r} 2.7 \\ + 2.8 \end{array}$ **12** $\begin{array}{r} 4.2 \\ - 1.4 \end{array}$ **13** $\begin{array}{r} 3.56 \\ + 1.06 \end{array}$ **14** $\begin{array}{r} 4.56 \\ - 3.64 \end{array}$ **15** $\begin{array}{r} 2.65 \\ + 4.76 \end{array}$ **16** $\begin{array}{r} 5.00 \\ - 3.14 \end{array}$

17 0.14 + 0.35   **18** 7.8 − 2.3   **19** 4.09 + 1.97   **20** 4.15 − 1.15

21 0.30 + 0.40 + 0.10   **22** 1.04 − 1.04   **23** 2.4 + 1.2 + 1.3

Algebra Use the properties of addition and subtraction to find the missing number.

24 2.5 + 1.2 = 1.2 + ■   **25** 4.2 − ■ = 4.2

26 1.3 + 4.2 + 6.8 = 6.8 + ■ + 4.2   **27** ■ − 1.5 = 0

············· **Make It Right** ··················

28 Gilda added 1.5 and 3.7.
Find the error and correct it.

$\begin{array}{r} 1.5 \\ + 3.7 \\ \hline 4.2 \end{array}$

29 Kate has $15. She wants to buy a kite for $11.75 and a ball of string for $1.75. Does she have enough money?

30 Hank's kite flies 34.5 m high. Cassie's kite flies 44.5 m high. Whose kite flies higher? How much higher?

31 Logical reasoning Sol, Gina, Yi, and Ira are flying kites. Yi's kite is higher than Sol's but lower than Gina's. Ira's kite is higher than Gina's. Whose kite is highest?

32 Write a problem that takes more than one step to solve. Both steps should involve adding or subtracting decimals. Solve it. Give it to others to solve.

33 Each side of a square kite measures 0.75 m. What is the perimeter of the kite?

34 Mel has a roll of ribbon 5.1 m long. He needs 2.5 m for the tail of his kite. How much ribbon will be left on the roll?

Cultural Connection Chinese Rod Numerals

By 300 B.C., the Chinese were using a place-value system of numbers. Sets of ivory or bamboo rods called *chou* were arranged on a counting board to represent numbers. Calculations were performed by moving the rods around the board.

Compare the rod numerals to these numbers.
14   406   3,790

1 How is zero shown in the rod numerals?

2 Look at the position of the rods. What pattern do you notice?

3 Choose a number. Write it using rod numerals.

Conduct an Experiment

Read | **What if someone places either 2 blue cubes and 6 yellow cubes, or 6 blue cubes and 2 yellow cubes in a bag. How could you tell how many cubes of each color there are without looking in the bag?**

Plan | You can conduct an experiment to solve the problem.

Solve | Work with a group. Take turns picking a cube from the bag. Record the result each time. Put the cube back. Shake the bag and pick again. Do this 40 times. Display the results in a bar graph.

Here are the results of one experiment.

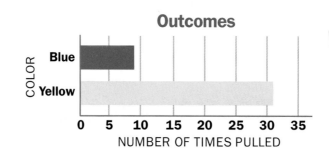

Outcomes

COLOR

Blue

Yellow

0   5   10   15   20   25   30   35
NUMBER OF TIMES PULLED

Yellow was pulled more than three times more often than blue was. You can predict there are 6 yellow cubes and 2 blue cubes in the bag.

Look Back | How can you check your experiment?

Check for Understanding

1 **What if** you had picked blue 28 times and yellow 12 times. What cubes can you predict are in the bag?

THINK CRITICALLY: Generalize

2 Explain how you can use the results of an experiment to predict what cubes are in the bag.

Problem Solving

1 Without anyone else looking, have someone place 5 cubes of one color and 1 cube of another color in a bag. Conduct an experiment to find what cubes were put in the bag.

2 Pete is planning a counter-toss game for his party. Describe an experiment he can conduct to find how far away from the throwing line he should place the cup to catch the counters.

Use the bar graph for problems 3–5.

3 Which color did the spinner stop on the most?

4 How many times was the spinner spun?

5 What do you think the spinner looked like? Draw it. Explain your reasoning.

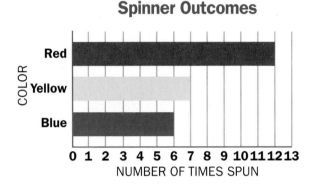

Spinner Outcomes

COLOR: Red, Yellow, Blue

NUMBER OF TIMES SPUN: 0 1 2 3 4 5 6 7 8 9 10 11 12 13

6 **Make a decision** In the game of "10," you pick number cards to try to make a sum as close to 10 as you can without going over it. You pick a 6. The cards for 1, 2, 3, 4, and 5 are left in the deck. Should you pick another card? Why or why not?

7 **Spatial reasoning** Here are two views of the same number cube. What is the number on the bottom? How do you know?

8 Val uses 24 counters in his game. There are 3 times as many red counters as there are blue counters. How many of each color counter does Val use?

9 **Write a problem** that can be solved by conducting an experiment. Solve it. Ask others to solve it. Compare your results.

10 For a game, Mary needs to put 3 red cubes and 4 blue cubes in each of 8 bags. How many cubes does she need?

11 Jay's school bus gets him home on time 4 out of 5 days. Should he expect his bus to be on time tomorrow? Why or why not?

Probability

When you and a friend play a game, you want it to be fair. Each of you should have an equal chance of winning.

Probability is the chance, or likelihood, that something will happen.

You will need
- *2-color counter*
- *graph paper*

Work Together

Work with a partner. Use a 2-color counter to explore probability and fairness.

Each of you pick a color. Take turns tossing a counter 50 times. The player whose color comes up the most wins.

Record each outcome in a tally chart. Find the total for each outcome. Then, display the results on a bar graph.

▶ Did the counter come up more often yellow, more often red, or about the same?

▶ Do you think the game is fair? Why or why not?

Compare your results with those of others.

Make Connections

Here are the results of an experiment.

24 out of 50 tosses came up red.
26 out of 50 tosses came up yellow.

The chances of the counter coming up red or yellow are equally likely. So the game is fair.

▶ **What if** you tossed the counter 50 more times. What do you think the result would be? Try it.

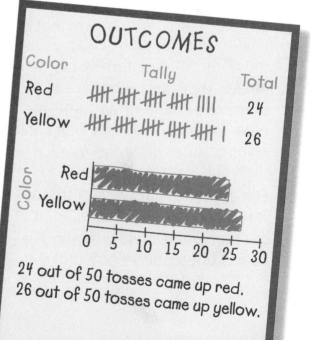

OUTCOMES

Color	Tally	Total
Red	⧼⧽	24
Yellow	⧼⧽	26

24 out of 50 tosses came up red.
26 out of 50 tosses came up yellow.

You can write the probability of the counter coming up red in two ways.

As a sentence

The probability that the counter will come up red is 1 out of 2.

As a fraction

$\frac{1}{2}$ ← number of chances it will be red
← total number of outcomes

▶ What is the probability of the counter coming up yellow?

Check for Understanding

Use the spinner for ex. 1–5.

1 Are the outcomes equally likely? Why?

2 What is the probability of the spinner stopping on red? How do you know?

3 What are the probabilities of other colors?

4 **What if** you play a game in which you get a point each time the spinner stops on your color. Is it a fair game? Why or why not?

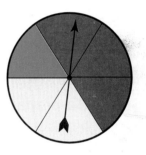

THINK CRITICALLY: Analyze **Explain your reasoning.**

5 What is the probability of the spinner stopping on white?

Practice

Use the spinner for ex. 1–3.

1 Would it be fair to use this spinner in a game? Why or why not?

2 What is the probability of spinning an 8?

3 Pick any number. Predict how many times the spinner will stop on it in 50 spins. Use a spinner like this one to test your prediction.

4 Draw your own spinner that can be used in a fair game. Give the probability of one result.

Problem Solvers at Work

Read
Plan
Solve
Look Back

Part 1 Use Alternate Methods

Henry and May are playing a game. May places 8 marbles in a bag. She gives Henry hints about what the colors of the marbles are.

Hints:

▶ $\frac{1}{2}$ of the marbles are green.

▶ You have an equal chance of pulling a red marble or a blue one.

▶ There are 2 fewer yellow marbles than there are green marbles.

Work Together

Solve. Be prepared to explain your methods.

1 What are some of the strategies that you could use to find the number of green marbles?

2 How many green marbles are there?

3 Find the number of the other color marbles. Solve the problem another way to check your answer.

4 **What if** May added a red and a blue marble to the bag. What would the probability of picking a green marble be?

5 **Take a stand** Kate says, "There is always only one best way to solve a problem." Tell whether you agree or disagree with Kate's statement. Give an example.

Part 2   Write and Share Problems

Christine counted the marbles Kim put in a bag. She wrote a problem using a line plot of the results.

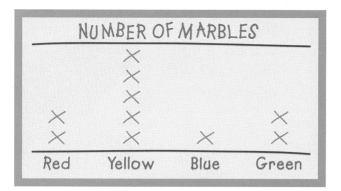

NUMBER OF MARBLES

Red	Yellow	Blue	Green

6 Solve Christine's problem.

7 Tell how you solved the problem. Solve it another way.

8 Which method do you prefer to use? Why?

9 **Write a problem** of your own that uses the information in the line plot.

10 Trade problems. Solve at least three problems written by your classmates.

11 Which problem was the most interesting? Why?

Kim had ten marbles. She put them in a bag. Shawn is going to pull one out. What do you think Shawn will pull out?

Christine Cruz
Shaughnessy Humanities School
Lowell, MA

Turn the page for Practice Strategies.

Menu

Choose five problems and solve them. Explain your methods.

1 You can fold this figure into a number cube. Is the probability of rolling each number the same? Why or why not?

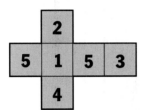

2 The weather report says there is a 1 out of 10 chance of rain today. Should you bring your umbrella? Why or why not?

3 Moesha plans to run 10 km today. She ran 2.4 km to the top of the hill. Then, she ran 6.7 km more before she stopped. How much farther does she need to run to reach her goal?

4 Loni has 3 pennies and 3 nickels in her pocket. She pulls out 3 coins. What is the greatest amount she can have if she pulls out at least one of each type of coin?

5 Kim gives 10 of the figures she has carved to Claude. This is twice as many as she gives to Sue. She keeps the last 4 figures. How many figures did Kim carve?

6 Ira places statues along the 4 walls of a gallery. The gallery measures 20 ft by 20 ft. He places a statue in every corner and one every 5 ft. How many statues are in the gallery?

7 Estimate to complete the prices and solve.
Ian buys a pad of drawing paper for ▨ and 2 markers for ▨ each. About how much does he spend?

8 Uri uses poster paint to make 4 pictures. He uses watercolors to paint 3 other pictures. What fraction of his pictures are watercolors?

**Choose two problems and solve them.
Explain your methods.**

9 There are 6 cards in a set. Each card may have the number 1, 2, or 3 written on it. Study the tally chart. Write three facts you can find from the results of the experiment.

Outcomes of Pick-a-Card Experiment		
Number	**Tally**	**Total**
1	~~IIII~~ ~~IIII~~ ~~IIII~~ ~~IIII~~ ~~IIII~~ ~~IIII~~ II	32
2	~~IIII~~ ~~IIII~~ ~~IIII~~ II	17
3		0

10 **Spatial reasoning** Can you get all the cups right side up? You must make three moves, no more and no less. You must turn over two cups each time you move.

11 Fold an 8-in. by 8-in. square diagonally in half. Color $\frac{1}{2}$ red. Continue to fold the paper diagonally. Unfold the paper each time to find other fractions equivalent to $\frac{1}{2}$. Do you think $\frac{32}{64}$ is equivalent to $\frac{1}{2}$? Why or why not?

12 **At the Computer** You can run probability experiments by making the computer simulate the tossing of two coins.

What is the probability of both coins showing heads?

Predict how many times this should occur in 40 tries; 80 tries; 120 tries.

Run the simulations to check your predictions.

Language and Mathematics

Complete the sentence. Use a word in the chart.

1 A ■ is made up of a whole number and a fraction.

2 A ■ names equal parts of a whole.

3 Fractions that name the same number are ■.

4 Four tenths can be written as a fraction or as a ■.

5 The chance, or likeliness, that something will happen is its ■.

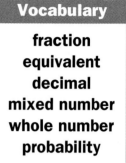

Vocabulary
fraction
equivalent
decimal
mixed number
whole number
probability

Concepts and Skills

Write a fraction or mixed number for the part that is shaded.

6

7

8

Write a fraction or mixed number.

9 5 out of 9

10 three fourths

11 six and two thirds

Complete to name the equivalent fraction.

12

$$\frac{1}{3} = \frac{\blacksquare}{12}$$

13

$$\frac{2}{5} = \frac{\blacksquare}{10}$$

14

$$\frac{2}{8} = \frac{\blacksquare}{4}$$

Compare the fractions. Write >, <, or =.

15 $\frac{6}{7} \bullet \frac{3}{7}$

16 $\frac{1}{2} \bullet \frac{3}{6}$

17 $\frac{5}{6} \bullet \frac{5}{8}$

18 $\frac{1}{4} \bullet \frac{3}{5}$

Write a decimal for the part that is shaded.

19 **20** **21**

Add or subtract.

22
$$0.65$$
$$+0.17$$

23
$$0.74$$
$$-0.36$$

24
$$1.6$$
$$+3.2$$

25
$$4.1$$
$$-3.2$$

Think critically.

26 Analyze. Ollie says the probability of spinning red is 1 out of 3. Find the error and correct it.

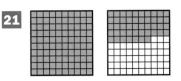

MIXED APPLICATIONS

Problem Solving

Pencil & Paper Calculator Mental Math

27 Roger paints 6 stripes on his wall. He paints 2 stripes blue, 2 stripes green, and 2 stripes red. What fraction of the stripes are blue?

28 Hal used 2.75 kg of clay in his sculpture. Eva used 3.25 kg in hers. Who used more clay? how much more?

29 The weather report says there is an 8 out of 10 chance of snow today. Should you wear your snow boots? Why or why not?

30 Ken used $\frac{3}{4}$ of a can of paint. Marge used $\frac{3}{8}$ of a can. Who used less paint?

Use the jar for problems 31–33.

31 What is the probability of picking a red ball? a blue ball? a yellow ball?

32 Predict which ball you will pick most often if you pick 50 times and return the ball each time. How do you know?

33 How can you make the outcomes equally likely?

Fractions, Decimals, and Probability **439**

Write a fraction or mixed number for the part that is shaded.

1

2

3

Complete to name the equivalent fraction.

4

$$\frac{1}{4} = \frac{\blacksquare}{12}$$

5

$$\frac{10}{12} = \frac{\blacksquare}{6}$$

6

$$\frac{2}{5} = \frac{\blacksquare}{10}$$

Compare the fractions. Write >, <, or =.

7 $\frac{4}{5} \bullet \frac{2}{5}$

8 $\frac{1}{5} \bullet \frac{2}{10}$

9 $\frac{1}{3} \bullet \frac{5}{9}$

Write a decimal for the part that is shaded.

10

11

12

Add or subtract.

13   0.54
     + 0.28

14   0.85
     − 0.28

15   2.7
     + 5.2

16   5.2
     − 3.4

Solve

17 Pat wants to know if the number-cube tosser in her game is fair. Describe an experiment she can conduct to check it.

18 Joe used 2.50 cups of flour in his cake. Lea used 2.25 cups in hers. Who used more flour? How much more flour?

Use the spinner for problems 19–20.

19 What is the probability of the spinner stopping on blue?

20 Predict which color the spinner will stop on the least if you spin 50 times. Explain.

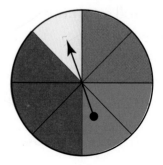

What Did You Learn?

Look at a 0–9 spinner. Answer these questions.

▶ What part of the spinner is covered by odd numbers? Write it as a fraction and as a decimal.

▶ **What if** you spin 50 times? Predict if the spinner will stop on numbers 5 or greater more or fewer times than it stops on numbers less than 5.

▶ Conduct an experiment to test your prediction. Record your work in a graph. Write a conclusion based on your results.

······················ **A Good Answer** ······················
- shows the fraction and decimal names for the parts of the spinner
- gives your prediction based on the probability of the spinner stopping on the number 5 or greater
- clearly shows the results of your experiment and your conclusions

You may want to place your work in your portfolio.

What Do You Think❓

1 Do you think you know what a fraction is?
How do you identify what fraction of the whole a part is?
If you are unsure, what do you do?

2 List all the ways you might use to find equivalent fractions.
- Use fraction strips.
- Use patterns.
- Draw a picture.
- Other. Explain.

Fabulous Fibers

Cultural Note

Fibers can be woven into cloth on a *loom.* The first automatic loom was invented in 1804 by Joseph Jacquard in France. It used punched cards to program the loom to make fabric.

1 Among the oldest examples of cloth are pieces of linen found in Switzerland. They are about 7,000 years old. Linen is a cloth made from flax.

2 Other types of cloth made from plant fibers include cotton and burlap, which is made from jute.

3 Several types of fibers come from animals. Wool from sheep is the most common. Cloth is also made from the hair of llamas, alpacas, and rabbits and from the cocoons of silkworms.

4 Until this century, all fabrics came from natural sources. Today, many fibers are created in laboratories. The first synthetic fiber, rayon, was made from wood. Most synthetic fibers are made from the chemicals found in oil.

▶ Why are different kinds of clothing made from different fibers?

▶ Why do you think scientists create new synthetic fibers?

Finding Fiber Fractions

Several types of fibers are often blended together. Mixing different amounts of each type of fiber makes cloth with different characteristics.

1 If a sweater is made from 2 parts silk and 1 part rayon, what fraction of the sweater is made from silk?

2 If a shirt is made from 6 parts cotton and 4 parts nylon, what fraction of the shirt is made from cotton?

3 Check the labels on your clothes. What types of fibers are you wearing?

4 Survey your class. What type of fabric is most common? least common? What fraction of your class is wearing each type of fiber?

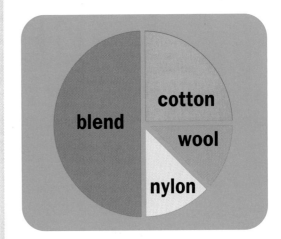

5 Use graphing software to make a table and circle graph of the fibers worn by your class.

6 Write two statements about your class based on the graph.

THEME Entertainment

In this chapter, you will see people gather in groups to put on shows and to go to shows. Multiplying and dividing help them to plan entertainment.

What Do You Know ?

Explain how you solved problems 1–2.

1 There are 4 sections of seats in a small theater. Each section has 3 rows. There are 5 seats in each row. How many rows are there in the theater? How many seats?

2 If each row seats 5 people, how many rows will a group of 45 people need? 50 people? 55 people?

3 **Portfolio** Design your own 72-seat theater. Tell how many equal rows there are and how many seats are in each row. Find another way to arrange the seats.

Multiplication Patterns

Where do cartoons come from? Animators draw on cels and then film them. How much would it cost to buy 8 light tables, 6 packs of cels, and 3 animation disks?

Studio needs:
8 light tables	$100 each
6 packs of cels	$50 each
3 animation disks	$400 each

Use what you know about basic facts to multiply mentally. You can use patterns to help.

8 light tables	6 packs of cels	3 animation disks
8 × 1 = 8	6 × 5 = 30	3 × 4 = 12
8 × 10 = 80	6 × 50 = 300	3 × 40 = 120
8 × 100 = 800		3 × 400 = 1,200

Think: 8 × 1 ten = 8 tens
8 × 1 hundred = 8 hundreds

Think: 6 × 5 tens = 30 tens

Think: 3 × 4 tens = 12 tens
3 × 4 hundreds = 12 hundreds

The light tables cost $800.

The cels cost $300.

The disks cost $1,200.

Check for Understanding

Complete. Describe the pattern.

1 6 × 1 = ■
6 × 10 = ■
6 × 100 = ■

2 5 × 3 = ■
5 × 30 = ■
5 × 300 = ■

3 4 × 5 = ■
4 × 50 = ■
4 × 500 = ■

Multiply mentally. Explain your method.

4 7 × 10   **5** 9 × 20   **6** 60 × 8   **7** 9 × 200   **8** 8 × 500

THINK CRITICALLY: Generalize   Explain your reasoning.

9 How would you find 3 × 4,000? 6 × 5,000?

Practice

Complete.

1 9 × 1 ten = 9 tens = ■

2 8 × 4 tens = ■ tens = 320

3 5 × 9 tens = ■ tens = ■

4 5 × 2 tens = ■ tens = ■

Copy and complete the pattern.

5 7 × 1 = ■
7 × 10 = ■
7 × 100 = ■

6 6 × 3 = ■
6 × 30 = ■
6 × 300 = ■

7 2 × 5 = ■
2 × 50 = ■
2 × 500 = ■

Multiply mentally.

8 3 × 10

9 2 × 40

10 3 × 100

11 3 × 200

12 2 × 200

13 4 × 70

14 6 × 800

15 4 × 100

16 7 × 800

17 90 × 7

18 600 × 6

19 9 × 900

20 7 × 60

21 3 × 300

22 8 × 800

MIXED APPLICATIONS
Problem Solving
Pencil & Paper | Calculator | Mental Math

23 In an animation studio, the cel painters finish 100 cels a day. How many cels get painted in 3 days?

24 An animator films cels for 1 hour 30 minutes. If the film shoot begins at 9:30 A.M., at what time does it end?

25 There are 30 video pictures, or frames, in every second of a cartoon. How many frames are in a 4-second spaceship landing?

26 An art show has an $80 budget. Programs cost $25.75. Food costs $29.90. About how much will be left?

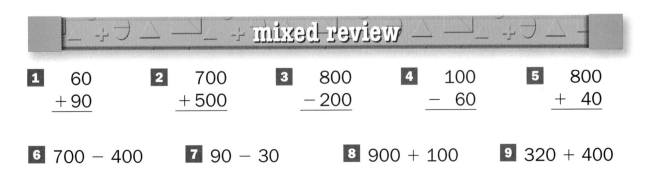

mixed review

1 60
+ 90

2 700
+ 500

3 800
− 200

4 100
− 60

5 800
+ 40

6 700 − 400

7 90 − 30

8 900 + 100

9 320 + 400

Estimate Products

At Ballet Folklórico de Mexico, dancers rehearse before a major production. About how many hours will the dancers rehearse before they perform?

Rehearsal Schedule	
Hours of practice per day	6
Days of practice	68

Estimate: 6 × 68

Understanding how to multiply by tens and hundreds can help you estimate products. Round the factor that is greater than 10. Then multiply mentally.

Think: Round to the nearest ten.
$$6 \times 68$$
$$\downarrow \quad \downarrow$$
$$6 \times 70 = 420$$

The dancers will rehearse about 420 hours.

Cultural Note
Ballet folklórico is the traditional dance of Mexico. Many companies practice and perform in Mexico and in the United States.

More Examples

A Estimate: 2 × 291

Think: Round to the nearest hundred.
2 × 300 = 600

B Estimate: 6 × 549

Think: Round to the nearest hundred.
6 × 500 = 3,000

Check for Understanding
Estimate the product. Tell how you rounded.

1 4 × 18   **2** 6 × 53   **3** 9 × 623   **4** 8 × 472   **5** 7 × 394

THINK CRITICALLY: Generalize Explain your reasoning.

6 How do you use basic facts to help you estimate products?

Practice

Estimate the product by rounding.

1 4 × 72　**2** 2 × 16　**3** 6 × 29　**4** 8 × 67　**5** 4 × 39

6 7 × 96　**7** 5 × 24　**8** 8 × 77　**9** 5 × 483　**10** 3 × 411

11 4 × 650　**12** 5 × 829　**13** 3 × 169　**14** 8 × 361　**15** 5 × 623

16 6 × 739　**17** 4 × $982　**18** 7 × $68　**19** 3 × $902　**20** 9 × $252

Algebra **Estimate. Write > or < to make a true sentence.**

21 2 × 43 ● 76　　**22** 6 × 87 ● 675　　**23** 5 × 76 ● 356

24 8 × 146 ● 460　　**25** 3 × 286 ● 600　　**26** 4 × 631 ● 3,082

MIXED APPLICATIONS
Problem Solving

27 At intermission, each of the 50 students buys a cup of Mexican hot chocolate for $1.25 and sweet bread for 75¢. About how much do the students spend in all?

28 **Spatial reasoning** A stage is 25 ft wide. The stage is about as wide as:
a. a door.
b. a classroom.
c. a football field.

Estimate the cost.

29 37 music CDs

30 47 woven wallets

31 183 folklóric dolls

32 99 dozen bracelets

Souvenirs	
Type of Souvenir	**Wholesale Price**
Music CD	$9 each
Folklóric doll	$7 each
Woven wallet	$5 each
Friendship bracelet	$3 per dozen

mixed review

1 86 + 12 + 32　　**2** 301 + 163 + 422　　**3** 59 + 27 + 43 + 65

4 90 + 37 + 41　　**5** 800 + 192 + 351　　**6** 729 + 510 + 220

Multiply by 1-Digit Numbers

Imagine traveling the world with a children's choir! Part of a choir director's job is to audition new singers. Suppose a choir director wants 3 rows of 16 students at a tryout. How many students will he audition?

Work Together
Work in a group. Use place-value models to find 3×16. Record your work.

Note: 3×16 means 3 groups of 16.

▶ How many students will he audition?

Choir director leading
the chorus in a concert

▶ Use place-value models to find two other ways the students can be arranged in equal rows. What do you notice about the products?

▶ Use place-value models to find the product.
   a. 4×18 **b.** 5×14 **c.** 3×32 **d.** 2×45 **e.** 6×13

Talk It Over

▶ How did you use the models to find the products?

▶ How can you use the multiplication facts you know to find the products of greater numbers?

You will need
• *place-value models*

Make Connections

Here is how two groups found 3×16.

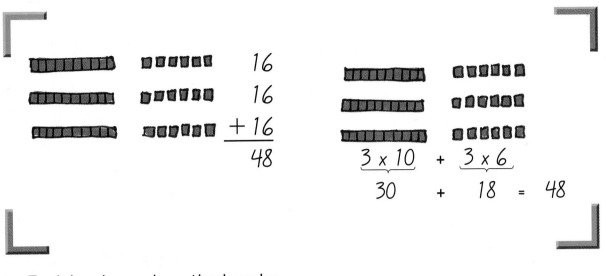

$$16$$
$$16$$
$$+ 16$$
$$48$$

$$\underbrace{3 \times 10}_{} + \underbrace{3 \times 6}_{}$$
$$30 + 18 = 48$$

▶ Explain why each method works.

Check for Understanding

Write the multiplication sentence. Find the product.

1.

2.

Multiply. You may use models.

3. 2×31

4. 3×43

5. 7×11

6. 5×15

7. 7×12

8. 4×14

9. 5×21

10. 3×31

11. 6×13

12. 8×11

THINK CRITICALLY: Analyze

13. **Journal** Explain how this recording tells about the model.

$$15$$
$$\times\ 4$$
$$20$$
$$+ 40$$
$$60$$

Turn the page for Practice.

Practice

Complete. Use place-value models if you need to.

1 3 groups of ■ = ■

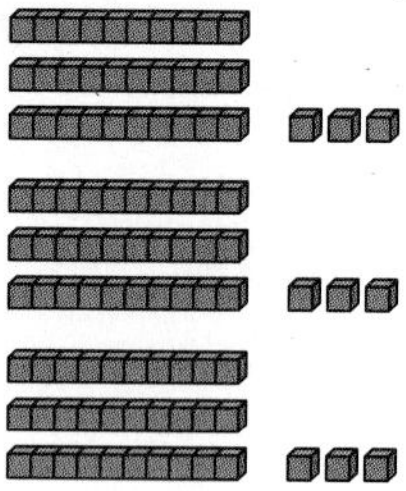

2 3 groups of ■ = ■

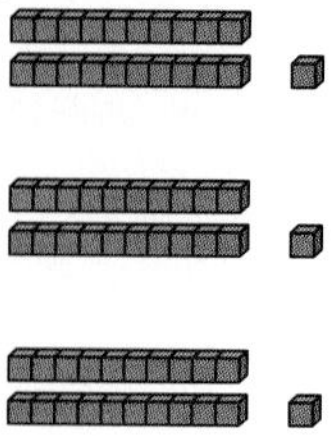

3 4 groups of ■ = ■

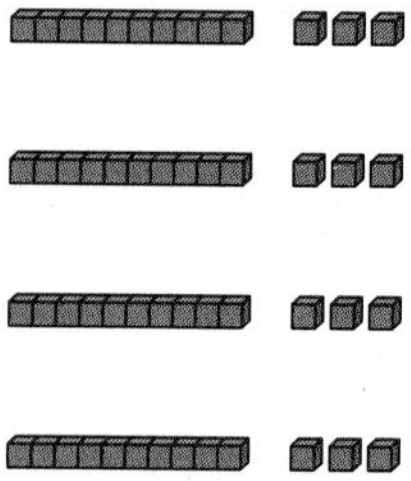

4 ■ groups of 42 = ■

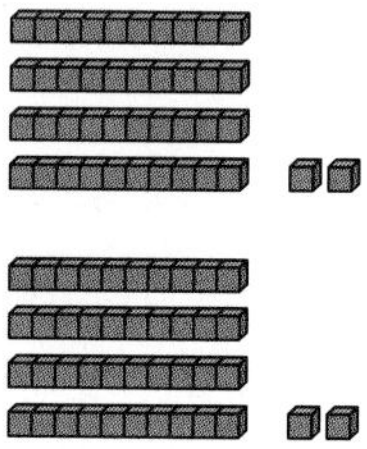

5 ■ groups of 35 = ■

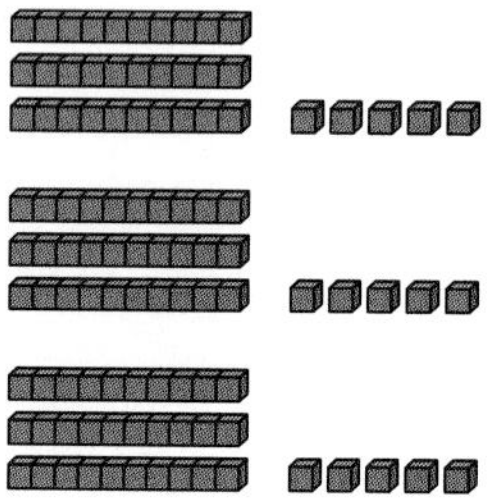

6 ■ groups of ■ = ■

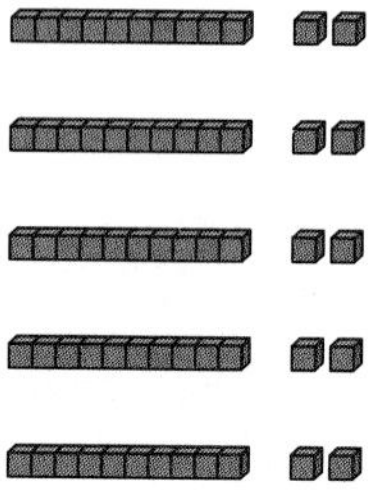

Multiply using any method.

7 3 × 13　　**8** 2 × 32　　**9** 3 × 23　　**10** 3 × 32　　**11** 5 × 19

12 4 × 22　　**13** 9 × 11　　**14** 6 × 15　　**15** 7 × 14　　**16** 8 × 21

17　12
　　× 3

18　43
　　× 2

19　22
　　× 3

20　13
　　× 5

21　44
　　× 2

22　36
　　× 2

Estimate to match the multiplication with a product in the box.

23 4 × 83　　**24** 9 × 77　　**25** 8 × 59

26 9 × 99　　**27** 3 × 49　　**28** 7 × 39

Products		
332	273	147
472	693	891

················· **Make It Right** ·················

29 This is the way Lorenzo recorded how he found the product of 3 x 18. Find the error and correct it.

```
   18
 × 3
   24
 + 3
   27
```

Use the poster for problems 30–33.

30 Mr. Hansen buys 4 adult tickets to the show. How much does he spend?

31 The Music Club has $50. Do they have enough to buy 6 children's tickets? Explain your reasoning.

The Fabulous
Cory School Chorus
See the show at 7:30 P.M.
Tickets: Adults $14
          Children $8
Buy 10 tickets and get 1 free!

32 The chorus's performance ends at 9:30 P.M. There is one 15-minute intermission. How long does the chorus perform?

33 Mrs. Hart wants to take a group of 10 students to the show. What is the cost of tickets for herself and the students?

Cultural Connection   The Yoruba Number System

The Yoruba people live in Nigeria. In the Yoruba number system, 14 is described as 10 plus 4. Numbers 15 or higher are based on 20.

A Yoruba person thinks how many groups of 20 are in a number and how much is added or subtracted. Here are some examples.

    15 = one group of 20, minus 5
    24 = one group of 20, plus 4
    45 = three groups of 20, minus 10, minus 5

Describe the number in the Yoruba system.

1 43   **2** 12   **3** 49   **4** 55   **5** 90

6 What mental math skills help you to understand the Yoruba way of describing numbers?

Multiply by 1-Digit Numbers

There is a lot to watch at a 3-ring circus. The entire cast comes out for the opening act. Suppose there are 25 performers in each ring. How many performers are in the act?

Multiply: 3×25

In the last lesson, you saw that you can multiply by using models and by recording the tens and ones separately.

$$
\begin{array}{r}
25 \\
\times\ 3 \\
\hline
15 \\
+\ 60 \\
\hline
75
\end{array}
$$

Here is another way to multiply.

Step 1

Multiply the ones.
Regroup if necessary.

$$
\begin{array}{r}
\overset{1}{2}5 \\
\times\ 3 \\
\hline
5
\end{array}
$$

Think: 3×5 ones $= 15$ ones
15 ones $= 1$ ten 5 ones

Step 2

Multiply the tens.
Add all the tens.

$$
\begin{array}{r}
\overset{1}{2}5 \\
\times\ 3 \\
\hline
75
\end{array}
$$

Think: 3×2 tens $= 6$ tens
6 tens $+ 1$ ten $= 7$ tens

There are 75 performers in the act.

Talk It Over

▶ After regrouping the ones, how do you show it on your paper?

▶ How can you estimate to check that 75 is a reasonable answer?

Suppose you take a backstage tour after the circus. There are 2 tour groups. Each group has 65 people. How many people are on the tour?

Estimate: 2 × 65   **Think:** 2 × 70 = 140

Multiply: 2 × 65

Step 1
Multiply the ones.
Regroup if necessary.

$$\begin{array}{r} \overset{1}{6}5 \\ \times\ 2 \\ \hline 0 \end{array}$$

Think: 2 × 5 ones = 10 ones
10 ones = 1 ten 0 ones

Step 2
Multiply the tens.
Add all the tens.

$$\begin{array}{r} \overset{1}{6}5 \\ \times\ 2 \\ \hline 130 \end{array}$$

Think: 2 × 6 tens = 12 tens
12 tens + 1 ten = 13 tens
13 tens = 1 hundred 3 tens

There are 130 people on the tour.

▶ How many times did you need to regroup?
How did you show the regrouping on your paper?

More Examples

A
$$\begin{array}{r} 43 \\ \times\ 2 \\ \hline 86 \end{array}$$

B
$$\begin{array}{r} \overset{2}{1}8 \\ \times\ 3 \\ \hline 54 \end{array}$$

C
$$\begin{array}{r} \$72 \\ \times\ 4 \\ \hline \$288 \end{array}$$

D
$$\begin{array}{r} \overset{3}{\$5}5 \\ \times\ 6 \\ \hline \$330 \end{array}$$

Check for Understanding
Multiply using any method. Estimate to check the reasonableness of your answer.

1
$$\begin{array}{r} 41 \\ \times\ 4 \end{array}$$

2
$$\begin{array}{r} 29 \\ \times\ 3 \end{array}$$

3
$$\begin{array}{r} \$92 \\ \times\ 6 \end{array}$$

4
$$\begin{array}{r} 84 \\ \times\ 2 \end{array}$$

5
$$\begin{array}{r} \$15 \\ \times\ 8 \end{array}$$

6
$$\begin{array}{r} 75 \\ \times\ 2 \end{array}$$

THINK CRITICALLY: Compare

7 Explain how these two methods are alike.

$$\begin{array}{r} \overset{1}{6}5 \\ \times\ 2 \\ \hline 130 \end{array} \qquad \begin{array}{r} 65 \\ \times\ 2 \\ \hline 10 \\ +\ 120 \\ \hline 130 \end{array}$$

Turn the page for Practice. ➥

Practice

Multiply using any method. Remember to estimate.

1 22
× 3

2 13
× 3

3 29
× 2

4 43
× 5

5 86
× 4

6 73
× 2

7 81
× 7

8 54
× 5

9 91
× 8

10 48
× 3

11 18
× 4

12 32
× 4

13 $35
× 6

14 $41
× 7

15 $13
× 9

16 56
× 6

17 43
× 6

18 64
× 6

19 7 × 61   **20** 4 × $34   **21** 4 × 52   **22** 6 × $47   **23** 7 × 52

Estimate first. Find only the products that are greater than 200. Write *under 200* for the others.

24 3 × 48   **25** 8 × 27   **26** 4 × 62   **27** 7 × 18   **28** 5 × 42

Algebra Copy and complete the table.

29

Rule: Multiply by 60.				
Minutes	1	2	6	7
Seconds	▨	▨	▨	▨

30

Rule: Multiply by 12.				
Cartons	1	3	5	8
Eggs	▨	▨	▨	▨

MIXED APPLICATIONS
Problem Solving

Pencil & Paper   Calculator   Mental Math

31 The largest big-top circus tent was 300 ft longer in length than in width. The tent was 200 ft wide. How long was it?

32 Danny has been a clown with a truck circus for 14 years. How many months has he toured with the circus? See INFOBIT.

33 **Write a problem** using the information in the INFOBIT. Trade problems with a classmate and solve them.

INFOBIT
Truck circuses usually tour 7 months a year. Railroad circuses stay on tour for over 10 months a year.

Big Top Adventure Game!

Use the game board to travel around the circus grounds.

Play the Game

▶ Play with a partner or in teams.

▶ Spin three numbers. Write a 1-digit number and a 2-digit number. Find their product. Have your partner check.

▶ If you are correct, take that amount of money out of the bank. Then move either 1 or 2 spaces on the game board.

▶ Take turns.

▶ The player with the greatest amount of money at the end is the winner.

What strategies did you use to play the game?

You will need
- *0–9 spinner*
- *play money*
- *game marker pieces*

---

more to explore

Using Front Digits to Estimate

Here is another way to estimate a product.

Estimate: 7 × 64   **Think:** Multiply the front digits. 7 × 60 = 420

Use the front digits to estimate the product.

1 5 × 62   **2** 7 × 85   **3** 8 × 46   **4** 4 × 77   **5** 6 × 62

Multiply mentally.

1 4 × 40   **2** 9 × 100   **3** 5 × 20   **4** 6 × 600

5 7 × 20   **6** 8 × 300   **7** 3 × 900   **8** 4 × 80

Estimate the cost.

9 29 adult tickets bought in advance

10 41 children's tickets bought in advance

11 58 adult tickets bought at the door

12 18 children's tickets bought at the door

Community Talent Night

Ticket Prices
Tickets in advance
Adult $8
Child $3
Tickets at the door
Adult $9
Child $4

Multiply using any method.

13 21 × 7   **14** 62 × 9   **15** 39 × 2   **16** 90 × 6   **17** 47 × 5

18 3 × 31   **19** 6 × 83   **20** 8 × 65

Solve. Use mental math when you can.

21 Mrs. Martinez reserved 6 rows of 18 theater seats. There are 120 members of her group who want to go. Did she reserve enough seats? Why or why not?

22 Mrs. Jackson and six helpers make decorations for the Spring Concert. They each make 20 paper flowers. How many paper flowers do they make in all?

23 The Student Council wants to raise $50. They have 16 cakes to sell at the Spring Concert. Should they sell the cakes for $3, $4, or $5 each? Why?

24 Evan and 4 friends each buy tickets for the circus setup in the park. The tickets cost $13 each. How much do they spend in all?

25 Journal Explain as many different ways as you can to find 3 × 62.

Graph a Function

For a spring play, 20 in. of crepe paper is needed to decorate each sunflower dancer's face. How much crepe paper is needed for 4 dancers? for 5 dancers?

You can multiply. You can also use a graph to "see" the products.

Graph the ordered pairs from the table. Then draw a line through and beyond the points.

Sunflower Dance Costumes	
Number of Dancers	**Inches of Crepe Paper**
1	20
2	40
3	60
4	■
5	■

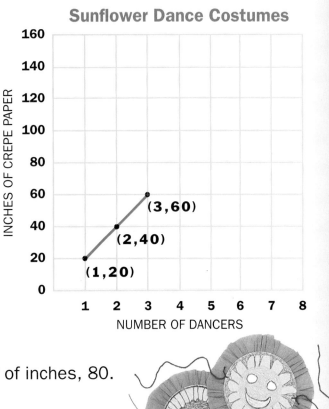

Sunflower Dance Costumes

Use the line to find 4 × 20. Read up from 4 to the line.

Then read across to find the number of inches, 80.

Now find 5 × 20.

Four dancers need 80 in. of crepe paper. Five dancers need 100 in.

Solve.

1 Use the crepe-paper graph. How many inches are needed for 6, 7, or 8 dancers? How can you tell?

2 Each costume vest needs 25 sequins. Copy and complete the table. Draw the graph. Find how many sequins are needed for 3, 4, and 5 vests.

Costume Vests	
Number of Vests	**Number of Sequins**
1	25
2	50
3	■
4	■
5	■

Produce a Show

Suppose you are the producer of a school show. You get to make the decisions.

▶ What kind of a show will you do? A talent show? A musical?

▶ When and where will you perform the show?

▶ How many people do you think will come?

▶ When will the performances be?

In this activity, you will work in teams to plan a school show.

Think about where you could perform your show and who would want to see it.

▶ What space is available in your school?

▶ When can other students, parents, and members of the community come to see the show?

▶ How many performances will you do?

Planning Your Show

1 As a team, decide where to perform your show.

2 Estimate the total number of people you expect to come.

3 Decide on when to perform the show, the number of performances needed, and a ticket price.

4 You could survey parents to find the best time or day for them to come or to find what price parents and students think is fair.

Report Your Findings

5 **Portfolio** Prepare a report on what you learned. Include the following:

▶ Make a sign to advertise your show. Include the dates and the ticket prices.

▶ Explain how you made your decisions. If you took a survey, include the results of the survey.

▶ Show any math that you did to determine the number of performances and to find the number of seats needed.

6 Compare your report with the reports of other teams.

Revise your work.

▶ Is your sign neat and easy to read? Is all the necessary information there?

▶ Is all of your math correct?

▶ Did you proofread the report?

MORE TO INVESTIGATE

EXPLORE how performing arts groups decide on the number of performances to give.

PREDICT the amount of money your show could raise.

FIND out what other schools charge for performances.

Solve a Simpler Problem

Read | **Donna Ling is the lighting designer for the Acadia Theater. How much does she plan to spend on lighting equipment?**

Lighting equipment

Buy: 8 stage lights for $77 each

Rent: Spotlight for 6 days for $85 per day

Plan | You can sometimes see how to solve a problem by first solving a simpler problem.

Solve | Try using smaller or easier numbers instead of the numbers in the original problem.

Buy 2 stage lights at $10 each.

Rent spotlight for 2 days for $5 per day.

Solve the simpler problem.

Cost of stage lights:
2 × $10 = $20

Cost of spotlight:
2 × $5 = $10

Total cost:
$20 + $10 = $30

Now solve the original problem the same way.

Cost of stage lights:
8 × $77 = $616

Cost of spotlight:
6 × $85 = $510

Total cost:
$616 + $510 = $1,126

Donna plans to spend $1,126 on lighting equipment.

Look Back | How could you solve this problem another way?

Check for Understanding

1 Donna hired an electrician twice. The first time, he worked 4 hours, and the second time, he worked 5 hours. He charges $38 an hour. How much did she pay him in all?

THINK CRITICALLY: Analyze **Explain your reasoning.**

2 Tell how you could use a simpler problem to help you see how to solve problem 1.

1 Auditions for the new show begin at 10 A.M. There are 75 people scheduled to perform. If each person takes 3 minutes, at what time will the auditions be over?

2 On Saturday, the Acadia Theater box office sells 59 children's tickets for $6 each and 43 adult tickets for $9 each. How much money does the box office take in that day?

Use the pictograph for problems 3–4.

3 The Acadia Theater took a survey to see which play people would most like to see. How many people did they survey in all?

Which Play Would You Prefer to See?	
Sleeping Beauty	🧍 🧍 🧍 🧍 🧍
Pinocchio	🧍 🧍 ♪
Hansel and Gretel	🧍 ♪
Little Women	🧍 🧍 🧍 ♪

Key: Each 🧍 stands for 10 people.
♪ stands for 5 people.

4 **Write a problem** using the information in the pictograph. Trade problems with at least three other classmates. Solve them and check each other's answers.

5 At intermission, the snack bar sells 6 dozen oatmeal cookies, 42 small cups of lemonade, and 55 large cups of coffee. How many items does the snack bar sell in all?

6 For a recent production of *Peter Pan*, 5,000 programs were printed. After the run of the show, there were 279 programs left over. How many programs were used?

7 Look at the table below. About how much do the costumes for the four characters cost?

Character	Costume Cost
Captain Hook	$79.58
Wendy	$23.26
Tiger Lily	$32.69
Peter Pan	$27.15

8 **Logical reasoning** The theater snack bar sells pieces of 2 cakes. Each cake is the same size. The carrot cake is cut into 12 equal pieces. The chocolate cake is cut into 8 equal pieces. The same number of pieces are sold from each cake. Which cake has more left over? Explain your thinking.

Division Patterns

Do you think it would be fun to make your own TV show? Suppose you have a 240-minute videotape. Your class breaks into 6 crews. If you share the tape equally, how many minutes does each crew get?

You can use what you know about basic facts to divide mentally. You can use patterns to help.

24 ÷ 6 = 4   **Think:** 24 ones ÷ 6 = 4 ones
240 ÷ 6 = 40   24 tens ÷ 6 = 4 tens

Each crew gets 40 minutes.

What if there are 200 students who want to make TV programs. They must work in teams of 5 students each. How many different TV programs will there be?

20 ÷ 5 = 4   **Think:** 20 ones ÷ 5 = 4 ones
200 ÷ 5 = 40   20 tens ÷ 5 = 4 tens

There will be 40 programs.

Check for Understanding

Complete. Describe the pattern.

1 8 ÷ 2 = ■ 　　　　**2** 40 ÷ 8 = ■ 　　　　**3** 24 ÷ 4 = ■
　 80 ÷ 2 = ■ 　　　　　　 400 ÷ 8 = ■ 　　　　　　 240 ÷ 4 = ■
　 800 ÷ 2 = ■

Divide mentally. Explain your method.

4 90 ÷ 3 　　**5** 80 ÷ 4 　　**6** 150 ÷ 5 　　**7** 200 ÷ 5 　　**8** 560 ÷ 7

THINK CRITICALLY: Generalize **Explain your reasoning.**

9 Does the number of zeros in the dividend tell you the number of zeros in the quotient? Give examples.

Practice

Complete.

1 6 tens ÷ 2 = 3 tens = ■

2 9 tens ÷ 3 = ■ tens = 30

3 42 tens ÷ 6 = ■ tens = ■

4 20 tens ÷ 4 = ■ tens = ■

Copy and complete the pattern.

5 6 ÷ 2 = ■
60 ÷ 2 = ■
600 ÷ 2 = ■

6 54 ÷ 9 = ■
540 ÷ 9 = ■

7 30 ÷ 5 = ■
300 ÷ 5 = ■

Divide mentally.

8 60 ÷ 2

9 70 ÷ 7

10 100 ÷ 5

11 630 ÷ 9

12 160 ÷ 8

13 150 ÷ 3

14 420 ÷ 7

15 480 ÷ 6

16 240 ÷ 3

17 120 ÷ 2

18 400 ÷ 5

19 350 ÷ 7

20 490 ÷ 7

21 540 ÷ 9

22 450 ÷ 9

MIXED APPLICATIONS
Problem Solving

Pencil & Paper   *Calculator*   *Mental Math*

23 Spatial reasoning Do you think that the blue segments are congruent? Test your answer.

24 Mara watched her friend's Hollywood vacation video from 9:35 P.M. to 10:15 P.M. How many minutes long was the video?

25 Make a decision Tickets for a local TV show cost $5. Seats in the front cost $9.50. Front-row seats include a free program worth $1.50. Which tickets would you buy? Explain.

26 You have a 180-minute videotape. You want to shoot about the same amount every day of your 9-day vacation. About how many minutes is that each day?

mixed review

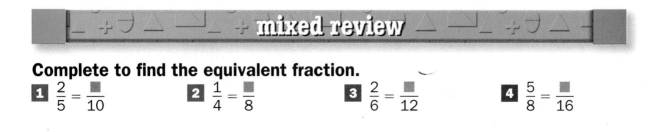

Complete to find the equivalent fraction.

1 $\frac{2}{5} = \frac{■}{10}$

2 $\frac{1}{4} = \frac{■}{8}$

3 $\frac{2}{6} = \frac{■}{12}$

4 $\frac{5}{8} = \frac{■}{16}$

Divide by 1-Digit Numbers

Twenty-six shadow puppets are being made ready for a play. The puppets are equally divided among 3 work areas. How many puppets are at each work area? How many are left over?

Work Together

Work in a group. Use place-value models to find 26 ÷ 3. Record your work.

Note: 26 ÷ 3 means 26 divided into 3 equal groups.

▶ How many puppets are at each area? How many are left over?

What if the head puppeteer packs the 26 shadow puppets in storage boxes for shipment. He puts 3 puppets in each box. How many boxes are full? How many puppets are in the last box?

Cultural Note

Shadow puppets are used in Indonesian plays. The plays tell stories and legends. A performance may last all night.

Use place-value models to find 26 ÷ 3. Record your work.

Note: 26 ÷ 3 means 26 divided into groups of 3.

▶ How many boxes are full? How many puppets are in the last box?

You will need
• *place-value models*

▶ Use place-value models to find the quotients and remainders.
  a. 46 ÷ 3   **b.** 36 ÷ 3   **c.** 23 ÷ 2   **d.** 51 ÷ 4   **e.** 55 ÷ 5

Talk It Over

▶ How did you use models to find the quotients and remainders?

▶ How do you know when you have a remainder?

Make Connections

Here is how Andrea used models to find 46 ÷ 3.

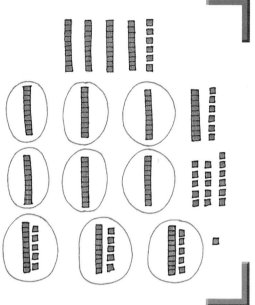

Divide the tens into 3 equal groups. Have 1 ten and 6 ones left.

Regroup 1 ten as 10 ones to get 16 ones.

Divide the ones into 3 equal groups. Have 1 one left over.

▶ Did you model 46 ÷ 3 the same way or in a different way? Explain.

You can also use what you previously learned about division with remainders to record your work. Compare the examples.

```
     8 R2              12              15 R1
  3)26             3)36             3)46
  − 24             − 3↓             − 3↓
     2                6               16
                   − 6             − 15
                     0                1
```

··

Check for Understanding

Divide. Use models, drawings, or pencil and paper.

1 7)74   **2** 3)62   **3** 5)53   **4** 2)72   **5** 4)76   **6** 4)83

THINK CRITICALLY: Generalize

7 [Journal] Carl says that he can check the answer to 46 ÷ 3 this way. Explain his method. Give other examples.

```
    15            45
  × 3           + 1
    45            46
```

Turn the page for Practice. ▶

Practice

Draw a picture of how you would put the models into 4 equal groups.

1 ‖ ‖ ‖ □□□□

2 ‖ ‖ ‖ ‖ □□□

3 ‖ ‖ ‖ ‖ ‖ □□

4 ‖ ‖ ‖ □□□□

5 ‖ ‖ ‖ ‖ □□□ □□

6 ‖ ‖ ‖ ‖ ‖ ‖ ‖ □□

Divide. Use models, drawings, or pencil and paper.

7 $4\overline{)42}$　　**8** $5\overline{)60}$　　**9** $2\overline{)31}$　　**10** $6\overline{)66}$　　**11** $2\overline{)47}$　　**12** $3\overline{)45}$

13 $4\overline{)57}$　　**14** $2\overline{)29}$　　**15** $3\overline{)77}$　　**16** $6\overline{)96}$　　**17** $3\overline{)64}$　　**18** $5\overline{)85}$

19 $37 \div 2$　　**20** $70 \div 5$　　**21** $46 \div 3$　　**22** $62 \div 5$　　**23** $93 \div 7$

24 $87 \div 8$　　**25** $96 \div 7$　　**26** $60 \div 4$　　**27** $98 \div 4$　　**28** $95 \div 8$

Algebra **Complete the table.**

29

Rule: Divide by 5.						
Input	62	63	64	65	66	67	68
Output	12 R2	▦	▦	▦	▦	▦	▦

30 What remainders are possible when the divisor is 5?

31 What do you think the possible remainders are when the divisor is 6? Explain your reasoning.

····················· **Make It Right** ·····················

32 Rita used models to find $62 \div 3$. Explain the mistake and correct it.

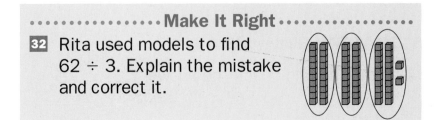

Problem Solving

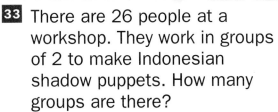

33 There are 26 people at a workshop. They work in groups of 2 to make Indonesian shadow puppets. How many groups are there?

34 An auditorium has 8 chairs in a row. How many rows will 95 students fill? How many students will there be in an unfilled row?

35 Suppose that during one 6-month period in Sumatra it rained 60 in. How much more would it need to rain to set a new record? See INFOBIT.

36 Mrs. Teng spent $37.49 for a new shadow puppet and $5 a yard for 9 yd of colorful batik fabric. About how much did she spend in all?

INFOBIT
One year, it rained a record 104 in. in Sumatra, one of the islands in Indonesia.

37 **Data Point** During Mrs. Teng's trip to Indonesia, there were 51 tremors and earthquakes. About how many days was she in Indonesia? See the Databank on page 541.

38 **Data Point** Sue Ann is 5 ft tall. About how many times taller than Sue Ann was the tidal wave produced by the eruption of Krakatoa? See the Databank on page 541.

---

more to explore

Using a Compatible Number to Estimate

Here is a way to estimate a quotient.

Estimate: $75 \div 7$ **Think:** Look for a number that is easy to divide by 7. 75 is close to 70.

$70 \div 7 = 10$, so $75 \div 7$ is about 10.

Which quotients are about 10? Explain your reasoning.

1 $26 \div 3$ **2** $97 \div 5$ **3** $53 \div 2$ **4** $38 \div 4$

Problem Solvers at Work

Read
Plan
Solve
Look Back

Part 1 Interpreting Remainders

Would it be fun for you to be among the first people to see a movie that everyone has been waiting to see?

At a sneak preview, the first 74 people will be admitted free. After that, tickets cost $3 each. PTA parents will take students. They can fit 5 students in each car.

Work Together

Solve. Be prepared to explain your methods.

1 Some students want to get there very early to get all of the free tickets.
   a. How many cars are needed for them?

   b. Shawn says that only 14 cars are needed because $74 \div 5 = 14$. Is he correct or incorrect? Why?

2 **What if** only 4 students ride in each car. How many cars will be needed?

3 The PTA donates $95 so that more students can go. How many more students can go? How much money will be left over?

4 How did you use remainders to solve problems 1–3?

5 **Make a decision** One hundred students want to go to the movie. There are 2 sneak preview showings today. At least 15 cars are available to get students to each showing. How would you get all the students to the 2 showings?

Part 2 Write and Share Problems

Ashlee wrote this problem.

6 Solve Ashlee's problem.

7 How did you use the remainder to solve her problem?

8 **Write a problem** that can be solved by dividing 50 by 4 and whose answer is:
a. 12. **b.** 13.

9 Trade problems. Solve at least two problems written by your classmates.

10 What was the most interesting problem that you solved? Why?

Mary has 5 friends and 80 candies. She gives each friend the same amount. How many candies does each friend get?

Ashlee Tognarelli
Southland Elementary School
Riverton, VT

Turn the page for Practice Strategies.

Part 3   Practice Strategies

Menu
**Choose five problems and solve them.
Explain your methods.**

1 At Kathie's school, each class makes an 8-minute video about the school. The best videos will be shown one after the other at an assembly from 9:00 A.M. to 10:30 A.M. How many videos can be shown?

2 Amber and Jamie spend $5 each on movie tickets. They buy 2 bags of popcorn for $1.25 each and 2 drinks for $1 each. How much money do they have left from $20?

3 Tanner made 25 puppets. He displays them equally on 6 tables. How many puppets are on each table? How many puppets are left over?

4 Paul sells 4 adult tickets to a talent show for $9 each and 3 children's tickets for $5 each. How much money does he receive?

5 Carrie is stamping a border around the edge of a poster. She repeats this pattern of figures: red heart, blue flower, pink heart, purple flower. The card has room for 30 figures. What will the last two figures be?

6 **What if** someone put 8 marbles of one color and 3 marbles of another color in a bag. Conduct an experiment to find what marbles are in the bag without looking in it.

7 Fatima practices the piano 5 hours a week. Her lesson is 1 hour a week. About how many hours does Fatima spend at the piano each year?

8 The perimeter of Cara's rectangular garden is 26 yards. The longer sides are 3 yards longer than the shorter sides. How long is a shorter side?

Choose two problems and solve them. Explain your methods.

9 The Sunshine Club receives 15 free tickets to the circus. Extra tickets cost $5. To make it fair, each person going pays $2. How many people must go for it to be fair?
(Hint: You must have enough money to pay for the extra tickets.)

Number of People	Amount Paid	Total Cost of Extra Tickets
15	$30	$0
16	$32	$5
17	$34	$10

10 **Logical reasoning** A group of students is waiting backstage to perform in a school talent show. Use these clues to determine how many students are backstage.

Clue 1: 20 students play musical instruments.

Clue 2: 12 students dance.

Clue 3: 6 students play musical instruments *and* dance.

11 Copy the figure. Fill in each circle with one of the numbers from 1 through 6 so that the sum on each side of the triangle is 9. Use each number only once.

12 **At the Computer** Use a spreadsheet to help you solve this problem. You need to earn $1,000. Your pay doubles each day. The first day, your pay is 1 cent. The second day, it is 2 cents. The third day, it is 4 cents, and so on.

a. How much would you earn after 1 week? after 2 weeks?

b. How long will you need to work to earn $1,000?

Day	Pay
1	$0.01
2	$0.02
3	$0.04
4	
5	

Language and Mathematics

Complete the sentence. Use a word in the chart.

1 The remainder is always ▮ than the divisor.

2 The ▮ of 56 ÷ 2 is 28.

3 The ▮ of 89 ÷ 3 is 2.

4 The ▮ of 51 and 2 is 102.

Vocabulary
remainder
less
greater
quotient
product
dividend

Concepts and Skills

Multiply mentally.

5 3×80　　**6** 5×50　　**7** 6×200　　**8** 4×600

9 7×60　　**10** 9×90　　**11** 8×500　　**12** 2×700

Estimate the product.

13 3×17　　**14** 9×39　　**15** 4×162　　**16** 6×537

17 4×370　　**18** 5×67　　**19** 8×342　　**20** 7×689

Multiply.

21 $\begin{array}{r} 17 \\ \times\ 4 \\ \hline \end{array}$　　**22** $\begin{array}{r} 21 \\ \times\ 5 \\ \hline \end{array}$　　**23** $\begin{array}{r} \$36 \\ \times\ \ 3 \\ \hline \end{array}$　　**24** $\begin{array}{r} 43 \\ \times\ 2 \\ \hline \end{array}$　　**25** $\begin{array}{r} 55 \\ \times\ 8 \\ \hline \end{array}$

26 9×81　　**27** 6×27　　**28** 7×63

Divide mentally.

29 $8)\overline{80}$　　**30** $7)\overline{420}$　　**31** $3)\overline{150}$　　**32** $6)\overline{180}$　　**33** $5)\overline{250}$

Divide.

34 $7)\overline{79}$　　**35** $3)\overline{38}$　　**36** $2)\overline{58}$　　**37** $4)\overline{63}$　　**38** $5)\overline{77}$

39 $65 \div 5$　　**40** $70 \div 6$　　**41** $48 \div 4$

Think critically.

42 Analyze. Explain what went wrong. Then correct it.

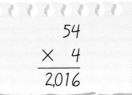

$$\begin{array}{r} 54 \\ \times\ 4 \\ \hline 2,016 \end{array}$$

43 Generalize. Write *always, sometimes,* or *never.* Give examples to support your answer.

  a. When the remainder is equal to the divisor, you have made a mistake.

  b. Quotients have remainders.

MIXED APPLICATIONS

Problem Solving

Pencil & Paper   Calculator   Mental Math

Use the price list for problems 44–47.

44 About how much does it cost to buy 15 old movies?

45 Calvin has $90. Can he buy 11 old movies? Tell why.

46 Mrs. Taylor spent $48. What tapes could she have bought?

47 How much does it cost to buy 5 children's tapes and 3 recent movies?

Sale price list for VCR sales:

BIG VCR Tape Sale in Every Department!

Children's **$10** each

Old Movies **$8** each

Recent Movies **$15** each

Nature **$5** each

Exercise **$5** each

48 There are 34 students going to a concert. Each car takes 3 students. How many cars are needed?

49 Inés has 38 jars of poster paint. She puts 8 jars on each shelf. How many shelves are full? How many jars are on the last, unfilled shelf?

50 Tom places 66 clay animal figures in 7 trays to dry. Some trays hold 6 figures. The rest of the trays hold 12 figures. How many of each kind of tray does he use?

chapter test

Multiply mentally.

1 2×30　　**2** 4×90　　**3** 7×300　　**4** 5×500

Estimate the product.

5 4×18　　**6** 8×27　　**7** 5×177　　**8** 9×325

Multiply.

9
$$
\begin{array}{r}
16 \\
\times\ 5 \\
\hline
\end{array}
$$

10
$$
\begin{array}{r}
\$46 \\
\times\ \ \ 3 \\
\hline
\end{array}
$$

11
$$
\begin{array}{r}
35 \\
\times\ 5 \\
\hline
\end{array}
$$

12
$$
\begin{array}{r}
24 \\
\times\ 4 \\
\hline
\end{array}
$$

13
$$
\begin{array}{r}
53 \\
\times\ 3 \\
\hline
\end{array}
$$

14
$$
\begin{array}{r}
\$67 \\
\times\ \ \ 6 \\
\hline
\end{array}
$$

15 8×64　　**16** $7 \times \$93$　　**17** 6×82

Divide mentally.

18 $4\overline{)40}$　　**19** $5\overline{)450}$　　**20** $7\overline{)490}$　　**21** $8\overline{)480}$

Divide.

22 $6\overline{)68}$　　**23** $2\overline{)49}$　　**24** $5\overline{)75}$　　**25** $9\overline{)97}$

26 $96 \div 3$　　**27** $40 \div 3$　　**28** $85 \div 4$　　**29** $87 \div 7$

Solve.

30 Xavier has $47.75. He wants to buy 3 shirts that cost $14.65 each. Does he have enough money?

31 Jo wants to pack 8 tapes in each box. There are 94 tapes. How many boxes does she need?

32 There are 6 boats on the Old Mill ride. Each boat holds 12 people. How many people can ride at one time?

33 Tickets to a show cost $6 each. Iris has $96. Can she buy 16 tickets to the show? How do you know?

What Did You Learn?

You are helping plan a party for your class. You need to rent enough tables and chairs so that everyone has a seat.

There are 3 table arrangements available. For each type of table, find how many tables your class needs.

Find how much using each type of table would cost. Decide which tables you would rent. Tell why.

$36

$48

$24

·················· **A Good Answer** ··················
- clearly explains how each answer was found
- gives a complete explanation of your decision
- shows all your work and is clearly organized, labeled, and accurate

Portfolio You may want to place your work in your portfolio.

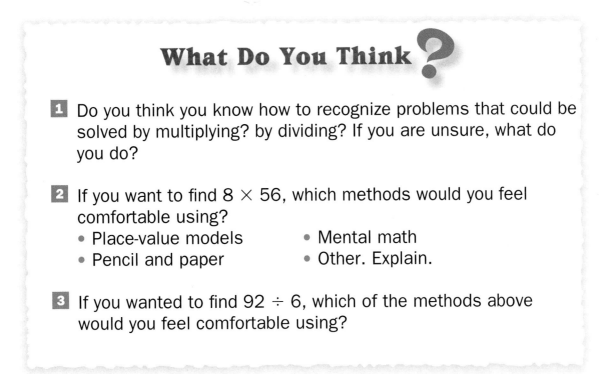

What Do You Think?

1 Do you think you know how to recognize problems that could be solved by multiplying? by dividing? If you are unsure, what do you do?

2 If you want to find 8 × 56, which methods would you feel comfortable using?
- Place-value models
- Mental math
- Pencil and paper
- Other. Explain.

3 If you wanted to find 92 ÷ 6, which of the methods above would you feel comfortable using?

MOVING PICTURES

Cultural Note

Roman soldiers used to draw pictures around the perimeter of their shields and then spin them to see the figures move. This is the earliest known example of animation.

How does Bugs Bunny move?

If you look at a piece of movie film, you will see that it is made of many pictures. These pictures are flashed before you very quickly—24 pictures each second.

They seem to move because your eyes continue to see an image for about a tenth of a second after it is gone.

Follow the directions below to make a simple "moving picture."

1 Cut a strip of good-quality writing or typing paper. Fold the strip lengthwise.

2 Draw a picture of a dog on the front. Press down hard so you can see the outline on the inside.

3 Open the folded paper and trace the outline. Draw the dog with its mouth open as if it were barking.

4 Roll the top picture back with a pencil so that it is curled. Then, use your pencil to move the top picture back and forth.

How Many Pictures?

When artists make a cartoon, each picture is used twice. So it takes 12 different pictures to make 1 second of a cartoon.

You may wish to use a calculator to help you solve these problems. Explain your reasoning.

1 If each second needs 12 pictures, how many pictures must be drawn for 5 seconds of film? 10 seconds? 1 minute?

2 If there were 4 artists working at a cartoon studio, how many pictures would each have to draw for 5 seconds of film? for a 1-minute cartoon movie?

3 If an artist can draw 5 pictures in an hour, how long will it take 1 artist to draw 5 seconds of film? a 1-minute cartoon?

At the Computer

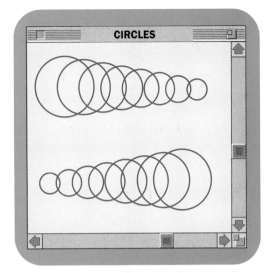

CIRCLES

4 Use drawing or geometry software to help you make a series of slightly different drawings of the same object.

5 Make a "flip book" using your drawings. Print them out. Then, cut out each drawing so all are on the same-size piece of paper. Staple one end. When you flip the open end of the book, the figure should look as if it is moving.

Chapters 1–12

Choose the letter of the correct answer.

1 Estimate 7 × 38.
- **a.** 21
- **b.** 35
- **c.** 210
- **d.** 280

2 Divide 97 ÷ 4.
- **a.** 21 R3
- **b.** 24
- **c.** 25
- **d.** not given

3 Find the perimeter.

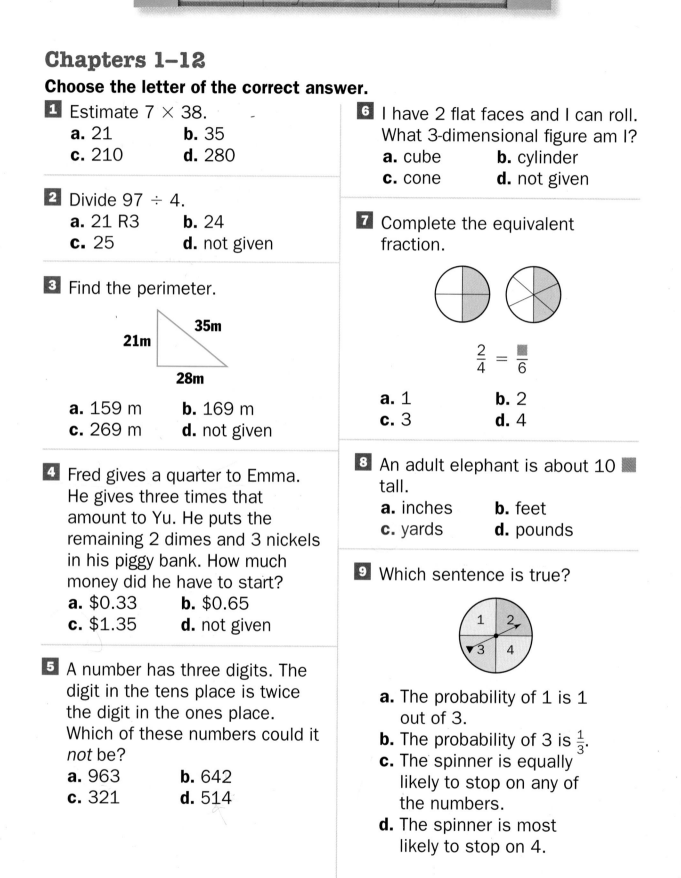

- **a.** 159 m
- **b.** 169 m
- **c.** 269 m
- **d.** not given

4 Fred gives a quarter to Emma. He gives three times that amount to Yu. He puts the remaining 2 dimes and 3 nickels in his piggy bank. How much money did he have to start?
- **a.** $0.33
- **b.** $0.65
- **c.** $1.35
- **d.** not given

5 A number has three digits. The digit in the tens place is twice the digit in the ones place. Which of these numbers could it *not* be?
- **a.** 963
- **b.** 642
- **c.** 321
- **d.** 514

6 I have 2 flat faces and I can roll. What 3-dimensional figure am I?
- **a.** cube
- **b.** cylinder
- **c.** cone
- **d.** not given

7 Complete the equivalent fraction.

$$\frac{2}{4} = \frac{\blacksquare}{6}$$

- **a.** 1
- **b.** 2
- **c.** 3
- **d.** 4

8 An adult elephant is about 10 ▓ tall.
- **a.** inches
- **b.** feet
- **c.** yards
- **d.** pounds

9 Which sentence is true?

- **a.** The probability of 1 is 1 out of 3.
- **b.** The probability of 3 is $\frac{1}{3}$.
- **c.** The spinner is equally likely to stop on any of the numbers.
- **d.** The spinner is most likely to stop on 4.

10 Add 303 + 25 + 86.
- **a.** 314
- **b.** 408
- **c.** 414
- **d.** 1.413

11 Find the missing number.
$$35 + 46 + 28 = 46 + \blacksquare + 35$$
- **a.** 0
- **b.** 28
- **c.** 81
- **d.** 109

12 Betty Sue begins baby-sitting at 11:30 A.M. If she charges $4 per hour and earns $32 baby-sitting, what time does she stop baby-sitting?
- **a.** 7:30 P.M.
- **b.** 5:30 P.M.
- **c.** 6:00 P.M.
- **d.** 8:00 P.M.

13 How many lines of symmetry does the figure have?

- **a.** 2
- **b.** 4
- **c.** 6
- **d.** 8

14 Complete the pattern.
$$3 \times 4 = 12$$
$$3 \times 40 = 120$$
$$3 \times \blacksquare = 1,200$$
- **a.** 40
- **b.** 400
- **c.** 4,000
- **d.** not given

15 Find the volume in cubic units.

- **a.** 6
- **b.** 8
- **c.** 12
- **d.** 16

16 Find $4.70 − $1.89.
- **a.** $6.59
- **b.** $2.81
- **c.** $2.90
- **d.** $281

17 Kara has 87 glass animals. She packs 6 animals in each box. How many boxes does she need to pack all the animals?
- **a.** 12 boxes
- **b.** 13 boxes
- **c.** 14 boxes
- **d.** 15 boxes

18 Choose the symbol to make a true statement.
$$4.3 \; \bullet \; 3.7 = 8$$
- **a.** >
- **b.** +
- **c.** <
- **d.** −

Use the graph for ex. 19–20.

Favorite Entertainment	
Movies	🧍🧍🧍🧍🧍🧍🧍🧍🧍🧍🧍🧍
Television	🧍🧍🧍🧍🧍🧍🧍🧍🧍🧍🧍🧍🧍🧍
Sports	🧍🧍🧍🧍🧍🧍🧍🧍🧍🧍🧍

Key: Each 🧍 stands for 6 people.

19 Which statement is not true?
- **a.** More people chose movies than chose television.
- **b.** 66 people chose sports.
- **c.** 18 fewer people chose sports than chose television.
- **d.** not given

20 How many 🧍 do you need to show that 60 people chose reading?
- **a.** 6 figures
- **b.** 10 figures
- **c.** 12 figures
- **d.** 60 figures

Addition Facts page 5

Add.

1 8 + 2 **2** 9 + 1 **3** 6 + 7 **4** 3 + 3 **5** 8 + 7

6 5 + 4 **7** 2 + 4 **8** 7 + 9 **9** 8 + 8 **10** 9 + 9

11 6   **12** 3   **13** 8   **14** 2   **15** 6   **16** 7   **17** 7
    +9   +4   +6   +9   +5   +3   +7

18 What is the sum of 5 and 7? **19** How much is 9 + 4?

Solve.

20 One whale swam near a boat for 8 minutes. It dove under the water and came up. Then it swam near the boat for 9 more minutes. How many minutes did it swim near the boat altogether?

21 There were 6 adults and 5 children on Carol's tour. There were 8 adults and 3 children on Rico's tour. Whose tour had more people? Explain how you know.

More Addition Facts page 7

Add.

1 7 + 8 **2** 3 + 7 **3** 6 + 4 **4** 9 + 2 **5** 6 + 8

6 9 + 4 **7** 7 + 2 **8** 6 + 6 **9** 5 + 8 **10** 8 + 4

11 7   **12** 8   **13** 7   **14** 5   **15** 5   **16** 4   **17** 6
    +7   +9   +5   +8   +2   +4   +7

18 What is the sum of 2 and 8? **19** How much is 7 + 9?

Solve.

20 There were 8 volunteers at the Nature Center on Saturday. There were 5 other volunteers on Sunday. How many volunteers were there in all?

21 **Spatial reasoning** Which shape does not belong? Why?

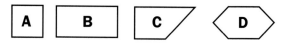

A B C D

Properties of Addition page 11

Add.

1 $0 + 1$ **2** $4 + 4 + 6$ **3** $5 + 6 + 0$ **4** $5 + 2 + 1 + 9$

5
$$\begin{array}{r} 3 \\ 7 \\ +2 \\ \hline \end{array}$$

6
$$\begin{array}{r} 6 \\ 0 \\ +3 \\ \hline \end{array}$$

7
$$\begin{array}{r} 0 \\ 1 \\ 7 \\ +5 \\ \hline \end{array}$$

8
$$\begin{array}{r} 1 \\ 3 \\ 5 \\ +7 \\ \hline \end{array}$$

9
$$\begin{array}{r} 4 \\ 8 \\ 2 \\ +0 \\ \hline \end{array}$$

10
$$\begin{array}{r} 3 \\ 2 \\ 9 \\ +4 \\ \hline \end{array}$$

11
$$\begin{array}{r} 6 \\ 1 \\ 2 \\ +5 \\ \hline \end{array}$$

Find the missing number.

12 $(6 + 4) + 7 = 6 + (\blacksquare + 7)$

13 $4 + 3 = 3 + \blacksquare$

14 $(4 + 3) + 5 = \blacksquare + 7$

15 $16 + \blacksquare = \blacksquare + 16$

Solve.

16 Shelby buys some stickers for $2 and a hat for $7 at the Nature Center gift shop. He also buys some postcards and stamps for $5 at a store outside the Center. How much money does he spend?

17 Lawanna saw sharks, jellyfish, and dolphins at the aquarium. She saw the dolphins last. She saw the jellyfish before she saw the sharks. Which animals did she see second?

Subtraction Facts page 17

Subtract.

1 $4 - 1$ **2** $10 - 5$ **3** $13 - 6$ **4** $9 - 0$ **5** $17 - 8$

6
$$\begin{array}{r} 11 \\ -\ 5 \\ \hline \end{array}$$

7
$$\begin{array}{r} 14 \\ -\ 7 \\ \hline \end{array}$$

8
$$\begin{array}{r} 16 \\ -\ 9 \\ \hline \end{array}$$

9
$$\begin{array}{r} 12 \\ -\ 3 \\ \hline \end{array}$$

10
$$\begin{array}{r} 15 \\ -\ 8 \\ \hline \end{array}$$

11
$$\begin{array}{r} 16 \\ -\ 8 \\ \hline \end{array}$$

12
$$\begin{array}{r} 15 \\ -\ 6 \\ \hline \end{array}$$

Write + or − to make a true number sentence.

13 $8 \bullet 4 = 12$ **14** $13 \bullet 5 = 8$ **15** $9 \bullet 6 = 15$ **16** $6 \bullet 5 = 11$

17 $12 \bullet 9 = 3$ **18** $7 \bullet 8 = 15$ **19** $16 \bullet 8 = 8$ **20** $10 \bullet 0 = 10$

More Subtraction Facts page 19
Subtract.

1 6 − 0   **2** 16 − 7   **3** 11 − 2   **4** 12 − 6   **5** 15 − 6

6 10 − 4   **7** 14 − 9   **8** 9 − 1   **9** 8 − 7   **10** 13 − 4

11
  4
−3

12
  13
− 5

13
  10
− 5

14
  11
− 8

15
  12
− 5

16
  15
− 8

17
  14
− 9

Solve.

18 A sunflower starfish is born with 5 arms. It grows more during its life. One sunflower starfish has 9 arms. How many new arms has it grown?

19 A razor clam can burrow 12 to 18 inches in the sand. One razor clam burrows 9 inches. How many more inches can it burrow?

Problem-Solving Strategy: Choose the Operation page 21
Solve.

1 A visitor to a wildlife park gave the clerk $12 to pay a $7 gate fee. The rest was a donation. How much was the donation?

2 Maurice waited in line 8 minutes for juice. He waited in another line 4 minutes to get a slice of pizza. How long did he wait in all?

3 There are 15 animals in the petting zoo. Carmine saw 6 adult and 8 baby animals. Did he see all the animals? Explain.

4 A wild turkey can run about 15 miles per hour. A chicken can run about 9 miles per hour. How much faster can a wild turkey run than a chicken?

5 Kyle is on a 2-week safari. He has been gone for 5 days. How many days longer will he be on the safari?

6 **Spatial reasoning** Draw the next picture to complete the pattern.

Fact Families page 25
Write a fact family for each group of numbers.

1 2, 3, 5   **2** 7, 8, 15   **3** 5, 6, 11   **4** 4, 9, 13   **5** 0, 0, 0

Find the missing number.

6 ■ + 5 = 14   **7** 3 + ■ = 11   **8** 8 − ■ = 6   **9** 16 − ■ = 7

10
$$\begin{array}{r} 6 \\ -\ \blacksquare \\ \hline 6 \end{array}$$

11
$$\begin{array}{r} \blacksquare \\ +\ 4 \\ \hline 9 \end{array}$$

12
$$\begin{array}{r} 13 \\ -\ \blacksquare \\ \hline 6 \end{array}$$

13
$$\begin{array}{r} 9 \\ +\ 9 \\ \hline \blacksquare \end{array}$$

14
$$\begin{array}{r} 5 \\ +\ \blacksquare \\ \hline 10 \end{array}$$

15
$$\begin{array}{r} 16 \\ -\ \blacksquare \\ \hline 8 \end{array}$$

16
$$\begin{array}{r} \blacksquare \\ +\ 9 \\ \hline 12 \end{array}$$

Solve.

17 Use the chart to find as many ways as you can to earn 6 or more extra credit points.

Extra Credit Activity	Points
Erasing board	1
Collecting papers	2
Leading group discussion	3
Helping another student	5

Problem Solvers at Work page 29
Solve. Explain your method.

1 A red squirrel has a litter of 6 babies. Earlier this year, she had another litter of 5 babies. How many babies were in the 2 litters?

2 Ashley has 8 glass horses. She receives some more for her birthday. She now has 13 horses. How many did she receive for her birthday?

3 A fox has 4 legs. A duck has 2 legs. Rocky sees both foxes and ducks as he counts 12 legs. How many foxes and ducks did he see?

4 The body of a Townsend mole can be 9 inches long. The mole can have a 2-inch-long tail. What operation could you use to find the total length of the mole?

5 Miguel has $5. He plans to save $2 each week so he can buy a circus ticket. How could you find how long it will take Miguel to save $15?

6 Lisa saw 6 trout in one tank and 8 trout in another. Write a question so that you will add to find the answer.

Numbers in the World page 39
Tell how the number is used.

1 I have 4 puzzles.　　**2** A tie costs 9 dollars.　　**3** It is 3:00 P.M.

Solve.

4 The 5 people in Al's family moved into their new house on 1/5/96. They live at 155 West Street. Tell how each number is used.

5 Write sentences that use 21 as a measure, as a name, for a count, and as a money amount.

Ordinals page 41
Name the position of the store. Start on the left.

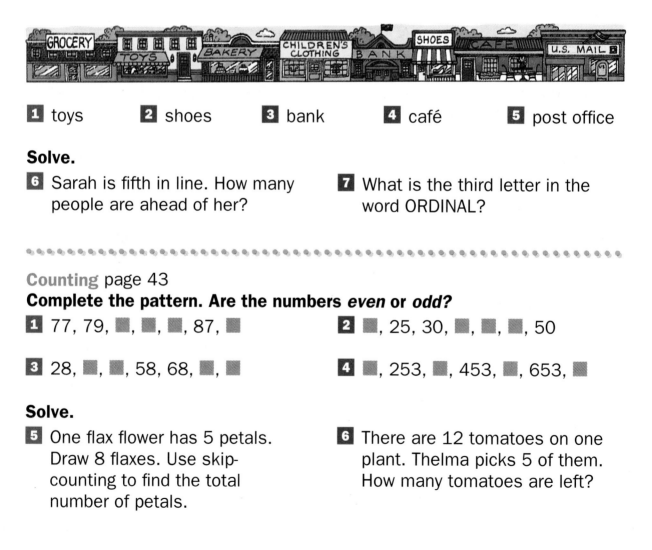

1 toys　　**2** shoes　　**3** bank　　**4** café　　**5** post office

Solve.

6 Sarah is fifth in line. How many people are ahead of her?

7 What is the third letter in the word ORDINAL?

Counting page 43
Complete the pattern. Are the numbers *even* or *odd?*

1 77, 79, ■, ■, ■, 87, ■

2 ■, 25, 30, ■, ■, ■, 50

3 28, ■, ■, 58, 68, ■, ■

4 ■, 253, ■, 453, ■, 653, ■

Solve.

5 One flax flower has 5 petals. Draw 8 flaxes. Use skip-counting to find the total number of petals.

6 There are 12 tomatoes on one plant. Thelma picks 5 of them. How many tomatoes are left?

Building to Hundreds page 45
Write the number.

1 8 tens 9 ones

2 4 hundreds 3 ones

3 15 tens 9 ones

4 6 hundreds 3 tens 4 ones

5 3 hundreds 7 ones

Solve.

6 List your first name and the first names of ten other students in alphabetical order. In which position is your name?

7 Pencils come in boxes of 100. How many pencils are in 5 boxes?

Ones, Tens, and Hundreds page 47
Write the number.

1 twenty-five

2 7 hundreds 2 tens

3 200 + 10 + 3

4 eight hundred ninety-five

5 600 + 20 + 7

Solve.

6 Use the digits in *three hundred fifty-four* to write as many different numbers as you can.

7 Flutes are shipped in boxes of 10. How many boxes are needed to ship 80 flutes?

Compare and Order Numbers page 49
Compare. Write >, <, or =.

1 76 ● 70   **2** 132 ● 87   **3** 456 ● 473   **4** 108 ● 108   **5** 91 ● 97

Write in order from least to greatest.

6 66, 50, 60

7 325, 223, 224

8 98, 301, 103, 130

Solve.

9 **Logical reasoning** José, Harv, and Amy live at 741, 702, and 127 May Lane. Harv's address is a number less than José's but greater than Amy's. Who lives at each address?

10 There are 857 people in Laurelton and 903 people in Elmhurst. Which town has the greater number of people?

Problem-Solving Strategy: Make a Table page 51

Organize this data on favorite colors in a table. Solve problems 1–2.

Carl: Red   Ann: Blue   Lisa: Blue   Raisa: Green   Ivan: Red

Jorge: Green   Carol: Green   Maria: Red   Tom: Blue   Len: Blue

1 Which color is the most popular?

2 Write a question that can be answered by using the table.

Round Numbers page 59

Round to the nearest ten or ten dollars.

1 58   **2** 12   **3** $28   **4** 34   **5** $82

Round to the nearest hundred or hundred dollars.

6 67   **7** 512   **8** $380   **9** 731   **10** $867

Solve.

11 Sally bought a hat for $5. She had $3 left. How much did she start out with?

12 Write a newspaper headline that uses 592 rounded to the nearest hundred.

Thousands page 63

Write the number.

1 8 thousands 6 hundreds 5 ones

2 7,000 + 400 + 30 + 8

Write the value of the underlined digit.

3 <u>2</u>,168   **4** 8,<u>2</u>16   **5** 6,1<u>2</u>8   **6** 1,86<u>2</u>

Solve.

7 **Spatial reasoning** Draw the next shape in the pattern.

8 Callie saved 672 pennies. Her mother gave her 100 more pennies. How many pennies did Callie have in all?

Numbers to Hundred Thousands page 65

Write the word name.

1 37,605

2 206,541

Solve.

3 Find 1,000 more than 63,789.

4 Find 1,000 less than 321,908.

5 The population of Bakersfield is 174,820. This is 1,000 more than the population of Fremont. What is Fremont's population?

6 The population of Coral Bay is 23,564. One hundred people leave town. What is the population now?

Compare and Order Greater Numbers page 67

Compare. Write >, <, or =.

1 72,496 ● 72,496

2 126,999 ● 127,009

3 672,591 ● 671,952

Solve.

4 Sort these numbers two ways.

| 162,596 | 591 | 2,593 |
| 73,644 | 44 | 3,644 |

5 Write a number sentence that compares the cost of two different cars advertised in a newspaper.

Problem Solvers at Work page 71

Solve. Explain your method.

1 A car wash charges $3 for each car. Mauri washes 10 cars. Annie also washes 10 cars. How much money does Mauri bring in?

2 There were 5 bats and 4 jump ropes in Seiko's class. The PTA bought 3 new bats. How many bats are in the class now?

3 The difference between the first two digits of a 3-digit mystery number is 9. The last digit is even. Which numbers could be the mystery number?

4 This number rounds to 500 to the nearest hundred and to 550 to the nearest ten. The ones digit is the sum of the hundreds and tens digits. What is the number?

Add Whole Numbers page 83
Add mentally.

1 40
+ 20

2 36
+ 42

3 200
300
+ 500

4 605
+ 21

5 519
+ 380

6 50 + 60

7 25 + 22

8 700 + 800

9 205 + 760

Solve.

10 Which is more—1 hundred and 7 tens or 17 tens?

11 Complete the pattern. 105, 210, 315, 420, ▩, ▩, ▩

Estimate Sums page 85
Estimate the sum. Round to the nearest ten.

1 31 + 45

2 73 + 82

3 12 + 63

4 528 + 43

Estimate the sum. Round to the nearest hundred.

5 637 + 345

6 479 + 763

7 314 + 873

8 98 + 394

Solve.

9 A bakery sold 328 pies one day and 286 pies the next. About how many pies were sold in all?

10 **Logical reasoning** Ken says he is close to 50 or close to 100 depending on how you round. How old is Ken?

Add 2- and 3-Digit Numbers page 87
Add. Explain your method.

1 68 + 31

2 86 + 47

3 517 + 392

4 355 + 438

Solve. Explain your method.

5 Di's class sold 136 raffle tickets. Jay's class sold 122 tickets. How many tickets were sold in all?

6 A grocer bought 45 pounds of apples, 23 pounds of peaches, and 16 pounds of cheese. How many pounds of fruit did he buy?

Add 2-Digit Numbers page 89
Add. Remember to estimate.

1   67
   + 35

2   90
   + 49

3   48
   + 23

4   56
   + 58

5   89
   + 8

6 48 + 53   **7** 24 + 37   **8** 85 + 67   **9** 29 + 59

Solve.

10 Kaya rides 56 miles to the new mall. Then she rides 35 more miles. How far does she ride in all?

11 Joel has $15 in one pocket and $27 in the other. Nan has $42. Who has more money?

Add 3-Digit Numbers page 93
Add. Remember to estimate.

1   635
   + 42

2   356
   + 138

3   705
   + 497

4   569
   + 230

5   399
   + 8

6 466 + 204   **7** 219 + 183   **8** 754 + 471   **9** 394 + 827

Solve.

10 Alice worked 12 hours at an expo. Elise worked 14 hours. Who worked longer?

11 A square is worth 100 points, a circle 25 points, and a triangle 50 points. Make a drawing that has a value of 750 points.

Column Addition page 95
Add. Remember to estimate.

1 34 + 50 + 32   **2** 851 + 222 + 505   **3** 740 + 346 + 421

4 13 + 24 + 31 + 42   **5** 254 + 102 + 390 + 400

Solve.

6 Jeff buys 530 wheat rolls, 650 white rolls, and 425 rye rolls. How many rolls does he buy in all?

7 Find three 3-digit numbers that have a sum of 1,000. Can you find another answer?

Problem-Solving Strategy: Draw a Picture page 97

Solve. Explain your methods.

1 Dan, Juan, and Tía are standing in line. Dan is not first. Tía is in front of Juan. In what order are they standing?

2 **Spatial reasoning** Which shape does not belong in the group? Explain.

3 It is 324 miles from Lee's house to Miami. How many miles would Lee travel to Miami and back?

4 Jill lives 35 miles from Cara's house. Nick lives 8 miles farther down the same road. Jill visits Cara and Nick, then returns home. How far does she travel?

Add Greater Numbers page 99

Add. Remember to estimate.

1 2,321 + 4,682   **2** 1,289 + 2,900   **3** 5,103 + 2,498

Solve.

4 A pilot flies 2,905 miles across the United States and 3,010 back. How far does she fly in all?

5 There are 14,516 people at a card show. Round the number to the nearest thousand.

Count Money and Make Change page 107

Write the coins and bills needed to make the amount.

1 50¢   **2** 72¢   **3** $1.36   **4** $5.24   **5** $8.90

Find the amount of change. List the coins and bills.

6 Cost: $2.75
You give: $5.00

7 Cost: $0.45
You give: $1.00

8 Cost: $3.80
You give: $5.00

9 Cost: $4.80
You give: $5.00

10 Cost: $1.45
You give: $2.00

11 Cost: $2.20
You give: $3.00

Compare, Order, and Round Money page 109

Write in order from least to greatest.

1 $3.92, $3.15, $2.85 **2** $6.09, $6.94, $6.49 **3** $0.51, $0.15, $1.50

Solve.

4 Which of these numbers rounds to $6?
$4.99, $5.26, $5.45, $5.51, $5.92, $6.06, $6.39

5 Jeremy wants to buy a paint set that sells for $8.95 and a brush for $2.45. Which costs more?

Add Money page 111

Add. Remember to estimate.

1 $0.75	**2** $0.90	**3** $3.48	**4** $5.09	**5** $8.35
+ 0.25	+ 0.57	+ 2.63	+ 0.65	+ 1.25

6 $0.56 + $0.82   **7** $3.21 + $5.99   **8** $5.71 + $6.35

Solve.

9 Uta spent $1.65 at the dime store, $3.56 at the toy store, and $6.26 at the grocery. How much money did she spend in all?

10 Uta gave the clerk 3 one-dollar bills and 3 quarters for her $3.56 purchase. What coins did she get in change?

Problem Solvers at Work page 115

Solve. Explain your methods.

1 Round 145 to the nearest ten and to the nearest hundred. Which is greater?

2 Jan spent $4.76. Ho spent $4.67. Who spent more? Explain.

3 Rewrite this problem leaving out the extra information. Alex paid $3 for 2 green apples and 2 red apples. How many apples did he buy in all?

4 Evan rides 10 miles to the farmer's market. Then he rides 5 miles farther to the feed store and comes home by the same route. How far does he ride?

Subtract Whole Numbers page 129

Subtract mentally.

1	70	**2**	57	**3**	900	**4**	486	**5**	218
	−40		−24		−200		−33		−110

Solve.

6 A bike tour is 276 miles. The bikers have gone 120 miles. How much farther do they have to ride to complete the tour?

7 Carter flies 423 miles to Chicago. He changes planes and flies 246 more miles to visit his aunt. How many miles does he fly?

Estimate Differences page 131

Estimate the difference. Round to the nearest ten.

1 73 − 21   **2** 67 − 15   **3** 92 − 78   **4** 248 − 31

Estimate the difference. Round to the nearest hundred.

5 496 − 235   **6** 544 − 223   **7** 792 − 411   **8** 963 − 98

Solve.

9 Jason saved $84 for a new bicycle. The bike costs $193. About how much more does he need to save?

10 **Spatial reasoning** How many triangles are there?

Subtract 2-Digit Numbers page 133

Subtract. Explain your methods.

1	84	**2**	54	**3**	76	**4**	50	**5**	58	**6**	92
	−26		−13		−49		−31		−44		−68

7 65 − 52   **8** 32 − 17   **9** 43 − 16   **10** 81 − 38

Subtract 2-Digit Numbers page 135
Subtract. Remember to estimate.

1   46
   − 18

2   72
   − 56

3   54
   − 21

4   85
   − 9

5   63
   − 16

6   78
   − 69

7 81 − 14   **8** 72 − 45   **9** 53 − 32   **10** 90 − 27

Solve.

11 It takes the bus 25 minutes to travel from Lido to Reno. An express bus makes the same trip in 17 minutes. How much faster is the express bus?

12 It will cost $594 to repair Jason's boat and $275 to repair his car. About how much will it cost Jason to make the repairs?

Problem-Solving Strategy: Solve Multistep Problems page 137
Solve. Explain your methods.

1 A store sells solar-powered cars for $15. Tyler bought 2 cars and gave the clerk 2 twenty-dollar bills. How much change did Tyler receive?

2 David walked 2 blocks north, 2 blocks east, 2 blocks south, and 2 blocks west. How many blocks did he walk in all? How far is he from his starting point?

3 A used-car lot has 21 cars and 12 trucks. A delivery of 14 cars arrives. How many more cars does it have than trucks now?

4 Aki was 13 when she learned how to skate. Two years later, she won her first medal. That was 14 years ago. How old is Aki now?

Subtract 3-Digit Numbers page 145
Subtract. Explain your methods.

1   286
   − 173

2   429
   − 132

3   567
   − 209

4   835
   − 592

5   742
   − 315

6   923
   − 268

7 664 − 351   **8** 528 − 319   **9** 874 − 391   **10** 421 − 196

Subtract 3-Digit Numbers page 149
Subtract. Remember to estimate.

1 573
   − 8

2 629
   − 76

3 825
  − 153

4 740
  − 327

5 862
  − 775

6 937
  − 289

Solve.

7 A ferry had 636 riders on Friday. On Sunday, it had 341 riders. How many more people rode on Friday than on Sunday?

8 Glenda has 6 coins worth $1.15 altogether. None of the coins have a value greater than 25¢. What are the coins?

Subtract Across Zero page 151
Subtract. Remember to estimate.

1 306
  − 135

2 907
  − 392

3 604
  − 119

4 405
  − 258

5 800
  − 705

6 600
  − 238

7 706 − 143

8 803 − 507

9 905 − 839

10 400 − 251

Subtract Greater Numbers page 153
Subtract. Remember to estimate.

1 4,296
   − 145

2 7,649
   − 186

3 5,428
   − 472

4 9,436
  − 3,519

5 6,732
  − 2,517

6 2,510 − 901

7 5,826 − 3,915

8 9,015 − 4,816

Solve.

9 The Wright brothers flew their first aircraft in 1903. How many years ago did that flight occur?

10 **Logical reasoning** Tom, Kim, and Sol each read a different kind of book. Tom reads poetry. Kim does not read mysteries. Who reads about sports?

Subtract Money page 155
Subtract. Remember to estimate.

1	$0.46 − 0.25	2	$0.93 − 0.74	3	$0.84 − 0.79	4	$6.53 − 2.38	5	$8.28 − 4.75

6	$5.21 − 1.47	7	$7.00 − 1.79	8	$9.05 − 3.62	9	$24.86 − 12.75	10	$64.39 − 46.46

11 $9.38 − $6.27   **12** $4.00 − $1.56   **13** $56.11 − $39.00

Solve.

14 Taxi fare to the port is $18.00. Bus fare to the port is $6.75. How much more is the taxi fare than the bus fare?

15 Val bought a sticker for $0.59. He gave the clerk $0.75. How much change should he receive?

16 Sara rode the ski lift 6 times one day and 7 times the next. How many times did she ride in all?

17 A driver went 55 miles per hour. The speed limit was 65 miles per hour. Was the driver speeding?

Problem Solvers at Work page 159
Solve. Explain your methods.

1 Write the information that is needed to solve the problem. Then solve it. Adrian's family takes a ship and a train to visit relatives. They travel 2,404 miles on the ship. How far do they travel in all?

2 Write the road mileage between Washington, D.C., and these cities in order from greatest to least: New Orleans, 1,078 miles; Dallas, 1,319 miles; Tulsa, 1,189 miles; and Minneapolis, 1,076 miles.

3 Mick bikes 3 miles to Ada's house. They ride to the park and back. Then Mick rides home. Mick rides a total of 8 miles. How far is the park from Ada's house?

4 The space shuttle *Columbia* was in orbit about 336 hours. *Endeavor* was in orbit about 260 hours. How much longer was *Columbia* in orbit than *Endeavor*?

Estimate Time page 169
Choose the more reasonable time.

1 Practice the piano—
30 minutes or 30 hours?

2 Play a soccer game—
1 minute or 1 hour?

Solve.

3 Evelyn buys a coat for $43 and a scarf for $12. How much does she spend altogether?

4 Lester runs for 30 minutes each day. How many minutes does he run in 4 days?

Tell Time page 173
Write the time using A.M. or P.M. Then show one way to say the time.

Elapsed Time page 175
How much time has passed?

1 Begin: 7:10 P.M.
End: 7:50 P.M.

2 Begin: 10:05 A.M.
End: 11:15 A.M.

3 Begin: 4:40 P.M.
End: 11:50 P.M.

Solve.

4 Melvin's scout meeting lasts for 1 hour. It is over at 5:15 P.M. When did it begin?

5 Jo spends 50 minutes on homework. She starts at 4:15 P.M. At what time does she finish?

Use a Calendar page 177
Use the calendar for ex. 1–8. What is the date for:

1 the first Monday?

2 Thanksgiving Day?

3 the Tuesday after Veterans Day?

4 the third Wednesday?

What day of the week is:

5 November 9?

6 November 30?

7 November 19?

8 November 25?

November

S	M	T	W	TH	F	SA
			1	2	3	4
5	6	7	8	9	10	11 Veterans Day
12	13	14	15	16	17	18
19	20	21	22	23 Thanksgiving	24	25
26	27	28	29	30		

Solve.

9 Victoria's birthday is June 14. One year, Victoria celebrated her birthday on a Friday. What was the date of the Friday after Victoria's birthday?

10 Sam started his math project on January 31. He finished it 18 days later. On what day did he finish?

Problem-Solving Strategy: Guess, Test, and Revise page 179
Solve. Explain your methods.

1 Lulani buys a radio and a video tape for $21. The radio costs $13 more than the tape. How much does each cost?

2 Write the information that is needed to solve the problem. Then solve it. Jane spent 3 hours at the mall. At what time did she go home?

3 Jeb gets home at 3:00. He takes one hour to do his homework. Then he watches television for a half hour. How much time does he have for playing before dinner at 6:00?

4 Celeste rode 5 miles from school to home. Then she rode 3 miles to her friend's house and home again. How far did she ride after school?

5 There are 2 more boys than girls in one class. There are 20 students in the class. How many are boys? How many are girls?

6 **Spatial reasoning** What is the next shape in the pattern?

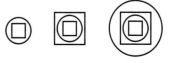

Tallies and Line Plots page 185
Use the tally for problems 1–4.

1 Copy the table. Complete the table using this data: Club members walked 10 miles during Week 5.

2 Use the tally to make a line plot.

3 How many miles did club members walk in all during the 5 weeks?

4 Did club members walk more miles the first week or the third week? How many more? How do you know?

Walkers' Club		
Week	Tally	Number of Miles Walked
Week 1	𝍷𝍷𝍷 𝍷𝍷𝍷𝍷	9
Week 2	𝍷𝍷𝍷 𝍷𝍷𝍷 𝍷	11
Week 3	𝍷𝍷𝍷 𝍷𝍷𝍷 𝍷𝍷𝍷	15
Week 4	𝍷𝍷𝍷 𝍷𝍷𝍷	8
Week 5		

Pictographs page 187
Use the table and the pictograph for problems 1–4.

1 Use the data in the table to copy and complete the pictograph.

2 Which activity had the greatest number of campers? How many symbols are needed?

3 How many more campers took the cooking class than took the pottery class?

4 You and a friend select one camp activity. Tell which activity you choose and how this changes the graph.

Camp Activities	
Activity	Number of Campers
Drawing	16
Swimming	20
Pottery	14
Cooking	18

Camp Activities	
Drawing	𝍢𝍢𝍢𝍢𝍢𝍢𝍢𝍢
Swimming	𝍢
Pottery	
Cooking	

Key: Each 𝍢 stands for 2 campers.

Bar Graphs page 191
Use the tally and the bar graph for problems 1–5.

1 Use the data in the tally to copy and complete the bar graph. Write a title for the graph.

2 In which week was the computer used most often? How can you tell without reading the scale of the bar graph?

3 During which week was the computer used exactly 10 hours?

4 How many hours was the computer used during Week 4?

5 How many hours was the computer used over five weeks?

Angelica's Computer Use		
Week	**Tally**	**Hours of Computer Use**
Week 1	////	4
Week 2	ŁĦŦ /	6
Week 3	ŁĦŦ ŁĦŦ	10
Week 4	ŁĦŦ //	7
Week 5	ŁĦŦ ŁĦŦ ///	13

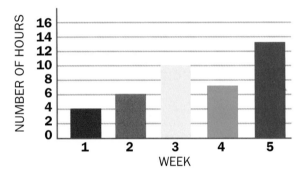

Problem Solvers at Work page 195
Solve. Use the line plot for problems 1–2.
Explain your methods.

1 How many people have 1 brother or sister? How many have 4 brothers or sisters?

2 How many people were surveyed in all?

3 One square table can seat one person on each side. How many people can be seated when 2 tables are pushed together?

Number of Brothers and Sisters

```
                x
                x
        x       x
        x       x       x
        x       x       x
        x       x       x               x
        0       1       2       3       4
```

4 **Logical reasoning** Put these sentences in order. Explain your answer.
a. See you later.   **b.** Hello.
c. How have you been?

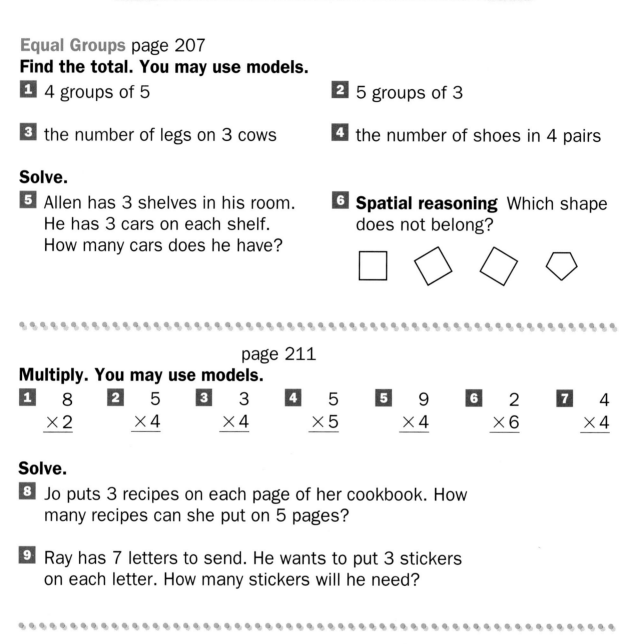

Equal Groups page 207
Find the total. You may use models.

1 4 groups of 5

2 5 groups of 3

3 the number of legs on 3 cows

4 the number of shoes in 4 pairs

Solve.

5 Allen has 3 shelves in his room. He has 3 cars on each shelf. How many cars does he have?

6 **Spatial reasoning** Which shape does not belong?

page 211
Multiply. You may use models.

1 $\begin{array}{r} 8 \\ \times 2 \\ \hline \end{array}$
2 $\begin{array}{r} 5 \\ \times 4 \\ \hline \end{array}$
3 $\begin{array}{r} 3 \\ \times 4 \\ \hline \end{array}$
4 $\begin{array}{r} 5 \\ \times 5 \\ \hline \end{array}$
5 $\begin{array}{r} 9 \\ \times 4 \\ \hline \end{array}$
6 $\begin{array}{r} 2 \\ \times 6 \\ \hline \end{array}$
7 $\begin{array}{r} 4 \\ \times 4 \\ \hline \end{array}$

Solve.

8 Jo puts 3 recipes on each page of her cookbook. How many recipes can she put on 5 pages?

9 Ray has 7 letters to send. He wants to put 3 stickers on each letter. How many stickers will he need?

Multiplication Properties/Facts for 0 and 1 page 213
Multiply. Then use the Order Property to write a different number sentence.

1 1×6
2 4×3
3 5×2
4 7×0
5 4×6

Solve.

6 Kyle writes 2 jokes on each page of his joke book. How many jokes can he write on 4 pages?

7 Mia sold 4 baseball cards for $1 each. She also sold a hockey card for $2. How much did she earn?

2 and 5 as Factors page 219

Multiply.

1 5   **2** 4   **3** 1   **4** 8   **5** 9   **6** 7   **7** 4
$\times 2$ $\times 5$ $\times 2$ $\times 5$ $\times 2$ $\times 5$ $\times 2$

8 2×6 **9** 0×5 **10** 2×9 **11** 6×5 **12** 5×9

13 2×2 **14** 5×1 **15** 2×3 **16** 5×5 **17** 5×2

Solve. Use the tally for problems 18–19.

18 How many more people collect models than stamps?

19 How many people were asked about their collections?

Class Collections	
Models	ЖІ ЖІ ІІІ
Cards	ЖІ ЖІ
Stamps	ІІІІ

Problem-Solving Strategy: Use Alternate Methods page 221

Solve. Explain your methods.

1 Write the information that is needed to solve the problem. Then solve it. Kathy buys 3 puzzles at the mall. How much does she spend?

2 There are 5 baseball cards in one pack. Each pack sells for 25¢. Jack has 3 quarters. How many cards can he buy?

3 There were 324 tickets sold to the hobby show in the first hour. Round the sales to the nearest ten and nearest hundred.

4 Palani keeps his stones in a box with 3 rows. There are 6 stones in each row. How many stones does Palani have?

5 Sal collects quarters and dimes. His collection is worth $1.70. He has three times as many quarters as dimes. How many of each coin does he have?

6 Linus had 4 baskets of apples. There were 2 apples in each basket. He gave one basket to Jenny. How many apples did he have left?

7 Richard rode 17 miles to the park. Then he rode another 12 miles to the mall. How far did he ride in all?

8 Mallory has 3 daisies. She has twice as many roses. How many flowers does she have in all?

3 as a Factor page 223
Multiply.

1 2
  $\times 3$

2 3
  $\times 6$

3 1
  $\times 3$

4 3
  $\times 3$

5 8
  $\times 3$

6 9
  $\times 3$

7 4
  $\times 3$

8 0×3 **9** 4×3 **10** 3×5 **11** 3×7 **12** 9×3

13 3×6 **14** 3×3 **15** 2×3 **16** 8×3 **17** 1×3

Solve.

18 Identify the extra information. Then solve. Mary bought 3 postcards for 40¢ each. She gave the clerk $1.25 in quarters. How much change did she receive?

19 **Logical reasoning** June and her friends bought a pack of baseball cards, a model ship, and a model car. April did not buy a model. May bought a model ship. What did June and April buy?

4 as a Factor page 225
Multiply.

1 4
  $\times 0$

2 4
  $\times 6$

3 1
  $\times 4$

4 4
  $\times 4$

5 8
  $\times 4$

6 5
  $\times 4$

7 9
  $\times 4$

8 3×4 **9** 4×2 **10** 9×4 **11** 4×7 **12** 5×4

13 4×4 **14** 4×0 **15** 4×3 **16** 8×7 **17** 1×4

Solve. Use the pictograph for problems 18–20.

18 How many books are in the collection?

19 How many more comedy books are there than mystery and science books together?

20 How would you show that 5 mystery books were added to the collection?

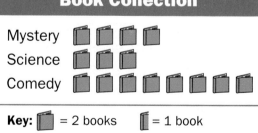

Book Collection

Mystery
Science
Comedy

Key: = 2 books   = 1 book

Use a Multiplication Table page 227

Multiply.

1
$$\begin{array}{r} 8 \\ \times 5 \\ \hline \end{array}$$
2
$$\begin{array}{r} 0 \\ \times 4 \\ \hline \end{array}$$
3
$$\begin{array}{r} 9 \\ \times 3 \\ \hline \end{array}$$
4
$$\begin{array}{r} 4 \\ \times 7 \\ \hline \end{array}$$
5
$$\begin{array}{r} 7 \\ \times 5 \\ \hline \end{array}$$
6
$$\begin{array}{r} 5 \\ \times 5 \\ \hline \end{array}$$
7
$$\begin{array}{r} 2 \\ \times 2 \\ \hline \end{array}$$

8 2×9 **9** 6×5 **10** 7×3 **11** 4×9 **12** 8×1

Write >, <, or = to complete the number sentence.

13 $3 \times 3 \bullet 2 \times 4$ **14** $4 \times 4 \bullet 2 \times 8$ **15** $5 \times 6 \bullet 4 \times 8$

16 $9 \times 0 \bullet 1 \times 1$ **17** $3 \times 2 \bullet 6 \times 1$ **18** $3 \times 5 \bullet 3 \times 4$

Solve.

19 Jason rides a total of 6 miles to and from school each day. How many miles does he ride in one week?

20 Complete the pattern.
4, ■, 12, ■, 20, 24, 28, ■, ■

Problem Solvers at Work page 231

Solve. Explain your methods.

1 Marco has 4 bags of marbles. There are 6 marbles in each bag. He gives 1 bag to Tyson. How many marbles does Marco have now?

2 Ashley has $2. Jaime has twice as much money as Ashley. Kelly has twice as much money as Jaime. How much money does Kelly have?

3 Calvin has 5 quarters, 3 dimes, and 4 pennies. Arnetta has $1.60. Who has more money? How do you know?

4 Juliette has $13. Anthony has $23. Sabrina has $15. About how much money do they have altogether?

5 A store has a sale on stuffed animals. A bear sells for $16 less than the original price. It is on sale for $16. What was the original price?

6 One album has 234 stickers. Another album has 342 stamps. Which album has more items? How many more?

6 and 7 as Factors page 245

Multiply. Explain your method.

1 $3 \times 7 = \blacksquare$
$6 \times 7 = \blacksquare$

2 $6 \times 5 = \blacksquare$
$7 \times 5 = \blacksquare$

3 $4 \times 6 = \blacksquare$
$8 \times 6 = \blacksquare$

Multiply.

4 $\begin{array}{r} 2 \\ \times 6 \\ \hline \end{array}$
5 $\begin{array}{r} 7 \\ \times 4 \\ \hline \end{array}$
6 $\begin{array}{r} 1 \\ \times 6 \\ \hline \end{array}$
7 $\begin{array}{r} 6 \\ \times 8 \\ \hline \end{array}$
8 $\begin{array}{r} 2 \\ \times 7 \\ \hline \end{array}$
9 $\begin{array}{r} 6 \\ \times 7 \\ \hline \end{array}$
10 $\begin{array}{r} 7 \\ \times 7 \\ \hline \end{array}$

11 $\begin{array}{r} 9 \\ \times 6 \\ \hline \end{array}$
12 $\begin{array}{r} 6 \\ \times 3 \\ \hline \end{array}$
13 $\begin{array}{r} 6 \\ \times 6 \\ \hline \end{array}$
14 $\begin{array}{r} 0 \\ \times 7 \\ \hline \end{array}$
15 $\begin{array}{r} 8 \\ \times 7 \\ \hline \end{array}$
16 $\begin{array}{r} 7 \\ \times 1 \\ \hline \end{array}$
17 $\begin{array}{r} 9 \\ \times 7 \\ \hline \end{array}$

Solve.

18 The sum of two one-digit numbers is 14. The product is 48. What are the two numbers?

19 Greg's family spent $5 to enter a state park. Then they bought 7 lunch specials at $3 each. How much did they spend in all?

8 and 9 as Factors page 249

Multiply.

1 $\begin{array}{r} 3 \\ \times 8 \\ \hline \end{array}$
2 $\begin{array}{r} 9 \\ \times 5 \\ \hline \end{array}$
3 $\begin{array}{r} 2 \\ \times 8 \\ \hline \end{array}$
4 $\begin{array}{r} 8 \\ \times 6 \\ \hline \end{array}$
5 $\begin{array}{r} 4 \\ \times 9 \\ \hline \end{array}$
6 $\begin{array}{r} 6 \\ \times 9 \\ \hline \end{array}$
7 $\begin{array}{r} 9 \\ \times 8 \\ \hline \end{array}$

8 $\begin{array}{r} 8 \\ \times 7 \\ \hline \end{array}$
9 $\begin{array}{r} 0 \\ \times 8 \\ \hline \end{array}$
10 $\begin{array}{r} 8 \\ \times 8 \\ \hline \end{array}$
11 $\begin{array}{r} 1 \\ \times 9 \\ \hline \end{array}$
12 $\begin{array}{r} 7 \\ \times 9 \\ \hline \end{array}$
13 $\begin{array}{r} 9 \\ \times 2 \\ \hline \end{array}$
14 $\begin{array}{r} 9 \\ \times 9 \\ \hline \end{array}$

15 8×4
16 5×8
17 9×3
18 9×0
19 9×8

Solve.

20 A party at a pizza shop costs $7 per child. How much will it cost to have a party for 8 children?

21 Sofia bought 30 ride tickets and Fred bought 35 ride tickets. How many tickets did they buy in all?

Problem-Solving Strategy: Make an Organized List page 251

Solve. Explain your method.

1 Byron is an actor. In one play, he can wear either a green or a red hat, and either a black or white shirt. He can choose to wear a fake beard. How many different ways can Byron look in the play?

2 Write the extra information. Then solve. Mary bought 4 postcards for 30¢ each. She gave the clerk $1.50 in quarters. How much change did she receive?

3 **Spatial reasoning** Use 7 toothpicks, or other objects of equal length, to make 2 squares.

4 The Jones family is driving 625 miles on their vacation. They drove 430 miles today. How much farther do they have to travel?

5 Use the data at the right to make a line plot showing the number of times students have ridden horses at State Park. Then write a question that can be answered using your line plot.

0 times	///
1 time	ℋℋ ////
2 times	ℋℋ /
3 times	///
4 times	
5 times	////

⦿⦿

Square Numbers page 257
Write the multiplication sentence.

1 **2** **3**

Draw the model and multiply.

4 6 × 6

5 9 × 9

6 7 × 7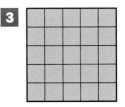

Solve.

7 The puppet theater sold 33 tickets on Friday, 97 tickets on Saturday, and 148 tickets on Sunday. How many tickets did they sell in all?

8 At the park, Peter went swimming for 30 minutes and canoeing for 45 minutes. How much time did he spend at the park?

Use a Multiplication Table page 259

Multiply. You may use the multiplication table on page 258.

1 4
×3

2 9
×6

3 8
×7

4 2
×9

5 5
×5

6 9
×9

7 7
×6

8 7 × 2

9 8 × 4

10 4 × 1

11 6 × 8

12 7 × 5

13 4 × 9

14 6 × 6

15 7 × 9

16 9 × 8

17 8 × 8

Solve.

18 Write the extra information. Then solve. Skates rent for $5 each hour and bikes rent for $8 each hour. How much will it cost to rent a pair of skates for 4 hours?

19 Wilfred has 3 discount coupons for lunch. Each coupon is good for 6 people. What is the greatest number of lunches Wilfred can buy at a discount?

Three or More Factors page 261

Multiply.

1 (4 × 1) × 8

2 9 × (3 × 2)

3 (2 × 2) × 6

4 5 × (0 × 8)

5 (3 × 3) × 7

6 8 × (2 × 4)

7 (1 × 1) × 1

8 7 × (4 × 2)

9 (2 × 3) × (4 × 2)

10 (3 × 1) × (4 × 2)

11 (3 × 2) × (3 × 3)

12 2 × (3 × 1) × (2 × 2)

13 (4 × 2) × (1 × 1) × 5

14 2 × (2 × 2) × (3 × 3)

Solve. Use the pictograph to answer problems 15–16.

15 How many lifeguards are on duty at Collier Beach? at Torres Beach? at North Beach? at all three beaches?

16 How many lifeguards would be on duty at Collier Beach if each symbol stood for 5 lifeguards?

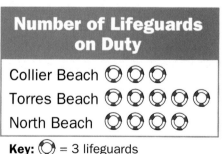

Number of Lifeguards on Duty

Collier Beach ◎ ◎ ◎
Torres Beach ◎ ◎ ◎ ◎ ◎
North Beach ◎ ◎ ◎ ◎

Key: ◎ = 3 lifeguards

Problem Solvers at Work page 265

Solve. Explain your methods.

1 The swim class keeps track of weekly attendance. Use the tally to copy and complete the bar graph. Write a title for the tally and the graph.

Week	Tally	Number of Swimmers
1	JHT IIII	9
2	JHT JHT II	12
3	JHT JHT III	13
4	JHT	5

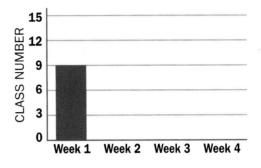

Use your bar graph for problems 2–5.

2 For which weeks did you draw bars that did not end on a line? Why?

3 Why do you think so few students attended class during Week 4?

4 There were 7 more students in Week 5 than in Week 1. How many students were in Week 5?

5 In Week 2, 17 students were supposed to attend class. How many students were absent?

Meaning of Division page 277

Complete. Explain your methods. You may use models.

1 18 in all
6 in each group
▨ groups

2 24 in all
3 groups
▨ in each group

3 25 in all
5 in each group
▨ groups

Solve.

4 One package of dog toys has 3 toys. Bob buys 12 toys. How many packages does he buy?

5 Katie walks her dogs 3 miles each day. How far do they walk in one week?

Relate Multiplication and Division page 279
**Write a pair of related multiplication and division
sentences for the group of numbers.**

1 2, 4, 8 **2** 3, 7, 21 **3** 6, 9, 54 **4** 5, 8, 40 **5** 6, 6, 36

Solve.

6 Duchess had 5 puppies in each
of her first 2 litters. She had 4
puppies in her third litter. How
many puppies has Duchess had
in all?

7 Marco could wear either his
blue or his yellow shirt to the
party, and either his blue or his
black pants. How many different
outfits could Marco wear?

8 It takes about 30 minutes to
run one lap in the park. About
how long will it take to run
3 laps?

9 **Logical reasoning** Jane is the
10th person in line. The same
number of people are in front of
her as behind her. How many
people are in line?

Divide by 2 and 5 page 281
Divide.

1 10 ÷ 2 **2** 35 ÷ 5 **3** 16 ÷ 2 **4** 15 ÷ 5 **5** 18 ÷ 2

6 5)30 **7** 2)14 **8** 5)45 **9** 2)6 **10** 5)40

Solve.

11 Each dog run at a kennel can
hold 2 dogs. There are 12 dogs
at the kennel. What is the
fewest number of dog runs that
can be used at one time?

12 Luisa started washing her dog
at 3:45 P.M. She finished at
4:30 P.M. It took 15 more
minutes to dry it. How long did
it take Luisa to bathe her dog?

13 In 5 days Dee's horse ran 35
miles. Each day it ran the same
distance. How many miles did it
run in 10 days?

14 Al rode his horse twice as far as
Julia. Julia rode 5 times as far
as Dean. Dean rode 2 miles.
How far did Julia and Al ride?

Divide by 3 and 4 page 283
Divide.

1 9 ÷ 3　　**2** 12 ÷ 4　　**3** 21 ÷ 3　　**4** 36 ÷ 4　　**5** 24 ÷ 3

6 4)16　　**7** 3)15　　**8** 4)28　　**9** 3)27　　**10** 4)32

11 Divide 6 by 3.　　**12** Divide 20 by 4.　　**13** Divide 18 by 3.

Solve.

14 Alvin works in the pet store. He wants to display 24 pet beds in 4 equal stacks. How many beds will he place in each stack?

15 Wendy has twice as many goldfish as Maggie. Maggie has 5 orange goldfish and 3 yellow goldfish. How many goldfish does Wendy have?

Divide by 6 and 7 page 285
Divide.

1 18 ÷ 6　　**2** 35 ÷ 7　　**3** 36 ÷ 6　　**4** 56 ÷ 7　　**5** 54 ÷ 6

6 7)21　　**7** 6)24　　**8** 7)63　　**9** 6)48　　**10** 7)42

Solve.

11 There are 18 horses in a parade. They march in equal rows. How many ways can the riders line up the horses in the parade? List all the ways.

12 **Logical reasoning** The beagle is to the right of the spaniel. The spaniel is to the left of the poodle and to the right of the boxer. Which dog is farthest from the poodle?

Divide by 8 and 9 page 287
Divide.

1 24 ÷ 8　　**2** 36 ÷ 9　　**3** 48 ÷ 8　　**4** 81 ÷ 9　　**5** 56 ÷ 8

6 9)45　　**7** 8)64　　**8** 9)54　　**9** 8)32　　**10** 9)72

Divide with 0 and 1 page 293
Divide.

1 $0 \div 2$ **2** $4 \div 1$ **3** $8 \div 8$ **4** $1 \div 1$ **5** $0 \div 5$

6 $1\overline{)6}$ **7** $3\overline{)3}$ **8** $1\overline{)9}$ **9** $7\overline{)0}$ **10** $5\overline{)5}$

Solve.

11 Sophie and 6 friends bought 7 tickets for pony rides. Each rode a pony. How many times did each person ride?

12 **Spatial reasoning** Connect all of the dots in every way. What shapes did you make?

Use a Multiplication Table to Divide page 295
Divide.

1 $12 \div 2$ **2** $18 \div 9$ **3** $45 \div 9$ **4** $56 \div 7$ **5** $28 \div 4$

6 $1\overline{)4}$ **7** $3\overline{)27}$ **8** $5\overline{)20}$ **9** $6\overline{)42}$ **10** $8\overline{)0}$

Solve.

11 A pet store has 8 brown and 7 multicolor guinea pigs. There are the same number of guinea pigs in each of 3 pens. How many guinea pigs are in each pen?

12 One symbol in a pictograph stands for 2 pet owners. There are 8 symbols for people owning birds. How many pet owners have birds?

Problem-Solving Strategy: Work Backward page 297
Solve. Explain your method.

1 Arlon gave Geoffrey 5 guppies. He gave Elena twice as many guppies as he gave Geoffrey. He has 23 guppies left. How many guppies did he start with?

2 Dylan was the 95th person to enter the Pet Show. How many more people must enter before the attendance is 1,000 people?

Fact Families page 301

Write a fact family for the group of numbers.

1 2, 5, 10   **2** 9, 6, 54   **3** 4, 7, 28   **4** 5, 5, 25

5 1, 3, 3   **6** 7, 6, 42   **7** 3, 4, 12   **8** 8, 9, 72

Solve. Use the line plot.

9 How much did Mato spend in all to buy the $2 fish? Write a fact family using these numbers.

10 How much did Mato spend to buy all the fish?

Cost of Mato's Aquarium Fish

```
        x
        x   x
    x   x   x       x
    x   x   x       x           x
   $1  $2  $3  $4  $5  $6  $7  $8
```

Divide with a Remainder page 305

Find the quotient and the remainder. You may use models.

1 $13 \div 2$ **2** $45 \div 7$ **3** $17 \div 3$ **4** $0 \div 5$ **5** $25 \div 8$

6 $4\overline{)34}$ **7** $1\overline{)9}$ **8** $6\overline{)28}$ **9** $9\overline{)23}$ **10** $5\overline{)37}$

Solve.

11 Ursi has 10 nut sticks to share equally among 3 birds. How many sticks will each bird get? How many will be left over?

12 Draw the next 2 figures in the pattern.

Problem Solvers at Work page 309

Solve. Explain your methods.

1 Jason buys 4 bottles of scented shampoo. Each bottle costs $5. Write a number sentence to find how much Jason spends on shampoo.

2 Viola had a $400 budget to adopt a pet. She spent $234 for the kitten, $141 at the vet, and $102 at the pet store. Did Viola spend more than her budget?

Length in Customary Units page 321

Estimate. Then measure to the nearest inch.

1 ⟨————————————————————⟩

Solve.

2 Billy Joe said the jungle bars were 3 units long. Which unit would be the best measure—inches, feet, or yards? Explain.

3 A running course is 2 miles long. Write a number sentence to find how far Uta runs if she runs the course every day for one week.

Length in Metric Units page 325

Estimate. Then measure to the nearest centimeter.

1

2 ⟨————————————⟩

Solve.

3 Would you use centimeters or meters to measure the distance run in a relay race? Explain.

4 Every three days, Neal plays the piano for 30 minutes. How many hours does he play in 12 days?

Perimeter page 329

Find the perimeter.

1
5 cm
5 cm   5 cm
5 cm

2
9 in.
9 in.   9 in.
9 in.   9 in.
9 in.   9 in.
9 in.

3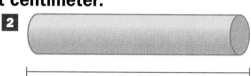
14 ft   8 ft
17 ft

Solve.

4 A rectangular painting is 4 feet long and 3 feet wide. What is the perimeter of the painting?

5 Mindy reads 3 books each week. How many books can she read in 8 weeks?

Area page 331
Find the area in square units.

 1

2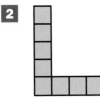

3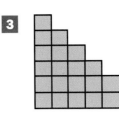

Solve.

4 Draw a square with 16 square units. Color three times as many of the square units blue as you color red.

5 Delaney scored 15 points in a basketball game. What is the greatest number of 2-point baskets she could have made?

Volume page 333
Find the volume in cubic units. Remember to count the cubes you cannot see.

1

2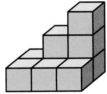

3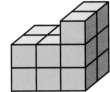

Solve.

4 **Spatial reasoning** What is the volume of the largest cube you can make using 50 cubes or less?

5 Dana bought 3 flowerpots for $3 each and potting soil for $1.98. How much did she spend in all?

Problem-Solving Strategy: Use Logical Reasoning page 335
Solve. Explain your methods.

1 Jewel, Molly, and Hector each like different types of music. Molly does not like country. Hector likes rap. Who likes rock and roll?

2 There were 2,405 people at the first football game, 2,054 at the second game, and 2,540 at the third. Write the attendance in order from greatest to least.

Capacity in Customary Units page 341

Write the containers in order from least to greatest capacity.

1 sport water bottle, pond, birdbath

2 water tank, cup, tub

Solve.

3 There was 1 gallon of orange punch and 4 quarts of red punch at the picnic. How many gallons of punch were there in all?

4 Kirk paid $48 for a season ticket to 8 home football games. How much will it cost Kirk to watch each game?

Capacity in Metric Units page 343

Complete. Choose a reasonable estimate.

1 Sven drinks ▊ mL of water after gym class.   **a.** 3   **b.** 30   **c.** 300

2 The fishbowl holds ▊ L of water.   **a.** 3   **b.** 30   **c.** 300

Solve.

3 Two jars each hold 270 mL of paint. Another jar holds 450 mL of paint. If you use all three jars, will you have used 1 L of paint? Explain.

4 Bruno trades baseball cards. He gave Ivan 6 cards and received 4 cards in return. He now has 68 cards. How many cards did he have before the trade?

Weight in Customary Units page 345

Estimate the weight of objects, from lightest to heaviest.

1 book, feather, pen, key chain

2 ruler, stapler, brick, thumbtack

3 One bag of trail mix weighs 12 ounces. Another bag weighs 5 ounces. Do the two bags combined weigh more than 1 pound? Explain.

4 **Logical reasoning** You have one pitcher that holds 2 liters and another pitcher that holds 5 liters. How can you measure 6 liters of water?

Mass in Metric Units page 347
Write the letter of the better estimate.

1
a. 1 g
b. 1 kg

2
a. 3 g
b. 3 kg

3
a. 1 g
b. 1 kg

Solve.

4 Darlene bought 5 kg of fruit, 2 kg of cheese, and a 625-g box of pasta. How many grams of food did she buy?

5 Vinnie has saved $103.45 from birthday gifts. He spends $72.91 at the sporting goods store. How much money does he have left?

6 **Spatial reasoning** Use graph paper to draw as many rectangles as you can with an area of 16 square units. Write the length of each side.

7 Write the extra information. Then solve. Jed has soccer practice from 3:15 P.M. until 4:30 P.M. Then he has a 1-hour violin lesson. How long does soccer practice last?

Problem Solvers at Work page 351
Solve. Use the tally chart to solve problems 2–5.
Explain your methods.

1 Rick has played 6 more games than Ruby. Ruby has played 3 fewer games than Basil. Basil has played 8 games. How many games has Rick played?

Sport Survey		
Sport	**Tally**	**Number**
Baseball	///	3
Soccer	Ж1 I	6
Swimming	//	2

2 How many were in the survey?

3 How many more people chose soccer than chose swimming?

4 Which sport is named the most often? the least often?

5 Use the data to make a table. Then make a bar graph.

3-Dimensional Figures page 365
Name the figure the object looks like.

1    **2**    **3**    **4**

5 It has 2 flat faces that are same-size rectangles and 4 flat faces that are same-size rectangles.

6 It has 2 flat faces, 2 edges, and no corners.

Solve.

7 Dessert is an orange and a glass of milk. What 3-dimensional figures do they look like?

8 Hakeem treated himself and 4 friends to lunch. He spent $5 for each person and has $2.30 left. How much did he have before they ate lunch?

2-Dimensional Figures page 367
Write the name of the shape.

1 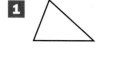   **2**   **3**   **4**

Draw the shape and name it.

5 It has 4 corners. The sides are all the same length.

6 It does not have any straight sides.

Solve.

7 **Spatial reasoning** If you trace around the face of a rectangular prism, you can make one of two shapes. What are those two shapes?

8 The sum of the digits in a two-digit number is 14. The product of the digits is 48. The ones digit is less than $63 \div 9$. What is the number?

Polygons page 369

**Write *yes* or *no* to tell whether the shape is a polygon.
If it is a polygon, name it.**

1 H

2 ∞

3

4

Solve.

5 Spatial reasoning Trace and cut out 6 triangles. Then make a hexagon.

6 The difference between the high and low temperatures was 18 degrees on Sunday. The low temperature was 58°F. What was the high temperature?

Lines, Line Segments, Rays, and Angles page 371

Tell if the angle is *less than*, *equal to*, or *greater than* a right angle.

1

2

3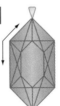

4

Problem-Solving Strategy: Finding a Pattern page 373

**Solve. Use the diagram for problems 1–3.
Explain your method.**

1 How many inches long is the ribbon?

2 Enrique made the design on the ribbon. How could he use words to describe the pattern so that Ashley could copy it? How could he translate the pattern into numbers?

3 Ashley copied the pattern onto a ribbon that was 15 inches long. She drew each shape the same size as in Enrique's pattern. How many circles did she draw?

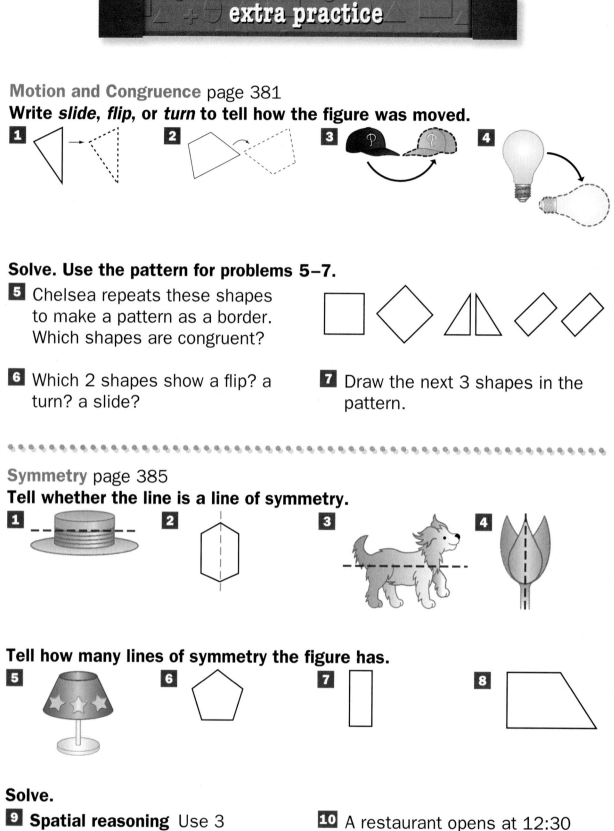

Motion and Congruence page 381

Write *slide*, *flip*, or *turn* to tell how the figure was moved.

1 **2** **3** **4**

Solve. Use the pattern for problems 5–7.

5 Chelsea repeats these shapes to make a pattern as a border. Which shapes are congruent?

6 Which 2 shapes show a flip? a turn? a slide?

7 Draw the next 3 shapes in the pattern.

Symmetry page 385

Tell whether the line is a line of symmetry.

1 **2** **3** **4**

Tell how many lines of symmetry the figure has.

5 **6** **7** **8**

Solve.

9 **Spatial reasoning** Use 3 triangles to make a design with one line of symmetry. Color your design.

10 A restaurant opens at 12:30 P.M. and closes at 9:15 P.M. How long is it open each day?

Ordered Pairs page 387

Write the ordered pair that tells the location of each item on the map.

1 bench

2 entrance

3 slide

4 bridge

City Park

Tell what is at the point on the map.

5 (6, 0)

6 (1, 2)

7 (2, 6)

8 (4, 3)

Solve. Use the map of City Park for problems 9–10.

9 What is the area of City Park in square units?

10 What is the perimeter of City Park?

11 Gary feeds 24 slices of bread to 6 ducks. How many slices does each duck eat?

12 Tami receives 8¢ for each bottle she recycles. How much will she receive for 9 bottles?

Problem Solvers at Work page 391

Solve. Explain your methods.

1 Ms. Lopez is putting a fence around her garden. The garden is 9 feet by 15 feet. She puts a fence post at each corner and every 3 feet. How many fence posts will she need?

2 Ms. Lopez is making bouquets from the roses in her garden. She can cut either red, yellow, or pink roses and put them in vases or baskets. What ways can she make the bouquets?

3 Arturo is going to save $2 each week. He has saved $23. If he doesn't spend any of his savings, how much will he have saved at the end of 8 weeks?

4 A stool has 3 legs and a table has 4 legs. Eldon counted 24 legs in the room. How many stools were in the room? How many tables?

5 Ami bought a sweater for $29.95 and a skirt for $21.99. Her change was $3.06. How much money did she give the clerk?

6 Miranda and her sisters spent 4 weeks at summer camp. How many days were they at the camp?

Meaning of Fractions page 401
Tell if the figure shows thirds. Tell why or why not.

 1 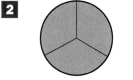 **2** **3** 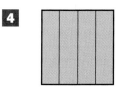 **4**

Draw a whole to match the description.

5 Ann rolls the dough into a circle and cuts it into eighths.

6 Bill has a piece of ribbon and cuts it into fourths.

Parts of a Whole page 403
Write a fraction for the part that is blue.

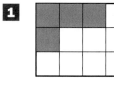 **1** **2**  **3**  **4**

Solve.

5 A leather band is divided into eighths. Stars are on 3 parts. The other parts are suns. What fraction of the whole are suns?

6 Supplies at Arts Ink cost $12.95. The same supplies cost $15.78 at Crafts Ink. How much more do the supplies cost at Crafts Ink?

Parts of a Group page 405
Write a fraction for the part that is blue.

4 7 of the 10 beads are blue.

5 5 of the 6 blocks are blue.

Equivalent Fractions page 409

Complete to name the equivalent fraction. You may use fraction strips.

1 $\frac{1}{2} = \frac{\blacksquare}{8}$ **2** $\frac{1}{3} = \frac{\blacksquare}{6}$ **3** $\frac{9}{12} = \frac{3}{\blacksquare}$ **4** $\frac{1}{4} = \frac{2}{\blacksquare}$ **5** $\frac{2}{6} = \frac{\blacksquare}{\blacksquare}$

Solve.

6 Peter uses a $\frac{1}{4}$-cup measuring cup to measure $\frac{1}{2}$ cup of milk. How many times will he fill the $\frac{1}{4}$-cup measuring cup? (Hint: How many fourths are in one half?)

7 **Logical reasoning** Hillary, Adano, and Que are making cookies, fudge, and brownies. Adano is not making cookies. Que is making fudge. Which student is making which treat?

Compare Fractions page 413

Compare the fractions. Write >, <, or =. Be prepared to explain your method.

1 $\frac{2}{3} \bullet \frac{1}{3}$ **2** $\frac{3}{6} \bullet \frac{3}{4}$ **3** $\frac{1}{2} \bullet \frac{3}{4}$ **4** $\frac{1}{4} \bullet \frac{2}{8}$ **5** $\frac{2}{10} \bullet \frac{2}{5}$

6 $\frac{3}{6} \bullet \frac{2}{6}$ **7** $\frac{2}{4} \bullet \frac{7}{12}$ **8** $\frac{1}{4} \bullet \frac{1}{6}$ **9** $\frac{5}{6} \bullet \frac{2}{3}$ **10** $\frac{1}{3} \bullet \frac{4}{12}$

Solve.

11 Jo uses $\frac{1}{2}$-inch yarn pieces in a design. Ty uses $\frac{1}{4}$-inch pieces. Who uses shorter pieces?

12 A package has 3 erasers. Ken has 3 packages. How many erasers does Ken have?

Mixed Numbers page 415

Write a fraction and a mixed number.

1  **2**   **3**

Solve.

4 Arturo and Amil were studying plant growth in science class. Arturo's plant grew $1\frac{3}{8}$ inches. Amil's plant grew $1\frac{4}{8}$ inches. Whose plant grew $\frac{11}{8}$ inches?

5 Flo has 36 quilt squares. Of these, her aunt made 8 squares and her mother made 10. Flo made the rest. How many squares did she make?

Decimals Less Than 1 page 423
Write a decimal.

1 $\frac{3}{10}$ **2** $\frac{1}{10}$ **3** $\frac{3}{100}$ **4** $\frac{43}{100}$ **5** $\frac{80}{100}$

Solve.

6 Chen drew a design. He colored 0.25 of the squares red, 0.6 blue, and 0.05 yellow. Use a hundred-square grid to show what the design could look like.

7 Sue can draw her teacher or her principal. She can use paints, markers, or charcoal. How many different kinds of pictures could she draw? List them.

Decimals Greater Than 1 page 425
Write a decimal.

1 $5\frac{3}{10}$ **2** $3\frac{7}{10}$ **3** $6\frac{5}{10}$ **4** $4\frac{2}{10}$

5 $2\frac{27}{100}$ **6** $8\frac{97}{100}$ **7** $4\frac{6}{100}$ **8** $3\frac{5}{100}$

9 one and two tenths

10 seven and fifty-four hundredths

Solve.

11 Lyle made two and three-tenths liters of paste. Use a decimal to show how much paste he made.

12 **Spatial reasoning** Draw a design using 10 congruent triangles that has at least one line of symmetry.

Add and Subtract Decimals page 429
Add or subtract. You may use models.

1
$$0.3 + 0.4$$

2
$$0.8 - 0.4$$

3
$$3.6 + 2.5$$

4
$$5.2 - 3.6$$

5
$$4.23 + 3.72$$

6
$$3.00 - 1.25$$

7 $2.3 + 3.5$ **8** $4.7 - 3.1$ **9** $7.28 - 4.36$ **10** $4.00 + 3.25$

Problem-Solving Strategy: Conduct an Experiment page 431

Solve. Use the pictograph for problems 1–3. Explain your method.

1 How many times was the experiment conducted?

2 Which color did the spinner stop on the least? the most?

3 What do you think the spinner looked like? Draw it. Explain your reasoning.

Spinner Outcomes	
Colors	
Green	↗ ↗ ↗ ↗ ↗ ╱
Blue	↗ ↗ ↗ ↗ ↗ ↗
Red	↗ ↗ ↗

Key: ↗ stands for 2 spins.
╱ stands for 1 spin.

4 Use your drawing from problem 3 to make a spinner. Spin 30 times to see how often you spin each color. Graph your results.

Probability page 433

Use the spinner for problems 1–3.

1 Are the outcomes equally likely? Why?

2 What is the probability of spinning a triangle? a square?

3 Would it be fair to use this spinner in a game if each player got a point each time the spinner stopped on his or her shape? Why?

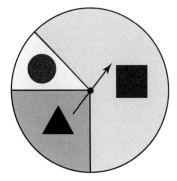

Problem Solvers at Work page 437

Solve. Explain your method.

1 Lil rolls a number cube. She has a 3 out of 6 chance of rolling a 10, a 1 out of 6 chance of rolling a 20, and a 2 out of 6 chance of rolling a 30. What are all of the numbers on the cube?

2 A punch is made by combining 1.50 liters of pineapple juice, 1.50 liters of orange juice, and 0.75 liters of ginger ale. How many liters of punch does this recipe make?

Multiplication Patterns page 447
Complete.

1 2 × 2 tens = ■ tens = ■

2 6 × 3 tens = ■ tens = ■

3 4 × 9 tens = ■ tens = ■

4 7 × 7 tens = ■ tens = ■

Multiply mentally.

5 5 × 40

6 3 × 200

7 900 × 6

8 8 × 700

Solve.

9 One employee at the animation studio earns $8 an hour. He works 5 hours each day. How much does he earn each day? How much does he earn in a 5-day work week? How much does he earn in 8 weeks?

10 **Logical reasoning** Connie, Alex, and Loretta each have a favorite hobby. One draws and another does origami. Connie and Alex do not make pottery. Alex uses a pencil. Which hobby does each have?

Estimate Products page 449
Estimate the product by rounding.

1 3 × 47

2 5 × 71

3 8 × 36

4 9 × 83

5 4 × 403

6 6 × 692

7 3 × 738

8 7 × 850

9 4 × $28

10 5 × $84

11 7 × $448

12 9 × $505

Solve.

13 A ballet is performed in a theater with 873 seats. Estimate how many people can attend 6 performances.

14 Acting students study for 1 hour and 30 minutes and have a 15-minute break. Class starts at 6:30 P.M. When does it end?

15 Vi walks 4 miles north, 8 miles east, 2 more miles north, 2 miles west, and then 6 miles south. How many miles is she from her starting point?

16 Vincent brought $\frac{1}{4}$ of his stamp collection to school. Kim brought $\frac{1}{4}$ of her collection. Did Vincent bring the same number of stamps as Kim? Explain.

Multiply by 1-Digit Numbers page 453
Multiply using any method.

1 2×12 **2** 3×23 **3** 4×32 **4** 6×21

5 5×11 **6** 8×31 **7** 5×34 **8** 4×44

9
$$\begin{array}{r} 14 \\ \times\ 2 \\ \hline \end{array}$$

10
$$\begin{array}{r} 22 \\ \times\ 4 \\ \hline \end{array}$$

11
$$\begin{array}{r} 23 \\ \times\ 5 \\ \hline \end{array}$$

12
$$\begin{array}{r} 32 \\ \times\ 3 \\ \hline \end{array}$$

13
$$\begin{array}{r} 42 \\ \times\ 7 \\ \hline \end{array}$$

Solve.

14 A play has 3 acts. Each act is 21 minutes. Is the play longer or shorter than one hour? How much longer or shorter?

15 **Spatial reasoning** Draw or trace some squares. Divide them into fourths in as many different ways as you can.

Multiply by 1-Digit Numbers page 457
Multiply using any method. Estimate to check the reasonableness of your answer.

1
$$\begin{array}{r} 12 \\ \times\ 2 \\ \hline \end{array}$$

2
$$\begin{array}{r} 61 \\ \times\ 7 \\ \hline \end{array}$$

3
$$\begin{array}{r} 26 \\ \times\ 3 \\ \hline \end{array}$$

4
$$\begin{array}{r} 45 \\ \times\ 4 \\ \hline \end{array}$$

5
$$\begin{array}{r} 72 \\ \times\ 3 \\ \hline \end{array}$$

6
$$\begin{array}{r} 43 \\ \times\ 5 \\ \hline \end{array}$$

7
$$\begin{array}{r} 34 \\ \times\ 8 \\ \hline \end{array}$$

8
$$\begin{array}{r} \$33 \\ \times\ 3 \\ \hline \end{array}$$

9
$$\begin{array}{r} \$82 \\ \times\ 4 \\ \hline \end{array}$$

10
$$\begin{array}{r} \$52 \\ \times\ 7 \\ \hline \end{array}$$

11 4×12 **12** 6×61 **13** 9×34 **14** $5 \times \$35$

Solve.

15 Guadeloupe and Lorenzo are tightrope walkers in the circus. They are partners in 2 matinee and 5 evening performances each week. How many times do they perform over a 24-week period?

16 On Saturday, 125 students from Bobby Ray's school went to the circus. On Sunday, Bobby Ray and 236 other students went to the circus. How many more students attended on Sunday than on Saturday?

Problem-Solving Strategy: Solve a Simpler Problem page 463

Solve. Explain your method.

1 The theater snack bar sells small boxes of popcorn for $2 each and large boxes of popcorn for $5 each. Cassandra sold 46 small boxes and 31 large boxes. How much money did she collect for popcorn?

2 Guillermo celebrates his birthday on Thursday, May 14. Jordan celebrates her birthday 10 days after Guillermo's. Which day will Jordan's birthday fall on? What is the date?

3 Theater tickets are $10 for adults and $5 for students. Nan sold 15 tickets. She sold twice as many student tickets as adult tickets. How much money did she collect?

4 Sal can wear either a blue coat or a brown coat. He can wear either sandals, loafers, or sneakers with the coat. What outfits can he wear?

Division Patterns page 465

Complete.

1 8 tens ÷ 2 = ■ tens = ■

2 18 tens ÷ 6 = ■ tens = ■

3 28 tens ÷ 4 = ■ tens = ■

4 35 tens ÷ 7 = ■ tens = ■

Divide mentally.

5 60 ÷ 2

6 120 ÷ 3

7 250 ÷ 5

8 320 ÷ 4

9 160 ÷ 4

10 360 ÷ 6

11 450 ÷ 9

12 560 ÷ 8

Solve.

13 Gwendolyn and Howard are making copies of the videotape of the class talent show. They have $120 to buy blank videotapes. Blank videotapes cost $3 each. How many videotapes can they buy?

14 **Spatial reasoning** Draw the next three shapes in the pattern.

Divide by 1-Digit Numbers page 469

Divide. Use models, drawings, or pencil and paper.

1 $3\overline{)31}$ **2** $6\overline{)86}$ **3** $5\overline{)75}$ **4** $4\overline{)53}$ **5** $2\overline{)25}$

6 $4\overline{)48}$ **7** $3\overline{)50}$ **8** $6\overline{)66}$ **9** $5\overline{)56}$ **10** $4\overline{)85}$

11 $31 \div 2$ **12** $44 \div 3$ **13** $72 \div 4$ **14** $80 \div 6$

Solve.

15 Crystal has 42 puppets. She displays them in three equal-size groups. How many are in each group?

16 Alejandro trades 32 quarters and 10 dimes for dollar bills. How many dollar bills does he receive?

17 Jonathan has 73¢. Katrina has 58¢. Together they have 14 coins. Which coins does Jonathan have? Which coins does Katrina have?

18 The total area of 6 congruent shapes is 72 square units. What is the area of each shape? Use graph paper to draw a picture of the 6 shapes.

Problem Solvers at Work page 473

Solve. Use the bar graph to answer problems 3–5.
Explain your method.

1 Matthew has 25 feet of yarn to frame the School Play signs. How many signs can he frame?

2 Carlotta visits her grandmother every 3 days. Her cousin, George, visits every 4 days. They both visit on a Monday. What is the next day that both Carlotta and George visit their grandmother?

3 How many more students like television than like concerts?

4 How many students were surveyed?

5 Copy the graph. Add a bar to show that 20 people like plays.

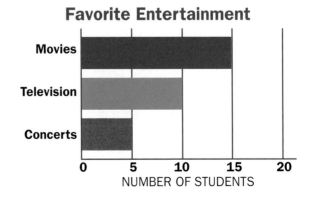

Databank

Average Animal Life Spans	
Animal	**Average Life Span (Years)**
Baboon	20
Black bear	18
Cat	12
Chipmunk	6
Cow	15
Dog	12
Elephant	37
Giraffe	10
Guinea pig	4
Kangaroo	7
Mouse	3

HOME RUN LEADERS

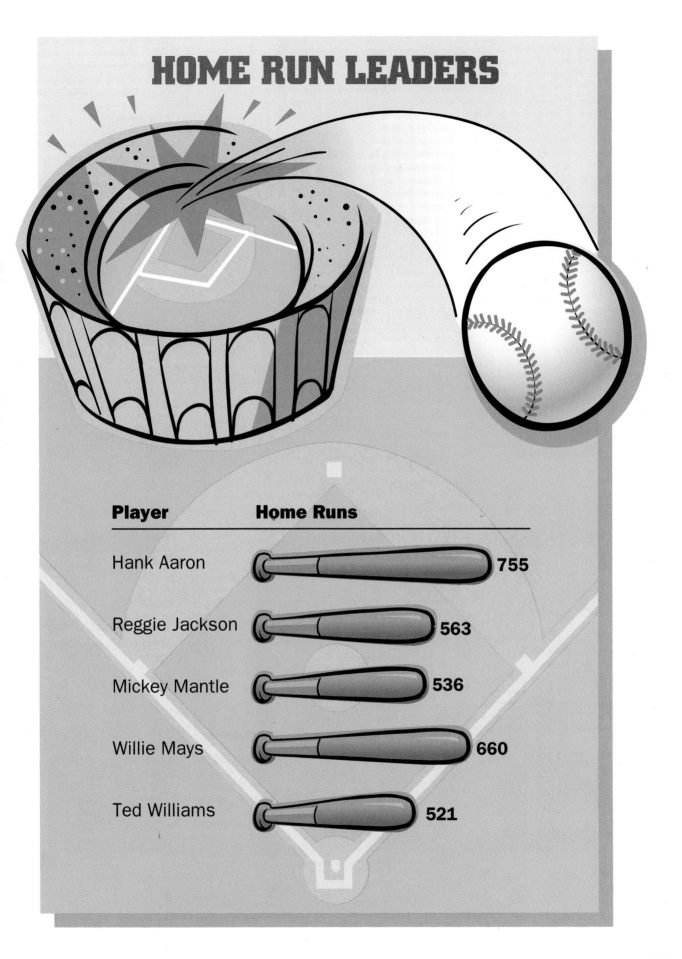

Player	Home Runs	
Hank Aaron		755
Reggie Jackson		563
Mickey Mantle		536
Willie Mays		660
Ted Williams		521

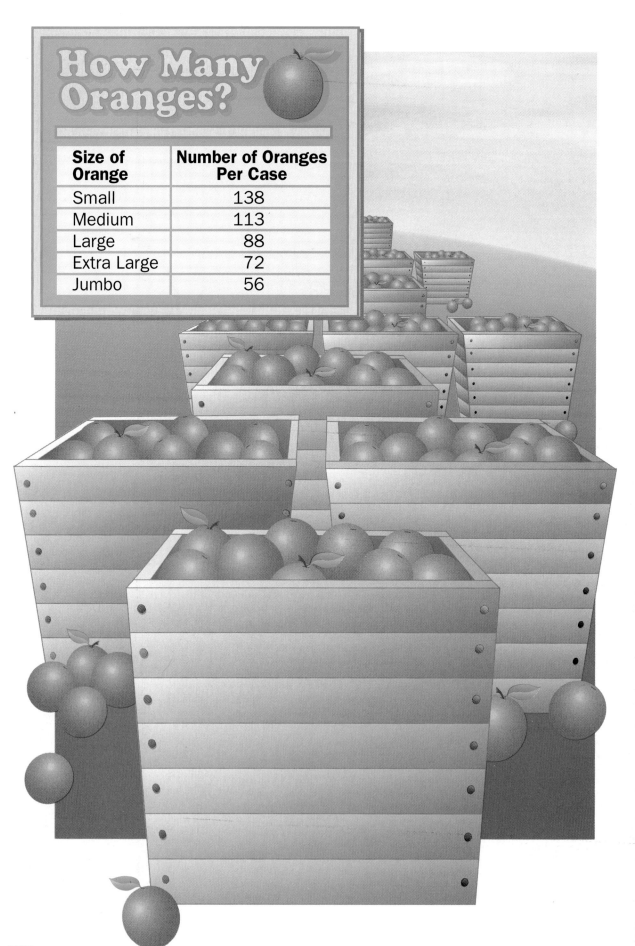

How Many Oranges?

Size of Orange	Number of Oranges Per Case
Small	138
Medium	113
Large	88
Extra Large	72
Jumbo	56

FASTEST U.S. PASSENGER TRAIN RUNS

From	To	Distance	Time
Baltimore	Wilmington	68 miles	43 minutes

From	To	Distance	Time
Metropark	Washington	201 miles	129 minutes

From	To	Distance	Time
New York	New Carrollton	216 miles	143 minutes

From	To	Distance	Time
Newark	Philadelphia	81 miles	57 minutes

BUBBLE BEACH AMUSEMENT PARK RIDES

Name of Ride	Waiting Time (in minutes)	Length of Ride (in minutes)
Cyclone	12	3
Sonic Rocket	6	4
Boat Ride	15	30
Power Tower	10	10
Ferris Wheel	15	15

PRICES FOR KELLOGG'S 1972 ALL-TIME GREATS ★ BASEBALL CARDS ★

Baseball Card	Current Price
Ty Cobb	$1.75
Eddie Collins	$0.40
Lou Gehrig	$1.75
Walter Johnson	$1.00
John McGraw	$0.40
Babe Ruth	$3.00
Cy Young	$0.60

Rides in Hershey Park

Name of Ride	Number of Passengers in Each Car	Number of Cars
The Comet	4	6
SooperDooperLooper	4	6
The Trailblazer	6	4
The Sidewinder	4	7
The Coal Cracker	5	30

American Kennel Club Dog Groups

Sporting Dogs

Pointer
Retriever
Setter
Spaniel
Weimaraner
Griffon

Hounds

Afghan
Basenji
Basset hound
Bloodhound
Foxhound
Wolfhound
Whippet
Borzoi

Working Dogs

Mastiff
Malamute
Boxer
Great Dane
Husky

Terriers

Airedale
Border
Bull
Cairn
Fox
Miniature schnauzer
Skye
Welsh
Irish
Scottish

Toy Dogs

Chihuahua
Maltese
Pekingese
Pug
Toy poodle
Papillon
Toy terrier
Yorkshire terrier

Non-Sporting Dogs

Boston terrier
Bulldog
Dalmatian
Chow chow
Poodle

Herding Dogs

Sheepdog
German shepherd
Collie
Corgi

LENGTHS OF PLAYING FIELDS
(in meters)

Volleyball	18
Basketball	26
American football	110
Canadian football	146
Gaelic football	146
Lacrosse	101
Soccer	110
Rugby	122
Polo	274

Native American Baskets

Many different grasses, roots, and stems were used to make baskets by the Native Americans of the Southwest. They used what was available in their area.

This is an Apache bowl basket. The black design is made from a weed with unusually long spines. ▶

This is a flat Pima basket. The Pima made their baskets of willow twigs. ◀

This is a covered container made by a Papago basket-weaver. The Papago make baskets from yucca plant fibers. ▶

HOW LONG IS EACH ONE?

ABOUT INDONESIA

Indonesia is the largest group of islands in the world. It stretches 3,977 miles between the Indian and Pacific Oceans. It includes 13,700 scattered islands. Only 6,000 of the islands are inhabited. Indonesia has 70 active volcanoes and experiences about 3 tremors and earthquakes a day.

INDONESIA

An Indonesian Volcano

In 1883, the Indonesian volcano of Krakatoa erupted. It was one of the biggest explosions in history. The explosion was so big that:
◆ it blew the island it was on to pieces.
◆ it caused a tidal wave 98 feet high that swept across the coast of the island of Java.
◆ the ash reached Singapore, 522 miles away.
◆ it flung rock and debris 17 miles into the sky.

Glossary

A

addend A number to be added to another number.

Example: 9 + 6 = 15
The addends are 9 and 6.

addition An operation that tells how many in all when you put together two or more numbers.

Example: 6 + 4 = 10 ← sum
　　　　　↑　↑
　　　　addends

A.M. A name for time between 12 midnight and 12 noon.

angle A figure formed when two rays meet at the same *endpoint*.

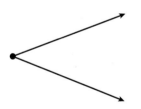

area The number of square units needed to cover a surface.

B

bar graph A *graph* that shows *data* by using bars of different lengths.

C

capacity The amount a container can hold.

centimeter (cm) A unit of *length* in the *metric system*. (*See* Table of Measures.)

circle A closed, curved *2-dimensional figure.* All the points on the circle are the same distance from the center.

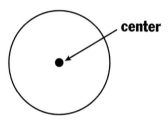

cone A *3-dimensional figure* whose base is a *circle.*

congruent figures Figures that have the same shape and size.

cube A *3-dimensional figure* with six square sides all the same size.

cubic unit A unit for measuring *volume.*

cup (c) A unit for measuring liquids in the *customary system.* (*See* Table of Measures.)

customary system A system of measurement. (*See* Table of Measures.)

cylinder A *3-dimensional figure* with two faces that are *circles.*

D

data Information.

day (d) A unit for measuring time that is equal to 24 hours.

decimal A number that uses *place value* and a decimal point to show tenths and hundredths.

Examples: 0.8, 1.7, 23.04
↑   ↑   ↑
decimal point

decimeter (dm) A unit for measuring *length* in the *metric system.* (*See* Table of Measures.)

degree Celsius (°C) A unit for measuring temperature in the *metric system.*

degree Fahrenheit (°F) A unit for measuring temperature in the *customary system.*

denominator The number below the bar in a *fraction.* It tells the number of equal parts in all.

Example: $\frac{3}{5}$ ← denominator

difference The number obtained by subtracting one number from another.

Example: $7 - 2 = 5$ ← difference

digit Symbols used to write numbers—0, 1, 2, 3, 4, 5, 6, 7, 8, and 9.

dividend A number to be divided.

division An operation on two numbers that tells how many groups or how many in each group.

Example: 4 ← quotient
divisor → 2)8̄ ← dividend

divisor The number by which the *dividend* is divided.

E

endpoint The point at either end of a *line segment.* The beginning point of a *ray.*

 ←— **endpoints** —→

equivalent fractions Different fractions that name the same amount.

Examples:
$\frac{1}{2}$ and $\frac{2}{4}$ $\frac{1}{3}$ and $\frac{3}{9}$ $\frac{1}{4}$ and $\frac{4}{16}$

estimate To find an answer that is close to the exact answer.

even number A number that ends in 0, 2, 4, 6, or 8.

expanded form A way of writing a number as the *sum* of the values of its digits.

Example: 364 can be written as $300 + 60 + 4$.

fact family Related facts using the same numbers.

Example:
$2 + 3 = 5$ $3 + 2 = 5$
$5 - 3 = 2$ $5 - 2 = 3$

factors Numbers that are multiplied to give a *product*.

Example: $4 \times 6 = 24$
        ↑   ↑
        factors

flip To move a figure over a line.

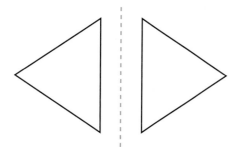

foot (ft) A unit for measuring *length* in the *customary system*. (*See* Table of Measures.)

fraction A number that names part of a whole or a group.

Examples: $\frac{3}{4}$ $\frac{4}{5}$ $\frac{1}{3}$

gallon (gal) A unit for measuring *capacity* in the *customary system*. (*See* Table of Measures.)

gram (g) A unit for measuring *mass* in the *metric system*. (*See* Table of Measures.)

graph A visual way to display *data*. (*See* bar graph and pictograph.)

grouping property When adding or multiplying, the grouping of numbers does not affect the result.

Examples:
  $3 + 5 + 7 = 15$ $2 \times 4 \times 5 = 40$
  $5 + 7 + 3 = 15$ $5 \times 2 \times 4 = 40$

hexagon A *2-dimensional figure* with six sides and six angles.

hour (h) A unit for measuring time that is equal to 60 minutes.

I

inch (in.) A unit for measuring *length* in the *customary system*. (*See* Table of Measures.)

is equal to (=) Symbol meaning "has the same value as."

is greater than (>) Symbol to show that the first number is greater than the second.

Example: 9 > 6

is less than (<) Symbol to show that the first number is less than the second.

Example: 13 < 64

K

kilogram (kg) A unit for measuring *mass* in the *metric system*. (*See* Table of Measures.)

kilometer (km) A unit for measuring *length* in the *metric system*. (*See* Table of Measures.)

L

length The measurement of distance between two *endpoints*.

line A straight path that goes in two directions without end.

Example:

line of symmetry A line on which a figure can be folded so that both sides match. (*See* symmetry.)

Example:

line plot A graph that shows *data* using symbols that are lined up.

Example:

What is Your Favorite Pet?

Dog	Cat	Fish	Snake
	X		
	X		
X	X		
X	X	X	
X	X	X	X

line segment A straight path that has two endpoints.

Example:

liter (L) A unit for measuring *capacity* in the *metric system*. (*See* Table of Measures.)

mass A measurement that indicates how much of something there is. It is measured by *kilograms* and *grams*.

meter (m) A unit for measuring *length* in the *metric system*. (*See* Table of Measures.)

metric system A system of measurement. (*See* Table of Measures.)

mile (mi) A unit for measuring *length* in the *customary system*. (*See* Table of Measures.)

milliliter (mL) A unit for measuring *capacity* in the *metric system*. (*See* Table of Measures.)

mixed number A number that has a *whole number* and a *fraction*.

Example: $5\frac{3}{4}$

month A unit for measuring time that is equal to about 30 days.

multiplication An operation that tells how many in all when equal groups are combined.

Example: $3 \times 7 = 21 \leftarrow$ product
$\qquad \uparrow \quad \uparrow$
$\qquad$ factors

net A flat pattern that can be folded to make a *3-dimensional figure*.

number sentence An inequality or an equation.

Examples: $14 > 11 + 1 \qquad 5 + 4 = 9$

numerator The number above the bar in a *fraction*. It tells the number of parts.

Example: $\frac{2}{5} \leftarrow$ numerator

odd number A number that ends in 1, 3, 5, 7, or 9.

order property When adding or multiplying, the order of the numbers does not affect the result.

Examples: $8 + 9 = 17 \qquad 4 \times 5 = 20$
$\qquad\qquad\; 9 + 8 = 17 \qquad 5 \times 4 = 20$

ordered pair A pair of numbers that gives the location of a point on a map or graph.

ordinal number A number used to tell order or position.

Example: second

ounce (oz) A unit for measuring *weight* in the *customary system*. (*See* Table of Measures.)

pattern A series of numbers or figures that follows a rule.

Examples: 1, 3, 5, 7, 9, 11, . . .

pentagon A *2-dimensional figure* with five sides and five angles.

perimeter The distance around a closed figure.

period Each group of three digits in a *place-value* chart.

Example:

Thousands Period			Ones Period		
Hundred Thousands	Ten Thousands	Thousands	Hundreds	Tens	Ones
5	2	7	0	0	0

pictograph A *graph* that shows *data* by using picture symbols.

pint (pt) A unit for measuring *capacity* in the *customary system*. (*See* Table of Measures.)

place value The value given to the place a *digit* occupies in a number.

P.M. A name for time between 12 noon and 12 midnight.

polygon A closed figure with straight sides. For example, a *pentagon* has five sides, a *hexagon* has six sides.

pound (lb) A unit for measuring *weight* in the *customary system*. (*See* Table of Measures.)

probability The chance of something happening.

product The result of *multiplication.*

Example: 3 × 4 = 12 ← product

pyramid A *3-dimensional figure* that is shaped by *triangles* on a base.

quart (qt) A unit for measuring *capacity* in the *customary system*. (*See* Table of Measures.)

quotient The result of *division.*

Example: 28 ÷ 4 = 7 ← quotient

range The difference between the greatest and least numbers in a group of numbers.

ray A *2-dimensional figure* with one *endpoint* that goes without end in one direction.

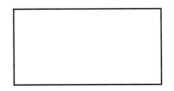

rectangle A *2-dimensional figure* with four sides and four square corners. The opposite sides are the same *length*.

rectangular prism A *3-dimensional figure* with six rectangular faces.

remainder The number left over after dividing.

Example: $64 \div 7 = 9$ R1 ← remainder

right angle An *angle* that forms a square corner.

rounding Finding the nearest ten, hundred, thousand, and so on.

Example: 53 rounded to the nearest 10 is 50.

second (s) A unit for measuring time. 60 seconds = 1 minute

skip-count Counting by twos, threes, fours, and so on.

Examples: 2, 4, 6, 8, 10, . . . 3, 6, 9, 12, . . . or 4, 8, 12, 16, . . .

slide To move a figure along a line.

sphere A *3-dimensional figure* that has the shape of a round ball.

square A *2-dimensional figure* that has four equal sides and four square corners.

square number The *product* of multiplying a number by itself.

square unit A unit for measuring *area.*

standard form The usual or common way to write a number.

subtraction An operation on two numbers that tells how many are left when some are taken away. Subtraction is also used to compare two numbers.

Example: $13 - 2 = 11$ ← difference

sum The result of *addition.*

Example: $5 + 2 = 7$ ← sum

survey A method of gathering *data* by asking people their opinion on a subject.

symmetry An exact matching of two parts along a fold line.

tessellation Repeated shapes that cover a flat surface without leaving any gaps, for example, the design on a checkerboard.

3-dimensional figure A figure that has *length, width,* and *height.*

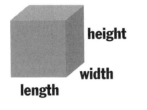

total The result of *addition* or *multiplication.*

Examples:
$$6 + 16 + 22 = 44 \leftarrow \text{total}$$
$$3 \times 6 = 18 \leftarrow \text{total}$$

triangle A *2-dimensional figure* with three sides and three corners.

triangular prism A *3-dimensional figure* with two triangular faces and three rectangular faces.

turn To move a figure in a curved path.

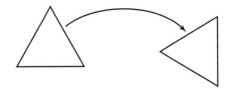

2-dimensional figure A figure that has only *length* and *width.*

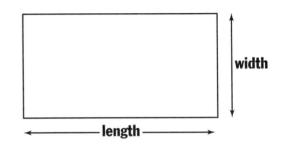

volume The number of cubic units that fit inside a *3-dimensional figure.*

week (wk) A unit for measuring time that is equal to 7 days.

weight A measurement that tells how heavy an object is.

whole number Any number, such as 0, 1, 2, 3, 4, 5, 6, 7, . . .

yard (yd) A unit for measuring *length* in the *customary system*. (*See* Table of Measures.)

year A unit for measuring time that is equal to 365 days (366 days in a leap year).

zero property of addition When one of two addends is zero, the *sum* is equal to the other *addend.*

zero property of multiplication When one *factor* is zero, the *product* is zero.

Table of Measures

Time

60 minutes (min) = 1 hour (h)
24 hours = 1 day (d)
7 days = 1 week (wk)
12 months (mo) = 1 year (y)
about 52 weeks = 1 year
365 days = 1 year
366 days = 1 leap year

Metric Units

LENGTH
10 centimeters (cm) = 1 decimeter (dm)
10 decimeters = 1 meter (m)
1,000 meters = 1 kilometer (km)

MASS
1 kilogram (kg) = 1,000 grams (g)

CAPACITY
1 liter (L) = 1,000 milliliters (mL)

TEMPERATURE
0° Celsius (°C) . . . Water freezes
100° Celsius . . . Water boils

Customary Units

LENGTH
1 foot (ft) = 12 inches (in.)
1 yard (yd) = 36 inches
1 yard = 3 feet
1 mile (mi) = 5,280 feet
1 mile = 1,760 yards

WEIGHT
1 pound (lb) = 16 ounces (oz)

CAPACITY
1 pint (pt) = 2 cups (c)
1 quart (qt) = 2 pints
1 gallon (gal) = 4 quarts

TEMPERATURE
32° Fahrenheit (°F) . . . Water freezes
212° Fahrenheit . . . Water boils

Symbols

<	is less than	°	degree	⟶	ray
>	is greater than	⟷	line	∠	angle
=	is equal to	•—•	line segment	(5, 3)	ordered pair 5, 3

Index

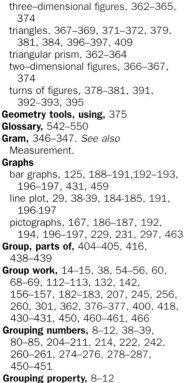

34–35, 76–77, 120–121, 164–165, 200–201, 236–237, 270–271, 314–315, 356–357, 396–397, 442–443, 478–479. *See also* Calculators; Computers.

Technology sense, developing
number puzzles, 13
use a geometry tool, 375
use counters and a table, 215
use place–value models, 53

Telling time, 170–175, 180. *See also* Time.

Temperature, 348–351, 353, 354

Ten
division by, 464–465
factor of, 446–452

Ten thousands, 64–65

Tens
addition of, 80–91, 94–95, 98–99
division by, 464–467
grouping, 44–45, 446–452, 464–465
multiplication of, 446–452, 454–455
regrouping, 134–135, 142–144, 146–148, 150–153, 454–455, 464–467
subtraction of, 126–131, 134–135, 142–144, 146–148, 150–153

Tenths, 420–427. *See also* Decimals; Fractions.

Tessellations, 381

Thermometer, 348–349

Thousands, 60–64, 446–447

Three
as factor, 222–223
division by, 282–283

Three addends, 95, 101

Three factors, 260–261, 266–267

Three–digit numbers
in addition, 86–87, 90–93, 100, 116–117, 135, 173, 175
in subtraction, 142–148, 150, 160–161, 175, 227

Three-dimensional figures, 362-365, 374

Time
A.M. and P.M., 170–175, 180
applying, 182–183
elapsed, 174–175, 283
estimating, 168–169, 176–177, 180
reading, 170–175, 180

telling, 170–175, 180
using a calendar, 176–177, 180
writing, 170–175

Time line, 177

Triangles, 367, 368–369, 371, 372, 379, 381, 384, 396-397, 409. *See also* Geometry.

Turns of figures, 378–380, 391, 395. *See also* Geometry.

Two
as factor, 218–219
division by, 280–281

Two–digit numbers
in addition, 86–89, 92, 100, 116–117, 135, 155
in subtraction, 132–135, 138, 148, 155, 160–161

Two dimensional figures, 366-367, 374

U

Units
cubic, 332–333
of measurement, 318–325, 336, 340–349, 352–353, 356–357
square, 330–331, 336, 351

V

Volume, 332–333, 336, 352–353. *See also* Measurement.

W

Week (wk), 176–177, 180. *See also* Time.

Weight in customary units, 344–345, 352–353. *See also* Measurement.

Whole numbers
addition of, 80–83, 100, 116–117
naming, 46–47, 52, 61–62, 64–65
subtraction of, 126–129, 138, 160–161
written names for, 46–47, 52, 61–62, 64–65

Whole, parts of, 402–403, 416. *See*

also Fractions.

Word names of numbers, 46–47, 52, 61–62, 64–65

Work together, 5, 6, 8, 18, 26, 38, 44, 54, 56, 60, 68–69, 86, 104, 112–113, 132, 142, 156–157, 168, 182–183, 184, 186, 188, 192, 204, 208, 228–229, 256, 258, 260, 262, 274, 278, 302, 306–307, 318, 322, 326, 330, 332, 348, 362, 366, 370, 376–377, 378, 382, 388, 400, 404, 406, 410, 418, 420, 426, 430–431, 432, 450, 457, 460–461, 466. *See also* Cooperative learning.

Working backward, 296–297. *See also* Problem-solving skills and strategies.

Writing money amounts, 104–117

Writing number sentences, 5–11, 17, 22–25, 29, 139, 209–210, 212–214, 219, 223, 227, 242–244, 248, 252, 259, 260, 266, 278–279, 287, 298–299, 302, 306–311

Writing problems, 11, 13, 21, 27, 33, 41, 51, 67, 69, 89, 97, 109, 113, 135, 137, 157, 173, 175, 179, 193, 219, 221, 229, 249, 251, 260, 263, 281, 283, 287, 297, 307, 309, 325, 335, 341, 347, 349, 373, 387, 389, 415, 425, 429, 431, 435, 456, 463, 471

Y

Yard (yd), 318–320. *See also* Measurement.

Year (yr), 176–177. *See also* Time.

Z

Zero factor, 212–214, 226-227, 258, 281

Zeros
in addition, 9, 10, 85
in division, 292–293, 310–311
in multiplication, 212–214, 226–227, 258–259, 281
in subtraction, 19, 149, 150–151, 160–161

(continued from page ii)